*The New Racism*

LIONEL LOKOS

# THE

# NEW

# RACISM

*Reverse Discrimination in America*

ARLINGTON HOUSE          *New Rochelle, N.Y.*

For My Mother and Father
and Laura

# Contents

# The New Racism

# Introduction

THE SUBJECT OF MY BOOK IS GENERALLY DISCUSSED ONLY in resentful whispers, when it is discussed at all. It is the sort of subject that makes one look around him, and then, satisfied that the audience is "safe," and "the others" are out of earshot, begin to pour out the angry grievances to which few public officials would dare even listen. Once this conversation begins, almost everyone in the group can relate similar experiences, with an equal sense of grim outrage. But rarely does the discussion venture any further. Having spontaneously surfaced for the moment, the resentments are again quickly submerged. and doggedly hidden away from public view—until the next opportunity arises when the subject can again be "safely" discussed.

In the belief that this subject must be brought out into the open—dissected, analyzed, and, yes, criticized—I have written this book.

The subject is racism—but not the old racism that is periodically linked to almost every white man, woman, and child in this country; not the old racism that is being pummeled to a jelly by so many Court decisions, executive orders, and civil rights laws that the mind reels at the thought of enumerating them. My subject is the New Racism—the New Racism that refuses even to acknowledge its name; the New Racism that can summon many of the most respected personages in America to swear that it really is not racism at all; the New Racism that considers it the highest public good to seek out and admit more and more Negroes to the best colleges—and employ more and more Negroes in the best companies—not because of ability or achievement but, quite frankly, because of the color of their skin. And to those who object that this is tantamount to discrimination against whites, the answer seems to be that it is racist to *call* this racist.

With messianic zeal, the New Racism is fervently convinced that it can use the tools of discrimination to find equality; that the "positive discrimination" that today favors Negroes is somehow more saintly than the discrimination that favored whites in the past. But, throughout history every form of discrimination has had this same split personality—positive and negative—in the sense that one group has always been helped, but always at the expense of another group which has been hurt.

The whole point is that if discrimination is wrong, it is wrong no matter whom it helps or whom it hurts—black or white. If it were otherwise, the civil rights laws would be nothing more than quaint mementos of a bygone age—more honored in the breach than in the observance. Indeed if it were otherwise, it would be patently hypocritical to have any civil rights laws at all.

In the field of education, the New Racism has turned the Great American Dream inside out, then upside down, and proudly paraded it as "equal educational opportunity." But the glittering subterfuge deceives no one for very long—least of all a studious white high school senior who may find his higher grades *prevent* him from attending the college of his choice. In the scramble to make ghetto residents part of the Ivy League decor, the new criterion is not ability, but educational disability —not a good scholastic record, but poor or indifferent grades. In some cases, a high school diploma may be a handicap; a dropout may get first preference. Score as low as you can, be as truculent to school authorities as you please, give less than a damn about education in general, and you just might have college registrars practically beating a path to your door with flattering offers of admission to the most highly regarded institutions of higher learning.

At the same time that Herculean efforts are being made to entice more ghetto youngsters into some kind—any kind—of college curriculum, we are witnessing an escalation of black separatism on our campuses. It masquerades in many guises—"black control of black studies," "the right to hire and fire teachers of black courses," "autonomy for the black studies department"—but it is separatism just the same. It is a movement that could splinter every well-known college, with certain buildings, certain courses, certain departments turned into anti-white enclaves of black nationalism—off limits to white students, teachers, and administrators. If left unchecked, black separatism could eventually result in an educational apartheid as absolute as any in South Africa.

When it is discussed publicly—which is not very often—opinion on the New Racism cuts sharply across party, political, and ideological lines. At times, liberals and conservatives find themselves in astonished alliance on the subject, both pro and con. For example, William F. Buckley, Jr., in an unfortunate column written a few years ago and titled "The Brownsville Affair II," quite frankly favored black community control of ghetto public schools, to the extent of giving black superintendents "the power to fire whom they like." Asked if he would tolerate a teacher who "preaches the thought of Mao Tse-tung or advances the principles of Karl Marx," Buckley replied, "My inclination would be to say yes; tolerate it, say, over a period of two or three years." This rhetorical exchange followed a paragraph in which Buckley stoutly declared, "The teaching of race hatred should not be permitted. A useful definition of what is not to be permitted is embodied in the UN's Genocide Convention." In other words, a black teacher can teach Communist *class* hatred—but not *race* hatred, or at least not the *kind* of race hatred embodied in the Geneva Convention. In any case, it is difficult to perceive why, in Buckley's lofty view, communism can be inflicted upon the captive audience in the Harlem schoolrooms, while race hatred cannot.

In this same column, when queried, "Aren't you making recommendations which are in a sense racist?" Buckley replied, "Yes, but only in the sense that reverse discrimination is racist." It could hardly have been put more bluntly—and from the thunderous silence that greeted this column in usually friendly quarters, it could hardly have been more obvious that, on that day at least, William F. Buckley, Jr., did not speak for very many "On the Right."

In the first of this two-part discussion—"The Brownsville Affair I"—Buckley had stated, "We must in fact encourage a *pro-Negro discrimination*" (emphasis added), and candidly admitted that those who tend to make this point "tend to be immune from the practical consequences of it." As examples, he cited himself ("I am not likely to be summarily replaced by an editor or columnist merely because he is a Negro"), Daniel Patrick Moynihan ("hired by Richard Nixon away from M.I.T., and that shows how desirable his talents are"), and Garry Wills ("a doctored classicist in a major university, and a journalist whose talents are rated very high in the free marketplace—he is not going to be edged out of anything"). Buckley continued, "What we need to consider is the individual who stands to suffer . . . the butcher and the candlestick maker for whom, under tight competitive situations, it means that, if they yield their places to a Negro, they lose their jobs."

Something about that last sentence reminded me of a few lines from *The Walrus and the Carpenter:*

> With sobs and tears he sorted out
> Those of the largest size
> Holding his pocket handkerchief
> Before his streaming eyes.

To be sure, Buckley dutifully suffered with the butcher and candlestick maker; but before and after, they were just as unemployed, while he was just as gloriously immune from the consequences of his pro-Negro bias. About the best Buckley could offer was the forlorn plea that the first duty of the cities "is to provide for those who are dislocated." It was a rolling, sonorous phrase, but terribly inadequate and meaningless. One did not have to peer very intently to see Musical Chairs being played, with a Black militant at the piano—and those not in tune with the Soul Brother might well have their chairs yanked right out from under them. And if other chairs could not be provided for the baker and candlestick maker, they could always be directed to seats at the unemployment office. Barring outright welfare—or a reverse form of reverse discrimination —this is how the cities will end up providing "for those who are dislocated."

Perhaps only someone who has to depend on a weekly salary to pay the rent and buy the groceries can perceive the depths of the human tragedy that could follow in the wake of the Buckley program. Visualize a white worker in his 40's, with 5, 10, perhaps 15 years on the job. For most of his adult life, he has voted a straight Democratic Party ticket—the same party that has written most of the civil rights laws. He has built up a little seniority—gotten a few pay raises over the years—has a few dollars, but only a few dollars, in the bank—makes just about enough money to get by on, after taxes. And now, suddenly, he's going to be fired, through no fault of his own, for no business reason, but solely to make room for someone from the ghetto. Even assuming this fired white worker gets severance pay (and Buckley makes no mention of this at all), where will he go? What will he do when his money runs out? In our youth-oriented society, who will hire a man in his 40's, and give him the same salary he was getting in his old job? What if he has mortgage payments to keep up on a house—bank payments to make, to send his children through college—payments he first assumed, based upon the salary he was getting in his old job? The tragedy is only compounded if the white worker is in his 50's, too old to obtain equivalent work and wages, too young for retirement on a pension. "Dislocation" is hardly the word for it. Call it by its right name: chaos!

Page by page, chapter by chapter, I will seek to call all of it by its right name in my book. And in doing so, I will not rely solely upon white columnists or white newspapers, but will document as much information as practicable from the black press.

For quite some time now, I have been reading the *Amsterdam News, Jet, Muhammad Speaks,* and the *Black Panther.* I have also read most issues of *Ebony* and *Negro Digest.* In reading these black publications, I have read what Negroes say to other Negroes about race problems, which often differs in many respects from what Negroes say to whites or confide to the *New*

*York Times.* I have obtained some information from the black press that may never have appeared in the major white newspapers at all, and I have preferred direct quotes of black people to any white man's paraphrase.

And yet I have no illusions that this research has given me a glossy coating of expertise on the subject of race relations. I believe no white man fully understands the Negro, simply because no white man knows what it is to be a Negro—and, even though the New Racism admits of no such heresy, I believe that no Negro fully understands the white man, for a reason that is equally obvious.

How, then, could I presume to write this book at all? By noting a shelf filled with Negro critiques of white people, and asking for Equal Time. By stating quite frankly in this Introduction that what the black man says and does most definitely affects this country, of which I am a part; that the turmoil of the ghetto scars and sears the cities that make this country a world power; that the non-negotiable demands of the Black Students Unions affect our colleges and the new generation of intellectuals who some day will have a decisive voice in the governing and direction of this nation; that the black separatist groups, small in numbers though they may be, can have a calamitous effect upon the black youth of the ghettos, the guilt-ridden white liberals, and even some aspects of our foreign policy. Are we involved in all mankind? I cannot say. But I do know that every man, woman, and child in this country is most urgently involved in the New Racism that would put Reverse Discrimination on a pedestal considerably higher than the Bill of Rights.

Ironically, *white* minority groups are equally vulnerable. When the New Racism speaks of "equal job opportunity for minorities," it is really saying that some minorities are much more equal than others. After all, Jews are a much smaller minority in this country (Negroes outnumber them 2 to 1), but this fact will give them cold comfort if and when Jews are replaced by Negroes in certain positions.

We must acknowledge the plain fact that Negro-Jewish relations have rapidly deteriorated in the past few years. We must recognize the presence of an anti-Semitic fringe element in the ghetto. And yet I would be the first to agree that we must not say too much—that in speaking of black anti-Semitism we must choose our words very carefully. We should not blindly hurl the charge of bigotry at every Negro who happens to criticize a Jew —nor should we automatically read anti-Semitic nuances into the statements of every black zealot who is obsessed with whitey-phobia.

In other words, anti-Semitism in the ghetto must not be exaggerated or overstated—but neither should it be ignored. The growth of anti-Jewish feeling among a number of black militants is a clear and present reality that can no longer be denied. It does exist; it is there. It was responsible for at least some of the incredibly vicious conflict in Ocean Hill-Brownsville and other ghetto schools, and the situation will not get better, but infinitely worse. We may quickly be approaching the time when only specially screened "pet Jews"* will be allowed to hold teaching jobs in the ghetto. And if this does happen, it will almost certainly be condoned, supported, and glorified as enlightened public policy by the New Racism.

The New Racism strives to justify its existence by calling it all "compensatory"—compensation of Negroes for past wrongs. But it is a bizarre form of reimbursement that empties one man's wallet to pay another man's I.O.U.'s. I think it is in order to repeat the question I asked in an earlier work:

> How many Americans now living are responsible for the Negro's plight? Those who enslaved the Negroes have long since departed this earth, and it is a social absurdity to indict their progeny through a form of retroactive guilt. It is even more absurd to expect feelings of guilt in today's sons or grandsons of immigrants who came to this country long after the Civil War, and themselves had to struggle to make their way. We come back to the four or five percent who are activists, and it is simply standing reason on its head to use the deeds of a motley few to justify a blanket condemnation of the rest of the country.**

The doctrine of compensation comes close to implying that the vast majority of white Americans all but lie awake nights, thinking of new outrages to heap upon the Negro. But if, in our time, anti-Negroism had been this pervasive, this overwhelm-

---

*Years ago, "pet Jew" meant to Jews what "Uncle Tom" means to Negroes.
**Lionel Lokos, *House Divided: The Life and Legacy of Martin Luther King* (New Rochelle, N.Y.: Arlington House, 1968), p. 478.

ing, the poll-tax laws would have existed not in just ten or eleven states, but in every state in the country; Negro workers would have been denied membership not in some unions, but in all of them; Congress would have turned a deaf ear not just to some but to every single scrap of civil rights legislation; public school integration would not have been ordered, but forbidden by the Supreme Court. This is not to maintain that most white Americans were civil rights activists; they were not—but, for that matter, neither were most Negroes. It would be much more accurate to say that most white Americans didn't care about Negro problems one way or the other. They were apathetic— and this apathy redounded to the Negroes' benefit, because it deprived segregationists of desperately needed allies. It was precisely because of this that civil rights leaders were able to rack up that startling string of victories in the courts, the Congress, and the urban areas in the last ten years, because most whites were far too apathetic to place any obstacles in their path.

Silence gave consent, but now that consent is no longer given. Now many whites who once shrugged off the issues are beginning to take sides. They are beginning to form a nucleus of opposition, but that opposition has yet to take any permanent form. The more alienated whites voted for George Wallace for President in 1968, but I think at least part of his vote came from those who were simply thumbing their noses at both major parties. Less than one out of six Presidential votes was cast for the Alabamian—but it was more than enough to send cold shivers running up and down the spines of our leading political figures. Whether a candidacy of this type—with or without George Wallace—remains a limited affair, or gathers vastly increased political momentum at the polls, may depend in large part upon the inroads the New Racism makes in the schools, the colleges, the offices, and the factories of America. And, too, much will depend upon the response of the major parties. If they go on pretending the New Racism is all a figment of an overwrought imagination, they may soon have to reckon not with just disgruntled voters, but with those who rarely used to vote at all—the Silent Americans who used to make almost a fetish of staying home on Election Day.

In the fiercest Presidential contest of this century—the Johnson–Goldwater battle in 1964—almost forty percent of those eligible to vote did not even go to the polls. So the ranks of the lethargic are astonishingly large. But if a sizable number of Silent Americans now become aroused, and shed their apathy, and take an active part in the election process, they might well form an almost invincible balance of power in Congressional, Senate, and gubernatorial contests, and even in the White House itself. Admittedly, this train of thought could be derailed by the row of "ifs" that are unavoidably attached. But we live in an age in which Today's Improbability often becomes Tomorrow's Fact—and it is intriguing to speculate about the awesome impact on Election Day if Black Power in urban areas is suddenly challenged by the Vote Power of hundreds of thousands of hitherto Silent Americans.

It must be emphasized and reemphasized that basically the New Racism is not some remote Olympian campaign against "The Power Structure" or "The Affluent Society." It literally hits home—North, South, East, West—in virtually every town, city, and state in America, as no other civil rights campaign ever has before. It has two prime targets—the white teenager who wants to go to a good college, and the white wage earner trying to hold his own in a highly erratic economy. White wage earners will have to face the ugly fact that in looking for work, a promotion, or a transfer from one part of a plant to another, certain job opportunities may automatically be denied to some of them and certain promotions deliberately withheld from others, because, and solely because, they happen to be white. Many of these incidents are probably unreported, and fragmentary information about others can only be gleaned from business or management publications. But as word filters through that some positions have been tacitly classified "black help wanted; white workers need not apply," the reaction could be explosive.

Not very long ago, one of the highest-ranking officials of the World Council of Churches, the Reverend Eugene Carson Blake, warned that preferential hiring of Negroes was "one of the most dangerous things that any of the Negro action groups have called for." Blake said that if a white man found he could not get a job because he was white, "then you will really have violence." We clearly cannot exclude this grim possibility.

After all, we have seen an era in which violence followed hard on the heels of non-violence. But in any such tragic confrontation, no one would win—black or white—and our country would lose, and perhaps die a little. Violence is not the answer; but too many in high places have winked at black violence in the past, and the credibility gap would be just too insurmountable if they should denounce white violence in the future.

Beyond question, Negroes do have very real grievances, and obviously have known flagrant discrimination. Negroes have generally had lower incomes than whites, and few of them have gone on to college. But it is one thing to agree on a statement of the problems, and quite another to agree on the *cause* of the problems, or the *solution* to them. It is one thing to point out individual white racists, and quite another to deduce that all whites are racist until proven otherwise. I do not believe that a newborn baby coming out of the incubator should be presented with James Forman's bill for reparations. I do not believe that every white person in this country should be made to assume personal responsibility for each and every wrong ever inflicted upon each and every Negro, from 1619 to the present.

In the field of employment, I do not suggest for a moment that there is a color line that divides capability and incapability. I have seen some patently incompetent white workers, and some highly competent black workers. In one instance, a long-time white employee told me that the most conscientious copy boy in her department was black (hired under a job-training program), while she had only the most caustic criticism for his slovenly white co-worker. Quite obviously, other such cases could be cited as well. Unfortunately, however, even if many of the Negroes hired under these programs turn out to be capable workers, the point is largely irrelevant because that was *not* the reason they were hired. The same holds true for Negroes who are admitted to the best colleges, regardless of grades. In far too many cases, color comes first under the New Racism, and ability is secondary, if it is considered at all. This fact will not be lost upon white workers and college students—and, violence or no violence, the New Racism will usher in a period of bitterness and slowly simmering hostility, a hostility that will find expression, in many ways, for many years to come.

A few years ago, the New Racism was like so many flurries dotting the landscape. Today it is more like the proverbial snowball rolling downhill—and the end of that hill is nowhere in sight. In the chapters that follow, we will see just how far it has gone, just how much it has grown, and how it has rolled over seniority, experience, ability, and academic excellence. We will assess its impact upon our lives, our families, our country, and our country's future. And sometime before we finish these pages, we will have to come face to face with this cold, hard truth—if it is wrong to discriminate against a minority, any minority, how much more wrong is it to discriminate against the majority.

LIONEL LOKOS
*Brooklyn, N.Y.*

# CHAPTER 1

# Black Separatism

WHAT DO YOU SUPPOSE WOULD BE THE REACTION OF THE press, the government, the Academic Establishment, if a white group suddenly demanded that five states in this country be handed over to their organization? What would be the reaction if another group of whites trained its members in the use of small arms, and encouraged and incited assaults upon the police? What if still another group—a religious group—preached white supremacy and a world in which whites were the embodiment of all that is good, and blacks the embodiment of all that is evil? What if the members of these white groups were imbued with such hatred of this country that they did not even consider themselves Americans? What if they demanded a Communist form of government, or either *de facto* or *de jure* separation from "the mother country" (America), peacefully, if possible, by force of arms, if necessary?

How would the press, the government, and most of the Academic Establishment react to all this? You knew the answer, almost from the start, because these groups were *white.* But now re-read that first paragraph, color it all *black,* apply names like Black Muslims, Black Panthers, Republic of New Africa, and suddenly you find a more than 180-degree turn on the part of far too many leaders of stature in America. Suddenly, you find an incredible degree of unctuous deference to these views, a judge-not-that-ye-be-not-judged refusal to call sedition by its right name. Suddenly you find a substantial number of newspaper and magazine articles dripping with sympathy for these black revolutionaries, articles which sometimes strongly suggest, sometimes say in just so many words, that it is not the black revolutionaries but their opponents who are to be condemned.

It is one of the more lurid manifestations of the New Racism to defend in black supermilitants what you would denounce in whites, to excuse, condone, overlook, or rationalize any or all of the most fanatical excesses by some blacks, excesses that would be met with the most withering ridicule if advocated by whites.

In a semi-somnambulistic state, white apologists find themselves in front row center at a grisly game of Racist Roulette —never quite realizing that the stakes for which the black radicals are playing are our future and our country. Some few others, in a masochism worthy of the Grand Guignol, are so far submerged in the role of White Toms that they virtually act as cheerleaders for their own destruction.

A fact that many of us—white and black—never quite seem to grasp is that the black separatists mean exactly what they say. To many of us, it may be rhetoric, but to many of them, it is the very breath of life. To many of us, it may be visionary and too utterly fantastic to be deserving of serious comment. But to many of them, it is an ideal to strive for, to fight for, and perhaps even die for, "by any means necessary."

Black separatism is the jagged cutting edge of the New Racism, the Damoclean sword that hangs over the head of those who seek to make our cities livable. Black separatists have a hardcore membership that is numerically small, but there is no known method of calculating their following, especially among the young and very young. Their finances are irregular, but somehow funds can always be obtained for weapons. Apostles of violence and revolution, the separatists are surprisingly successful in cajoling various ministers to rush to their defense in the arena of public opinion. And when all else fails, they can always summon up their hate-riddled prose and their caches of verbal Molotov cocktails, ever held in readiness to hurl at the American Guilt Complex—that bleeding ulcer of white society.

Try to define black separatism, and the words divide and then subdivide into varying shades of meaning. There is the black separatism that any school child can recognize—that of the Republic of New Africa, which demands no less than five American states to comprise its own country (some of its devotees insist upon 13 states, in a mordantly ironic bow to the 13 colonies). There is the black separatism of the Black Panthers, which group disavows any allegiance to this country and dreams of a communized nation, or, at the very least, of a form of community control that would all but seal off the ghettos of the cities to the governing authority of the mayors and city councils. There is the black separatism of the Black Muslims, who seek a separation of black and white as absolute as anything ever proposed by the Ku Klux Klan (from opposite sides of the color line, one group is precisely as racist as the other).

Can the United States stay united if its cities become divided? The question may not seem quite so preposterous after you read this book. What you will read is fact—cold, stark, frightening fact, much of it taken from the black separatists' own speeches and publications.

Read it—and if it is true that any nation is only as strong as the devotion and loyalty of its citizens, it may be equally true that our country is now facing some of the most difficult and dangerous days in its history.

# CHAPTER 2

# The Black Muslims

IF YOU WERE TO LOOK AT IT ON A PURELY SUPERFICIAL level, never once removing the blinders you would require for the purpose, the Black Muslims might well emerge as the living embodiment of the old-fashioned American virtues: thrift, industriousness, fastidious neatness, sobriety, self-sufficiency, and even a notable absence of profanity.

The Black Muslims were black capitalists 20 or more years before anyone ever thought of the term. And by any criteria, the fruits of their labors have been most impressive. On November 7, 1969, the Black Muslim newspaper, *Muhammad Speaks*, gave its members a progress report. And the word *progress* in no way overstated their achievements. The front page of this special section contained some of the evangelistic exhortations of Black Muslim leader Elijah Muhammad:

> ... to my people, the so-called American Negro, Freedom, Justice, Equality, Happiness, Peace of Mind, Contentment, Money, Good Jobs, Decent Homes—all these can be yours if you accept your God, Allah, now and [*sic*] return to His (and your original) religion, Islam.

The rest of this section was interspersed with detailed listings of the accomplishments of the Black Muslims, among them:

# In Michigan, we have over 843 acres of pastures and other farm land costing in excess of $500,000.00 which was paid for in cash. A modern sanitary 110 cow milk dairy.... A modern, 10,000-eggs-per-day laying factory. ... Fertile pastures for over 200 head of cattle and over 600 head of sheep and a 1969 harvest of corn, beans, cabbage, wheat, navy beans, snap beans, apples, strawberries, squash and other crops. ...
# the Honorable Elijah Muhammad has stripped the profits from the live stock markets by independently building a modern 100-ton capacity, sanitary—United States Department of Agriculture approved meat processing and manufacturing plant, from which the Nation of Islam's cattles will be processed for marketing. The plant was built at a cost of more than $125,000, which was paid completely in cash. ...
# In Georgia, we have a half-million dollar farm of over 2200 acres of pastures and crop producing land paid for in cash. ...
# In Alabama, we have over 908 acres of farm land valued in excess of $350,000 paid for in cash.[1]

Few white organizations could boast of such phenomenal affluence.

In an article that sometimes sounded like a press agent's panegyric, *Time* raved about the Black Muslim movement. *Time* lamented that "in recent years, the militant Black Muslim movement has been saddled with a falsely fierce image."[2] And in another glowing paragraph, that magazine wrote:

Indeed, Muhammad, now 71, seems to have mellowed. Instead of inflaming Muslim passions, Muhammad (born Elijah Poole) is busily investing Muslim money. His energies are totally concentrated on building a Muslim-owned financial empire that some day, he predicts, will lead to a separate self-sufficient "Black Islam nation" within the continental United States.[3]

It is true that "the Muslims have become the nation's leading exponents of 'black capitalism'—a Nixonian term that they despise." It is equally true that Benedict Arnold was promoted to brigadier general and then major general, during the Revolutionary War. But just as the one statement does not tell the *whole* truth about Benedict Arnold, so the other statement does not tell the *whole* truth about the Black Muslims.

The whole truth about what Black Muslims believe, what they want, how they feel about whites and the United States, cannot fully be gauged by the analysis or interpretation of even the most well-intentioned white observers. To find out if Elijah Muhammad has really "mellowed," we must read his own weekly newspaper, *Muhammad Speaks,* and not just leaf aimlessly through one or two issues. We must read what he and his newspaper say, and not what others—white or black—may think he is saying.

In preparation for this section of the book, the author read *Muhammad Speaks,* week after week, for nearly a year. What he read substantially negated the *Time* image of Elijah Muhammad as a benign father-figure, a chairman of the board emeritus, totally immersed in credits, debits, and ledger sheets. The November 28, 1969, issue of *Muhammad Speaks* was about as typical as any. Its headlines speak eloquently of the contents of that issue:

FIRST AND TOUGHEST FOES OF GENOCIDAL WAR AND UNJUST DRAFT: THE OVERWHELMING BLACK MAJORITY

WHITE CHAMPIONS OF "FREEDOM OF THE PRESS" SILENCE FACTS BEHIND: THE MASSACRE AT PENDLETON REFORMATORY

DEPT. OF HUD SAYS SUBURBANITES WANT TO RELOCATE: WILL WHITES RETAKE CITY?

BLACK MARINES WHO SURVIVED WHITE MARINE LYNCH MOB ON TRIAL FOR: CONSPIRACY TO COMMIT SELF-DEFENSE

YOUNG URBAN LEAGUERS SAYS GROUP IS NOW PAWN OF ZIONISTS UPPER-CLASS WHITES

OEO TO SPEND BILLIONS FOR GENOCIDE PROGRAM[4]

Had Elijah Muhammad really "mellowed"? The most authoritative answer would have to come from Elijah Muhammad himself, from the continuing series of articles published in the center-fold of *Muhammad Speaks,* containing the leader's doctrine and dogma. Where you read the phrase "the Messenger of Allah," it refers to Elijah Muhammad. "Fard Muhammad" refers to D. W. Fard, the founder of the sect. "The devil" is the white man—virtually any and every white man since the dawn of time.

The following is Elijah Muhammad speaking for himself (in his disjointed and confusing style) in the pages of *Muhammad Speaks*.

*On the World of the White Man:*

If we would consider THE TIME that was set forth for the rule of the white man of the people of the earth; it was 6,000 years. The beginning of this time of 6,000 years brings us into THE TIME of its ending.[5]

****

The Father of the white race, (Mr. Yakub) made a race of people (white) to make war against the righteous (Black man) and to bring him into subjection; a slave to the will of the white man. . . . the Father of the white man, Mr. Yakub, at the age of six (6) was found by his uncle, PLAYING WITH STEEL. He learned how a steel magnet attracted steel. Mr. Yakub then said to his uncle that when he got to be an old man he was "going to make a people who shall rule you, uncle." Mr. Yakub and his uncle were both Black; not white. The white man is Mr. Yakub's idea . . . his made-man whom he would teach to rule the Black man. He taught his made-man (white race) the method by which a peaceful (Black Man) could be overcome and ruled until One Greater Than, Mr. Yakub, Come to our rescue [*sic*]. (Allah, God, Who Came in the Person of Master Fard Muhammad, to Whom Praises are due forever.)[6]

*On America:*

Let us take a look again at our own Black independence and how it came on this same day of 4th of July . . . at the Coming of Allah (God) Who Came in the Person of Master Fard Muhammad, to Whom Praises are due forever, on July 4, 1930. . . . His Presence meant the destruction of the independence of the white race and especially, America . . . over the Black Man. . . . EVER since that day, the 4th

of July, 1930, has meant the doom of American Independence of the Black Man of America and the Black People
of the earth. Ever since that day, America has been fall-
ing.[7]

\*\*\*\*

What has been known as America is threatened today,
with total destruction. America is destroying herself, in
her effort to destroy her Black slave.[8]

\*\*\*\*

THE country of America is now being Divinely Plagued
and hundreds of millions of dollars are needed for repara-
tion of damage caused by storms and other catastrophies
and revolution. There is dissatisfaction and disagreement
going on hourly between citizen and citizen and between
heads of state and the government but THE WORST IS
YET TO COME. There will be no jobs with high salaries
paid to men. There will hardly be any jobs at all. A very
small percentage of the people will be employed. The war
will continue in Europe after America is out of Asia.
America must come out of Asia or be thrown out with
greater loss. America will be deprived of every post that
she has outside of the borders of America. . . . America's
outposts will fall one by one and what few men she has left
will return to America. But they will not have the power
to ever again set up a powerful and respected government.
America will come to shame and disgrace.[9]

*On the Black Man:*

EVERYWHERE the white man may be, even in Europe,
the earth belongs to the Black Man[10] the rule must be
restored to the Black People, for they are the Owners of
the earth.[11] THE TIME of the Rise of THE BLACK MAN of
America is NOW! It is not a Time to come—the Time of our
Rise is NOW! . . . THE devil knows that THE BLACK MAN
who follows him is headed for hell. The devil knows himself and he knows his hell (doom). But his foolish Black
slave, even though he is one hundred (100) years up from
servitude Black slavery—he wants to be beloved by his
white slave-master's children. . . . THE BLACK MAN will
never be free of the white man as long as THE BLACK
MAN is willing to be called by the white man's name. Nor

will THE BLACK MAN be able to obtain the Acceptance of
Allah (God) himself as long as THE BLACK MAN believes
in the white man's religion, Christianity, and goes in the
white man's name.[12]

Virtually every "liberation" movement in Africa finds fervent support in the pages of *Muhammad Speaks,* a fact that
presumably led one Philip Edward Alley to write:

I am black and an avid reader of MUHAMMAD SPEAKS
Newspaper. The trend of *Muhammad Speaks* to unite
Black people in America with Black people in Africa is
very necessary and very encouraging. In reference to articles written on the African Freedom Wars, I and others
would appreciate very much if you would give us the address, or any other possible means in which we could have
a direct line of communication with FRELIMO, the guerrilla movement fighting in Mozambique, SWAPO fighting
in South West Africa and MPLA fighting in Angola. We
feel that the liberation and salvation of Black People is
necessary in America as well as in Africa.[13]

Alley's letter was published in *Muhammad Speaks,* along
with an editor's note that "current addresses on these organizations [sic] local offices can be obtained by writing: Organization
for Solidarity of the Peoples of Africa, Asia and Latin America,
Havana, Cuba."[14]

Ever ready to ascribe racism to others, did Black Muslims
consider themselves racist? The answer seemed to be Yes and
No, with equal emphasis on each, according to these comments
of Elijah Muhammad, in an article titled "Hate Teachings":

The origin of hate teachings comes from the devil, who is
the originator of hate. . . . The devil hates Truth, because
he is not made of Truth. Therefore, he calls Truth hate
teachings, because the truth is against his works of evil,
and it brings them, manifestly before the eyes of the
Righteous. . . . They were the originators of racism, not you
and me. And any race that thinks anything of its race is a
racist. . . . It is an intelligent person who loves his own race
and wants his own race to stand out for itself, and not mix
itself up with other races. This is intelligent and decent.
This, the white man knows. We all are racists who have
two cents worth of knowledge, because racism is only the
love of your own race. . . . The Racist; and you are right.[15]

To Elijah Muhammad, the equation was this simplistic: love of the Messenger of Allah, plus love of Allah, equalled the hope —the only hope—of the Black Race. Or as he expressed it:

ALLAH (God) Has Come and Brought the Black slave the truth. If the Black slave refuses to accept the truth, he will be destroyed for willingly and knowingly rejecting the truth when the truth has come in his midst. . . . I have the Power of Allah (God) the heavens, and the earth and the whole universe on my side to help you in and onto your Own. . . . BLACK Man, who was once a slave in America, you have a way of escape. The way out is not on your own terms. It is on the condition that you submit to Allah (God) and come, follow me. This is the only way out. I am the door and I have the key to your salvation. Reject it and die.[16]

When the Black Muslims refer to "white devils," they are not engaging in rhetoric or symbolism. They mean literally and exactly what they say, and consider it a statement of both religious conviction and historical fact. Thus, the October 31, 1969, issue of *Muhammad Speaks* carried a comic strip of a tough black youth and a young Black Muslim, looking at a white boy. This was the dialogue:

*Tough Black Youth:* There goes a Whitey! . . . Let's *get* him!
*Young Black Muslim:* No, brother.
*Tough Black Youth:* How come? Ain't you a Muslim?
*Young Black Muslim:* Right! And Mr. Muhammad teaches us never to be an aggressor! Oh, sure—after all they've done to us . . . our foreparents . . . 400 years of slavery . . . 100 years of free slavery . . . our people burned and lynched by them! . . . no citizenship! . . . We've got plenty of reasons not to like them! But Mr. Muhammad says when a thing behaves according to its nature, we shouldn't be surprised at its actions! For instance, a wolf— once we understand the wolf's nature, we know him—and stay out

|                        |                                                        |
|------------------------|--------------------------------------------------------|
|                        | of his way! Same with the white man! Since Mr. Muhammad has taught us about their nature and history, we don't waste time hating him—we just know him! And we don't want to integrate with him! |
| *Tough Black Youth:*   | Well, since he's the devil why shouldn't we do him in? |
| *Young Black Muslim:*  | Because Mr. Muhammad says a righteous person never is the aggressor—we don't start fights—we fight only those who fight with us! Brother, I'm going to take you to the mosque so you can get some understanding![17] |

In another issue of the Black Muslim newspaper—three weeks after his comic strip appeared—Elijah Muhammad praised white efforts to help Negroes further their education, but hastened to add that "the white slavemaster's children . . . cannot help from doing evil because their nature is made of evil and not of good."[18] And the author hastens to add that Elijah Muhammad was not speaking about some whites, many whites, or even most whites, but *all* whites.

This was Elijah Muhammad's doctrine—and this was what he sought to instill into the minds of black youths in the Muslim schools. In 1931, Elijah Muhammad had first started the University of Islam educational system in Detroit and 38 years later, to obtain financial support for the new Muhammad University of Islam No. 7 in Harlem, an Educational Banquet was held in the Waldorf-Astoria's Grand Ballroom, on September 14, 1969.[19] It was announced that the stellar event of the evening would be the opportunity to see and hear "The Honorable Elijah Muhammad" in a special film on proper education for the black student.[20] An ad for the event, which appeared in the *Amsterdam News,* noted that "these distinguished community leaders" would be present at the banquet:

Basil Paterson
State Senator

Al Vann
Pres. Afro-American Teachers Assoc.

Percy Sutton
Manhattan Boro President

Charles Rangel
Assemblyman

Judge William Booth

Rev. Milton Galamison

Leonard Weir
Pres. National Society
of Afro-American Policemen

Harcourt Dodds
Deputy Commissioner
N.Y.C. Police Dept.

Livingston Wingate
Exec. Director of
N.Y. Urban League

Isaiah Robinson
N.Y.C. Board of Education

Betty Lomax
Harlem Prep.[21]

It was quite abhorrent enough to contemplate the avid support given the Black Muslim banquet by the chief executive of the Borough of Manhattan, a state senator, an assemblyman, a judge, and even a member of the Board of Education. But it was a staggering act of mindless irresponsibility that among those in attendance would be a high-ranking police official of the city of New York. (Defenders of Deputy Police Commissioner Dodds might well have turned the other side of the coin, and asked themselves if they would have as blithely condoned some white police official's attendance at a Ku Klux Klan social function.)

Some indication of what would be taught black students at this newest University of Islam was given by the minister of Harlem Mosque No. 7, Louis Farrakhan. It was in the kindergarten, said the Black Muslim minister, that "through nursery rhymes and fairy tales, the seeds of falsehood, mysticism and spookism are sown," manifesting themselves later in the black child's inability to cope with reality and his willing acceptance of religious dogma which was based on the unreal and the untruth. Farrakhan went on to state:

> The religion that white people have taught Black people has not been for the good of Black people. It has been to make you and me tools of service for white America. By the time the Black child is 7 years old, he or she is well on

the way to mental and psychological destruction. Mommy
and daddy work and slave all year long to give their child
gifts, but on Christmas eve they give the credit to Santa
Claus. And you wonder why grown men and women sit up
in a church, drooling at the mouth, before a blue-eyed
blond-haired Jesus Christ.[22]

At this $25-a-plate dinner, over 1,200 guests saw a special
20-minute color film featuring Elijah Muhammad, who asserted, "We must build independent educational centers
throughout the country, centers in which the Black Student will
be taught in a manner that will create peace and unity among
ourselves."[23]

Considering that *Muhammad Speaks* had carried a number
of laudatory articles on black militant student revolts on the
campus, there were overtones of irony in the Black Muslim
leader's lament that

the schools of the entire white race today in North America are confused and are in revolt among themselves. Can
my child or your child be sent to such schools where the
teachers and superintendent of schools and of the government are all dissatisfied with each other and cannot form
a good way of carrying out their own schooling? They are
fighting each other and if they are fighting each other can
we go there and seek these dissatisfied teachers who are
in revolution with self for education? No! We want to be
able to compete with the civilized world of education. In
competing with the civilized world, we must have the
knowledge of education that they have—that we may be
able to compete with them.[24]

One of those at the dinner was Bill Patterson, an academic
counselor for the Black Students Union at Pennsylvania State
University. Patterson stated:

The awareness that is sweeping our people today bears
witness to the fact that the Honorable Elijah Muhammad
is an idea whose time has come. A lot of black students
coming up today are going to be teachers. They want to
teach the kind of knowledge that Mr. Muhammad spoke
about tonight. The problem is they are running out of
places to do it. I come here to ask you to help us help
ourselves by helping Mr. Muhammad establish the Uni-

versity of Islam in all the major cities of America. And we
ask you to be in a hurry.[25]

After a question-and-answer period, the audience at the Muslim Education Banquet heard from various political and community representatives, including State Senators Basil
Paterson and Waldaba Stewart, Assemblyman Hulan Jack,
Judge William Booth, Isaiah Robinson, Leonard Weir, Livingston Wingate, Rhody McCoy of the Ocean Hill–Brownsville
School District, and Albert Vann.[26]

No matter how these gentlemen tried to rationalize it (assuming some of them were even willing to make the effort), the
fact remained that knowingly and willingly they were guests at
a dinner sponsored by a sect that was vehemently anti-white,
anti-Christian, anti-Jewish, and anti-American. And if any
prominent white liberal in New York City uttered so much as
a peep of protest, or a syllable of condemnation, the author has
yet to hear about it.

What exactly did the Black Muslims want? For the price of
a copy of *Muhammad Speaks,* one could easily ascertain the
answer, simply by turning to the back page of almost any issue,
where it was all spelled out, point by point. Devotees of the-
Black-Muslims-are-mellowing school of thought would be well
advised to read and re-read this verbatim reprinting of The
Muslim Program, especially the italicized paragraphs:

1. We want freedom. We want a full and complete freedom.
2. We want justice. Equal justice under the law. We
   want justice applied equally to all, regardless of
   creed or class or color.
3. We want equality of opportunity. We want equal
   membership in society with the best in civilized society.
4. *We want our people in America whose parents or*
   *grandparents were descendants from slaves, to be*
   *allowed to establish a separate state or territory of*
   *their own—either on this continent or elsewhere.*
   *We believe that our former slave masters are obli-*
   *gated to provide such land and that the area must*
   *be fertile and minerally rich. We believe that our*
   *former slave masters are obligated to maintain and*
   *supply our needs in this separate territory for the*

*next 20 to 25 years—until we are able to produce
and supply our own needs.*

*Since we cannot get along with them in peace and
equality after giving them 400 years of our sweat
and blood and receiving in return some of the worst
treatment human beings have ever experienced, we
believe our contributions to this land and the suffering forced upon us by white America, justifies our
demand for complete separation in a state or territory of our own.*

5.  *We want freedom for all Believers of Islam now
held in federal prisons. We want freedom for all
black men and women now under death sentence in
innumerable prisons in the North as well as the
South.*

*We want every black man and woman to have the
freedom to accept or reject being separated from the
slave master's children and establish a land of their
own. We know that the above plan for the solution
of the black and white conflict is the best and only
answer to the problem between the two people.*

6.  We want an immediate end to the police brutality
and mob attacks against the so-called Negro
throughout the United States.

We believe that the Federal government should in-
tercede to see that black men and women tried in
white courts receive justice in accordance with the
laws of the land—or allow us to build a new nation
for ourselves, dedicated to justice, freedom and liberty.

7.  As long as we are not allowed to establish a state or
territory of our own, we demand not only equal justice under the laws of the United States, but equal
employment opportunities—NOW!

We do not believe that after 400 years of free or
nearly free labor, sweat and blood, which has helped
America become rich and powerful, that so many
thousands of black people should have to subsist on
relief, charity or live in poor houses.

8.  *We want the government of the United States to
exempt our people from ALL taxation as long as we
are deprived of equal justice under the laws of the
land.*

9.  We want equal education—but separate schools up to
16 for boys and 18 for girls on the condition that the
girls be sent to women's colleges and universities.
*We want all black children educated, taught and*

*trained by their own teachers.*
Under such schooling system [*sic*] we believe we will make a better nation of people. The United States government should provide, free, all necessary text books and equipment, schools and college buildings. The Muslim teachers shall be left free to teach and train their people in the way of righteousness, decency and self-respect.

10. *We believe that intermarriage or race mixing should be prohibited.* We want the religion of Islam taught without hindrance or suppression.

These are some of the things that we, the Muslims, want for our people in North America.

When the Black Muslims spoke about equality, they were most assuredly thinking in terms of "separate and equal." The proof of that statement is in the contents of The Muslim Program, and in these articles of separatist faith from "What the Muslims Believe":

*We believe that the offer of integration is hypocritical and is made by those who are trying to deceive the black peoples into believing that their 400-year-old open enemies of freedom, justice and equality are all of a sudden their "friends." Furthermore, we believe that such deception is intended to prevent black people from realizing that the time in history has arrived for the separation from the whites of this nation.*
If the white people are truthful about their professed friendship toward the so-called Negro they can prove it by dividing up America with their slaves.[27]

If any white organization, with equal bluntness, had condemned "intermarriage" and unleashed such vehement broadsides against "integration," it would have been denounced from coast to coast and from pulpit to pulpit—as the ultimate in racism. But in keeping with the politically fashionable New Racism, reaction to the Black Muslim doctrine evoked little more than a raised eyebrow, and a rather gentle shaking of the head.

Can this Black Muslim program really be taken seriously? Not if its approach is "all or nothing." But perhaps some of it can, if its approach is a piecemeal one—a small victory here and a small victory there—geared to the art of the practical and the possible. And quite possibly, this may be the key to those controversial land purchases in Alabama.

In a half-dozen Southern states, agents for the Progressive Land Development Corporation were scouting rural areas for prospective land purchases. The corporation purchased 907 acres in central Alabama, and spoke of increasing its Alabama holdings to about 100,000 acres in a year's time. The company paid about $223,000 for their acquisitions in St. Clair County— a 1-acre sawmill in Pell City, and a 376-acre ranch and a nearby 431-acre farm in Ashville, about 18 miles north of Pell City. The sellers of the farm were a white automobile dealer, Ray Wyatt, and a white dentist, Robert McClung, who racked up a tidy $20,000 profit on the transaction. This farm surrounded the small Pine Forest Missionary Baptist Church and cemetery.[28]

Rumors erupted that the land had been bought by Negroes. Wallace Wyatt, a deacon of the church, asked his brother, Ray Wyatt, about it. Later, Wallace Wyatt said he had been forced to break a pledge of confidence he had made to his brother "in order to uphold the family honor and the honor of this state and nation" after he found out that his brother had been acting as an agent for the Black Muslims.[29] The Progressive Land Development Corporation was actually owned by the Black Muslims.[30]

Both Ray Wyatt and Dr. McClung claimed that at the time they didn't know the buyer, a Negro named Walter Turner— national director of public relations for the Black Muslims— was representing Elijah Muhammad. But few of their white neighbors believed them. Ray Wyatt said his auto dealer business "is off at least 90 percent. I had been selling 75 to 100 cars a month and now I'm not selling anything."[31]

The Muslims insisted that their Alabama land purchases were strictly business ventures and had nothing to do wih black separatism. The Muslims insisted that they were raising not an army but merely crops and cattle to supply their supermarkets and restaurants in Chicago and elsewhere. But most local whites were convinced the real aim was to make St. Clair County the capital of the new Nation of Islam.[32] Edwin Strickland, the staff director of the Alabama Legislative Commission to Preserve the Peace, told an audience of whites at a local high school that Black Muslims had an announced goal of setting up a separate black nation, and that their farm purchases were a form of blockbusting.[33]

At the Pine Forest Missionary Baptist Church, the Reverend James H. Bishop said the Black Muslims "are after one thing. These Southern states of ours. Our deepest conviction is that they are going to train people to start their new nation here, and that's why we're fighting them." Reverend Bishop vowed, "I for one am willing to lay my life down for the cause, if necessary."[34] Muslim spokesman Walter L. Turner responded, "We have not broken any laws. If they attempt any violence against us, we will send 1,000 Black Muslims in there."[35] Which was no inconsequential threat, considering that the two towns involved had a combined population of only about 5,000.[36]

The state of Alabama filed four suits against the Progressive Land Development Corporation, charging that the land purchases were invalid because the corporation was not registered to do business in the state.[37] In the county itself, two Hereford cows in the Black Muslim herd were killed by gunfire. Acid was poured on 12 new cars parked in a lot beside the Ray Wyatt Co., causing $5,000 in damage.[38] Wyatt said he planned to begin laying off his 30 employees and liquidating the business. He stated that he, his wife, and children were the target of constant telephone death threats.[39] Dr. McClung fled to Mobile to try to start anew, but returned to the county. He severed all business ties with Ray Wyatt and swore never to have anything to do with Muslims again. A few days before, he had been ousted as head of the local unit of the John Birch Society. Said McClung: "For the first time in my life, I know what it feels like to be black."[40] At about this time a group called RID (Restore Integrity to Development) sprang up to run the Black Muslims out. It was headed by Wallace Wyatt, who said of the Muslims, "We can't live with them because they don't believe in Christ. I know the Jews don't believe in Christ either, but they're not a militant race."[41]

Was the land purchase made simply to supply products for their restaurants and supermarkets, as the Black Muslims contended? Or was the purpose a more insidious one—to establish a beachhead for the Nation of Islam, as most Alabama whites feared? The answer was by no means certain, but the whole affair provided a chilling preview of what conceivably could happen in this country if the Black Muslims ever try to practice the black separatism they preach.

# CHAPTER 3

# Malcolm X

THE DOCTRINE OF BLACK SEPARATISM IS HARDLY A NEW arrival on the American scene. As far back as 1811, wealthy Negro ship-owner Paul Cuffe went to Sierra Leone in his own vessel to investigate possibilities of taking free Negroes back to Africa; four years later, Cuffe took 38 Negroes to Africa at his own expense, paying what was then the immense sum of three or four thousand dollars.[1] Shortly before the Civil War, a leading Negro physician and author, Martin R. Delany, expressed the view that Negroes would prosper in Central and South America.[2] In our own century, the now legendary Marcus Garvey said the only hope for American Negroes was to flee America and return to Africa, to buld a country of their own. "Wake up, Ethiopia!" Garvey cried. "Wake up, Africa! Let us work toward the one glorious end of a free, redeemed and mighty nation. Let Africa be a bright star among the constellation of nations."[3]

But in one of those curious twists and turns of history that defy the descriptive powers of a dozen thesauruses, black separatism has reached its intellectual zenith at a time of es-calating civil rights legislation. At a time when more black political leaders hold elective office on the city, state, and fed-eral level—and a black judge sits on the Supreme Court—embittered black men and women talk more openly of one or another form of black separatism.

Their words may differ, their doctrines may vary, their proposals may seem contradictory and even conflicting, but they are all branches on the same tree—a tree that was planted and nurtured, painstakingly, lovingly, by one remarkable man, out of the fears, the hates, and the agonies of the ghetto.

Almost alone, at a time when others predicted the Civil Rights Act of 1964 would inspire an almost otherworldly sense of brotherhood, this one man, Malcolm X, predicted more violence, more estrangement, more bitterness. Almost alone, this one Evangelist of Chaos, Malcolm X, stumped the ghettos with a fiercely worded message of impending disaster. Denunciation served only to strengthen his appeal. He became a folk hero of the ghetto, a black St. George, day after day, in speech after speech, slaying and then re-slaying the white dragon in its power-structure lair. An ex-convict and ex-hustler, Malcolm X was a towering original in life, and his influence is, if anything, even more powerful in death.

Sixty blacks marched through an old Roxbury slum neighborhood in Boston, and announced plans to name one of its intersections "Malcolm X Square."[4] At Northwestern University, black students tacked his poster portrait over the mantel at their house, and called him "St. Malcolm."[5] At the University of California's Santa Cruz branch, the mostly white Academic Senate unanimously approved a proposal to name one of the campus's seven colleges for Malcolm.[6] There were Malcolm X T-shirts, buttons, and posters in the ghettos and on the campus, all over the country. His autobiography sold 800,000 paperback copies—selling, at one time, at a rate of 100,000 a month.[7]

But today, in death as in life, it is the spoken word that is the ultimate weapon of Malcolm X: the words he spoke before countless groups and meetings, from the streets of Harlem to Cairo and Accra (Ghana), from a socialist forum to one at the Harvard Law School—words that inflamed the imagination, words that plunged a red-hot iron into the black psyche. It was a psychedelic prose whose dazzling verbiage nearly blinded logic and fact. And if black militants today adore "St. Malcolm," it is surely because of the hymn of hate he chanted about his country, almost until the very moment of his death.

The black militants' emulation of Malcolm X transcends words and dogma. You not only read it and hear it, but you can see it in their faces. The grim caricature rarely, if ever, varies. There is the scowl of utter hostility, the supersensitivity that assumes any white man a racist until proven innocent (and then they may very well proceed to denounce the proof as racist in itself). There is the implacable, unalloyed hatred of virtually every institution in this country, from the *Mayflower* to the present. There is their own version of the Berlin Wall—in their minds and souls—in which the black "brothers" are aligned on one side, and the white "devils" on the other (with only a few White Toms allowed to scale the fortress, if they all but take a blood oath of unquestioning servility to The Cause). This is today's black militant, and as a photo of his fierce-visaged appearance will testify, this is a virtual carbon copy of Malcolm X.

What did Malcolm X want? What did he believe in? What did he drive a generation of black militants to believe in? Why do many of the most vehement black revolutionaries in the country all but worship him? Inevitably, one returns to the spoken words of Malcolm X, and perhaps it would be well to begin with the speech he made at Cory Methodist Church in Cleveland. The speech came during a turning point in his life, four months after Elijah Muhammad had suspended Malcolm X for commenting that the "chickens had come home to roost" in the assassination of John F. Kennedy. At the time Malcolm delivered his speech, he had just recently announced his decision to leave the Nation of Islam and to organize a new movement.[8] There was high interest in what he might say about the Civil Rights Act of 1964, which had just begun to be debated in Congress. A few months later, civil rights leaders would urge a "broad curtailment if not total moratorium" on all mass demonstrations until after the Presidential election,[9] but there was not the slightest curtailment of Malcolm's hypermilitant invective in his speech in Cleveland:

If we don't do something real soon I think you'll have to agree that we're going to be forced either to use the ballot or the bullet. It's one or the other in 1964. It isn't that time is running out—time has run out! 1964 threatens to be the most explosive year America has ever witnessed. . . . The year when all of the white political crooks will be right back in your and my community with their false promises, building up our hopes for a letdown, with their trickery and their treachery, with their false promises which they don't intend to keep. As they nourish these dissatisfactions, it can only lead to one thing, an explosion; and now we have the type of black man on the scene in America today . . . who just doesn't intend to turn the other cheek any longer.[10]

Malcolm tore into the black electorate:

It was the black man's vote that put the present administration in Washington, D.C. Your vote, your dumb vote, your ignorant vote, your wasted vote put in an administration in Washington, D.C., that has seen fit to pass every kind of legislation imaginable, saving you until last, then filibustering on top of that.[11]

And he kept fanning the flames at the Militant Labor Forum, sponsored by a socialist weekly:

The job of the Northern Democrat is to make the Negro think that he is our friend. He is always smiling and wagging his tail and telling us how much he can do for us if we vote for him. But at the same time that he's out in front telling us what he's going to do, behind the door he's in cahoots with the Southern Democrat setting up the machinery to make sure he'll never have to keep his promise.[12]

But Malcolm X had a very special hell reserved for the winner of the 1964 election:

In 1964, 97 percent of the black American voters supported Lyndon B. Johnson, Hubert Humphrey, and the Democratic Party. Ninety-seven percent! No one minority group in the history of the world has ever given so much of its uncompromising support to one candidate and one party. No one group, no one group, has ever gone all the way to support a party and its candidate as did the black people in America in 1964. . . . And the first act of the Democratic Party, Lyndon B. included, in 1965, when the representatives from the state of Mississippi who *refused* to support

Johnson came to Washington, D.C., and the black people of Mississippi sent representatives there to challenge the legality of these people being seated—what did Johnson say? Nothing! What did Humphrey say? Nothing! What did Robert Pretty-Boy Kennedy say? Nothing! Nothing! Not one thing! . . . [The Democrats] get all the Negro vote, and after they get it the Negro gets nothing in return. All they did when they got to Washington was give a few big Negroes big jobs. Those big Negroes didn't need big jobs, they already had jobs. That's camouflage, that's trickery, that's treachery, window-dressing.[13]

Again and again, Malcolm returned to the theme: The ballot or the bullet:

. . . The Negro in this country holds the balance of power, and if the Negro in this country were given what the Constitution says he is supposed to have, the added power of the Negro in this country would sweep all of the racists and the segregationists out of office. It would change the entire political structure of the country. It would wipe out the Southern segregationism that now controls America's foreign policy, as well as America's domestic policy. And the only way without bloodshed that this can be brought about is that the black man has to be given full use of the ballot in every one of the fifty states. But if the black man doesn't get the ballot, then you are going to be faced with another man who forgets the ballot and starts using the bullet.[14]

Seven months before the Los Angeles riots, Malcolm X seemed clairvoyant:

1964 was not a pie-in-the-sky Year of Promise, as was promised in January of that year. Blood did flow in the streets of Harlem, Philadelphia, Rochester, some place over in New Jersey, and elsewhere. In 1965 even more blood will flow. More than you ever dreamed. It'll flow downtown as well as uptown. Why? Why will it flow? Have the causes that forced it to flow in '64 been removed? Have the causes that made it flow in '63 been removed? The causes are still there. . . . Black people in 1965 will not be controlled by these Uncle Tom leaders, believe me; they won't be held in check, they won't be held on the plantation by these overseers, they won't be held on the corral,

they won't be held back at all. . . . So in 1965 we should see
a lot of action. Since the old methods haven't worked,
they'll be forced to try new methods. . . .[15]

Who were "they"? What percentage of the black people did
"they" comprise? Malcolm X never really made that clear, and
quite probably could not have cared less. Because in his own
implacable vocabulary of vitriol, "they" were the *real* black
men, even if only a minority within a minority, while the moderates were Uncle Toms, even if 80 percent of the black population happened to agree with their abhorrence of force and
violence.

Malcolm X was on more solid ground when he talked about
black pride. Few, if any, civil rights leaders could fault him
when he told a meeting in Detroit sponsored by the Afro-American Broadcasting Company:

> Number one, you have to realize that up until 1959 Africa
> was dominated by the colonial powers. Having complete
> control over Africa, the colonial powers of Europe pro-
> jected the image of Africa negatively. They always project
> Africa in a negative light; jungle savages, cannibals, noth-
> ing civilized. Why then naturally it was so negative that it
> was negative to you and me, and you and I began to hate
> it. . . . You can't hate your origin and not end up hating
> yourself. You can't hate Africa and not hate yourself. . . .
> You know yourself that we have been a people who hated
> our African characteristics. We hated our heads, we hated
> the shape of our nose, we wanted one of those long-dog-
> like noses, you know, we hated the color of our skin, hated
> the blood of Africa that was in our veins. And in hating our
> features and our skin and our blood, why we had to end up
> hating ourselves . . . it made us feel inferior; it made us feel
> inadequate; made us feel helpless.[16]

Again, civil rights leaders found it difficult to criticize Malcolm X for statements such as the following (although it must
be observed that the same statement—applauded as the inali-
enable right of self-defense on the part of Negroes—would
have been denounced as vigilantism if uttered by whites):

> How can you and I be looked upon as men with black
> women being beaten and nothing being done about it,

black children and black babies being beaten and nothing being done about it? No, we don't deserve to be recognized as men as long as our women can be brutalized in the manner that this woman [Fannie Lou Hamer of Mississippi] described, and nothing being done about it, but we sit around singing "We Shall Overcome."[17]

Much of what Malcolm X said has been paraphrased, only slightly, by the black militant student of today. What you are about to read evoked resounding echoes in the black student societies on a dozen college campuses, but Malcolm X said it in Harlem in December 1964:

When I was in Africa, I noticed some of the Africans got their freedom faster than others. Some areas of the African continent became independent faster than other areas. I noticed that in the areas where independence had been gotten, someone got angry. And in the areas where independence had not been achieved, yet, no one was angry. They were sad—they'd sit around and talk about their plight, but they weren't mad. And usually when people are sad, they don't do anything. They just cry over their condition. But when they get angry, they bring about a change. When they get angry, they aren't interested in logic, they aren't interested in odds, they aren't interested in consequences. When they get angry, they realize the condition that they're in—that their suffering is unjust, immoral, illegal, and that anything they do to correct it or eliminate it, they're justified. *When you and I develop that kind of anger and speak in that voice, then we'll get some kind of respect and recognition, and some changes from these people who have been promising us falsely already for far too long.*[18] [Emphasis added]

Malcolm X never had the copyright on the litany of vilification black militants use to describe America, but his words still serve as a macabre model for the angry young radicals of the ghetto:

This society is controlled primarily by the racists and segregationists who are in Washington, D.C., in positions of power. . . . That is a society whose government doesn't hesitate to inflict the most brutal form of punishment and oppression upon dark-skinned people all over the world. . . . This is the *worst* racist society on this earth. There is no country on earth in which you can live and racism be brought out in you—whether you're white or black—more so than this country that poses as a Democracy.[19]

To Malcolm X, racism was *white*—period. He didn't raise so much as an eyebrow over black racism, as shown in this answer to a question at the Harvard Law Forum, 2 months before his death:

Usually the black racist has been produced by the white racist. In most cases where you see it, it is the reaction to white racism, and if you analyze it closely, it's not really black racism. I think black people have shown less racist tendencies than any people since the beginning of history . . . if we react to white racism with a violent reaction, to me that's not black racism. if you come to put a rope around my neck and I hang you for it, to me that's not racism. Yours is racism, but my reaction has nothing to do with racism. My reaction is the reaction of a human being, reacting to defend himself and protect himself.[20]

Implicit in Malcolm's statement was the assumption that any man had the right to sit as judge, jury, and executioner in a case of racism. It was one thing to assert the right of any man, white or black, to defend himself from actual assault, and quite another matter to elevate "an eye for an eye, a tooth for a tooth" to virtually the status of the Bill of Rights. Once having that rope in their hands, where would black racists stop—or *would* they stop? And would they always fastidiously wait until a white racist had struck the first blow?

Malcolm X advocated no such bloody activity against white liberals, but his denunciation of them came uncomfortably close to their political jugular: "This government has failed the Negro. This so-called democracy has failed the Negro. And all these white liberals have definitely failed the Negro."[21]

On another occasion, he told a mostly white audience: "I know that all that have come in here tonight don't call yourselves liberals. Because that's a nasty name today. It represents hypocrisy."[22]

It was a theme he returned to, again and again, with obvious relish:

You're white. You can go and hang out with another white liberal and see how hypocritical they are. A lot of you sitting right here know that you've seen whites up in a Negro's face with flowery words, and as soon as that Negro walks away you listen to how your white friend talks. We have black people who can pass as white. We know how you talk.[23]

The white liberal who seemed to inspire Malcolm's greatest contempt was Robert Kennedy, principally in his onetime role of U.S. Attorney General:

I remember the exposé that *Look Magazine* did on the Meredith situation in Mississippi. *Look Magazine* did an exposé showing that Robert Kennedy and Governor Barnett had made a deal, wherein the Attorney General was going to come down and try to force Meredith into school, and Barnett was going to stand at the door, you know, and say, "No, you can't come in." He was going to get in anyway, but it was all arranged in advance and then Barnett was supposed to keep the support of the white racists, because that's who he was upholding, and Kennedy would keep the support of the Negroes, because that's who he'd be upholding. It was a cut-and-dried deal. And it's not a secret; it was written, they write about it. But if that's a deal, how many other deals do you think go down? What you think is on the level is crookeder, brothers and sisters, than a pretzel which is most crooked.[24]

Where Malcolm X was willing to accept white allies, it was with the none-too-subtle proviso that they be political automatons—unquestioningly rubber-stamping whatever action the black militants took:

The black man has to be shown how to free himself, and the white one who is sincerely interested has to back whatever that black group decides to do. . . . Nowadays, as our people begin to wake up, they're going to realize they've been talking about Negro revolt. Negro revolution—You can't talk that stuff to me unless you're really for one. . . . And most of you aren't. When the deal goes down, you back out every time.[25]

Toward the end of his life, Malcolm seemed to be inching slowly toward the idea of a possible alliance with sufficiently groveling white sympathizers. But the way in which he approached it suggested that he would have handled it, if at all, with one 10-foot pole firmly attached to another 10-foot pole. Commenting on the difficulty of getting militant whites and blacks together, Malcolm told Marlene Nadle, of the *Village Voice*:

> The whites can't come uptown too easily because the people aren't feeling too friendly. The black who goes downtown loses his identity, loses his soul. He's in no position to be a bridge because he has lost contact with Harlem. Our Negro leaders never had contact, so they can't do it. The only person who could is someone who is completely trusted by the black community. If I were to try, I would have to be very diplomatic, because there are parts of Harlem where you don't dare mention the idea.[26]

If Malcolm X had even the slightest feeling for this country, he carried the secret with him to his grave. The same day he spoke of "the ballot or the bullet," Malcolm, completely in character, told his audience:

> I'm not a Democrat, I'm not a Republican, and I don't even consider myself an American. If you and I were Americans, there'd be no problem. Those Hunkies that just got off the boat, they're already Americans; Polacks are already Americans; the Italian refugees are already Americans. Everything that came out of Europe, every blue-eyed thing is already an American. And as long as you and I have been over here, we aren't Americans yet.[27]

It must have been a source of wry amusement to those European immigrants who had known considerable discrimination in this country to be told that they were Americans as soon as they got off the boat.

Expanding on his theme, Malcolm argued:

> Being here in America doesn't make you an American. Being born here in America doesn't make you an American. Why, if birth made you American, you wouldn't need any legislation, you wouldn't need any amendments to the

Constitution, you wouldn't be faced with civil-rights filibustering in Washington, D. C., right now. They don't have
to pass civil-rights legislation to make a Polack an American. . . . I'm speaking as a victim of this American system.
And I see America through the eyes of the victim. I don't
see any American dream; I see an American nightmare.[28]

Years before James Forman started billing the churches and
synagogues for "reparations"—and long before the Republic of
New Africa had submitted a bill in the millions to our Department of State—Malcolm X had planted the seed:

Three hundred and ten years we worked in this country
without a dime in return—I mean without a *dime* in return. You let the white man walk around here talking
about how rich this country is, but you never stop to think
how it got rich so quick. It got rich because you made it
rich. . . . Your and my mother and father, who didn't work
an eight-hour shift but worked from "can't see" in the
morning until "can't see" at night, and worked for nothing,
making the white man rich, making Uncle Sam rich.[29]

His indictment was a powerful one; the problem was that the
defendants, including Simon Legree, had died a long time ago.
Like a black Don Quixote, Malcolm X was tilting with the wind-
mills of a long-dead past. Malcolm declared:

This government should feel lucky that our people aren't
anti-American. They should get down on their hands and
knees every morning and thank God that 22 million black
people have not become anti-American. You've given us
every right to. The whole world would side with us, if we
became anti-American. You know, that's something to
think about.[30]

Malcolm's opinion of policemen went beyond the usual cries
of "brutality." He conceived of them as little more than storm
troopers, inflicted upon a community which wanted no part of
them:

A black man in America lives in a police state. He doesn't
live in any democracy, he lives in a police state. That's
what it is, that's what Harlem is . . . the police in Harlem,
their presence is like occupation forces, like an occupying

army. They're not in Harlem to protect us; they're not in Harlem to look out for our welfare; they're in Harlem to protect the interests of the businessmen who don't even live there.[31]

If one's critical faculties were suspended long enough to swallow the claim that Harlem was being occupied by an enemy force, one was almost prepared to hear the next non sequitur:

In Harlem, for instance, all of the stores are owned by white people, all of the buildings are owned by white people. The black people are just there—paying rent, buying the groceries but they don't own the stores, clothing stores, food stores, any kind of stores; don't even own the homes that they live in. These are all owned by outsiders, and for these run-down apartment dwellings, the black man in Harlem pays more money than the man down in the rich Park Avenue section. It costs us more money to live in the slums than it costs them to live down on Park Avenue. Black people in Harlem know this, and that the white merchants charge us more money for food in Harlem—and it's the cheap food, the worst food; we have to pay more money for it than the man has to pay for it downtown. So black people know that they're being exploited and that their blood is being sucked and they see no way out.[32]

In the case of exorbitant grocery prices, there was a very simple way out, a boycott of such stores until their prices were rolled back to an equitable level. In the case of exorbitant rents, there again was a way out for Harlem tenants: insist that the rent-control laws on the books be strictly enforced under pain of political reprisals on Election Day if the city fathers should refuse. Of course, it also needed to be said, though Malcolm X would probably have been the very last person to admit it, that if there were cases of rent-gouging landlords, other cases could be cited of ghetto tenements so profitless that the landlords had simply abandoned them.

Malcolm continued:

When the thing is finally sparked, the white man is not there—he's gone. The merchant is not there, the landlord is not there, the one they consider to be the enemy isn't there. So they knock at his property. This is what makes them knock down the store windows and set fire to things, and things of that sort.... It's a corrupt, vicious, hypocritical system that has castrated the black man and the only way the black man can get back at it is to strike it in the only way he knows how.[33]

In the world of Malcolm X, the torch of liberty was a Molotov cocktail, not only burning black militants' bridges behind them, but also helping them blaze a bloody trail to revolution.

This is a real revolution. Revolution is always based on land. Revolution is never based on begging somebody for an integrated cup of coffee. Revolutions are never fought by turning the other cheek. Revolutions are never based upon love-your-enemy and pray-for-those-who-spitefully-use-you. And revolutions are never waged singing, "We Shall Overcome." Revolutions are based upon bloodshed. Revolutions are never compromising. Revolutions are never based upon negotiations. Revolutions are never based upon any kind of tokenism whatsoever. Revolutions are never even based upon that which is begging a corrupt society or a corrupt system to accept us into it. Revolutions overturn systems. And there is no system on this earth which has proven itself more corrupt, more criminal, than this system that in 1964 still colonizes 22 million African-Americans, still enslaves 22 million Afro-Americans.[34]

How would the black man wage his revolution? What means would he use to achieve his ends? "Our objective is complete freedom, complete justice, complete equality, *by any means necessary*"[35] (emphasis added).

There was not the slightest equivocation in Malcolm's use of "by any means necessary." He meant exactly what he said, and referred to it again and again in his own no-quarter-asked, no-quarter-given brand of black Machiavellism:

You get freedom by letting your enemy know that you'll do anything to get your freedom; then you'll get it. It's the only way you'll get it. When you get that kind of attitude, they'll label you as a "crazy Negro," or they'll call you a "crazy nigger"—they don't say Negro. Or they'll call you an extremist or a subversive, or seditious, or a red or a radical. But when you stay radical long enough, and get

enough people to be like you, you'll get your freedom. . . .
You've got to take something in your hand and say, "Look,
it's you or me." And I guarantee you he'll give you freedom
then. He'll say, "This man is ready for it." I said something
in your hand—I won't define what I mean by "something
in your hand." I don't mean bananas.[36]

If the black militants had never heard him make a single
speech, those four words—"by any means necessary"—would
have told them all they needed to know about the thoughts of
Malcolm X. Certainly, the meaning was clear enough, in his
famous Appeal to African Heads of State:

> Out of frustration and hopelessness our young people have
> reached the point of no return. We no longer endorse pa-
> tience and turning-the-other-cheek. We assert the right of
> self-defense by whatever means necessary, and reserve
> the right of maximum retaliation against our racist op-
> pressors, no matter what the odds against us are. From
> here on in, if we must die anyway, we will die fighting
> back and we will not die alone. We intend to see that our
> racist oppressors also get a taste of death. We are well
> aware that our future efforts to defend ourselves, by reta-
> liating—by meeting violence with violence, eye for eye
> and tooth for tooth—could create the type of racial conflict
> in America that could easily escalate into a violent, world-
> wide, bloody race war.[37]

Explicitly or implicitly, those four words were the underpin-
nings of virtually his every major speech:

> Nobody can give you independence. Nobody can give you
> freedom. Nobody can give you equality or justice or any-
> thing. If you're a man, you take it. If you can't take it, you
> don't deserve it.[38]

When it suited his purposes, Malcolm could, with pseudo-
reverence, cite the actions of the Founding Fathers:

> If George Washington didn't get independence for this
> country nonviolently, and if Patrick Henry didn't come up
> with a nonviolent statement and you taught me to look
> upon them as patriots and heroes then it's time for you to
> realize that I have studied your books well. . . .[39]

But not well enough. Unless he just chose to ignore that basic document of American democracy, the Declaration of Independence, which spoke out against "absolute despotism," and "an absolute Tyranny over these States"—all very much different from the revolution against majority rule, and against the democratic form of government that was envisioned by Malcolm X.

Which brought him back to the words, "by any means necessary":

I read a little story once, and Mau Mau proved it. I read a story once where someone asked some group of people how many of them wanted freedom. They all put up their hand [*sic*]. Think there were about 300 of them. Then the person says, "Well, how many of you are ready to kill anybody who gets in your way for freedom?" About fifty put up their hands. And he told those fifty, "You stand over here." That left 250 sitting who wanted freedom, but weren't ready to kill for it. So he told this fifty, "Now you wanted freedom and you said you'd kill anybody who'd get in your way. You see those 250? You get them first. Some of them are your own brothers and sisters and mothers and fathers. But they're the ones who stand in the way of your freedom. They're afraid to do whatever is necessary to get it and they'll stop you from doing it. Get rid of them and freedom will come naturally."[40]

Malcolm X commented, "I go for that. That's what the Mau Mau learned. The Mau Mau realized that the only thing that was standing in the way of the independence of the African in Kenya was another African. So they started getting them one by one, all of those Toms. One after another they'd find another Uncle Tom African by the roadside. Today they're free."[41]

Speaking to a Harlem audience, Malcolm X declared: "In Mississippi we need a Mau Mau. In Alabama we need a Mau Mau. In Georgia we need a Mau Mau. Right here in Harlem, in New York City, we need a Mau Mau."[42]

To Malcolm X, Hitler was not dead, but alive and well in America:

. . . If you and I don't waken and see what this man is doing to us, then it will be too late. They may have the gas ovens built before you realize that they're already hot . . . You'll be in one of them, just like the Jews ended up in gas ovens

over there in Germany. You're in a society that's just as
capable of building gas ovens for black people as Hitler's
society was. . . . [43]

In espousing the attitude, "by any means necessary," Malcolm was not dismayed by the massive numbers and power of
his opposition:

I find you can get a whole lot of small people and whip hell
out of a whole lot of big people. They haven't got anything
to lose, and they've got everything to gain. And they'll let
you know in a minute: "It takes two to tango; when I go, you
go."[44]

And in a speech to a predominantly socialist audience in the
Militant Labor Forum Hall, Malcolm X observed:

The people of China grew tired of their oppressors and the
people rose up against their oppressors. They didn't rise up
nonviolently. It was easy to say that the odds were against
them, but eleven of them started out and today those
eleven control 800 million. . . . When Castro was up in the
mountains of Cuba, they told him the odds were against
him. Today he's sitting in Havana and all the power this
country has can't remove him.[45]

In noting Malcolm's remarks, the author was reminded of an
occasion, some years ago, when he went to Union Square in
Manhattan to debate with some of the local Communist ora-
tors. One of these Red spellbinders was regaling his audience
with stories of the paradise on earth that was the Soviet Union,
and how wildly popular its government was. "If that's the
case," the author mildly inquired, "could you tell me who ran
against Stalin in the last election, and how many votes he got?"
After giving the author a look that went through him like an
acetylene torch, the Communist orator abruptly changed the
subject. In like manner, what Malcolm X was speaking about
was not democracy but dictatorship, not freedom, but a power
so absolute as to approach political slavery, with a violent
death clearly indicated for "Uncle Tom" dissenters.

With singular adroitness, Malcolm X even found a way to
turn the words *majority* and *minority* against his opponents:

They [black nationalists] look upon themselves as a part of dark mankind. They see the whole struggle not within the confines of the American stage, but they look upon the struggle on the world stage. And, in the world context, they see that the dark man outnumbers the white man. On the world stage, the white man is just a microscopic minority . . . when the 22 million black Americans see that our problem is the same as the problem of the people who are being oppressed in South Vietnam and the Congo and Latin America, then—the oppressed people of this earth make up a majority, not a minority—then we approach our problem as a majority that can demand, not as a minority that has to beg.[46]

It was a theme he kept pounding on:

As long as we think we're over here in America isolated and all by ourselves and underdogs, then we'll always have that hat-in-hand begging attitude that the man loves to see us display. But when we know that all of our people are behind us—as he said, almost 500 million of us—we don't need to beg anybody. All we need to do is remind them what they did to us; that it's time for them to stop; that if they don't stop, we will stop them. Yes, we will stop them.[47]

To Malcolm X, "Black Power" were words to be painted on a world canvas:

If your power base is only here, you can forget it. You can't build a power base here. You have to have a power base among brothers and sisters. You have to have your power base among people who have something in common with you.[48]

For reasons as obvious as these, there were few more avid supporters of the UN than Malcolm:

Politically, Africa as a continent, and the African people as a people, have the largest representation of any continent in the United Nations. Politically, the Africans are in a more strategic position and in a stronger position whenever a conference is taking place at the international level. Today, power is international, real power is international; today, real power is not local. . . . When you see that the African nations at the international level comprise the largest representative body and the largest force of any continent, why, you and I would be out of our minds not to identify with that power bloc.[49]

Malcolm X did far more than just "identify" with the African bloc of nations. On July 9, 1964, he left the United States for Africa and the Middle East, primarily to attend the second meeting of the Organization of African Unity, which had been formed to bring about joint action by the independent African governments. The OAU conference was held in Cairo July 17–21, and was attended by most of the heads of the thirty-four member states. The welcoming address was made by President Gamal Abdel Nasser of the United Arab Republic, who hailed the Civil Rights Act of 1964 that had recently been enacted in the United States. As an observer at the conference, Malcolm X was permitted to submit to the delegates an eight-page memorandum urging their support of the Negro struggle in the United States, and their help in bringing the problems of the American Negro before the United Nations. The memorandum was delivered to the delegates on July 17, one day before the Harlem riots.[50]

Here, in part, is what Malcolm X wrote:

Your Excellencies:
The Organization of Afro-American Unity has sent me to attend this historic African summit conference as an observer to represent the interests of 22 million African-Americans whose *human rights* are being violated daily by the racism of American Imperialists. . . . The Organization of Afro-American Unity (OAAU), has been formed by a cross-section of America's African-American community, and is patterned after the letter and spirit of the Organization of African Unity (OAU). . . . Since the 22 million of us were originally Africans, who are now in America not by choice but only by a cruel accident in our history, we strongly believe that African problems are our problems and our problems are African problems. . . . We, in America, are your long-lost brothers and sisters, and I am here only to remind you that our problems are your problems. As the African-Americans "awaken" today, we find ourselves in a strange land that has rejected us, and, like the prodigal son, we are turning to our elder brothers for help. We pray our pleas will not fall upon deaf

ears. . . . During the past ten years the entire world has witnessed our men, women and children being attacked and bitten by vicious police dogs, brutally beaten by police clubs, and washed down the sewers by high-pressure water hoses that would rip the clothes from our bodies and the flesh from our limbs. And all of these inhuman atrocities have been inflicted upon us by the American governmental authorities, the police themselves, for no reason other than we seek the recognition and respect granted other human beings in America. Your excellencies: The American government is either unable or unwilling to protect the lives and property of your 22 million African-American brothers and sisters. We stand defenseless, at the mercy of American racists who murder us at will for no reason other than we are black and of African descent. . . . your problems will never be fully solved until and unless ours are solved. You will never be fully respected until and unless we are also respected. You will never be recognized as free human beings until and unless we are also recognized and treated as human beings. Our problem is your problem. It is not a Negro problem, nor an American problem. This is a world problem; a problem for humanity. It is not a problem of civil rights but a problem of human rights. . . . If South Africa is guilty of violating the human rights of Africans here on the mother continent, then America is guilty of worse violations of the 22 million Africans on the American continent. And if South African racism is not a domestic issue, then American racism also is not a *domestic* issue. . . . The United States Supreme Court passed a law ten years ago, making America's segregated school system illegal. But the federal government has yet to enforce this law even in the North. If the federal government cannot enforce the law of the highest court in the land when it comes to nothing but equal rights to education for African-Americans, how can anyone be so naive as to think all the additional laws brought into being by the civil-rights bill will be enforced? . . . We beseech the independent African states to help us bring our problem before the United Nations, on the grounds that the United States government is morally incapable of protecting the lives and the property of 22 million African-Americans. And on the grounds that our deteriorating plight is definitely becoming a threat to world peace. . . . In the interests of world peace and security, we beseech the heads of the independent African states to recommend an immediate investigation into our problem by the United Nations Commission on Human

Rights. . . . May Allah's blessings of good health and wisdom be upon you all. Salaam Alaikum.

Malcolm X, Chairman
Organization of Afro-American Unity[51]

The Organization of African Unity did, in fact, pass a resolution, "Racial Discrimination in The United States of America." The resolution noted "with satisfaction the recent enactment of the Civil Rights Act designed to secure for American Negroes their basic human rights," while declaring that the OAU conference was "deeply disturbed, however, by continuing manifestations of racial bigotry and racial oppression against Negro citizens of the United States of America." The resolution concluded by restating the OAU's "belief that the existence of discriminatory practices is a matter of deep concern to member states of the Organization of African Unity," and by urging "the government authorities in the United States of America to intensify their efforts to ensure the total elimination of all forms of discrimination based on race, color, or ethnic origin."[52]

On August 13, 1964, the *New York Times* printed a dispatch by M. S. Handler, who reported:

Malcolm's eight-page memorandum to the heads of state at the Cairo conference requesting their support became available here only recently. After studying it, officials said that if Malcolm succeeded in convincing just one African government to bring up the charge at the United Nations, the United States government would be faced with a touchy problem. The United States, officials here believe, would find itself in the same category as South Africa, Hungary, and other countries whose domestic policies have become debating issues at the United Nations. The issue, officials say, would be of service to critics of the United States, Communist and non-Communist, and contribute to the undermining of the position the United States has asserted for itself as the leader of the West in the advocacy of human rights.[53]

Malcolm's proposal was not acted on at the United Nations session that began in the fall of 1964. But later that year, in a UN debate over the Congo, the spokesmen of some African states accused the United States of being indifferent to the fate of the blacks, and cited as evidence the attitude of the United States government toward the civil rights struggle in Mississippi. Handler noted that Malcolm X had been urging the Africans to employ "the racial situation in the United States as an instrument of attack in discussing international problems," because "such a strategy would give the African states more leverage in dealing with the United States and would in turn give American Negroes more leverage in American society."[54]

That Malcolm X has become a folk hero—"Saint Malcolm"— to the Old Left, the New Left, black radicals, and black revolutionaries is one of the few certainties in a highly uncertain world. Equally certain is the infinite power of self-delusion of most of Malcolm's admirers and worshipers, their ability to comprehend every twist and turn of his incredible life, but their inability to comprehend the meaning of his death; their ability to remember his conflicts with white America, but their obvious desire to forget his conflicts with he Black Muslims. Their grief over his death is real and deeply felt, but they cannot, or dare not, face the fact that Malcolm X was murdered by *black* men in a *black* community, before an audience that was virtually *all black.*

Preferring to turn off, or tune out, unbearable truths, the black militants pointedly overlook a cavernous gap—a gap that exists between the day Malcolm X left the Black Muslims and the day he was murdered, a gap only partially filled by an accounting of his speeches, his radio appearances, his trips to Africa and elsewhere. Invariably ignored are the questions:

- Did Malcolm's break with the Black Muslims cause a crisis of confidence in the leadership of Elijah Muhammad?
- Did the conflict between Malcolm X and the Black Muslims intensify after his defection?
- Did Malcolm X openly voice the fear the Black Muslims would kill him?
- Were those convicted of his murder members of the Black Muslim movement?

For the most part, Black militants bitterly resent these questions, and even more bitterly resent the unavoidable answers. For the facts are all but overwhelming, and are a matter of open and public record.

While Malcolm lived, there was no more caustic critic of the Black Muslims, in general, and their leader, Elijah Muhammad, in particular. On one occasion, he told a Detroit audience:

> The thing that you have to understand about those of us in the Black Muslim movement was that all of us believed 100 percent in the divinity of Elijah Muhammad. We believed in him. We actually believed that God, in Detroit by the way, that God had taught him and all of that. I always believed that he believed it himself. And I was shocked when I found out that he himself didn't believe it.[55]

In this same speech, Malcolm X commented:

> Elijah Muhammad had taught us that the white man could not enter into Mecca in Arabia and all of us who followed him we believed it. . . . When I got over here and went to Mecca and saw these people who were blond and blue-eyed and pale-skinned. . . . there was a difference between them and the white ones over here. And the basic difference was this: in Asia or the Arab world or in Africa, where the Muslims are, if you find one who says he's white, all he's doing is using an adjective to describe something that's incidental about him, one of his incidental characteristics; there is nothing else to it, he's just white.[56]

Probably one of Malcolm's bitterest attacks on Elijah Muhammad occurred shortly before his assassination, in an article by Marlene Nadle of the *Village Voice.* The subject was "con men," and Malcolm made this comment:

> Muhammad is the man, with his house in Phoenix, his $200 suits, and his harem. He didn't believe in the black state, or in getting anything for the people. That's why I got out.[57]

After Malcolm's defection, he and his family continued to live in Queens, in the house which the Black Muslims had bought for the use of their New York ministers. In September

1964, the Black Muslims—who had retained title to the house—obtained an eviction order, directing him to vacate the premises by January 31, 1965. He defied the order, and filed an appeal which was still pending on February 14.[58] On that date, Malcolm X and his family escaped injury when a firebomb attack wrecked the house; bottles of gasoline with fuses had been hurled through the windows of his living room. The explosion took place at about 2:45 a.m. approximately 10 feet from the bedrooms in which he, his wife, and four daughters were sleeping. Awakened by the first explosion, he rushed his wife and children through the kitchen door into a small paved areaway behind the house and out of the range of the fire.[59]

The following day, evicted from the ruined house by a court order, Malcolm X charged that his home "was bombed by the Black Muslim movement on the orders of Elijah Muhammad." He said, "I have no compassion or mercy or forgiveness for anyone who attacks sleeping babies. The only thing I regret is that two black groups have to fight and kill each other off."[60]

After the firebombing, Malcolm X applied for a pistol permit to protect himself and his family. He informed the police he was going to carry a pistol, with or without a permit.[61]

It is sometimes forgotten that Malcolm's defection set off a chain reaction of resignations that could have had fateful consequences for the Black Muslim movement. Not long after Malcolm X was read out of the Black Muslim movement, Wallace Muhammad, a son of the Black Muslim leader, and Hassan Sharrieff, a nephew, got out of the organization.[62] A month before the firebombing, another son of Elijah Muhammad, Akbar Muhammad, announced that he had quit the Black Muslim group. Interviewed in a Cairo hotel, Akbar said he was no longer able to agree with "my father's concocted religious teachings, which are far from and in most cases diametrically opposed to Islam and secondarily because of his politically sterile philosophy of the Afro-American struggle." A 25-year-old student of Islamic law at Al Azhar University, Akbar Muhammad made it clear that his sympathies lay with efforts of Malcolm X, and others, to establish an orthodox Muslim movement among American Negroes. Akbar said that in the past year, about 300 persons had left the Black Muslim movement. He estimated Black Muslim strength at about 7,000, but said that

there were many members who were dissatisfied with his father's leadership and teachings. Akbar said of Elijah Muhammad, "I know there are members of the top echelon in the
movement who do not go along with him. But they stay because
they are getting good salaries."[63]

Akbar got out of the Black Muslim movement unscathed;
others were not so fortunate. In the six months prior to Malcolm's death, at least two Muslim defectors had been beaten in
Boston. Kenneth Morton, an apostate Muslim, died of injuries
sustained in a beating, and Benjamin Brown, a New york correction officer, was shot.[64] One of the most public of all attacks
was upon Leon 4X Ameer, a ranking Muslim official, in a Boston
hotel lobby. On Christmas night Ameer, once Malcolm's bodyguard, was again attacked, this time in his hotel room. The next
day, a Boston police sergeant found Ameer unconscious in his
bathtub and rushed him to Boston City Hospital, where he remained in a coma for three days.[65] Ameer denounced the Black
Muslim movement, and escaped two further attacks only on
the strength of the chain on his hotel room door.[66]

Vowing "to carry on Malcolm's work" after the assassination,[67] Ameer himself had only three more weeks to live. On
March 12 he addressed a meeting of the Socialist Workers Party
in Boston. United Press International reported that one person
at the meeting said Ameer had told the group: "This will probably be the last time you'll see me alive."[68]

The following day, Leon 4X Ameer was found dead in his
hotel room. The medical examiner said that death was due to
natural causes. But Ameer's estranged wife, still a loyal Black
Muslim, said she did not know what to think about the cause of
his death. "I don't know," she stated. "He was afraid of being
killed, but I'm not accusing anyone."[69]

The *New York Times* reported a statement by Leon Ameer
that after the firebombing, Malcolm X was preparing to offer
fresh evidence of financial links between Elijah Muhammad
and the Ku Klux Klan, and other groups.[70] And indeed, Malcolm
X had openly announced that he had "shifted my attack to
George Lincoln Rockwell and the [Ku Klux] Klan in the past
month," because he had seen Elijah Muhammad make agreements with the American Nazi Party leader, and the Klan, that
were not in the interests of Negroes.[71]

The murder of Malcolm X took place a week before the sched-

uled opening of an annual Black Muslim convention. Ameer stated, "Malcolm was pretty concerned last week, because he knew that the Savior's Day convention was coming up, and the Muslims like to clean up loose ends and embarrassing people before they all get together."[72]

In a two-hour interview with a *New York Times* reporter three days before his assassination, Malcolm X stated, "I live like a man who's already dead. I'm a marked man. It doesn't frighten me for myself as long as I felt they would not hurt my family." Asked who "they" were, Malcolm X replied, "those folks down at 116th Street and that man in Chicago." He quickly confirmed that his references were to the Black Muslims and Elijah Muhammad.

He said of his break with the Black Muslim movement, "No one can get out without trouble, and this thing with me will be resolved by death and violence." He noted, "I was the spokesman for the Black Muslims. I believed in Elijah Muhammad more strongly than Christians do in Jesus. I believed in him so strongly that my mind, my body, my voice functioned 100 percent for him and the movement. My belief led others to believe. Now I'm out. And there's the fear if my image isn't shattered, the Muslims in the movement will leave. Then, they know I know a lot." Malcolm said that he knew many things that made him a "dangerous man to the movement." Nodding his head and rubbing his small goatee, Malcolm said, "I know brothers in the movement who were given orders to kill me. I've had highly placed people within tell me, 'be careful, Malcolm.' " He added, "The press gives the impression that I'm jiving about this thing. They ignore the evidence and the actual attempts."[73]

Later, his widow told a press conference that the preceding night, and the morning of the day he was murdered, Malcolm X had received phone calls warning that he had "better wake up before it's too late."[74]

Deputy Police Commissioner Walter Arm disclosed that on 20 specific occasions the police department had offered protection to Malcolm or other leaders of his group, only to be turned down. He said that 17 times the New York City Police Department had offered to station uniformed men at meetings at the Audubon ballroom. The last such offer of police protection was made on the day Malcolm X died.[75]

That day was Sunday, February 21, 1965. The place was the

Audubon Ballroom on West 166th Street in Manhattan's Washington Heights. The occasion was a regular Sunday affair of
Malcolm's Organization of Afro-American Unity. With only a
few scattered exceptions, virtually everyone in the ballroom
was black. No attempt was made to search anyone for weapons
at the meeting.[76]

Gene Simpson, a WMCA newsman, said he was sitting in the
front row when Malcolm X was introduced. He said Malcolm
gave the traditional Arabic greeting, *Salaam Aleikum* ("peace
be unto you"). Simpson continued, "The crowd responded *Aleikum Salaam,* and then there was some disturbance about eight
rows back. Everybody turned, and so did I and then I heard
Malcolm saying, 'Be cool now, don't get excited.' And then I
heard this muffled sound, and I saw Malcolm hit with his hands
still raised and then he fell back over the chairs behind him.
And everybody was shouting, and I saw one man firing a gun
from under his coat behind me as I hit it [the floor] too." Simpson recalled that the gunman "was firing like he was in some
Western, running backward toward the door and firing at the
same time."[77]

Stanley Scott, a United Press International reporter, said he
had been admitted with this admonition by an aide of Malcolm
X: "As a Negro, you will be allowed to enter as a citizen if you
like, but you must remove your press badge." Later, Scott reported, "There was a scuffle at the back of the auditorium,
possibly to distract attention from the assassins. Shots rang out.
Men, women and children ran for cover. They stretched out on
the floor and ducked under tables. Malcolm's wife, Betty, who
was in the audience, ran about screaming hysterically, 'They're
killing my husband!' "[78]

The police said seven bullets had struck Malcolm. Three
other Negroes were shot. The Medical Examiner's office said
that bullets of two different calibers as well as shotgun pellets
had been removed from the body of Malcolm X.[79]

Shortly before midnight, a 22-year-old Negro was charged
with the killing of Malcolm X. The accused was charged under
the name of Thomas Hagan, but he was soon identified on the
basis of F.B.I fingerprint data as Talmadge Hayer, alias
Thomas Hayer.[80]

Sergeant Alvin Aronoff and Patrolman Louis Angelos, who

were in a radio car, heard the shooting. Aronoff said he and his partner got to the Audubon Ballroom just in time to see four or five persons run out, followed by a mob of perhaps 150, many of them pummeling Hagan. "I've been shot—help me!" he shouted. Sergeant Aronoff fired a warning shot into the air to halt the crowd, then pushed Hagan into the police car. The sergeant said that "in the car, I found four unused .45 cartridges in Hagan's pocket." From the station house, Hagan was taken to the hospital, and later to the Bellevue prison ward. Hagan had been shot in the left thigh and his left leg was broken, apparently by kicks.[81] Aronoff stated, "If we hadn't grabbed Hagan and gotten him away from that crowd, they would have kicked him to death."[82]

At 126th Street and Seventh Avenue in Harlem, a hawker of the Black Muslim newspaper, *Muhammad Speaks,* said of Malcolm's death, "When you go against the Elijah Muhammad— God—this will happen. He disobeyed the Messenger of God."[83]

In an interview on WOR-TV, Leon Ameer threatened that the same fate that "befell Malcolm X will eventually befall Elijah Muhammad." He said that Elijah Muhammad was responsible for Malcolm's death and that there would be "some type of retaliation."[84]

The following morning, a Black Muslim building in the heart of Harlem went up in flames, after a firebomb was tossed through one of its windows. The four-story building at Lenox Avenue and 116th Street was virtually demolished an hour after the fire broke out. No one was reported to have been in the building at the time of the blaze.[85]

In Brooklyn's Bedford-Stuyvesant section, police guarded another Black Muslim mosque and ten businesses owned by the Nation of Islam (the Black Muslims' formal name). In Chicago, police squads maintained 24-hour vigils outside the mansion of Elijah Muhammad, while others watched its mosque, university, newspaper, and restaurants.[86]

A week after the assassination, at the annual meeting of the Black Muslims, Elijah Muhammad warned followers of Malcolm X that "we will fight" if necessary to combat attacks on mosques. At this meeting, Elijah Muhammad's eldest son, Wallace Delaney Muhammad, recanted his defection from the Black Muslims and begged forgiveness for having said that his father had betrayed Allah's teachings. But perhaps the highest emotional voltage of the evening was generated when two brothers of Malcolm vowed their faith in Muhammad and assailed their slain brother. One of Malcolm's brothers, Philbert X, said he had vainly tried to convince Malcolm to change his "dangerous course." In explaining why he would stand by Muhammad rather than be at Malcolm's funeral, Philbert X replied, "Now that he is dead there is nothing I can do—or anybody else." The other brother, Wilfred X of Detroit Temple No. 1, said his brother went off on a "reckless path," and that "no doubt is what brought him to his early death."[87]

There were seats for 7,500, but the audience filled only half the hall. The year before, the same hall was jammed.[88]

How large was Malcolm's organization, at the time of his death? The *New York Times* came up with some rather pallid calculations:

> While his own group withheld data, responsible outside quarters estimated Malcolm's movement had perhaps only 40 "hard core" or "full-fledged" members and 200 more "hangers-on." This was a decline from an estimated total of 400 members at its start. . . .[89]

Be that as it may, the deification of "St. Malcolm" had already begun. The police estimated that a total of 22,000 people viewed the body of Malcolm X at the Unity Funeral Home in Harlem.[90]

On February 27, 1965, Malcolm X was buried as Alhajj Malik Shabazz, and though some aspects of the funeral contradicted Islamic laws, he was buried as a Muslim.[91]

By December of that year, the *New York Times* was commenting that Malcolm X had "become a dominant influence in the intellectual life of the Northern ghettos." Some of his admirers were given to wearing Malcolm memorial buttons captioned, "Our Black Shining Prince—Freedom By Any Means Necessary," and the black fur astrakhan hats he favored.[92]

Now the trial was under way—the trial of the three men charged with shooting down Malcolm X in the Audubon Ballroom: Thomas Hagan or Talmadge Hayer; Thomas 15X Johnson; and Norman 3X Butler. All three were charged with murder in the first degree, and all three pleaded not guilty.[93]

Three months later, Talmadge Hayer took the witness stand

and confessed his guilt. At the same time, he tried to absolve his two co-defendants. Hayer stated, "I just want to testify that Butler and Johnson had nothing to do with it. I was there. I know what happened, and I know the people who were there." Hayer quoted Butler and Johnson as saying, "We wondered when you were going to do this."[94]

Hayer said he had been approached early in the month of February and offered money to do the job, but he declined to say by whom and how much. One thing he did know, Hayer said, was that no one involved in the murder of Malcolm X was a member of the Black Muslims.[95] The prosecution found Hayer's whitewash (or blackwash) of the Muslims something less than convincing; the week before, it had introduced photographs showing Hayer taking part in a karate demonstration at Black Muslim Mosque No. 25 in Newark. Furthermore, Butler and Johnson were both admitted members of the Fruit of Islam, the Muslims' paramilitary auxiliary.[96] In all, Assistant District Attorney Vincent J. Dermody presented 26 witnesses. Five testified they had seen Hayer in the ballroom with a gun in his hand. Four gave similar testimony about Butler, and two said they had seen Johnson, who allegedly emptied both barrels of a sawed-off shotgun into Malcolm's chest.[97]

Was the killing of Malcolm X ordered by the national headquarters of the Black Muslims? The answer depended upon one's definition of the outer limits of coincidence. During the cross-examination of Norman 3X Butler, Assistant District Attorney Dermody said that John Ali, the Black Muslims' National Secretary, had checked into a New York City hotel on February 19, 1965, and left on the evening of February 21—the same day that Malcolm X was murdered.[98]

All three men charged with the killing of Malcolm X were found guilty of first-degree murder. The jury deliberated for 20 hours and 20 minutes before reaching the verdict, which was delivered by George S. Carter, the jury foreman. Carter was one of three Negroes on the jury.[99] On April 14, 1966, in a heavily guarded locked courtroom that was opened only to permit the widow of Malcolm X to enter, Hayer, Johnson, and Butler were sentenced to life in prison.[100]

A week after the assassination, Elijah Muhammad asserted that "Malcolm got just what he preached," and referred to him as a "star" who had "gone astray." Muhammad insisted that Malcolm X "had no right to reject me. They knew I didn't harm Malcolm, but he tried to make war against me." Muhammad maintained that if Malcolm had stayed with the Black Muslims and had died a natural death he would have received "the most glorious of burials." Instead, he said, "We stand beside the grave of a hypocrite. Malcolm, who was he leading, who was he teaching?" the Black Muslim leader asked. "He has no truth. We didn't want to kill Malcolm. His foolish teaching would bring him to his own end."[101]

The assassins' bullets indelibly inscribed the name of Malcolm X into the pages of history; it was not the end, but the beginning of the larger-than-life legend of militant martyrdom. The hatred that gunned him down triggered not the end, but the beginning of the reverence in which he now is held by black militants, most especially by those in the high schools and on the college campuses.

The gauntlet Malcolm X threw down at the Black Muslims in life still lies at the feet of Elijah Muhammad in death. It is still there for all to see, and all the old battles against Malcolm's words and thoughts must be fought and fought again.

Witness the two-page article that ran in the October 3, 1969, issue of *Muhammad Speaks,* four and a half years after the assassination, titled "Whiteman [sic] and the Hypocrites Love Malcolm." The lead paragraph read:

> A great affront has been made to the Black people of Chicago and America by naming a school after Malcolm right in the home of the Honorable Elijah Muhammad. Long have we witnessed the efforts to make a martyr out of Malcolm Little, known better as Malcolm X. Many times people have said—nothing should be said about or against Malcolm X as this brings about an element of division in the Black community.

The Black Muslim newspaper denounced what it called "this effort throughout the country to glorify Malcolm by the former slavemaster and his puppets," as "a great attempt to weaken the leadership position of Messenger [Elijah] Muhammad or to embarrass him and finally to make and fester a bed of opposition to Messenger Muhammad."

The Black Muslim newspaper denied any sensitivity about opposition, declaring, "Muhammad's opponents are considered by him and God as a gnat chewing at a mountain." But never did a mountain labor more mightily to overwhelm a gnat, if these passages are any criterion:

> It was only after Malcolm turned hypocrite to the religion of Islam and his teacher, the Honorable Elijah Muhammad, did the white man take up the exportation of Malcolm as an example for black people. Why didn't the white man do this before the fall of Malcolm from the graces of Islam, the religion he professed to be in and taught during the more than nine years he followed the Honorable Elijah Muhammad? Malcolm, himself, acknowledged that his awareness of Black and the preachings of it all came from the Honorable Elijah Muhammad and many examples of his speeches or writings prior to his fall as a hypocrite (a religious term used to describe one who turns away from that which he professed or believes; *militarily, they are called traitors; and politically, they are called turncoats*).[102] [Emphasis added]

In writing the past few pages, it was not necessary for the author to search through subterranean crypts for the facts about the murder of Malcolm X. It was all a matter of public record. And yet, most black militants have simply put these facts out of sight and out of mind. With a highly selective amnesia, they conveniently forget Malcolm's own warnings that Black Muslims had been ordered to kill him; they gloss over the unchallengeable fact, backed by black eyewitnesses, that Black Muslims had killed him and Black Muslims were found guilty of his murder by a jury that included three Negroes. The evidence is not just persuasive; it is overwhelming. But in the face of all this, fiction may yet triumph over fact and ghetto gossip may yet override the public, documented record, as suddenly the murder of Malcolm X is touted as a conspiracy of the white power structure, with the fiendish C.I.A. pulling the strings. And like the Big Lie of another era, if this arrant nonsense is repeated often enough, to enough people, over a long enough period of time, it may yet become accepted as a kind of Divine Militant Revelation, both in and out of the ghetto.

In the court of militant public opinion, Whitey is guilty of the murder of Malcolm X until proven innocent, and all facts to the contrary are simply "irrelevant." In the colleges, the case was succinctly stated by Martin L. Kilson, Jr., assistant professor of government at Harvard, and adviser to the Harvard Association of African and Afro-American Students. In Kilson's words, "Malcolm X had a tremendous influence on the militant outlook among Negro students. Many of them considered his death the work of 'white devils' (e.g., the F.B.I., the C.I.A., white racists) and this reaction has certainly aided the spread of militancy among black students since 1965."[103]

One can only wonder how many of these student militants realize that in the end, Malcolm X fell victim to his own doctrine; that in the hail of gunfire that cut him down that February day in 1965 in the Audubon Ballroom, his black opponents made good their determination to silence him "by any means necessary."

# CHAPTER 4

# Republic of New Africa

A FEW YEARS AGO, THE IDEA WOULD PROBABLY HAVE BEEN laughed into oblivion; today it is at times the subject of ponderous discussion. A few years ago, it would have sounded like an inane plot for a third-rate farce; today, it is at times the subject of in-depth articles and probing analyses in many of our most prestigious publications.

More than 100 years after the Civil War, this scheme envisions what would, in effect, be a black confederacy, one nation racially divisible, with five states or more torn away from the United States of America to form the Republic of New Africa.

In a sense, any discussion of the Republic of New Africa should begin with Malcolm X and his speech in Detroit a week before his death, in which he delivered this glowing testimonial:

> Milton Henry and the brothers who are here in Detroit are very progressive young men, and I would advise all of you to get with them in any way that you can to try and create some kind of united effort toward common goals, common objectives.[1]

Milton Henry, a prominent attorney and former city councilman in Pontiac, Michigan, and a personal friend of Malcolm
X's, accompanied Malcolm on his visit to Africa.[2] Milton and
his brother, Richard Henry, who had worked as a technical
editor for the federal government with a secret clearance,
helped found the Malcolm X Society, after the assassination.[3]
The Republic of New Africa was an outgrowth of the Malcolm
X Society, and in the words of an *Ebony* writer, "It was in the
spirit of Malcolm X that black people came together to establish the Republic of New Africa."[4]

The Republic of New Africa was established at a National
Black Government Conference held in March 1968 at the
Shrine of the Black Madonna—Central United Church of
Christ—in Detroit. Between 150 and 200 delegates and some
2,000 to 3,000 observers heard the Henry brothers outline their
plans to form an all-Negro nation in five Southern states. Milton Henry summed it up in three words: "We want out."[5]

Two months later, the following letter was sent to the State
Department:

The Republic of New Africa
May 29, 1968

Hon. Dean Rusk,
Department of State, The United States of America,
Washington, D. C.

GREETINGS: This note is to advise you of the willingness of the Republic of New Africa to enter immediately into negotiations with the United States of
America for the purposes of settling the long-standing
grievances between our two peoples and correcting
long-standing wrongs.

The wrongs to which we refer are those, of course,
which attended the slavery of black people in this country and the oppression of black people, since slavery,
which continues to our own day. The grievances relate
to the failure of the United States to enter into any
bilateral agreements with black people, either before or
after the Civil War, which reflect free consent and true
mutuality. Black people were never accorded the
choices of free people once the United States had
ceased, theoretically, its enslavement of black people
and this constitutes a fatal defect in the attempt to im-

pose U. S. citizenship upon blacks in America.

The existence of the Republic of New Africa poses a realistic settlement for these grievances and wrongs. We offer new hope for your country as for ours. We wish to see an end to war in the streets. We wish to lift from your country, from your people, the poorest, most depressed segment of the population, and with them, work out our own destiny, on what has been the poorest states in your union (Mississippi, Louisiana, Alabama, Georgia, and South Carolina), making a separate, free, and independent black nation.

Our discussions should involve land and all those questions connected with the prompt transfer of sovereignty in black areas from the United States to the Republic of New Africa. They must also involve reparations. We suggest that a settlement of not less than $10,-000 per black person be accepted as a basis for discussion. We do assure you that the Republic of New Africa remains ready instantly to open good faith negotiations, at a time and under conditions to be mutually agreed. We urge your acceptance of this invitation for talks in the name of peace, justice, and decency.

> Milton R. Henry
> First Vice President[6]

The second vice president of the Republic of New Africa was Betty Shabazz, widow of "the father of our revolution, Brother Malcolm."[7]

In a 16-page booklet entitled, "Now We Have a Nation, the Republic of New Africa," the language was considerably more blunt. Under "How Shall We Get Control of Our Land," it read:

### By Black Determination

The first step is to decide in our hearts and minds that the land in the South (the black counties) and the land in the North (the black ghettos) are ours and that in these areas we will not be oppressed or controlled by anyone.

### By Adhering to International Law

The next step in gaining control is to hold elections among ourselves in the black ghettos and the black counties, before the eyes of the world, with United Nations world observers to take our consent from the government of the United States, and give that consent to the Republic of New Africa. Under international law, government "derives from the consent of the governed." We have a right to chose [sic] whether we want the old, oppressive government of the United States or our own new government. The Republic of New Africa, brimming with great hope and promise.

## By Arms if Necessary

The Republic of New Africa doubled its reparations demands in one year—from about $200 billion to $400 billion, plus all the gold in Fort Knox.[9] One could guffaw at the patent absurdity of its money demands, and still conclude that the gut issue of national allegiance that it posed was no laughing matter.

At the outset, the president of the Republic of New Africa was Robert F. Williams—who had been living in exile for the past seven years. In August 1961 Williams fled the country after being indicted by a grand jury in Monroe, North Carolina, on charges of kidnaping a white man and his wife, and holding them hostage during a race riot. The grand jury heard testimony from Mr. and Mrs. G. Bruce Stegall, that they had been held captive in Williams' home for two and a half hours. Local officials and Mrs. Stegall said the capture of her and her husband had been part of an attempt to force the police to release some Freedom Riders who were demonstrating to end segregation in transportation. Mrs. Stegall said she and her husband had been forced from their car at gunpoint, taken to Williams' home, and bound back to back with tape from a venetian blind. She said Williams had called Chief A. A. Mauney of the Monroe police and told him that if those in jail were not released the Stegalls would "be killed or sacrificed or done away with" within thirty minutes. Chief Mauney was quoted as having said that he had received the call, and had recognized Williams' voice.[10]

Williams escaped to Cuba, and eventually turned up in Red China, where he published intermittently a newsletter called *The Crusader*. The September–October 1967 issue of *The Crusader* calmly gave specific instructions for spreading revolution and destruction in America:

Afro-American revolutionary forces must create a top-notch agency. This agency must be responsible for the establishment of an efficient and extensive intelligence network. It must infiltrate the armed forces, the National Guard, the police, the FBI, the CIA, public utility services and all political groups, right, center, and left. The power structure's facilities must be utilized to advance the cause of Afro-American liberation. . . . The most aggressive and irrepressible arm of the over-all organization would be the fire teams. . . . The mission of these thousands of active teams would be setting strategic fires. They could render America's cities and countryside impotent. . . . The fire teams roving in automobiles would find unguarded rural objectives even more accessible. A few teams could start miles and miles of fires from one city to another. The psychological impact would be tremendous. By day the billowing smoke would be seen for miles. By night the entire sky would reflect the holocaust and emit a feeling of impending doom. . . .[11]

Williams kept up this murderous motif in the May 1968 issue of *The Crusader,* which featured his own bloody version of "The Star Spangled Banner." His title: "The Nationalist Anthem":

Oh, say can you see by the devil's dim light What so proudly he hailed at his twilight's last gleaming?
Whose blood stripes and deep scars, through our perilous fight
O'er the ramparts they watch so arrogantly dreaming?
And the killer cop's cold glare, violence bursting in air
Gives proof day and night that Jim Crow is still there. Oh, say does that blood-spangled banner yet wave O'er the land of white hate and the home of the slave?
And where is that klan who so vauntingly swear That havoc of war and the battle's confusion, A home and a country shall lead us nowhere! Their blood shall wash out their foul deeds polution.
No refuge can save whitey's flight from the slave From the terror of the night or the doom of the grave;
And the blood-spangled banner no longer will wave O'er the land of white hate and the home of the slave!
OH! thus be it ever, when bondmen shall stand Between their loved homes and the city's desolation! Blest with courage and anger, gas bombs firm in hand Praise Black Power, the battlecry sweeping the nation.

Burn baby we must, insurrection is just,
And this be our cry: "In Guns is our trust."
And our glorious new flag in triumph shall wave O'er a
Black people free, never more to be slave.

Appearing directly beneath the poem were the initials
"R.F.W.,"[12] Robert F. Williams, president in exile of the Republic of New Africa.

In September 1968 a drive was under way to get ghetto dwell-
ers to sign petitions asking for payment to blacks for past injustices, and for recognition of the Republic of New Africa. The
petitions reiterated the $10,000-per-person reparations figure
Milton Henry had stressed in his letter to the State Department,
only now it was revealed that of this sum, $6,000 was to go to
the Republic of New Africa, and $4,000 to the person. Primarily
operating in Detroit, the petition drive was not a roaring success. After almost two months of effort, only 4,500 signatures
were collected in that city.[13]

The idea of a Negro state, per se, did not spring full-grown
from the brows of the Henry brothers. As early as 1885, a Fort
Smith, Arkansas, Negro lawyer, S. H. Scott, started a movement
to establish an all-Negro community.[14] And in 1889, Edwin P.
McCabe, former state auditor of Kansas, attempted to set up an
all-Negro state in the Oklahoma territory.[15] In our own century,
in 1933, "a group of educated, intelligent black men in Chicago
who more nearly resembled members of the establishment
than bristle-bearded radicals, were seriously pushing a program for the establishment of the '49th state.' "[16] (At that time,
there were only 48 states in the union, and this was to be a
Negro state.) But for the most part, such movements envisioned
statehood *within* the United States, and *within* the framework of the Constitution.

One of the few proposals for a black state *separate and apart*
from this country was recalled by Bella Dodd, a onetime member of the National Committee of the Communist Party in the
U. S. Miss Dodd noted that in 1946, she and her fellow Communists on the party's National Committee set up a blueprint for
" 'self-determination' of the Negro in the Black Belt." Said Miss
Dodd:

Only the intelligence and patience of Negro leaders in
America have made possible resistance to this mischie-

vous theory which was contrived by Stalin.... Briefly told, it is the theory that the Negroes in the South form a nation, a subjugated nation with the desire to become a free one, and that the Communists are to give them all assistance."

Miss Dodd stressed that the theory was not for the benefit of the Negroes, "but to spur strife, and to use the American Negro in the world Communist propaganda campaign to win over the colored peoples of the world. Ultimately, the Communists proposed to use them as instruments in the revolution to come in the United States."[17]

There is no definitive evidence, of which the author is aware, that would prove the Republic of New Africa was inspired by the Communist party proposal of 1946. Nevertheless, it is decidedly worthy of mention that the Republic of New Africa's minister of health and welfare, Queen Mother Moore, was elected to the State Committee of the New York State Communist Party in 1945, and remained in the Communist Party until at least 1950.[18]

From all reports, the finances of the Republic of New Africa were in a rather anemic condition. Their meetings were generally held in Negro churches and other places that could be prevailed upon to accept modest rentals. One of the few occasions the officials of the Republic of New Africa met under plush circumstances took place in August 1968. The event was described in matter-of-fact fashion by Detective Sergeant Thomas J. Courtney of the office of the chief of detectives of the New York City Police Department. Sergeant Courtney was appearing before the Senate Subcommittee on Investigations of the Committee on Government Operations, and his testimony was a bombshell:

August 17 and 18, 1968—Held a convention at the Hotel Delmonico, Park Avenue, New York City. This convention was sponsored by *Esquire* Magazine, who published a feature story on the organization and its officers in its January 1969 issue.
*Senator Griffin.* You say this convention of the Republic of New Africa was actually sponsored by the Esquire Magazine?
*Sergeant Courtney.* It is our understanding it was sponsored by Esquire so that they could get material for a feature article.

*Senator Griffin.* Can you give us any more information beyond what you have said here? Can you elaborate?
*Sergeant Courtney.* I am afraid not, Senator. I think the article will be offered in evidence at the proper time.

****

*Senator Griffin.* I think this is a very important item because there is a great deal of concern generally about the impact of the news media—publications, television, and so forth—on much of this activity; the fact that sometimes incidents, even riots on a small scale, seem to be instigated or generated for publicity purposes. Sometimes the publicity is wanted by the people who are participating. Then we have had insinuations or charges leveled from time to time that various news-gathering agencies are actually generating some of the activity. I think it is a pretty serious charge and it ought to be backed up, if it is true.
*Sergeant Courtney.* We will see that the material is provided the committee, sir.[19]

The material was subsequently provided, and the committee's own investigation fully substantiated Sergeant Courtney's testimony. Its findings were printed in the committee hearings.

Based on information given in testimony by Sergeant Courtney and other information provided subsequently by the New York City Police Department, the subcommittee on July 2, 1969, issued a subpoena to the general manager, Delmonico Hotel, 502 Park Avenue, New York City, calling for the production of certain records relating to a conference held at that hotel by certain officials of the Republic of New Africa on or about August 17 and 18, 1968. In response to this subpoena, the hotel provided documentation and information which showed that Esquire Magazine, 488 Madison Avenue, New York City, had made arrangements for room accommodations for certain individuals identified in testimony before this subcommittee as officials of the Republic of New Africa. Payment for these rooms was made by Esquire Magazine under a "due bill" arrangement, whereby the hotel owed Esquire for advertising by the hotel in the magazine. Bills for the following individuals in this party were paid for by Esquire Magazine:
    1. Wilber Grattan, August 17, $29.40
    2. T. R. Kenyatta, August 17, $32.00

   3. Obaboa Alowo, August 17-18, $59.80
   4. John Taylor, August 17, $35.05
   5. Mr. and Mrs. Richard Henry, August 17 and 18, $101.50
   6. Mr. and Mrs. Milton Henry, August 17 and 18, $286.51
   7. Mae Mallory, August 17, $29.80
   8. Mr. and Mrs. O. Adefunmi, August 17, $30.39
   9. Miss Joan Franklin, August 17, $101.13
  10. Mr. and Mrs. Leo Sklarz, August 17 and 18, $110.00
  11. Mr. L. Simons, August 17, $49.31[20]

It had been one of the best-kept secrets—that for two days, in one of New York's most posh hotels, one of America's most widely read magazines, in effect, *subsidized* black separatists. It need only be added that the *Esquire* Magazine article about the Republic of New Africa oozed sympathy and admiration from every journalistic pore.

Discussing his first trip to Africa, Milton Henry stated, "I got off the plane in Dakar and instead of white people trampling me the way it had been in New York, there were black people trampling me. Everyone was black—immigration, the police, the whole thing. I almost cried. For the first time I saw black people being a part of things."[21]

Considering his love for old Africa, it was difficult to understand why Henry preferred to cast his lot with new Africa. And his explanations only compounded the difficulty:

Q.  Well, why don't you get completely away from it all by moving to Africa? You like Africa, don't you?
A.  I love it. Every time I go over there, I feel a peace, which is an important thing for me. For myself, I would personally like to go to Africa and say to hell with it.

                                   ****

Q.  Then why don't you load up your people and go back to your fatherland instead of heading South?
A.  It's a good idea, but logistically it is very unsound because of the difficulties of moving people, furniture, mastering the culture. Anyway, could you tell me what nation we might be able to move back to? It's easier to put furniture on a truck than to get it across that ocean.[22]

And it was even easier to see that, like the proverbial tourist in Manhattan, Milton Henry may have enjoyed visiting old Africa, but wasn't terribly enthusiastic about living there.

Quite evidently, the supporters of the Republic of New Africa not only marched to a different drummer, but also gave their allegiance to a very different flag—the red, green, and black flag of separatism. Explaining the meaning of the colors, Milton Henry said the green was for the land, for grass, trees, crops. The black was for the dignity of the black man. As for the red, Henry added:

> "You know, we have to go through blood, there can be no land, no nation without bloodshed. That is what the red is for."[23]

Where would the black separatist flag be raised? In the tormented ghetto area of Ocean Hill-Brownsville, in Brooklyn, if Brother Imari (Richard Henry) had anything to say about it.

In May 1968, in the midst of the battle over community control of ghetto schools, the Ocean Hill–Brownsville Governing Board ordered ten teachers transferred. The teachers later were cleared by a trial examiner of charges that they had tried to sabotage community school control or had done unsatisfactory work. But the Ocean Hill–Brownsville Governing Board opposed taking back the 10 teachers and 100 others who had stayed out of school to support them. Since they were members of the powerful United Federation of Teachers, it became a union issue—a fight to protect what it considered the legal rights of the school personnel. In September the U.F.T. called a citywide teachers' strike to require the reinstatement of the teachers by the Ocean Hill–Brownsville Governing Board. On September 29, after a 16-hour negotiating session with the mayor, and three weeks on the picket line, it was finally agreed —over the strenuous objections of the governing board—that all 110 teachers would be returned to Ocean Hill–Brownsville. Because some of them feared for their physical safety, it was agreed that policemen would be on duty in the district to make sure these teachers would not be prevented from entering the schools.[24]

To Richard Henry, the mayor's action amounted to "a police

occupation of the schools of the Ocean Hill–Brownsville District. . . ." He urged that the Republic of New Africa become involved "in a do-or-die battle for New African sovereignty in Ocean Hill–Brownsville," for these reasons:

> First, we opt for Ocean Hill *because it is possible* to win sovereignty there;
> second, we opt for Ocean Hill because by winning sovereignty here *we may shorten our ultimate war in America,* victouriously [*sic*], and *save many New African lives.*

Richard Henry elaborated on his change in strategy from Southern counties to Northern ghettos:

> The issue was clearly—if narrowly—drawn. It was narrowly drawn because it involved directly, only education. It was clearly drawn because the Ocean Hill–Brownsville School District has been set up with a local school board elected from the district and with "power" to run its own affairs. (This included power to hire, assign, re-assign, and transfer teachers.) It *represents a last stage before separation: the giving of community control*—within the United States system—to people who see control of their own lives as the only means of ending their victimization. Stop here. The first thing that made Ocean Hill–Brownsville more advanced than Mississippi—or Detroit or Atlanta, or any other place in the U. S.—was that leaders in Ocean Hill–Brownsville already understood not just in their heads but in their gut-bottom emotions, that *community control* (that is *black* control; this includes Puerto Ricans) is the *only* answer to their misery and oppression, to their victimization. This fact is not just important, it is crucial. Ocean Hill–Brownsville was already to the point to which we could hope to get people in Mississippi after months—indeed, perhaps, years—of steady, hard, and certainly costly (in human terms) work. What Mayor Lindsay did when he sent in the police to occupy the District and force a white decision down black throats was to *prove* that community control *within* the United States system is impossible. He *proved* that whenever decisions of the local black community are not to the liking of the larger white-controlled community, the larger white-controlled community will walk in and slap down the local black community.[25]

To link Ocean Hill–Brownsville to the Republic of New Africa, the black separatist group arranged for an "election" to be held on March 21, 1969. The voting requirements were something less than minimal; any person 16 or older, who had lived in Ocean Hill–Brownsville at least six months prior to March 1, might nominate, and vote, and run in the election.[26]

As a matter of unfortunate fact, this Republic of New Africa "election" had impressive community support and participation. Among those serving on the "election commission" were: Clara Marshall, vice chairman of the Ocean Hill–Brownsville Governing Board; Keith Baird, director of the Afro-American Studies Center, in Ocean Hill; Thelma Hamilton of the Brownsville Community Council; and Louis A. De Fritas, an assistant principal in the Ocean Hill School District.[27]

The Republic of New Africa's minister of education, Herman Ferguson, was free on an appeal bond after being convicted of conspiracy to commit murder in New York. Ferguson had worked in the New York City school system. He had served as an assistant principal in Jamaica, and later been hired by the I.S. 201 Planning Board in Harlem. He was based in Ocean Hill–Brownsville at 125 Hopkinson Avenue—the same address given for the Republic of New Africa's Ocean Hill–Brownsville Independence Project.[28]

Since the "election" was wholly a one-party affair, the campaign literature was directed more at getting out the vote than telling the electorate whom to vote for. This is how one handbill expressed it:

*Why Vote Friday, March 21st?*

Because you *care* about the future of Ocean Hill–Brownsville.
Because—even if you have not yet made up your mind about voting for independence later, and making Ocean Hill–Brownsville a part of the Republic of New Africa— the Republic is so sure that people here will eventually do so that Ocean Hill–Brownsville has been authorized ten representatives in the Republic's National Council of Representatives (the Congress), which meets in Detroit on March 28–30.
Because, while your vote will not bind you to independence it *will* insure that you have a voice in shaping the black

nation—not only for Ocean Hill–Brownsville, should this community later vote for independence within the Republic, but for all black people who one day may live under our own government. The Ocean Hill–Brownsville Independence Project, 125 Hopkinson Avenue, Brooklyn, N. Y., Republic of New Africa.[29]

With or without the hoped-for voter turnout in Ocean Hill–Brownsville, the largely self-elected government and representatives of the Republic of New Africa met in Detroit, as announced. On Friday, March 28, 1969, over 200 persons from various parts of the country registered for the convention held at 13305 Dexter.[30] The following day, the Republic of New Africa's Congress convened, and "laws" were passed relating to health and education, state and foreign affairs. That night at 7:00 p.m., the meeting adjourned, and an announcement was made that everyone was to meet at the New Bethel Baptist Church.[31] So far, all perfectly routine. But soon, it would be the scene of a cold-blooded and brutal murder. And the killing would come as no great surprise to anyone who had read Robert Williams' November 1968 issue of *The Crusader*—an issue in which he predicted, "The year of '69 is to be a year of unmitigated terror," and wrote, "BEST WISHES FOR UNITY, SUCCESS, AND STRAIGHT SHOOTING IN 1969!"[32]

Traditionally, such meetings were held behind closed and guarded doors. But a staff writer for the *Detroit News,* Michael Maharry, interviewed scores of persons about the meeting, and was able to piece together one of the few available reports of the evening's events. Maharry wrote that the Republic of New Africa meeting at the New Bethel Baptist Church "was staged to win converts and financial support for an organization which regards the white man as a mortal enemy. And it was, by the accounts of some who were there, a flop. Few converts were won over at the meeting because only a handful of nonmembers showed up."[33]

By secret ballot, Richard Henry was chosen speaker, and Herman Ferguson was elected deputy speaker. *Muhammad Speaks* noted as a highlight of the meeting an announcement about the "vote on Black secession in Ocean Hill–Brownsville, New York, in which they had got 13% of the eligible Black voters to participate. In national elections, the major parties get only 25% of the eligible voters out."[34] Ferguson spelled it out in more specific detail for the *Amsterdam News*. He claimed that 1,047 community residents voted in the "elections" in Ocean Hill, and he asserted that six of their elected representatives attended the legislative conference in Detroit.[35]

Among the speakers was Wilber Grattan, Sr., "minister of state and foreign affairs," who sent the words of Malcolm X ringing through the hall as he raged: "What has the white man ever given us but slavery and handouts? All I know is that we will fight for what is ours and take back all that belongs to us by any means necessary."[36]

Maharry reported that Grattan, Milton Henry, and the other speakers, were flanked on the church altar by a half-dozen members of the paramilitary Black Legion dressed in military-style uniforms and armed with carbines and M-1 rifles. Other Black Legionnaires stood guard at the entrance to the church, frisking each non-member who entered to make sure unauthorized weapons were not brought into the meeting. Only the guards who surrounded the speakers were carrying rifles. As the three-hour meeting went on, the altar guards were spelled by other Black Legionnaires who took the rifles from the men they replaced.[37]

What happened after the meeting ended? Much of it is a matter of record—on a trunk-sized nine-track tape recorder at Detroit police headquarters, which recorder reveals the roaring sounds of a life-and-death police battle. The recording—a series of police calls marked off against the mechanical voice of a telephone operator calling off the time every ten seconds —began with an almost casual report by 22-year-old Patrolman Michael Czapski that men with guns were on the street at Linwood Avenue, just north of Euclid Avenue. He and his partner, 28-year-old Patrolman Richard Worobec, had approached the New Bethel Baptist Church in a police scout car as the Republic of New Africa meeting was breaking up. It was the Republic's armed guard, the Black Legion, that was reported on the street with rifles. On the recording, Patrolman Czapski, in a calm voice, at first blurred with static, stated he was investigating "guys with a rifle." The police dispatcher called for a precinct support unit car and another 10th precinct scout car to join the investigation. On the tape recording, an electronic siren was heard, and voices said, ". . . on the way." Patrolman's Worobec's voice broke in, shouting and shaken, with gunshots in the background, "Help, help . . ." The dispatcher was heard calling, "All units." A gasping shout was heard from Patrolman Worobec, apparently hit at that moment by one of three shots that wounded him. Gunfire could be heard on the recording as he shouted. The dispatcher called, "Officer in trouble, Linwood and Euclid. All units, officer in trouble. Linwood and Euclid. They're shooting at them." At 11:48 p.m. the dispatcher stated: "Information from ten-six that one officer was shot at from the church at that corner. The officer was shot at from that church at Linwood and Euclid . . . they're inside that church, according to the officer in the scout car that was shot at. . . ." He added, ". . . the persons responsible for the shooting are supposed to be inside that church, information from ten-eighteen." The scout car was heard to report, "Between 10 and 12 of them and they're armed with carbines." The dispatcher repeated, "There's about 10 or 12 of them inside the church that did the shooting and they're armed with carbines."[38]

There was some dispute about whether or not shots had in fact been fired from inside the church. *Muhammad Speaks* printed the stories of four purported eyewitnesses who asserted that no one had fired any shots from inside the New Bethel Baptist Church.[39] But Mayor Jerome Cavanagh said that the police "conclusively believe and know" that members of the Republic of New Africa's armed "Black Legion" had fired from inside the building at entering police officers.[40]

What was not in any dispute was the fact that Patrolman Michael Czapski was killed by eight bullets in his chest and head.[41] Patrolman Richard Worobec had been shot three times in the back and right leg.[42] Four Negroes were wounded in the shootout.[43]

The Reverend C. L. Franklin, pastor of New Bethel Baptist Church, said, "I'd rent the church again to the same group if I'm assured they don't have guns. . . . I do not denounce these people. Their goals are the same as ours, only they approach them from different directions."[44]

Brother Imari (Richard Henry) said that while the RNA "would not be ashamed to admit to a self-defense shooting," the group did not really know who had done the shooting.[45] But *Jet* flatly described it as "the rifle killing of one white policeman and the wounding of another *in an altercation with armed guards of the Republic of New Africa*"[46] (emphasis added).

Witnesses of the shootings said that the policemen had *not* drawn their guns before they were shot,[47] and yet *Muhammad Speaks* wrote that the shootings appeared "to have been self-defense shootings." The Black Muslim newspaper contended that by law "if a man reasonably feels his life is threatened and defends himself in light of this reason, he is justified in killing another man."[48] Since the policemen had not drawn their guns, it was simply ludicrous to maintain the killers' lives were threatened. But perhaps it was simply the Black Muslim way of declaring open season on white patrolmen.

Later, in the auditorium of Junior High School 271 in Ocean Hill–Brownsville, a Brooklyn member of the Republic of New Africa, attired in a black beret and a military olive-green uniform with a lieutenant's bar on his shirt, was rolled onto the stage in a wheelchair. The young separatist, Larry Edwards, told the audience that at the New Bethel Baptist Church, "Four pigs walked over to me, shot me three times in the left arm and right hip." Edwards asserted that as he fell to the ground, one of the police barked, "I ought to kill you, nigger." Edwards said his reply was, "Why don't you? Go ahead and kill me." Youths in the audience gave him a standing ovation as he raised a clenched fist and shouted "Power!"[49] And if the old specter of police brutality had been invoked by Larry Edwards in a wheelchair, few black militants displayed any concern at the separatist brutality that had put a policeman who had not even drawn his gun—Patrolman Michael Czapski—on a marble slab. And few knew, or cared, of the grief of Tekla Czapski, who sobbingly repeated, "I don't understand it; I just don't understand it," when she spoke of the murder of her son, 15 minutes before he was to go off duty.[50]

After the shootout at the New Bethel Baptist Church, police forced open the doors, arrested 142 persons and confiscated several rifles, pistols, and ammunition containers.[51] Early the next morning, Recorders Court Judge George W. Crockett, a Negro, was roused by a state legislator, and C. L. Franklin. Judge Crockett went to police headquarters, set up a makeshift court, and within hours released 139 of the 142 suspects arrested at the scene.[52] His action aroused shock and outrage in a city where racial tensions had almost become a way of life since the Detroit riot of 1967.

Judge Crockett's explanation revealed a mind that was not merely closed, but hermetically sealed. He stated, "I understand, of course, why the hue and cry arose. An angry prosecutor, lacking police evidence or testimony which might produce a probable suspect, and resentful that ordinary and undemocratic police practices were challenged, chose to divert public attention to Judge Crockett."[53] And yet Crockett knew that among those freed were six whom police sought to hold for investigation after nitrate tests indicated they had fired guns. The dispute chiefly involved release of these six.[54]

When Judge Crockett heard that these nitrate tests had been given, he became incensed. In his words, "I said . . . that I wanted these people brought directly before me without any nitrate test. . . . That is a factor that I will take into consideration in exercising my discretion that the statute gives me with respect to the release [of the suspects]." Judge Crockett ruled that the nitrate tests—given to determine whether the suspects had recently fired a weapon—would be unconstitutional, since they were taken before the suspects were afforded legal counsel.[55] Crockett allowed the police to hold only three suspects in custody: one identified by police as having fired on them; another caught illegally possessing a canister of Chemical Mace; the third accused of possessing marijuana.[56] Among those whose release was ordered were three people who had been convicted two years before for participating in a conspiracy to murder Roy Wilkins and Whitney Young.[57]

Carl Parsell, president of the Police Officer Association, said the judge's action "had given people a free license to shoot policemen . . . without fear of punishment."[58]

In a generally ecstatic review of Judge Crockett's activities, the *New York Times* reported that he was "widely supported in the Negro community and considered the finest expert on the Constitution on the Detroit bench."[59] Crockett also could claim some expertise on the subject of prison life, having once spent four months in a federal jail for contempt of court.[60] The *New York Times* article did admit that "it seems sometimes as if he does not trust the police, particularly if a charge of police brutality is involved—an attitude that is mirrored in the Negro community."[61] Though the article did not say it, Crockett's distrust was of *white* policemen; his relations with black policemen were apparently quite cordial. In fact, a crowd of more than 2,500 that demonstrated to support his actions included "a number of black policemen."[62] Judge Crockett could not find a particle of racism in the black support of a black judge, who had speedily and arbitrarily freed hundreds of black suspects in the murder of one white policeman, and in the wounding of another—but he could, and did, denounce as racist almost every criticism of his judicial actions.

Two months later, Judge George Crockett made the keynote speech before the National Conference of Black Lawyers and Law Students at the University of Chicago. What Judge Crockett told his audience of some 250 black lawyers was a judicial blueprint for the New Racism:

> Fifty percent of what judges do is discretionary. Black judges are there [on the bench] to be responsive to the black community; we cannot afford to have black judges who are not responsive. If they aren't, get rid of them. We are on the bench to shake up the community, within the law. Do your homework, give us a peg to hang our decisions [on] to do justice, and you won't have anything to worry about.[63]

It was of considerable interest to note Crockett's order of priorities. First came the "discretionary" powers of the judge. Responsiveness "to the black community" came second. A desire "to shake up the community" came third. "A peg to hang our decisions [on]" came fourth, and finally, bringing up the rear, almost as an afterthought—the idea of doing justice.

Judge Crockett's distrust of white policemen was surpassed only by his trust in the Communist Party. On one occasion, he asserted, "So far as the Communist Party is concerned, it is probably more accurate to say that Negroes have used the Communist Party [rather than vice versa]. It is the one party in which they feel free to speak and to act like Americans. It is the only party that seemingly cares about the plight of the Negroes in this country." Crockett also called the party the "conscience of America."[64] The anti-Communist publication *Combat* disclosed that Crockett had been a sponsor of the Civil Rights Congress, cited as a Communist front by the Subversive Activities Control Board, Attorney General, House Committee on Un-American Activities, and Senate Internal Security Subcommittee. For over twenty years Crockett had been a member of the National Lawyers Guild, cited as the "foremost legal bulwark of the Communist Party" by the House Committee on Un-American Activities, and cited as a Communist front by the Senate Internal Security Subcommittee. Crockett was a defense attorney at the trial of the eleven Communist Party leaders in New York City in 1949, and it was his contemptuous courtroom manner that impelled a federal judge to sentence him to four months in jail.[65]

Given this background, his mistrust of white policemen, his compulsion to bend over backwards to be "responsive" to the black community, in a court of justice that is supposed to be color-blind—it is perfectly clear that George Crockett not only should have disqualified himself from trying a case involving a white policemen, but should have declined to preside in any court at all.

At about this time, a white judge in Pontiac, Michigan, was being totally unresponsive to Milton Henry and the Republic of New Africa. Henry, acting as defense attorney in a heroin case, told the judge that he, Henry, was not a citizen of the United States. The judge ruled that Henry, as a non-citizen, was not eligible to practice law in his court. In reply, Attorney Henry (or Brother Gaidi) angrily retorted, "The law of the land says I am [a citizen] despite what I might think." The judge wired the state supreme court, asking it to bar Henry from practicing law in the state of Michigan. But Henry pointed out that he had never renounced his citizenship. And coming to the rescue, *Muhammad Speaks* quoted a U. S. Justice Department official to the effect that since Henry continued to practice law within the United States and to defend clients on the basis of domestic instead of international law, the Republic of New Africa's first vice president was prescribing to "the laws of the land."[66]

And where was Robert Williams during this time? Still in self-imposed exile, still publishing his incendiary *Crusader,* still vowing an early return to the United States. As early as September 20, 1968, associates of Williams asserted that he would "return imminently to his people," but declined to give a definite time of arrival.[67] The primary reason for this vagueness was given by Milton Henry, who complained that "the United States Government has refused to issue President Williams the documents necessary for his return to these shores or to guarantee his person against malicious persecution by racist Federal and state officials."[68]

It was not until ten months later—June 1969—that his return really became imminent. Both *Jet* and *Muhammad Speaks* broke the story—from Dar es Salaam in Tanzania—that the U. S. embassy had issued Robert Williams a passport good for a single journey to America to face the kidnapping charges against him. "I am not guilty of any crime," said Williams. "I am not a criminal and I refuse to be intimidated on the grounds that I am. Those white people who are trying to frighten and oppress us cannot be allowed to get away with this." He stated, "I am going home to do whatever my people want me to and not with the intention of leading."[69]

In September 1969, after a self-imposed exile of eight years, Robert Williams flew back to Detroit—a trip which cost the airline about $20,000. A T.W.A. spokesman said the flight had been made "in response to a request from the United States government."[70] He was immediately arrested by federal authorities on a fugitive warrant issued by North Carolina. Williams was quickly taken to the federal building in downtown Detroit where Judge Fred W. Kaess, during a seven-minute hearing, released him on bail.[71]

The *New York Times,* which seemed charmed by Williams' "soft-spoken, accommodating manner," reported his denial that he had kidnapped the Stegalls in 1961. "Some men were actually crying, 'Let me kill them, let me kill them,' and I had to fight the crowd to keep them from killing the couple," was Williams' version, adding that it was probably a "mistake" to have interceded.[72] And probably it took Williams eight years in exile to reach the point where he could make these statements with a straight face.

In his "soft-spoken, accommodating manner," Williams said the only way he would go back to North Carolina would be by "a fight and when I say fight I mean war." At this point, several of Williams' followers, in their soft-spoken, accommodating manner, shouted, "right on," and "teach, brother."[73]

The *Washington Post* account of Williams' return was even more ecstatic. Carried on page one, the article gushed:

> Now, looking much as he had before he left, having aged little in the Cuba and China years, he sat in his Mao-styled suit and spoke of himself as a changed man, a man who has seen a different light through the window. . . . "If a man can rid himself of selfishness, this will abolish most of the evils of the world," he said. "But this is the most difficult fight of man, to be selfless." . . . Taking gentle exception to the emotional appeals of some black nationalists, Williams said: "I've learned that we have to be less emotional about this thing . . ."[74]

It was all just a little too much for columnist James Jackson Kilpatrick, who called the *Washington Post*'s 1,500-word article "a bucket of mush. It was the old snow job."[75] Which neatly sums up the author's own reaction to the article.

It was really not necessary to ask the real Robert Williams to stand up. He was there for all to see, in all his glowing admiration of Red China, in his first full interview which was carried as an exclusive by *Muhammad Speaks.* Here, he spelled out his conception of a "selfless society":

> The idea of the Cultural Revolution [in Red China] was to create a selfless man, one who considers the collective good of all. He doesn't work to gain a specific item like a better car; he tries to construct a society where all people will get equal benefits. For example, in some factories the workers turn in what they consider to be excessive pay to the communes which run them. Or they may bring in blankets and sleep in the factories until they finish a product or a quota so that they don't waste time traveling to and from home.[76]

Of course, in centuries past, the "Selfless Society" had gone under another name; it had been called slavery. The only difference was the pittance Mao's workers received as wages, part of which they returned to the commune as "excessive." And it required no great imagination to divine the fate of any worker who *refused* to turn in part of his pay or sleep in the factory until his masters told him he could go home.

Williams himself had not exactly been a model of selfless-
ness during his sojourn in Red China, and his life there had
been far superior to the lot of the Chinese peasants. While in
Red China, Williams had "an automobile at my disposal and a
chauffeur and I could go any place in the country I wanted to
go and they never let me go without anything. . . ."[77]

In the interview, Williams conceded that most black people
did not agree upon the need for a separate territory at that time.
But in his overriding desire to build a united front, Williams
was willing "to go to people and see what they need and want.
If most people think that struggling within the system will
bring them what they want, the united front should press those
struggles that people think are necessary."[78]

To Williams, it was all merely a means to an end—a way
station on the road to rebellion. In his words, "if you want
liberation, you need the MASS POWER of your people."[79]

John Woodford of *Muhammad Speaks* asked Williams:

> From your experiences, do you think that African-Ameri-
> cans and Africans can build strong and effective unity
> between them? Most of the white news media and the
> Negroid news media have spread the CIA line that our
> people here and in Africa don't have enough in common to
> support each other actively.

This was Williams' reply:

> The masses of African people, the real Africans, are 100
> percent with us. We can rest assured of that. They wel-
> come any contact with us and follow our situation here as
> closely as they can. But in Africa you have the same prob-
> lems as everywhere—Judases. Some leaders are merely
> puppets of the USA, Britain, France, Portugal, and South
> Africa. They work to prevent international unity between
> us. It's a mistake to think governments or leaders are good
> just because they're black. I couldn't enter several African
> states which are presently considered very progressive.[80]

Possibly these African states were concerned about the kind
of news Williams was making—like this report in the *Zambia
Mail*:

> Although Mr. Williams and his colleagues, who claim many followers among the Afro-American population throughout the United States, declare their willingness to negotiate with white US leaders, they admit that there is little chance of black separation without a civil war in the United States. They expect such a violent upheaval in the next few years.[81]

Now that he was back in the United States, would Williams be found guilty of kidnapping that white couple in North Carolina? Milton Henry stated that eight other persons involved in the incident were convicted on similar charges, but the convictions were later overturned.[82]

What Henry conveniently forgot was that the convictions were overturned by the North Carolina Supreme Court not because of lack of evidence, but because of a finding that Negroes had been systematically excluded from the grand jury. In fact, the state supreme court took pains to emphasize that those whose convictions were overturned might be tried again if true bills were returned by "an unexceptionable Grand Jury. It does *not* follow that the defendants are entitled to dismissal of the charges"[83] (emphasis added).

On December 3, 1969, Robert F. Williams got off what he obviously considered a sinking ship. He announced he had resigned as president of the Republic of New Africa.

Williams' version of his designation as RNA president was one of arm-twisting on an international scale. He complained that he had been "pressured into it." In Williams' words:

> I was in Peking when I received the cablegram saying I had been unanimously elected president of the RNA and asking if I would accept. I said I would under these conditions: the organization would not fight Mr. Elijah Muhammad or the Black Muslims; that it would not create dissension among my people and that the organization would be willing to work with other groups (including whites) on projects that would advance the cause of our people.

Williams said the main reason he resigned was that he needed all his time to fight extradition proceedings against him but added that his philosophy differed substantially from that of the RNA:

> I was out of the country for eight years and since my return I have been unable to become active in the RNA. I'm listed as that organization's head, and I could be held responsible for its conduct. Daily papers are constantly referring to my being head of a race hate organization that is out to kill whites, babies, etc. . . . I have to release myself so I can fight the battle I know best, and it's a matter of common sense that I need a coalition of forces to help with that fight.[84]

Williams said he needed "a broader base of whites and blacks" to support him in fighting the extradition proceedings but that he and the RNA were "still on friendly terms."[85] The friendship, however, was discernibly one-sided. Richard Henry insisted that the RNA cabinet had asked Williams to resign. "I deeply regret that it is not possible for Robert Williams to continue as president. Personally, I am deeply disappointed and disturbed."[86]

No leopard ever labored more zealously to change his spots —but only created a wider credibility gap—than Robert F. Williams, in his overnight transformation into a model of semisweet reasonableness.

In any case—with or without Williams—quite probably, the most effective weapon the Republic of New Africa possesses is the fact that it requires no renunciation of American citizenship, that a supporter can have his black separatist cake and eat it too. He can denounce America, but never formally renounce it—cling to American citizenship, but pledge undying love for the RNA. Even participating in an election of the Republic of New Africa would not jeopardize the voter's American citizenship; such a voter could simply refer to the U.S. Supreme Court decision in *Afroyim* v. *Rusk*.

Beys Afroyim had voted in an Israeli election while holding American citizenship. Under earlier court decisions, this vote would have cost Afroyim his U. S. nationality. But on May 29, 1967, in a 5-to-4 decision, the high court held that one could only lose his American citizenship by voluntary renunciation.[87] This was a most unfortunate decision, in the author's opinion, for it could quite easily open the door for dual citizenship in the United States of America *and* the Republic of New Africa, or any other black separatist "government" that may come along to replace it, or for that matter, any African state.

It would be tempting to dismiss the Republic of New Africa merely as a study in ideological hyperbole—to dwell upon its surrealistic demands for billions in reparations and five or more states, to label it all "nonsense" and consign it to political limbo. But this would miss the central point—the point which continues to exist, even as the RNA's demands are summarily rejected by a federal government which is not yet prepared to commit national suicide.

In this country, sheltered under the paternalistic cloak of the New Racism, it is now possible for black separatists openly to advocate disloyalty, the destruction of the United States as a political entity, allegiance to a foreign government, and risk no greater penalty than a reproving glance. The point will undoubtedly lure some waverers into the black separatist camp, and exert a powerfully persuasive influence upon youthful black militants.

In the sea of racial troubles that beset us, a black separatist group like the Republic of New Africa is the tip of the iceberg. We should not magnify it beyond its true significance, but neither should we delude ourselves by simply ignoring it.*

*On August 22, 1970, the *Amsterdam News* reported that in Jackson, Mississippi, "national officers of the Republic of New Africa . . . confirmed plans for starting construction of the first New African community near here. . . . New Africans, native to the area, under Jackson RNA Administrator Carolyn Williams have been at work here a year."

# CHAPTER 5

# The Black Panthers

ON DECEMBER 4, 1969, 15 POLICEMEN, LED BY Sergeant Daniel Groth, surrounded the first-floor apartment in an old walkup building at 2337 West Monroe Street in Chicago. Policemen with helmets and rifles were stationed on nearby roofs and a cordon was set up around the block. In his initial report, Sergeant Groth said that he knocked on the door and someone shouted, "Who's there?" He identified himself as a police officer and said that he had a search warrant. Groth said the exchange was repeated several times. Then, he said, he pushed the door open, and inside the apartment he saw a woman lying on a bed pointing a shotgun at the door. Groth stated that she opened fire on the police. As firing began between the police and the inhabitants of the apartment, two other detectives, Edward Carmody and John Ciszewski, came in through the back door and also began firing.[1]

Several times during the gunfight, Sergeant Groth said, he ordered a cease-fire, but a voice from the dark shouted, "Shoot it out." Groth said, "There must have been six or seven of them firing. The firing must have gone on 10 or 12 minutes. If 200 shots were exchanged, that was nothing."[2]*

*Seven Black Panthers—including the woman, Brenda Harris—were indicted by a Cook County Grand Jury, on charges of attempted murder, armed violence, unlawful possession of weapons, and unlawful use of weapons. On May 8, 1970, all criminal charges against these defendants were dropped. In explanation for this highly unusual action, State's Attorney Edward V. Hanrahan, citing a faulty Chicago Police Department Crime Laboratory Report, also noted, "the

In this predawn shootout, two Black Panthers were killed, and four wounded. A policeman was shot in the leg, and another was cut on the hand by broken glass.[3]

Killed were Fred Hampton, 21-year-old Illinois chairman of the Black Panther Party, and Mark Clark, 22-year-old leader of the Black Panthers in Peoria, Illinois. Hampton was found dead on his bed in the rear bedroom of the apartment. The coroner's office said there were two bullet wounds in his head and one in his left shoulder. Detective Ciszewski said that a cocked .45-caliber automatic pistol was found on the floor near the bed and that "the whole front room floor was covered with shotguns and handguns."[4]

Two days later, a black Chicago alderman and attorneys for the Black Panther Party asserted that an independent autopsy performed on the body of Fred Hampton "confirms our theory that he was murdered while he was asleep." The Panthers charged that the police had burst into the apartment and opened fire, and that the occupants had had no opportunity to shoot back. The private autopsy was held at the funeral home owned by Alderman A. A. Rayner, where Hampton's body was awaiting burial. Francis Andrew, one of three attorneys for the Black Panthers who arranged and observed the examination, said that the autopsy had been conducted by "a leading pathologist, a renowned expert in forensic medicine. He was assisted by two other distinguished doctors." Andrew said that all three doctors were white, but he refused to identify them.

Andrew also stated,

"A bullet hole was found just below Fred Hampton's hairline above his right eye. An examination of the angle of the wound showed that if Hampton was lying on his back, the person who shot him would have been standing above him, slightly to the right and behind his head. Another bullet hole was below the right ear, with an exit hole on the left side of the lower neck, showing exactly the same angle as the other bullet hole. There were two other bullet

methods used to recover and identify evidence seized by our police in the apartment may prevent our satisfying judicial standards of proof." Hanrahan concluded, "Because of that, and because the indictment is so largely based on the original laboratory report, our adherence to fundamental legal principles compels us to dismiss the indictment—despite the fact that there is other evidence that the occupant fired at the police."

grazes, one of the front left shoulder again at the same angle, and one on the right arm.[5]

Meanwhile, Edward V. Hanrahan, state's attorney, announced that Alderman Rayner himself was under investigation for his connection with the Panthers. Hanrahan's office said that copies of the lease on the Panther headquarters had been signed by Rayner, and Bobby Lee Rush, the Panthers' deputy minister of defense. The alderman confirmed that he had co-signed the lease.[6] Later, *Jet* noted that "the lease now bares the names of a number of prominent persons."[7]

At a meeting held after a memorial rally for Hampton, Black Panther speakers said they would bring genocide charges against the United States before the United Nations. Nearly 5,000 people jammed into a church or stood outside listening to loudspeakers at the rally, held in suburban Maywood Park where Hampton had once been an honor student. The Reverend Ralph D. Abernathy, head of the Southern Christian Leadership Conference, delivered the main eulogy. He declared: "If the United States is successful in crushing the Black Panthers, it won't be too long before they will crush the S.C.L.C., the Urban League and any other organization trying to make things better."[8]

Twenty-five men and women prominent in the fields of civil rights, law, politics, and business joined Arthur J. Goldberg and Roy Wilkins in announcing the formation of an independent commission to "direct a searching inquiring" into clashes between the police and the Black Panthers. The name of the group was the Commission of Inquiry into the Black Panthers and Law Enforcement Officials. The commission asserted: "The past weeks' events in Los Angeles and Chicago have raised grave questions over the whole range of civil rights and civil liberties as applied to Black Panthers."

While deploring much of the Black Panther doctrine, particularly its violent aspects, Wilkins and Goldberg emphasized that agreement with, or support of, the Panthers, was not the aim of the commission. Wilkins told a news conference, "The process of justice cannot proceed on the basis of predawn raids, killing and by some stories that are not even plausible." He said that Hampton had been a former president of the Youth Council of the Maywood, Illinois, chapter of the N.A.A.C.P. "Although he strayed from the N.A.A.C.P. way," Wilkins said, "he was a fine young man who wanted for his people only what we want for everyone. To see him shot down under the pretext of a search for weapons is what spurred us."[9]

With Wilkins' statements giving every indication that he had prejudged the case, it was difficult to swallow Goldberg's assertion that the commission would conduct "an orderly and *dispassionate* inquiry"[10] (emphasis added). It was hardly any more encouraging to read that another convener of the commission, Whitney Young, had previously been quoted by the *Wall Street Journal* as suspecting a national plan to wipe out the Panthers.[11] And one had every right to wonder how "dispassionate" another of its conveners, the Reverend Jesse Jackson of Operation Breadbasket, could be in matters concerning the Chicago police. Just before the Democratic convention opened in Chicago in 1968, Jackson wrote Mayor Daley that Chicago was on the brink of a racial "eruption," and urged the mayor to "remove the white policemen from the black neighborhoods now, to insure their personal safety and to insure black people's collective security. . . . Remove white policemen, white firemen and other white employees now."[12] On occasion, Jackson had praised at least some activities of the Black Panthers and he had attended the Black Panther's United Front Against Fascism in Oakland.[13]

This was not to imply that the commission was riddled with Panther sympathizers—some distinguished people were on the panel—but few had distinguished themselves by active, public opposition to Panther ideology and activities. As a writer for the *National Observer* commented: "The new willingness of respectable Negro leaders to go to bat for the Panthers in demanding an investigation of the latest gun battles may be more important in the long run than anything that such investigations themselves may eventually reveal."[14] At one point, there were eight investigations under way.[15]

Possibly some of the commission's statements would have been more persuasive if some of its members had ventured, however timorously, beyond the *pro forma* "I disagree with the Panthers' goals but. . ." and actively, publicly condemned the fantasy world in which they lived—in which every police raid was considered part of a concerted conspiracy to wipe out the Black Panthers, their supporters, and sympathizers in a nation-wide bloodbath.

The pinnacle of Black Panther hysteria was reached in an address by Deborah Johnson, "revolutionary widow of Fred Hampton":

> All Power to the People. No power to the pigs. And all you mother—— who are pigs out there leave now cause my voice can carry better if you're not in here. Those of you out there who think the pigs aren't for real I'm ready to tell you they are. If you think the pigs vamped on that crib just cause members of the Black Panther Party were there, because the Deputy Chairman was there, I'm telling you, you're wrong. They'll kill you, your mama, and your mama's mama too. This is all part of a massive plan, you see, handed down from the top pig Nixon to wipe out Black people. First they wipe out the people's army, then eventually Black people completely. And I'm telling you, you're gonna have to pick up your guns to be men. Sisters, you're gonna have to pick up your guns and be sisters. Cause this struggle is a struggle involving everybody, not just the brothers. And as the sister said before, you don't need no man who ain't gonna be a man. You don't need no man who's scared to pick up a gun and deal on them pigs. And brothers, you don't need no sisters who are gonna just be there to wash the dishes, cause the pigs will come down on her. And when you find your other half that's for real, right on, go on and make those revolutionary babies. Make those revolutionary babies, cause the youth make the revolution. And we're gonna start a beat. The beat has already been started, but we're gonna keep this beat going on and it's going to continue all throughout Babylon [America]. We're going to stop talking about this relating to what's going on in Vietnam, cause that's far away. We're going to relate to this bull—— going on in Babylon cause it involved every mother—— out here. Every mother——. And those of you who are going to wait until tomorrow to get it together, I'm telling you tomorrow might not be here. Tomorrow might not be here. You'll wake up tomorrow and you'll be dead, and your man will be dead and your kids too. So now is the time to SEIZE THE TIME AND OFF THE SLIME.

*Power to the People*

The furor over the Hampton case overflowed the front pages, and seeped into the national consciousness, suspicion by suspicion, accusation by accusation—with charges and innuendos that had been reaching flood tide for over a year. In one form or another—in ghetto patois or white rhetoric—the questions came down to these:

\# Had the leadership of the Black Panther Party been picked off, one by one, by government authorities?

\# Was there, as a Black Panther attorney, Charles Garry, charged, "a national scheme by the various agencies of government to destroy and commit genocide upon members of the Black Panther Party"?[17]

\# Were the Black Panthers, as Ralph Abernathy indicated, comparable to "the Urban League and any other organization trying to make things better"? Or was it their aim to put the American government "up against the wall"?

\# Was Fred Hampton, as Roy Wilkins said, "a fine young man who wanted for his people only what we want for everyone"? Or, as a Black Panther, was he, by definition, a committed revolutionary, fully capable of shooting it out with the police?

\# From past experience, did the Chicago police have reasonable grounds to believe that a raid on Black Panther headquarters might trigger an armed confrontation?

The answers to these questions follow—not in quotes from only the white press, but, wherever possible, from the black press as well, including the *Black Panther.*

That the Black Panthers had been losing leaders at a dizzying pace was undeniable—as undeniable as the statement that these leaders had been found guilty by real judges and real juries of real crimes or real offenses against the court. Perhaps the logical starting point is with the gentleman whose incarceration has been celebrated in song, story, and the spate of "Free Huey" buttons that have become a scriptural *idée fixe* of the New Left litany. Let us therefore begin with Huey Newton, a founder and early leader of the Black Panthers.

The murder of Patrolman John Frey led to Newton's indictment on a charge of first-degree murder in Oakland, California. At the trial, Henry Grier, a Negro bus driver, testified that he saw Huey Newton pull a gun from inside his coat pocket, whirl, and fire after a struggle with Patrolman Frey.[18] Grier's testimony remained unshaken despite a showing of some inconsistencies in an earlier physical description of the killer that he had given to the police.[19] In his own defense, Newton testified that he did not remember anything after he watched Patrolman Frey draw his gun.[20] Assuming this to be true, it bordered on absurdity that Newton could have gone on to state he was certain he did not shoot Frey or a second patrolman who survived.

Medical evidence was introduced that three bullets passed through Frey's body. The second patrolman was hit by three shots. Newton was shot through the abdomen with one bullet.[21] Charles Garry, Newton's defense counsel, castigated Patrolman Robert Fredericks for handcuffing Newton to a bed at Kaiser Hospital, where he had gone for treatment of his wounds.

"You did because you hated him and wanted to see him die?" Garry insisted.

"No," the policeman said, "I had the right to handcuff him and I did."

"You were afraid?" Garry asked. "You had a gun?"

"So did Officer Frey," the policeman replied.[22]

A jury of seven women and five men elected their only Negro member as foreman.[23] The trial lasted eight weeks, and after four days of deliberation, on September 8, 1968, the jury found Huey Newton guilty of voluntary manslaughter in the killing of Patrolman Frey.[24] Newton was sentenced to a prison term of 2 to 15 years.[25]

Another Black Panther leader, Eldridge Cleaver, had been convicted in 1958 on two counts of assault with attempt to commit murder.[26] He had been paroled since 1966.[27] Cleaver was among a group of Black Panthers arrested on April 6, 1968, following a shooting incident with the Oakland police in which young Black Panther Bobby Hutton was killed. During the battle, Cleaver and two policemen were wounded.[28] The California Adult Authority revoked Cleaver's parole over the incident, and returned him to California Prison Medical Center to serve out the remainder of his term.[29] Judge Raymond Sherwin of Solano County Superior Court, however, overruled the Adult Authority, and released Cleaver on a writ of habeas corpus. Sherwin said in his decision that Cleaver was being held as a political prisoner.[30] The state district court of appeals reversed Judge Sherwin's decision and said the Adult Authority was empowered to hold hearings on parole violations without the right of counsel for a defendant.[31] The state supreme court, in a one-sentence decision, said that it would not interfere with the appellate court ruling.[32]

The state court of appeals ordered Cleaver returned to prison in 60 days.[33] That deadline came due on November 27. Cleaver's lawyers had asked the United States Supreme Court to stay the order, but were turned down.[34] On the day of the deadline, a fugitive warrant was issued for Cleaver's arrest, after he had failed to surrender himself to the authorities.[35] Two weeks later, a federal warrant was issued for Cleaver's arrest. U.S. Attorney Cecil Poole, a Negro, authorized the signing of the federal complaint, after agents of the F.B.I. presented him with "new evidence" in the case. An affidavit presented to Poole said that Cleaver's wife had recently withdrawn more than $33,000 from a local bank, and flew to New York City with the money.[36] The warrant would have had to be served in Havana, where Cleaver fled to avoid imprisonment. Hardly a prototype of poverty and deprivation, in January 1969 the absent Cleaver had a tax lien of $59,715.12 filed against him by the U. S. Internal Revenue Service.[37]

The next high-ranking Black Panther leader to see the cell doors clanging shut behind him was Bobby Seale. One of eight defendants charged with inciting a riot at the Democratic National Convention in Chicago, Seale subjected the presiding judge, Julius J. Hoffman, to a sustained barrage of verbal filth and invective unparalleled at any time in any court in this country. During the trial—on October 20, 1969—after calling Judge Hoffman "a fascist and a racist," the judge warned Seale that he had means to deal with a defendant who had refused to remain silent in court. Observers interpreted this as a warning that Seale would be shackled and gagged if the outbursts continued.[38]

A week later, when Judge Hoffman ordered Seale to be seated, he denounced the judge and the prosecution. "You represent the corruptness of this rotten government!" Seale shouted. The judge ordered the jurors to leave the courtroom. When the jury had left, Seale continued to denounce the judge. "You begin to stink," Seale told Hoffman. "Oink, oink."[39]

Seale contended that he was being deprived of the counsel of his choice because Judge Hoffman had refused to postpone the trial until Seale's attorney, Charles R. Garry, had recovered from a gallbladder operation. The judge had ruled that Seale was adequately represented by William M. Kunstler, one of the defense attorneys who had originally filed an appearance for him.[40] Kunstler was subsequently "fired" by Seale[41]—an action that deceived no one, presumably Kunstler least of all. An attorney for Black Panther defendants on many occasions, this white lawyer had been getting a worshipful buildup in *Life,* the David Frost TV show, the *New York Times,* etc., but one would have had to look elsewhere to find just how far-out Kunstler really was. The July 26, 1969, issue of the *Black Panther* reprinted a speech by Kunstler, describing an incident in Plainfield, New Jersey, in 1967:

> One white policeman by the name of John Gleason moved into the central wards of Plainfield on Saturday afternoon. He marched down a street leading under a railroad underpass and then he shot a black man by the name of Bobby Lee Williams through the stomach. Bobby Lee Williams fell to the ground at this intersection near the railroad underpass. Gleason began to retreat out of the ghetto. He was followed by a crowd of black men and women. And a block and a half past the intersection he was stomped to death. In my opinion he deserved that death. . . . The crowd, justifiably, without the necessity of a trial and in the most dramatic way possible, stomped him to death. . . .[42]

This speech by Kunstler appeared in the *Black Panther* about three months before Seale claimed to have "fired" Kunstler as his attorney, and "replaced" him with the ailing Charles R. Garry.

Seale extolled Garry as "the Lenin of the courthouse,"[43] a description that may have been more than mere rhetoric. On June 19, 1957, Dr. Jack Patten, once a member of the secret professional section of the Communist Party in San Francisco, testified before the House Committee on Un-American Activites that he knew Garry as a member of that Communist Party professional section.[44] Two days later, Garry appeared before the committee and took the 5th Amendment in refusing to respond.[45] Garry and Seale deserved each other, but Judge Hoffman certainly did not deserve the loathsome vituperation hurled upon him by the Panther chief.

On October 28, 1969, as Seale continued to shout accusations and questions at the judge and a government witness, Hoffman warned Seale that he had the power to "have you gagged and chained to your chair."[46]

The following day, Seale shouted more accusations and insults at Judge Hoffman and the prosecution. Twice federal marshals had to wrestle Seale into his seat. The second time a marshal twisted Seale's arm behind his back to hold him there. Judge Hoffman had had enough. He ordered Seale gagged and chained to his chair.[47] The gagging of a defendant is an extreme measure rarely used in American courtrooms. Lawyers consulted could recall only one recent case—a 1960 narcotics trial in a New York federal court—during which three defendants were gagged and shackled after one of them threw a chair at the prosecutor. Chaining is somewhat more common, particularly in murder trials where the defendant is considered dangerous.[48]

There was a clear precedent for Hoffman's actions in a recent case before the U. S. Court of Appeals for the Seventh Circuit (which included Chicago). In that case, the court of appeals overturned a lower court's decision because an obstreperous defendant had been removed from the courtroom. The court of appeals held that "the proper course for the trial judge was to restrain the defendant by whatever means necessary even if those means include his being shackled and gagged."[49]

The following day, although gagged and strapped to his chair, Seale still kept the trial of the Chicago 8 in turmoil. Once he managed to slip free of the leather strap on his left arm, and scuffled wildly with federal marshals. At one point, Seale's gag came completely loose, and he shouted at Judge Hoffman, "you fascist dog!"[50] The *New York Times* wrote that Seale "seemed determined to goad the court into imposing its sternest measures," and felt there had been "an air of calculation about the whole affair."[51]

The trial of the Chicago 8 was recessed so defense representatives could fly to San Francisco to consult with Charles R. Garry.[52] A few days later, the gag and shackles that bound Seale were removed. Seale was brought in to hear and respond to a report by the defense attorneys who had gone to California. Leonard Weinglass told the court that Garry would not enter the trial. He said Garry, still convalescing from the gallbladder operation, was not physically well enough to appear at that time. "But even if he were well enough he would not enter the case now," Weinglass said. "He feels he could not ethically or legally enter the case at this point."[53]

The next day, the confrontation between Hoffman and Seale resumed, with the Black Panther leader insisting upon the right to cross-examine witnesses. When Judge Hoffman again ruled that Seale was adequately represented by Kunstler, Seale replied, "I do not want this man as my attorney. You never asked me whether I wanted him as my lawyer." Ignoring federal marshals' warnings to be seated, Seale, referring to pictures of George Washington and Thomas Jefferson which hung on the wall, compared the judge to "those slave-owner Presidents on your wall."[54]

On November 5, 1969, Federal Judge Julius Hoffman handed down the longest sentence ever imposed for contempt of court. Judge Hoffman convicted Bobby Seale on 16 counts of contempt of court and sentenced him to four years in prison. Hoffman ruled that Seale's behavior over the course of the trial "consituted a deliberate and willful attack on the administration of justice and an attempt to sabotage the functioning of the federal judicial system."[55]

"I have tried—I have endeavored on many occasions to make it clear to the defendant that his conduct was contumacious," the judge said. "I feel it is necessary that I deal with his conduct at this time." Judge Hoffman said he had selected only the 16 "most flagrant" of Seale's violations during the trial. He said that each one constituted a "separate contempt of court." Then he sentenced Seale to three months on each count, for a total of four years.[56]

Alan Dershowitz, a professor at the Harvard Law School, said, "I recall no case in the entire history of Anglo-American jurisprudence in which a sentence of this length has been handed out for criminal contempt." He said that the longest previous case he recalled was three years for bail-jumping. Frank Greenberg, president of the Chicago Bar Association said that he would ask the American Bar Association for a study of what was needed to cope with "revolutionary tactics in the courtroom."[57]

No man had ever before been sentenced to prison for a term of this length in contempt of court—but then, no man had ever before called an American judge a "racist," "fascist," and "pig." Professor Robert A. Burt of the University of Chicago Law School felt the sentence was excessive and the judge could have acted differently and more swiftly. But he added:

> Seale was making a farce of the court. It's just like the new "confrontation politics" in which the people deliberately do things totally at war with the accepted proprieties. It's like throwing crap at the cops.[58]

In this confrontation in the courtroom, either Bobby Seale or the American judicial system would be bound and gagged. Either Bobby Seale or Judge Hoffman would be giving the orders in this federal trial. There is not the slightest doubt in the author's mind that Judge Hoffman had no other alternative, to prevent the administration of justice from being put "up against the wall."

At this point, the highest-ranking Panther official still functioning in his position was David Hilliard, Black Panther national chief of staff. Soon, Hilliard was to compel his own arrest and indictment on charges of threatening the life of the President of the United States.

The threat was made in a speech by Hilliard on November 15, Moratorium Day, before a crowd of thousands in a peace rally at Golden Gate Park, in San Francisco:

> Richard Nixon is an evil man. This is the mother—— that unleashed the counterinsurgent teams upon the BPP. This is the man that's responsible for all the attacks on the

Black Panther Party nationally. This is the man that sends his vicious murderous dogs out into the Black community and invade upon our Black Panther Party Breakfast programs. Destroy food that we have for hungry kids and expect us to accept sh—— like that idly. F—— that mother —— man. *We will kill Richard Nixon. We will kill any mother—— that stands in the way of our freedom.*[59] [Emphasis added]

The entire speech was proudly reprinted in the November 22, 1969, issue of the *Black Panther.*[60] Shortly thereafter, Hilliard was arrested by agents of the Secret Service on charges of threatening President Nixon's life.[61] Attorney Charles Garry was incensed at the arrest, and predicted that the government could never get a conviction. If Hilliard couldn't say that, Garry added, "then the First Amendment doesn't mean a damn thing."[62]

The Panthers have been called "the vanguard of the North American revolutionary movement"; they call themselves "the children of Malcolm." Many of their ideas were developed from those of Malcom X's later years, such as the readiness to work with whites[63]—a readiness that was the primary, some thought the only, outstanding feature of the National Conference for a United Front Against Fascism. The conference, called by the Black Panthers, was held in Oakland, California, on July 18–20, 1969. Black Panther official Raymond "Masai" Hewitt laid down only two rules for attendance: "First you've got to be against fascism, and second, you can't be anticommunist."[64]

As stated in the official Black Panther announcement of the meeting:

The freedom of all political prisoners and political freedom for all proletarian type organizations, the freedom and political work of all students, farmers, workers, and the lumpen must be developed into a national force, a front which answers the basic desires and needs of all people in fascist, capitalistic, racist America. *Primary objective will be community control of police to end fascism.*[65]

In terms of this primary objective, the meeting was a flop. Little, if anything was forthcoming in the way of hard results and accomplishments. But of far greater significance was the makeup of the audience—at one point, about 80 percent white[66] —and the most indulgent manner in which Communist Party stalwart Herbert Aptheker was allowed to drone on and on, at the podium, despite the sometimes audible protests of an increasingly restless audience. Some hecklers of the long-winded comrade were told by the Black Panther guards either to "cool it" or to get out.[67]

The Panthers' reverent regard for Communist sensitivities indicated a most significant change in ideology. For the Black Panthers, the enemy was no longer just Whitey; now the foe was capitalism, imperialism, and racism. Now the struggle was no longer racial; it was "the class struggle."[68]

The most graphic proof of this change of Black Panther heart could be found in their weekly newspaper, which laboriously followed every twist and turn of Panther party line. In the June 14, 1969, issue of the *Black Panther,* Point #3 of the Black Panther Party Platform and Program was worded, "We want an end to the robbery by the white man of our Black Community."[69] But in the August 2nd issue—after the formation of the United Front Against Fascism—Point #3 was now worded, "We want an end to the robbery by the CAPITALIST of our Black Community."[70]

This was the full platform and program:

1. *We want freedom. We want power to determine the destiny of our Black Community.*
[An accompanying cartoon showed a group of young black militants pointing guns and rifles at fleeing white police with piglike features.]

2. *We want full employment for our people.*
[This was not a plea for integrated hiring. The cartoon that went with it showed an all-black office staff.]

3. *We want an end to the robbery by the capitalist of our Black Community.*
[This was illustrated by a cartoon showing one policeman with the face of a pig holding up a black youth at gunpoint, while another white "pig" businessman made off with a sackful of money, and chanted, "Law and order, law and order, law and order."]

4. *We want decent housing fit for shelter of human beings.*
[The cartoon that accompanied it showed a poverty-

stricken black woman and three children living in a shanty while a piglike white landlord was saying, "Came for the rent $ $ $ oink."]

5. *We want education for our people that exposes the true nature of this decadent American society. We want education that teaches us our true history and our role in the present-day society.*

[The cartoon that was paired with this one showed a piglike white teacher pointing to a blackboard on which was written "Uncle Tom was a good nigger. Be like Tom and you will go a long way." The black student in the cartoon was ignoring the "lying teacher" and reading a book about Nat Turner, the leader of a slave revolt.]

6. *We want all black men exempt from military service.*

[The cartoon appended showed a Vietcong peasant with his arm around a black soldier, as a piglike white soldier, knife in hand, lay dying on the ground.]

7. *We want an immediate end to POLICE BRUTALITY and MURDER of black people.*

[There was a cartoon showing a pregnant black woman being punched, kicked, and slugged by two piglike white policemen.]

8. *We want freedom for all black men held in federal state, county and city prisons and jails.*

[The accompanying cartoon showed six black prisoners walking out of prison, while a white "pig" jailer quaked with rage and fright.]

9. *We want all black people when brought to trial to be tried in court by a jury of their peer group or people from their black communities, as defined by the Constitution of the United States.*

[The cartoon that went with it showed a black defendant and an all-black jury. The foreman, raising his clenched fist in what looked like a Black Power salute, was saying, "We find the brother NOT", as two white "pig" guards looked on, fearfully.]

10. *We want land, bread, housing, education, clothing, justice and peace. And as our major political objective, a United Nations–supervised plebiscite to be held throughout the black colony in which only black colonial subjects will be allowed to participate for the purpose of determining the will of black people as to their national destiny.*

An almost pathological hatred of the police ran like a jagged scar through the Black Panther doctrine. In each and every issue of the Panther paper, the policeman emerged as the fiendish *bête blanche* of their demonology. Ross K. Baker, assistant professor of political science at Rutgers, wrote, "Given the Panther definition of self-defense, the killing of a policeman is usually regarded as a case of justifiable homicide."[72] Huey Newton put it even more baldly when he told his followers, "Every time you go execute a white racist cop, you are defending yourself."[73]

One issue of the *Black Panther* showed photos of police assaulting black and white militants, along with such headlines as, "Fascist Pigs Brutalize the People," and, "Fascism is the Organization of Terrorist Vengeance Against the Working Class."[74] Another issue featured more atrocity photos, along with a call to arms by headlines that declared, "We must not only lay down our lives, we must pick up the gun," and, "Without a people's army, the people have nothing."[75]

One of the most gushing articles about the Black Panthers that the author has ever had the misfortune to read appeared in the *Washington Post.* It was titled, "Panthers at Home," written by Nicholas von Hoffman, and contained this classic bit of political myopia:

> Seemingly, the Panthers are able to do what the Black Muslims were doing a few years ago; that is, recruit young men who would otherwise lead demoralized, semi-criminal existences. The Panthers put down drugs, booze and personal dissolution while giving people pride, purpose and a structured way to live.[76]

About six months after von Hoffman had penned this love letter to the Black Panthers, the Philadelphia branch of the party hosted a three-day gang youth conference in the YMCA. Philadelphia Black Panther leaders called upon gang members to stop killing each other and "get together to form a 'People's Army.'" Some 200 young men were told to "clean and oil your pieces [weapons] and keep them stored in a safe place. And then when you need to use them in your own defense and in the defense of the people, they'll be ready."[77]

To the Black Panthers, "the key tool against Fascism in

America is community control of police."[78] The party faithful honed these tools by circulating a petition for community control. The petition provided for an amendment to a city charter that would give control of the police to community-elected neighborhood councils. A council could recall the police commissioner any time it decided he was no longer "responsive" to the community. By the same token, the council members themselves could be turned out of office, if the community found *they* were no longer "responsive." There would be one police department for the black community, another for "the predominantly white area," still another for the Mexican-American community, etc. . . . *The departments were to be separate and autonomous.*[79]

The black community might control its police—but if David Hilliard had anything to say about it, the Black Panthers would control the black community. In Hilliard's words:

> The work that we have cut out for us in our police petition, to control the pigs in our community we know that this is a very powerful weapon. This is a very powerful weapon because the control of the police in our communities would definitely mean that we control the guns in our communities, and to control the guns in our communities would insure the Black Panther Party a voice in the political realm.[80]

With the Black Panthers leveling an almost constant barrage of vilification at the police, friction and bitter hostility were inevitable—and it must be candidly conceded that there were a few occasions when some policemen overreacted in a way that dismayed their friends, and unwittingly gave aid and comfort to their foes.

A most disturbing example of this took place in Brooklyn, after the long simmering summer of 1968. Trouble between the police and the Panthers had been building all summer. On August 1, two Panthers were arrested on charges of assaulting a policeman.[81] On August 2, two patrolmen were seriously wounded in an ambush in the Crown Heights section of Brooklyn. Assistant District Attorney John J. Meglio later said he believed the ambush had been carried out by Black Panthers.[82] On August 21, three more Panthers were arrested, again on charges of assaulting a policeman.[83]

A hearing was held in Brooklyn Criminal Court for these three members of the Black Panthers. On the day of the hearing, about 150 white men, many of whom were off-duty and out-of-uniform policemen, attacked a small party of Black Panther Party members and white sympathizers on the sixth floor of the court building. Although newsmen present could not see any of the white men actually striking the Panthers and their white colleagues during the brief melee, they could see swinging hands holding blackjacks high in the air and, immediately after the clash, blood running from the heads of at least two of those attacked. A third member of the group claimed he had been kicked in the back "20 or 25 times."

The attack by the white men, some of whom were wearing Wallace-for-President buttons, was stopped when a detachment of uniformed men intervened and permitted the eight or nine Negroes and the three or four whites to get on an elevator. When they reached the ground floor, David Brothers, Brooklyn Black Panther leader, was granted a police escort as they left the immediate vicinity of the building. No arrests were made.[84]

Some of the attackers were known by newsmen to be policemen. Others were identified as policemen through their conversations about arrests and tours of duty, during the hour or so that they stood outside the courthouse before the attacks began. One unidentified policeman confirmed that the group included policemen, most of whom had gone to the court after completing the midnight to 8:00 a.m. shift.[85]

The following day, during a meeting with two top police commanders in Brooklyn, representatives from the office of the mayor, and the executive director of the Civilian Complaint Review Board, David Brothers stood up and removed his shirt. A participant at the meeting recalled, "His shoulders and upper back were a mass of ugly bruises."[86] Mayor Lindsay and Police Commissioner Howard Leary promised prompt action against the attackers. Lindsay said that the police commissioner had informed him that "off-duty policemen, as well as civilians, were involved" in the incident. The mayor said, "There can be absolutely no excuse whatever for a handful of police officers breaking the law. This kind of lawlessness undermines public confidence in our police." He added, "Commissioner Leary has assured me that he will take immediate and vigorous action against any individual member of the force who has violated the law or departmental regulations, including criminal prosecution if that is warranted by the facts."[87]

Preliminary reports had seemed to implicate a militant new policeman's organization, the Law Enforcement Group, in the incident. Five of the group's top members were questioned by Elliot Golden, the chief assistant district attorney in Brooklyn, and they repeated earlier denials that they had instigated the attack or urged their members to go to the courthouse for the hearing.[88]

Golden said that not one "alleged victim" had so far lodged a complaint with his office. "This investigation may take longer than it normally would," he said, "because of the apparent lack of cooperation." Golden added, however, that his investigators were out actively seeking witnesses and that "our people have talked with people associated with the Black Panthers."[89]

One of the highest-ranking Negro police officials in New York City, Assistant Chief Inspector Lloyd Sealy, stated that the Black Panthers "apparently believe we do not really want to get to the bottom of this incident and deal with the patrolmen involved." As a consequence, Sealy admitted that the Panthers refused to work with the police in efforts to point out the men involved in the harassment and assault.[90]

At a news conference, Joudon Ford, a captain of the Panthers, was asked about hostility between his group and the police. Specifically, he was asked whether the Black Panthers had been responsible for an ambush of some policemen in Brooklyn. Ford replied, "The Black Panther party did not order those two policemen shot. It should be clear to all that the Black Panther party was not involved because if we had been . . . the pigs would be dead."[91]

A police department investigation of the beatings was ordered by Mayor Lindsay. The chief inspector's investigating unit went to considerable lengths in its investigation of the incident; they interrogated virtually all of the patrolmen working in the 28 Brooklyn precincts on the midnight to 8:00 shift on the day of the incident. The report of the inquiry thoroughly deflated any theory of a sinister police conspiracy. The investigators did not believe that leaflets urging off-duty policemen to attend the court hearing had been printed by the Law Enforcement Group. The investigators also found that policemen were not the only group attending the hearing that day. Some firemen were also in the crowd. As for the persons who actively encouraged the off-duty officers to attend the hearing, they did not expect there would be a physical attack on the Panthers. Said one investigator, "From what we've learned so far, it appears the assault was a spontaneous thing, not anticipated by the organizers."[92]

The assault on the Black Panthers in the Brooklyn courthouse, and the death of Fred Hampton in Chicago, were page-one stories in the *New York Times.* The murder of a Chicago policeman by a Black Panther was consigned to journalistic oblivion—page 28.[93]

On November 13, 1969, a Chicago policeman and a Black Panther Party member were killed and eight policemen and a Black Panther were wounded in a gun battle on Chicago's South Side. Those slain were Patrolman Francis Rappaport and Spurgeon J. Winters, who was identified as a Black Panther. Patrolman Rappaport was shot by Winters. Witnesses said Winters then walked up to the wounded policeman and shot him again. Police said at that point another policeman arrived and shot Winters seven times with two pistols.

Shots were fired from the building at the first policeman to arrive at the scene. A number of additional squads were called in after many more shots had been fired. Two squad cars were so badly riddled they later had to be towed away. One of those wounded, Patrolman Ronald Comparia, recalled, "It was a nightmare. Gunfire poured on us and it seemed to come from everywhere." According to police, the first three patrolmen to arrive were fired upon before they could even unholster their guns.[94]

The following day, a second Chicago policeman died of his wounds—21-year-old Patrolman John Gilhooly, who had been paralyzed from four gunshot wounds in the face and neck.[95]

The shooting of these patrolmen in Chicago took place less than a month before the shooting of Fred Hampton, but the same Roy Wilkins, Whitney Young, Reverend Jesse Jackson, and Arthur Goldberg, all of whom waxed so rhapsodic over the fallen Black Panther leader, evinced little, if any, regret over the killing of the two policemen. Nor did these gentlemen utter a peep of protest over the full-page *Black Panther* cartoon that depicted a black militant ready to swing his pickax at a piglike Mayor Daley.[96] And one would have had to use a micrometer to measure the depth of their public indignation over a cache of 10 rifles, 71 sticks of dynamite, 100 instantaneous dynamite caps, and 50 feet of explosive primer cord, found by the F.B.I. in the apartment of one Black Panther in Chicago.[97]

From all that had happened, it was readily apparent that even with a search warrant, any Chicago policeman raiding a Black Panther headquarters was quite literally taking his life in his hands.

The typical newspaper account of Fred Hampton's life emphasized that he was "once an N.A.A.C.P. youth chairman, football player, and honor student," and casually added that at the time of his death, Hampton was "regarded as one of the most effective Panther leaders in circulation. . . ."[98] Conveniently forgotten was the Fred Hampton who declared, "No matter what anybody says, I am a revolutionary";[99] the Fred Hampton who encouraged blacks to arm themselves with the statement, "We are hip to the fact that they [police] want to play Germans. But we ain't going to play Jews";[100] the Fred Hampton who told his followers, "If you kill a few pigs, you get a little satisfaction. If you kill some more pigs, you get some more satisfaction. And when you kill all the pigs, you get complete satisfaction."[101]

In the first few days following the death of the Illinois Black Panther leader, it was commonly accepted that Hampton was one of 28 Panthers Charles Garry said were killed in run-ins with the police.[102] Challenged to name the 28 Panthers who had died in battles with the police, the list quickly dwindled to 19 —and of the 19 listed, four were killed by US (a rival black militant group), one was shot by a merchant, one was not known to the police at all, and one was said to have been killed by the Panthers themselves.[103]

This was the list of the 19 Black Panther deaths compiled by Bobby Seale's favorite lawyer, Charles Garry, along with his comments:

ARTRUS GLENN NORRIS, March, 1968, Los Angeles: Dead. No details [The Los Angeles Police Department reported no record of the violent death of Norris or Arthur Glenn Carter, another name he used.]

BOBBY HUTTON, April 6, 1968, Oakland: Police ambush— shot as he surrendered, with hands in air, unarmed, after 90-minute shootout involving over four dozen police. [The Police said Hutton was thought to be armed, and was shot while attempting escape.]

TOMMY LEWIS, Aug. 25, 1968, Los Angeles: Dead. Killed by the police. [Sources in Los Angeles said Lewis was one of three Panthers shot to death in a gunfight with police. The police said that Lewis was one of three who were stopped for a routine check, but came out of their car firing. During the battle, two white police officers were wounded, one critically.]

ROBERT LAWRENCE, August 25, 1968, Los Angeles: Dead. Killed by the police.

STEVE BARTHOLOMEW, August 25, 1968, Los Angeles: Dead. Killed by the police.

WELTON (BUTCH) ARMSTEAD, October 15, 1968, Seattle: Dead. As Armstead was tinting the windows of his car, police drove up, questioned and harassed him about a stolen car. Armstead decided to defend himself and get his rifle—asked the police to leave him alone. Officer Buttedahl was standing face to face with Armstead, shot in the heart. At inquest, Buttedahl claimed Armstead turned to run; witnesses claim this is not true. Verdict: Justifiable homicide. [Sources in Seattle said that the fatal shot was fired by Erling J. Buttedahl, a policeman who testified at an inquest that Armstead threatened him with a rifle. The officer was exonerated at a coroner's inquest.]

SIDNEY MILLER, November 7, 1968, Seattle: Dead. Killed outside grocery store in West Seattle by merchant who claimed he thought Miller was going to rob the store. No attempt had been made to rob the store. [Witnesses said that Miller and a companion were attempting a robbery at gunpoint. The storekeeper said that when Miller turned his head for a few seconds, he grabbed a pistol from beneath the counter and shot him. The shopkeeper was exonerated at a coroner's inquest.]

FRANK (FRANKO) DIGGS, Dec. 30, 1968, Los Angeles: Dead. [Diggs was found dead six months before in Los Angeles County, shot by a foreign-made gun.]

ALPRENTICE (BUNCHY) CARTER, Jan. 17, 1969, Los Angeles: Dead. Killed by US-UCLA.

JOHN HUGGINS, Jan. 17, 1969, Los Angeles: Dead. Killed by
    US-UCLA.
ALEX RACKLEY, May 21, 1969, New Haven, Conn.: Dead.
    [Garry said he believed that Rackley was killed by
    the police or by agents of some armed agency of the
    government. But police indicted Bobby G. Seale, and
    others, for murder and conspiracy to commit mur-
    der, contending that Rackley was assassinated.]
JOHN SAVAGE, May 23, 1969, San Diego: Dead. Killed by US.
SYLVESTER BELL, Aug. 25, 1969, San Diego: Dead. Killed by
    cultural nationalist. [Savage and Bell were allegedly
    shot by members of US. One suspect in the shooting
    is at large, and the others are currently standing
    trial in San Diego.]
LARRY ROBERSON, Sept. 4, 1969, Chicago: Dead. Died of
    wounds received in July 17, 1969, shootout with po-
    lice—charged...with attempted murder and interfer-
    ing with officer. [Sources in Chicago said Roberson
    died in jail after being wounded in shootout during
    police raid the previous summer.]
NATHANIEL CLARK, Sept. 12, 1969, Los Angeles: Dead. Killed
    by police agent.
WALTER TOURE POPE, Oct. 18, 1969, Los Angeles: Dead.
    Killed by metro squad. [Police sources in Los Angeles
    said that Pope died in a gunfight with officers after
    he and another man attempted to ambush them,
    opening fire with a shotgun and a carbine.]
SPURGEON J. WINTERS
FRED HAMPTON
MARK CLARK[104]

As four dead Panthers proved, the story of the Black Panthers
and US was like the story of the snake and the mongoose. The
head of US, Ron Karenga was one of the very few black militants regularly denounced as a "pig" in the *Black Panther*. In
a spate of invective ordinarily reserved for the police, Karenga
was blasted as a "boot licking pig—tool of the fascists."[105]

The deep enmity between the groups came fatally to the fore
in January 1969 at the University of California at Los Angeles.
The Black Panther Party and Ron Karenga's US organization
were brought together for the choosing of a director of the
school's newly founded Afro–American Studies Center. Karenga's candidate for the job was loudly opposed by John Jerome

Huggins and Alprentice (Bunchy) Carter, who were both UCLA students and Panthers. (The Panther version was that Huggins and Carter opposed Karenga's "cultural nationalism.") After the meeting, students were filing out, laughing and talking. Then without warning, gunfire broke out and Huggins and Carter fell dead.[106]

After secret two-day Los Angeles County Grand Jury hearings, tightly guarded and designed to eliminate any possibility of retaliation against witnesses, five high-ranking members of US were indicted on charges of conspiracy and murder of the two Panthers. Among those arrested were US members George Stiner and his brother Larry.[107] The Stiner brothers had been enrolled at UCLA as part of a special program that permitted persons with felony records to study at the university. The brothers had been scheduled to stand trial the following month on charges of armed robbery, attempted murder, and assault with a deadly weapon.[108]

In November, the Stiner brothers were sentenced to life in prison for the slaying of Huggins and Carter.[109] Two more Panthers—Sylvester Bell and John Savage—were killed by US members in San Diego, a city described by the *Black Panther* as "a known Karenga stronghold."[110]

But beyond any doubt, the most vile and brutal murder of a Black Panther member was committed not by a member of US, and certainly not by a member of any police department, but, according to all the evidence, by some of his own "brothers" and "sisters" in the Black Panther Party.

On May 21, 1969, the body of a black man was found at about 5:00 p.m., in a shallow portion of the Coginchaug River in Middlefield, a small town 22 miles north of New Haven, Connecticut. The body bore all the savage marks of interrogation by torture and death by execution. There were burns made by cigarettes and scalding water, rope marks at the wrists and multiple ice-pick punctures. Large-caliber pistol slugs had torn through the head and chest. The victim was identified as a 24-year-old Negro named Alex Rackley, a member of the Black Panther Party for the past eight months.[111]

New Haven police alleged that Rackley had been kidnapped, forcibly transported from New York to New Haven, and held captive in a basement in the party's headquarters. It was in this basement that a kangaroo trial and the torturing of Rackley was said to have occurred.[112]

Eight members of the Black Panther Party—six women and two men—were arrested and charged with Rackley's murder. The arrests were made in coordinated raids by the New Haven police shortly after 1:00 a.m. The police said the raids had also uncovered tape recordings of the "trial" of Rackley that had preceded his murder.[113]

In August, Bobby Seale was arrested in connection with Rackley's death. New Haven Police Chief James Ahern said that Seale was in New Haven at the time of the murder. Seale spoke in New Haven at Yale on May 19, two days before Rackley's death. The police said that Seale had ordered Rackley's death,[114] a charge which had been made in an 11-page statement by George Sams, Jr., a Panther who said he had participated in the slaying. In this statement, Sams said he was ordered from Berkeley, California, to take part in a purge of Black Panther chapters in the East. Sams admitted torturing Rackley with scalding hot water.[115] Seale said Sams was "outright lying," and denounced it as "a frameup operation connected with the fascist tactics used by black racists and the racist police. I remember Sams was kicked out of the party for stabbing a brother in the leg. A little while later, Stokeley Carmichael came out and begged me to let him back in."[116]

Seale denied that he had visited the Black Panther's New Haven headquarters, saying he arrived in New Haven on May 19 for a speech at Yale, and left early the next morning (a day before the murder).[117] Seale added, "My probation officer has records of all my travel, and can back that up."[118] Yet Seale did disclose that one of the Black Panther Party members in New York called him up prior to his Connecticut trip, and discussed George Sams with him.[119]

On August 27, Bobby Seale was indicted by a grand jury on a charge of first-degree murder in the death of Alex Rackley.[120]

In December, George Sams pleaded guilty to second-degree murder. He was the first of 14 defendants to admit his part in the kidnapping and torture-murder of Rackley.[121] Later that morning, a second defendant, Loretta Luckes, changed her plea to guilty of conspiracy to kidnap, resulting in death.* She then

*This was not the last of the confessions. On January 17, 1970, the *New York*

took the witness stand against five Black Panthers, and said that all 14 defendants had been at Panther headquarters at some time during the four days that Rackley was held prisoner. She also identified the voices of defendants on a tape-recorded interrogation of Rackley, a recording which, the state contended, was made by the local Black Panthers to justify Rackley's "discipline" to the national organization.[122]

In a hushed and heavily guarded courtroom, these tape recordings were played, over the strong objections of three defense lawyers. One tape included an introduction in the voice of a female, who identified herself as Ericka Huggins, one of the defendants. The voice described how "Brother Alex got some discipline" from beatings with a stick and from buckets of hot water. The voice was followed by the strained, almost sobbing voice of a male, who identified himself as Alex Rackley. The Rackley voice said that "pigs were put into the party to infiltrate the party." When another voice demanded, "Name, names, nigger," five names were given.[123]

New Haven Police Chief Ahern said there was a "direct link" between the killing of Alex Rackley, and the recent arrests of 21 Black Panthers in New York.[124]

On April 3, 1969, New Yorkers picked up their morning newspapers and read that 21 members of the Black Panther Party were indicted on charges of plotting to kill policemen and to dynamite city department stores, a police station, and a commuter railroad's right-of-way. District Attorney Frank S. Hogan announced that the Black Panthers had planned to plant bombs in the midtown department stores of Macy's, Alexander's, Bloomingdale's, Korvette's, and Abercrombie and Fitch at the height of the Easter-season shopping. The police, armed with shotguns and wearing bulletproof vests, arrested 12 of the defendants on charges of conspiracy to murder, arson, reckless endangerment, and possession of weapons and explosives.[125]

One of those seized in the early-morning raids was Robert S. Collier. Four years before, Collier had been convicted of conspiring with others to blow up national monuments, including the Statue of Liberty, and of smuggling dynamite from Canada.

*Times* reported that the head of the Black Panther chapter in New Haven, Warren Kimbro, pleaded guilty to a charge of second-degree murder in the shooting of Alex Rackley.

Released from prison in March 1968, Collier sought a job as a Parks Department employee in charge of recreational activities at the Tompkins Square Community Center in New York City. Subsequently an anonymous donor gave $5,750 to Mayor Lindsay's Commission on Physical Fitness to pay Collier for working at the center.[126]

The police said Collier had a high-powered rifle and "other contraband" at the time of his arrest. They described him as the Black Panther "minister of education" for the New York area.[127] District Attorney Hogan said the conspirators planned to dynamite the tracks of the New Haven branch of the Penn Central at six points north of 148th Street. He added that the Panthers had also planned to bomb the police station at Third Avenue and 160th Street in The Bronx as a diversionary action. Snipers with high-powered rifles were to pick off police as they fled the burning building.[128]

Chief of Detectives Frederick M. Lussen said that arms and ammunition had been seized during the arrests. The police also said they had confiscated three homemade pipe bombs, a five-pound can of blasting powder, bomb components, a switchblade knife, and a dagger.[129]

Over objections by defense counsel that the amount of bail was unconstitutional, Supreme Court Justice Charles Marks held the dozen in bail of $100,000 each. He emphasized that if the plot had been carried out, hundreds of deaths could have resulted in the crowded department stores.[130]

In an exclusive story, the anti-Communist newsletter *Combat* reported:

> A defector from the Black Panthers, shaken by realization that the Easter shopping rush bombing of New York department stores would probably mean death or injury to Negro women, provided the police with the first information on the bomb plot. Police say they aborted the scheme only hours before explosions were to rip through the five shopper-jammed stores, a police station and a commuter railroad line.... The Panther defector knew that members of his own family patronized one of the stores, and this realization triggered his conscience.[131]

The arrests were thought to have solved the series of bombing and shooting attacks that had plagued police stations for some time.[132] One of the bombs had exploded in the East 125th Street station, and another was discovered before it went off in the West 100th Street station.[133]

The court rejected pleas by defense lawyers for lower bail. When chief defense counsel William M. Kunstler called the bail "ransom," the charges "a frameup," and the indictment comparable to charges made after the Reichstag fire of February 7, 1933, Justice Marks accused him of airing his views "for the benefit of the press."[134]

At one point, four persons were arrested, as more than 800 Negroes, Yippies, and other youths besieged the Criminal Court Building to protest the conspiracy indictment of the 21 Black Panthers. More than 200 patrolmen guarded the building as the pickets massed for more than three hours, chanting, "Power to the people—off with the pigs." The mostly white protesters included about 100 members of the Black Panther Party, led by David Brothers, chairman of the New York State chapter of the party.[135] He and 70 other Panthers refused to submit to a search and were not allowed to enter the courtroom. Brothers called the charges against the New York City Black Panthers "absurd and outrageous." He declared that Panthers "would not waste dynamite on the blowing up of some jive railway stations and department stores simply because some of our own people would be killed and we know this is completely wrong when it comes to organizing the people against the demigod politicians and avaricious businessmen and the racist pig police forces."[136]

Two months later, everyone, including reporters, was searched before being allowed to enter the courtroom.[137]

Among those giving immediate support to the "Panther 21" in New York City was actor-playwright Ossie Davis, who served as MC at a rally in Central Park. Davis called for all concerned people to contribute to the defense of the Panther 21.[138] Another who offered speedy support was Robert Newton, of the coordinating committee of the New York High School Student Union and a pupil at Brandeis High School. Newton said that the "Panthers have been beaten, busted, murdered, and exiled all over the country," and accused the local police and press of executing the "plot" against the Panthers. He pledged that high school students would take to the streets in demonstrations to free the 21 Panthers.[139]

A most intriguing question was posed by *Muhammed Speaks:* "Was a Black judge shifted to another courtroom because a case involving Black Panthers might come before him?" The charge was made by William Kunstler, chief counsel for the Panther 21 in a press conference at the Panthers' Harlem headquarters. The judge was William Booth, a Lindsay protégé who had recently donned judicial robes. According to Kunstler, Judge Booth told him of his "strange and sudden shift, which only lasted about an hour." Kunstler said that Judge Booth was originally assigned to the part in which three black defendants were seeking preliminary hearings on charges brought in against them. (They were arrested in the police roundup of 21 indicted Panthers but not charged in that indictment against them). Judge Booth was said to have been moved to another courtroom and replaced in his old courtroom by a white judge who denied the request of the defendants for a preliminary hearing. Shortly after, Judge Booth was again assigned to his old courtroom.

In a preliminary hearing, details of charges against defendants are aired and can result in the dismissal of charges and the defendant for lack of, or no, evidence. *Muhammad Speaks* asked:

> Was somebody afraid that Judge William Booth of New York would render justice in the same manner that Judge George Crockett of Detroit did recently? Atty. Kunster [*sic*] indicated that Judge Booth is investigating as to why he was mysteriously moved and so is he. MUHAMMAD SPEAKS was unsuccessful in its efforts to reach Judge Booth for comment.[140]

In the case of the Panther 21, would Judge William Booth have become the George Crockett of New York City? *Muhammad Speaks* apparently thought so. And apparently, Judge Booth had a special fondness for some of the more far-out black extremist groups, as he was to demonstrate four months later when he attended that educational banquet sponsored by the Black Muslims, and featuring Elijah Muhammad as guest speaker.[141]

Were New York City prison authorities mistreating the Panther defendants? From the horrendous charges that were made, one visualized them in the throes of some medieval torture chamber. But the facts were really quite simple and reasonable, and were buttressed by an almost irresistible logic. The Department of Correction stated that 13 Black Panthers held on charges of conspiracy were being kept in special high-security observation cells in which they were checked every half-hour, made to sleep with the light on in their cell, and denied certain privileges given other prisoners. But George F. McGrath, commissioner of the department, made clear that there was no diabolical design behind it all. "This is the way we have to view these people," McGrath said. "They were committed to us as recognized militants, as part of a formal party which urges people to be anti-establishment. We view them as security risks. It's simply a matter of their proclivity for trouble, for stirring up trouble in the institution."[142]

The *Black Panther,* which at best considered law enforcement the political napalm of the power structure, was totally in character when it commented:

> The absurd nature of the charges against the 21 clearly indicate [*sic*] the intent of the arrests; to destroy the Panther Party and create a lynch-mob atmosphere in order to discredit the Panthers in the community. By their efforts to create a revolutionary movement in the black community and to turn the black struggle into a struggle against capitalism as well as racism, the Panthers represent a significant danger to the establishment. To charge the Panthers with conspiracy to blow up department stores—an act which would only hurt working people, not the power structure—can only be seen as an attempt to destroy the Panthers.[143]

But New York Supreme Court Justice Mitchell D. Schweitzer hardly mirrored the image of a ravenous capitalist oppressor. Appearing before his court, District Attorney Frank S. Hogan sought to obtain a separate or superseding grand jury indictment against the 21 Black Panther defendants. Then, in a proceeding that Judge Schweitzer called the first of its kind there, he allowed defense lawyers to question prospective grand jurors about their impartiality, bias, and prejudices. The Black

Panther defense challenged the seating of four jurors on the ground of their social and economic standards, holding that they did not represent a cross section of the community. Judge Schweitzer disallowed those challenges. But in two other instances, when prospective jurors declared opinions against "violence," challenges were allowed.[144]

A month later, a new indictment against the Panther 21 was handed down. This new 30-count indictment added charges that the Black Panthers conspired to blow up subway switch-control rooms and that they had possessed rifles, pistols, and bombs. The indictment also charged that defendants planned to place bombs in "ladies handbags" and "that they would be carried into the stores by women in order to avoid detection." The Panthers' contribution to the dialogue was to shout invective and obscenities, and to refer to the presiding judge, State Supreme Court Justice John M. Murtaugh, as "a white-haired racist pig."[145] By all accounts, Judge Murtaugh kept his urbanity and cool, and suffered no noticeable pangs of guilt or remorse about being over 30.

The violence, the terror, and the aura of fear and fanaticism that pervade the Black Panther Party have made membership in the Panthers a revolving door for many. Sometimes that door whirls around with dizzying rapidity, spewing out a number of defections and expulsions in one city after another. Thus, one issue of the *Black Panther* reported:

> The San Diego Branch of the Black Panther Party has exposed a foul element within our ranks. A sister—Lydia Runnels. She is guilty of committing the following undesirable acts: Liberalism and subjectivism. She let things slide for the sake of peace and friendship when she knew a person had clearly gone wrong; she indulged in irresponsible criticism in private instead of actively putting forward one's suggestions to the organization; she would be among the masses and fail to conduct propaganda and agitation; she also indulged in pleasure seeking.[146]

And from another *Black Panther* article, "The People's Pimp from New Haven", the following:

As of August 27, Theodore Spurlock, the most reactionary counter-revolutionary madman to ever hit the set here in New Haven has been expelled from the Black Panther Party. He has on many occasions proven himself to be a harmful corrosive to the peoples' revolution. He has perpetrated such evils as:

1. Individualism.
2. Subjectivism.
3. Disregard for organizational discipline.
4. Spreading erroneous information (lying to the people).
5. Liberalism.
6. Consciously cashing false checks in the Party's name.
7. He did not adhere to the policy and ideology laid down by the Central Committee.
8. Selfish departmentalism.[147]

And still another issue discussed a Black Panther purge in Philadelphia:

Willie McIntyre is no longer a participant in the people's vanguard. He has been ultra-democratic—he has been ultra-individualistic, and he has been a fool. There is no room for ultra-democracy in the Black Panther Party. There is no need for him. There is no room for individualism in the Black Panther Party! There will be no more![148]

Obviously, the grounds for expulsion said a very great deal about the Black Panthers.

In Oakland, California, twenty breakaway members described the Black Panther Party as a "Black Ku Klux Klan" that was "pimping and leeching off the black people." In a news conference that was held just two doors away from the Panthers' national headquarters, the defectors said that at least 100 party members had been expelled in recent months.[149]

Among those who left the Black Panther Party were Larry and Jean Powell, who testified before the Permanent Subcommittee on Investigations of the Senate Committee on Government Operations. Mrs. Powell told Chairman John McClellan:

The party began with the idea of helping black people. It originally began with approximately 4 men in Oakland. Since that time, only one is left of the original Huey P. Newton Party. The members have either been assassinated, set up to be killed, set up to be arrested, or ex-

pelled, which leaves only one person to run the Black Panther Party at present, David Hilliard. Bobby Seale is the
only original member left. Yet through certain minimal
strains, Bobby began to deteriorate and depend solely on
David Hilliard. After this dependence began, Bobby was
all of a sudden drugged day by day with Scotch and its
problems to the point that David got full control of the
Panther Party.[150]

Mrs. Powell, who had worked for the party as a secretary,
estimated that the national headquarters of the Black Panthers
"collects anywhere from $50,000 to $100,000 a month" from its
various activities. She added, "I have never known any of the
money to be used for the Party nor the people."[151] While she
hadn't kept the books on the money, she "knew what was coming in, like the sale of papers, the sale of buttons, the sale of
posters, donations, things like that."[152]

Larry Powell testified that the Black Panther Party received
a "third percent of everything liberated"[153] (which was Pan-
therese for a "third percent of everything stolen"). Powell
stated that the party received this third percent every day, and
that there was an average of two or three such robberies each
night. Powell told the subcommittee that one of his jobs was to
run off plans for the robberies, "how the place was, how it was
set up, where the exits and entrances were."[154] He said, "The
Black Panther Party central committee not only knew that we
were performing armed robberies, but the top officer, chief of
staff, David Hilliard, was setting up many of the robberies, such
as the one which I was arrested for."[155]

Powell was a section leader in the Black Panthers. He testified:

We were also instructed to tell people that when they got
into the party to think it over before they joined because,
once they joined there was no getting out. So it was best if
they discussed it with their mother, their father, or their
preacher. If you got in and you turned out to be a pig or a
snitch, we would kill you, your family or anybody related
to you, or burn your house down.[156]

Powell stated that he was nominated to the Black Guard,
which he described as

an armed body within the Black Panther Party which carries out disciplinary actions against members within the party or counterrevolutionaries or people who are a hindrance to furthering the revolution. They act as security for David Hilliard and Bobby Seale and others. They are prepared to perform acts of violence which include anything necessary to further what they called the revolution. These acts of violence might include such things as firebombing, dynamiting, killings, or anything considered necessary.[157]

Powell related the ease with which even the most impoverished Panther could "pick up the gun":

The guns in the [Black Panther] arsenal would at times be distributed to members who could not afford one but who [*sic*] they wanted to be armed. When a gun is distributed to a member, it is still the property of the party, although it is kept in his possession. When weapons are distributed, they are quickly replaced. Most of the weapons in the arsenal are purchased but many are stolen. The majority of the 357's and some silencers were purchased in Reno, Nev.[158]

Both Larry and Jean Powell testified that they had been set up to be murdered by the Black Panthers.[159] Larry Powell summarized:

For the fate of being called an Uncle Tom or house nigger seems much worse than the participation [in Black Panther activities] itself, and few are mature enough in mind to sense that it is more a mark of manhood to tell the advocates of a revolution to go to hell. Once people aren't taught that all men wearing a police uniform is [*sic*] to be automatically hated, then there is progress and hope for a better understanding between black people of the ghetto and law-enforcement agencies....Because senseless violence has become the main tool of a revolutionary, they clearly possess a potential of serious harm to this country, and it's all based on freedom, but freedom in its real sense is nothing more than the right of self-discipline. I feel this and Huey taught this, which is the reason I became a Panther.[160]

Wherever there is a breeding ground for racial hostility that can erupt into raging violence, there is a potential source of support for the Black Panther Party. It is from the ranks of these Violent Ones, steeped in hatred of our society, that the Black Panthers are most likely to find the sympathizers, hangers-on, and actual members they need to survive. The Violent Ones do not always wear black berets and dark glasses—sometimes they wear a military uniform. And the scene of racial conflict is not always a ghetto—sometimes it's a military installation where integrated living has only created new strains, new tensions, new misunderstandings.

In 1967, racial conflict broke out among U. S. troops in Germany. Thomas D. Morris, then assistant secretary for manpower and reserve affairs, quietly ordered all military installations to "take affirmative action" to preclude racial violence.[161] In 1968, there was more racial conflict in the armed services. In June, July, and August of that year, a series of racial eruptions occurred at Cam Ranh Bay in South Vietnam. A few months later, "a real donnybrook" of racial rioting erupted at Camp Tien Sha, a Navy base in Vietnam.[162]

Little publicity was given to these military outbreaks; America was simply too preoccupied with the racial agonies of the cities. And only minimal reporting was accorded the testimony of Joseph F. Cannon, acting director of the National Urban League's Office of Veteran Affairs. Appearing before the Senate Subcommittee on Veterans Affairs on June 25, 1969, Cannon made this ominous statement:

> We know that the average veteran, whatever his race, is dedicated to his country and wants to follow the American way of life. There is, however, a clear and present danger that many black veterans will be enlisted in the army of militants if he [sic] is disillusioned and frustrated in his attempt to find meaningful employment, housing, and educational opportunities.[163]

Asked by the subcommittee chairman, Senator Alan Cranston (D., Calif.), to expand on his warning, Cannon said he could not document the report.[164]

The following month, *Sepia* magazine published a series of letters from "Our Men in Viet Nam," and it was quite obvious that "the army of militants" had enlisted some of the most bitter black recruits. There was a letter from Sp/4 Nickson Dudley of the 100th Engineering Company:

Over here in the Nam, a brother goes through many changes. We definitely have two enemies—Charlie and Whitey. The white man over here is the same white man out of Mississippi and Alabama who has tried all of his days to keep my people down, but it's going to be a different version of the story when we brothers come back home. There won't be any Uncle Tomming and scratching heads and all that stuff. We don't have to see our thing on Huntley-Brinkley. We experience it every day, and woe unto the soul who isn't together. We don't want anybody to give us anything—open the door and we'll get it ourselves. If he doesn't open the door, then we will have to take other measures of entering because we have been promised too much, too long.[165]

And Sp/4 Coleman Ellis of Co. C, 1st Bn 8th Cav., 1st Cav. Div., wrote: "To a brother, a war is a lifetime occurrence, from Viet Nam to the U.S. only to engage in a bigger war."[166]

On July 20, 1969, that "bigger war" came to Camp Lejeune, North Carolina, home base of the Second Marine Division. Filled with Vietnam combat veterans, the First Battalion, Sixth Marine Regiment, was celebrating its imminent departure on a Mediterranean cruise. At the party, a white sailor was dancing with a girl, when a Negro marine attempted to cut in, and was refused. There was a scuffle on the dance floor, but it was stopped, and the couple left the service club. Corporal Edward Bankston, a 20-year-old white Mississippian, left the party shortly after 10:00, and with three other white marines began heading back across base to his barracks. He didn't get far. Suddenly a cry of "Fight! Fight!" rang out. Witnesses saw a gang of some 30 blacks and Puerto Ricans attack Bankston and his friends. Bankston was beaten with a tree limb; he fell, his skull fractured.[167]

Only a few blacks and Puerto Rican militants were involved. That night, some other Negros and Puerto Ricans actually saved some white marines from beatings. These courageous marines jeopardized their own safety by running through the area and telling white marines to get into their barracks, in order to avoid a confrontation with the angry and violent mob.[168]

But the mob of seething black and Puerto Rican assailants was not to be stopped. Before the night was over, a total of 14

whites had been mugged, two of them had been hospitalized
along with Bankston, and a half-dozen blacks and Puerto Ricans were taken into custody.[169]

A week later, Corporal Bankston, the survivor of three combat wounds in Vietnam, died from his wounds in the fight.
Bankston was so savagely beaten that had he lived, he would
have had to undergo months of plastic surgery and treatment
for the restructuring of his face.[170]

Three days after the racial conflict, at the request of members of a Marine Corps Reserve unit that was then training at
Camp Lejeune, Congressman Mario Biaggi (D., N.Y.) visited
and inspected that marine installation. A former Bronx policeman who had been injured 21 times in the line of duty, and who
had been included in the National Policeman's Hall of Fame,[171]
Biaggi was uniquely qualified to assess the gravity of conditions
at Camp Lejeune.

Biaggi's inspection "was prompted by the fact that members
of this particular reserve unit, known as the 6th Communications Battalion from Fort Schuyler, N. Y., expressed concern for
their safety because of conditions at Camp Lejeune." In a
speech on the floor of the House, Biaggi stated:

> While at Camp Lejeune, I spoke to many Reserves and
> Regular marines, to both commissioned and non-commis-
> sioned officers, and reviewed the matter with Maj. Gen.
> Michael Ryan, commanding officer of the 2nd Marine
> Division at Camp Lejeune, and Brig. Gen. Fred Haynes,
> legislative chief at Marine Corps headquarters in the Pen-
> tagon. My conclusion was inescapable. Yes, there was am-
> ple reason for concern at Camp Lejeune. I, therefore,
> recommended as an immediate measure that the Reserve
> unit from my district be moved to safer quarters away
> from a section of the installation that was obviously a
> trouble area. The morning after my inspection, General
> Haynes telephoned my office to inform me that there was
> compliance with my recommendation. He reported that
> the Reserve unit was moved to an area very close to base
> headquarters.[172]

Both generals acknowledged that "a pattern of trouble occasionally culminating in assaults has been developing at Camp
Lejeune for some months now."[173] The provost marshal told

Representative Biaggi that "190 assaults were reported on the base or in the nearby town of Jacksonville between Jan. 1 and the first week in August. Employees of the Seashore and Trailways bus lines which service Camp Lejuene have reported that Marines have been assaulted frequently aboard their buses."[174] Biaggi added that one employee reported, "We've had buses looking like a bucket of blood."[175] Of the 190 assaults, only four of these had been a Negro assaulting another Negro. Fifty had involved whites only. There were 136 involving blacks and whites—122 of these cases involving attacks by Negroes on whites, while 14 were attacks by whites on Negroes. Of these 136 cases, there were 114 attacks on base and 22 off base.[176]

To cope with the situation, General Ryan posted additional sentries, with side arms and rifles and shortwave radios, along the "lines of drift" (the bush-lined paths leading from the post movie houses and enlisted men's clubs to the barracks). At night, some of the sentries hid in the bushes. In addition, General Ryan created three "reaction forces"—25 men in one area, 15 in a second, and 10 in a third—and set a goal of three minutes for a force to reach the site of an assault or riot. The reaction forces were equipped with tear gas, arms, and cameras.[177]

What happened at Fort Lejeune was no isolated incident, it was simply the most widely reported of a chain of tragic events that had reached serious dimensions in other bases as well, among them, Fort Jackson, S. C.; Fort Belvoir, Va.; Fort Lee, Va.; Fort Gordon, Ga.; Fort Hood, Tex.; Fort Bragg, N. C.; Fort Dix, N.J.; Fort Carson, Colo.; Fort Sill, Okla.; Fort Sheridan, Ill.; and Fort Knox, Ky.[178]

Biaggi was compelled to comment, "It is sad but accurate to say at this time that American boys are not only dying on foreign soil, but their lives are also obviously being jeopardized needlessly right within the confines of some of our own military installations."[179]

Three months before Corporal Bankston was killed at Camp Lejeune, a committee of seven officers warned the camp's commanding general that "an explosive situation of major proportions has been created and continues to be aggravated." This Ad Hoc Committee on Equal Treatment and Opportunity laid the blame for the tense situation in large measure on officers of the Second Marine Division. The committee told the then commanding officer, Major General Edwin B. Wheeler, that "the lack of informed, courageous leadership in dealing with racial matters is widening the gulf of misunderstanding between the races," and stated that there had been "a general lack of compliance on the part of officers and non-commissioned officers with the existing policies, either by intent, in spirit or through ignorance."

The committee gave the following examples, among others, in support of its charge:

# "many white officers and non-commissioned officers retain prejudices and deliberately practice them," as evidenced by the racial stories they tell and the references to "blacks or black marines."
# Many facilities—barbershops, bars, and amusement centers—in towns near Camp Lejeune in southeast North Carolina were segregated, and patronage of them by white marines "is, in fact, condonation of discrimination."
# Black marines were "the special target for discriminatory actions by the military police"
# "Only results and never causes" seemed to the black marines to be the object of military investigation and discipline when any incident occurred involving them.

The committee felt that many racial tensions could be alleviated through a more effective "request mast." This was a privilege, in the Navy, under which any officer or enlisted man was permitted to take any grievance or problem to his superiors —to the commanding officer and in exceptional cases to the chief of naval operations, or in the case of a marine, to the commandant. The committee said:

The deterioration of the request mast procedure into a forum for defensive reaction is indicative of the inability or unwillingness of marines in positions of authority to recognize legitimate grievances and to quickly and fairly dispose of them.

The committee was convinced that, "generally speaking," the young white and black marines were "striving for mutual accommodation." But their attempts "are blocked and frustrated by the officers and non-commissioned officers," among whom "bigotry and prejudice are either overtly practiced or tacitly condoned."[180]

The committee reported to General Wheeler on April 22. Less than a month later, Wheeler was succeeded in command by Major General Michael P. Ryan. General Ryan was in command at Camp Lejeune for only two months when Bankston was attacked, and he was not yet familiar with "any report that was submitted."[181]

Even if General Ryan had known of the report, read it, and almost instantaneously taken remedial action, it was not all that certain that those tragic events would have been averted. During that long hot military summer, nearly 250 black and white marines at Kaneohe Marine Corps Air Station in Hawaii clashed, leaving 16 injured—*after* discussions between local N.A.A.C.P. representatives and the base commanders were getting under way.[182] In September, columnist Jack Anderson was writing, "Racial violence is so common at some bases that they have become as dangerous at night as encampments in the middle of Viet Cong country. Marines from Camp Lejeune, N.C., to the Kaneohe Air Station in Hawaii go to bed at nights with bayonets, pipes and chains to defend themselves from attack."[183]

General Ryan said that there were "indications" but "no tangible evidence" that Negro marines involved in the racial flareup at Camp Lejeune were members of the Black Panther Party.[184] The *New York Times* noted that no orders had been issued forbidding Negro marines to belong to the Black Panthers.[185]

Certainly, Black Panther Chairman Bobby Seale was making the most frenzied efforts to enlist the sympathy and support of black servicemen. In an article titled, "Black Soldiers as Revolutionaries to Overthrow the Ruling Class," Seale declared:

The Black brothers, Vietnam Black G. I.'s, must understand and feel desire to oppose oppression right here at home, domestically. . . . And we'll be glad when you come back, because here you must fight the pigs who occupy our community . . . these police forces have been tripled and quadrupled with machine guns, AR-15s (the same kinds of guns you brothers got and are carrying over there) .357 magnums (you can stand up and shoot 10 demonstrators with one bullet with a .357 or a .44 magnum) that these cops carry here. . . . It's important, brothers, that you understand that your fight is really right here at home in America. So when you come back, you'll be fighting against the oppression that we've been subjected to for 400 years. . . . So, power to the people, brothers. And please come on home, brothers. And when you get home, we'll be waiting for you.[186]

At times, some of the bitter-end white supremacists—through acts of callous stupidity—unwittingly played right into the hands of black extremists. That summer, black America, and much of white America, was rightly incensed by the despicable treatment accorded Private Bill Henry Terry, Jr. Private Terry, a black Alabamian, volunteered to serve in the Army in September 1968. Six months later, he was shipped to Vietnam. Less than a year after volunteering, and four months after arrival overseas, he was dead. Private Terry had a premonition that he would be killed, and asked his wife, Margaret, and his mother, Mrs. Jimmie Lee, to see that he was buried in Elmwood Cemetery, one of the oldest and largest burial grounds in Birmingham, Alabama. Terry's body was returned to his native Birmingham with the customary military escort. The grieving widow went to Elmwood Cemetery—which advertised space for cemetery lots, in the local news media. But Mrs. Terry was turned away. In the words of the N.A.A.C.P. Legal Defense and Educational Fund, "Having no alternative and having already made arrangements for the funeral," the woman "arranged to have Bill Henry Terry, Jr., buried at a Negro cemetery on July 19, 1969." Declaring his intention to file suit in federal court, an attorney for the N.A.A.C.P. group said that Terry's body would be exhumed if the court found that "Elmwood Cemetery wrongfully abridged plaintiff's rights."[187]

From time to time, one hears that human rights must be exalted above property rights—which is like saying that six of one must be exalted above half a dozen of the other. In the final analysis, property rights *are* human rights, the rights of a human being freely to use, retain, or dispose of his property as he sees fit. Nevertheless, as a matter of conscience, the author felt the most profound shame and fury that the Terry case could be happening in his time, in his country—that the owner of any cemetery could deny a place of burial to any serviceman who died, giving "the last full measure of devotion." Beyond any doubt, the day Elmwood Cemetery turned away Terry's widow and mother, a score of recruiting agents could not have done as much to swell the ranks of the Black Panthers as was done by this brutal segregationist insensitivity that followed a courageous black soldier to his grave.

Under the order of a federal judge, the body of Private Terry was later unearthed from the Negro cemetery and reburied in Elmwood, with full military honors.[188] But the irreparable racial harm had already been done.

Possibly it was with such a case in mind—along with the mushrooming racial tension in the armed forces—that a black civilian in Saigon asked: "Can that black cat [the Negro serviceman] walk like a dragon in Vietnam and like a fairy in the land of the big PX [America]? And can America expect him to?"[189]

The answer was quickly forthcoming—and the timing made it clear that the primary intent was to head off a racial polarization at Camp Lejeune, and elsewhere, over grievances, real or imagined. The Marine Corps commandant, General Leonard F. Chapman, conceded that "it is obvious we have been less successful than we thought" in stopping racial outbursts. "There is no question about it, we've got a problem," the general said. "We're tackling the problem, we're going to find out what are the valid complaints about discrimination and we're going to correct them. However, we are not going to, under any circumstances, tolerate either discrimination or lack of discipline or the use of violence."[190]

The *New York Times* found "a noticeable generation gap between the teenaged privates and privates first class and their older sergeants." Black and white sergeants complained about "the jitterbugs," the "beatniks," and "that bad 10 percent" of the youthful marines who, they said, caused most of the trouble. On the other hand, some black youths maintained that only a Negro Uncle Tom could be promoted in the Marine Corps, and some enlisted men wore their lack of rank like a badge of honor, as proof of their refusal to "tom for the man."[191] Proof of the decline and fall of battlefield cameraderie was evident in the suggestion boxes at one enlisted men's club at Camp Lejeune; among the suggestions were such requests as "keep niggers off the dance floor," "no more pink pigs in the club," and "coons, go back to Africa."[192]

Marine sources said that racial slurs had been practiced by both white and black marines. Instances were cited in which a number of Negroes would stand up and cheer when a white actor was killed on screen, during post movies. And white sergeants had been known in the course of garrison instructional courses to make racial jokes, with Negroes as the butt of the "humor."[193]

Black marines were prone to greet one another with the clenched fist, or Black Power salute, but denied that it had any racial connotations. And many white marines liked to display the Confederate flag, but denied just as strenuously that it had any white supremacist implications.[194]

A white Marine captain suggested that new Negro Marine enlisted men would naturally be more conscious of their rights and of discrimination than their predecessors were. "We're dealing with men who grew up during the civil rights movement," he said. "They grew up with the boob-tube [television] as their babysitters."[195] Several white officers and some Negro sergeants were certain that "outside" pressures—"the black power groups, the Black Panthers and the militants"—were influencing black marines. A Negro sergeant said "We know the militants are talking to the younger guys whenever they swoop up [take a trip] to Washington or New York."[196]

On September 3, a month and a half after Bankston's death at Camp Lejeune, General Chapman issued an order calling for an end to racial violence in the corps and outlining steps to eliminate discrimination against Negroes. In a message to all Marine Corps commands, Chapman stated:

Every marine must understand that the Marine Corps does guarantee equal rights, equal opportunity, and equal protection, without regard to race, and will continue to do so.... Some complaints about discrimination I have heard appear to be valid. But many are based on rumor or misapprehension. Nevertheless, some marines believe them to be true. Most are concerned with promotions, military justice, duty and assignments and request mast [direct appeal to a commander].... To come to grips with the problem of racial friction, the following actions will be immediately undertaken: . . . Every officer will review his request mast procedures to ensure that all marines understand clearly their right to air their grievances without hindrance or prejudice. I emphasize that no harassment, either real or implied, will be permitted to occur at any level. . . . Commanders will permit the Afro natural haircut providing it conforms with current Marine Corps regulations [neatly trimmed on the sides and in back and standing no more than three inches high on top]. No actions, signs, symbols, gestures, and words which are contrary to tradition will be permitted during formation or when rendering military courtesies to colors, the national anthem, or individuals. Individual signs between groups or individuals will be accepted for what they are—gestures of recognition and unity. . . . However, they are grounds for disciplinary action if executed during official ceremonies or in a manner suggesting direct defiance of duly constituted authority.[197]

This official authorization to give black marines more leeway in "doing their thing" produced some bizarre results at the Quantico (Va.) Marine base, where some black enlisted men met in a group during off-duty hours. This was *Jet*'s description of it:

An uninformed visitor might have thought he'd stumbled onto an underground black guerrilla base, where the invasion of a "honky stronghold" was being plotted in secret. There was brother Alan Roberson, 21 year old third prime minister of the Moormen, proudly strolling across the military compound, his Black Panthers-style beret cocked to one side of his head, a ring in one ear. At the junior noncommissioned officer's club entrance, where the soul children could be heard wailing on a juke box inside, he exchanged a smart black power handshake and salute with fellow Moorman Millard Johnson.

*Jet* acknowledged that "older black Marines wonder if the directive [of General Chapman] will create more dissension than harmony." The magazine quoted Gunnery Sergeant James H. Ball, who said, "The white marines won't like this any more than I'd like seeing them in Ku Klux Klan robes."[198]

In October, the *Amsterdam News* reported, "At long last, The Amsterdam News, Ebony, Jet, Muhammad Speaks and other publications published for, about, and by Black people will be in libraries and PX's at U.S. Army Posts."[199] The author is very much in favor of the widest practicable choice of reading matter in military installations but fails to understand how stocking libraries and PX's with the virulently anti-white *Muhammad Speaks* can be expected to ease racial tensions in the armed forces. Before civil libertarians rush in to defend the Army decision, they might ask themselves if they would condone the sale of Ku Klux Klan literature at these same Army bases. Their answer would be a most illuminating one—and perhaps might indicate whether they have begun to succumb to the blandishments of the New Racism.

Apparently, some black servicemen were avid readers of the *Black Panther.* The August 16th issue of that paper published a "Letter from Vietnam", which read in part:

> So brothers in the world, I John R. White, have 19 days left in the army, but right now my brothers need me to stand by them. I know for a fact that I want to get out of the white man's army to come home and join the Black Liberation Army. But before I come back to the States if it takes 19 days or 19 years, I will stand beside my Black brothers until I have used every breath in my body to fight those white dogs.[200]*

And the November 22nd issue of the *Black Panther* carried this:

> 801st Maint. Bn.
> APO S.F. 96383
> We the brothers of Vietnam would like to see our names in print in your Black Panther paper. And we the brothers of Vietnam say, "FREE HUEY."
>
>      The Brothers:[201]

SP/4 Isiah Davis                    SP/4 Gregory McClain
SP/4 Charles Calhoun                SP/4 George Williamson
SP/4 Needham Jefferson              Sgt. William Whitehead
SP/4 Kenneth Miles                  SP/5 Sir Walter Jones[sic]
All power to the people.

---

*On July 15, 1970, *Combat* reported that in the racial rioting in Asbury Park, New Jersey, "sniper fire reportedly came from black ex-GIs with Vietnam experience."

This fan mail for the Black Panthers put into fearful focus the warning of Urban League official Joseph F. Cannon that "the Office of Veterans Affairs had already estimated that some 100,000 minority servicemen would be returning to the cities of this nation in 1969–1970. Many of them will be approached by black militants eager to capitalize on their resentments and their skills in demolition, sabotage, hand-to-hand combat, discipline, and organizational ability."[202]

Equally appalling was the Black Panthers' growing hold on the minds of at least some children (or as the party called them, "little brothers and sisters") in the ghetto. The way to the hearts of these youngsters was through their stomachs—through the use of food donated to the Black Panther breakfasts for school children. The *Black Panther* gleefully reprinted a story from the Communist *Daily World* about a breakfast at All Saints Catholic Church in Harlem. As the *Daily World* made it perfectly evident, the Panther breakfast was an adroit mixture of eggs and propaganda, sausage and revolution, melted cheese and sizzling hatred of the police.* Before the meal was served, a team of Panthers circulated through the rows of tables, greeting the children and spreading the Panther program. One young Panther asked a six-year-old girl, "What is point number six of the 10-point program of the Black Panther Party? What do we want?" She replied, "We want all black men to be exempt from military service." The Panther asked a little boy, "And what is our point number seven?" The child snapped, "We want an immediate end to police brutality and murder of black people." An 11-year-old boy blurted out, "Pigs hate black people."[203]

In Oakland, California, a Black Panther named Charles Bursey was facing a life sentence on the charge of attempting to

---

*For the most part, the food for Panther breakfasts was "donated" by businessmen—small shopkeepers and supermarket managers who eventually caved in under pressure and terror tactics that virtually put their businesses "up against the wall." One issue of *Black Panther* told how a fire had destroyed a San Francisco meat-processing plant that had failed to contribute. And *Black Panther,* spearheading a boycott of Safeway Stores, acidly commented: "It is very insane for these avaricious fools to refuse to contribute $100 per week to the Free Breakfast for Children Program, while they are losing so much more per day." Later, the Panthers announced that Safeway had begun "donating" food. An excellent account of this thinly veiled extortion can be found in the July 15, 1969, issue of *Combat.*

murder a policeman. Young children at Panther "liberation schools" sent him loving letters, among them:

Free all political prisoners
My name April Cephas 9 years old. I go to liberation school in the Fillmore Area. Teachers are Jim Patrick and Kathy. We learn about Fascism and picking up the gun. We learn about the red Book [of Mao Tse-tung]. We sing revolutionary songs. We know about John Huggins and Alprintinc [*sic*] Carter. The Cleaver had a baby.
Revolution is the only Solution
April

                                            ****

Dear Charles Bursey,
I am a student at the Liberation School in Berkeley and I heard about the pig that put you in jail on August 7, 1969, and we just got through hearing about the lying pig telling lies on you, and you got put in jail. We will free you and Huey too and the rest of the Revolutionaries. So, right on, Charles, All Power to the People.
Panther Power
Teddy

                                            ****

Free all Political Prisoners
My name is Tina. I'm 7 years Old. I live in the Haight area. I've been going since July. I've been singing song. We have learn about the field nigger. We have learn about the house nigger. To get freedom is to get the gun and off the pigs. I am going to free all political prisoners by the Red Book, Huey teaches and the gun.
Free Rory and Landon
Comrade Tina[204]

On June 24, 1969, a San Francisco police inspector, Ben Lashkoff, told the McClellan Committee in Washington that members of the Black Panther Party had distributed at some breakfasts a *Black Panther Coloring Book*—a book which *Combat* said "could be appropriately subtitled *A Child's Garden of Murder.*"[205] Inspector Lashkoff said the coloring books were being distributed along with free breakfasts in at least three locations: the Sacred Heart Catholic Church, the South Ridge Methodist Church, and the Jedediah Smith Elementary School.[206]

The Reverend Eugene J. Boyle (a white priest) of Sacred Heart Church told United Press International: "It's obvious that the San Francisco police intelligence squad does not understand the black man if they are making such a big thing out of this."[207] But in reading the *Black Panther Coloring Book,* as the author did, there was not the slightest question of misunderstanding. It was all totally self-explanatory. Six of the cartoons purported to deal with historical themes, from the origins of slavery to the Nat Turner uprising. The 16 other cartoons, for the most part, depicted monstrous murders of policemen by black men and black children. One cartoon showed three black men, two with knives and one with an ax, hacking away at a "pig" policeman lying on the ground. The caption was, "Off the Pig Beautiful Black Men." Another cartoon showed a black youth shooting a white "pig" policeman through the throat, as two black children looked on. It was captioned, "Black brothers protect black children." Another cartoon showed two black youths killing a white "pig" businessman as a black woman held a gun, and a black child looked on. The caption read: "Brothers and sisters deal with the white store owner that robs black people." Another cartoon depicted a young black boy shooting a white "pig" policeman. The caption: "The Junior Panther defends his mother." In still another cartoon, a "pig" policeman was lying in a pool of blood, while a black child pointed a gun at another "pig" patrolman, whose hands were raised and who was shaking with fright. The caption: "The Pig is afraid of Black children because they are brave warriors." Another cartoon took its text from Chairman Mao: "Power Comes Through the Barrel of a Gun."[208]

A member of the McClellan Committee, Senator Karl Mundt, summarized it most aptly. "Here it is," Mundt said. "Color him dead. This is a blueprint for the murder of policemen in the hands of children....When you teach murder in the basement of our churches, you begin to see where some of the fault lies."[209]

J. Edgar Hoover said that of all the black extremist groups, "the Black Panther Party, without question, represents the greatest threat to the internal security of the country."[210] It would be well to bear this in mind, as more and more pressure is exerted to hamper the police in their surveillance and arrests of Panther members.

If it is proven that individual police exceed their lawful authority, these few must be speedily dealt with. If it is proven that individual policemen assume the role of *agent provocateur* in the Black Panther movement, the few law enforcement officers involved must be strongly criticized.

But the general principle of the police department's watchful observance of the Panthers, a no-nonsense enforcement of the law as it applies to these Marxist-Leninist revolutionaries, and a police presence that prevents the Black Panther Party from using fear and terror to impose its will upon any part of the ghetto must be vigorously supported by all who want to make our cities livable for black and white alike.

Congressman Edward Koch stated, "I don't agree with goals or methods of the Black Panthers, but civil liberties transcend the issue of the Panthers' goals."[211] To which the author would reply—repeating the phrase which can never be repeated too often: "The Bill of Rights was never meant to be a suicide pact."

Eldridge Cleaver, Stu Alpert, and Tom Hayden

# LEROI JONES

# A POLITICAL PRISONER

America is holding LeRoi Jones as a political prisoner for the following reasons:

1. He, as a Free Black Man, refuses to be judged by an all white jury and judge.
2. He demands to be judged by his PEERS - BLACK PEOPLE.
3. He has called for the awakening of black people to the evils of this white society.

BLACK PEOPLE, WE SAT BACK AND PERMITTED THOSE DEVILS TO KILL/MURDER

BROTHER MALCOLM X.

WE CANNOT ALLOW the EXTERMINATION of ANOTHER BLACK LEADER!!

DIPLOMAT MAGAZINE - July, 1966 - 75 cents - New York City Newsstands

LE ROI JONES

---

*College Center Board Presents:*

## "BLACK POWER"
### A Seminar Series

**For:** NEWARK STATE STUDENTS, FACULTY, ADMINISTRATORS AND STAFF ONLY.
(ADMISSION FREE, BY IDENTIFICATION ONLY!)

**Place:** LITTLE THEATRE - COLLEGE CENTER BUILDING

| | | |
|---|---|---|
| Thursday, February 29, 1968 | 7 p.m. | LECTURE #1. "History of Black Power, General Orientation." Mr. John Howard - Former Director Office of Economic Opportunity - Plainfield, N.J. |
| Thursday, March 7, 1968 | 7 p.m. | LECTURE #2 Panel Discussion – "Political Aspects of Black Power, Analysis of the Racial Situation in New Jersey, Black Militancy in Newark." Mr. Marshall Brown – Co-coordinator Olympic Boycott of Black Athletes. Mr. Kenneth Gibson – Mayoralty Opponent of Mayor Addonizio, Assemblyman George Richardson – Founder of Freedom Party – Essex County, Mr. Harry Wheeler – Former Campaign Manager for Mayor Addonizio. Co-coordinator against the Establishment of the Medical School Center in Newark. |
| Thursday, March 14, 1968 | 7 p.m. | LECTURE #3. "Extremist Militant View of Black Power" Mr. Le Roi Jones - Poet, Playwright, Author. |
| Thursday, March 26, 1968 | 7 p.m. | LECTURE #4: Panel Discussion – "Psychological Aspects of Black Power – Re. Education, Decentralized Schools" Reverend Dr. Nathan Wright – Executive Director Urban Studies Center for the Episcopalian Diocese, Newark. Coordinator – Newark Black Power Conference. Dr. Kenneth Clark – Professor of Psychology, City College of New York. Major Contributor to 1954 Supreme Court Desegregation Decision. |
| Thursday, April 4, 1968 | 7 p.m. | LECTURE #5: Summary: Speakers will consist of one or several of the following: Mr. Whitney Young – Executive Secretary, National Urban League. Senator Edward Brooke – United States Senator, Commonwealth of Massachusetts. Mr. Bayard Rustin – Director of A. Philip Randolph Institute of New York City. Coordinator, March on Washington. Mr. Tom Hayden – Director of Newark Community Union Project (NCUP). Dr. Richard Kessler – Professor – New York University Human Relations Center. |

---

## PLEASE

at St. Michael's Hospital

We accuse Mayor Hugh Addonizio and the Management of St. Michael's Hospital of being Wage earners and Union busters.

More than 300 Black workers are out on strike at St. Michael's Hospital.

- We are fighting for our rights
- We are fighting for justice
- We are fighting for a living wage
- We are fighting for equality with White workers.

The Hospital recognized a union of 15 White workers. But the Hospital refuses to recognize a Union of 350 Black workers.

We met with the Mayor and we met with the Hospital Management and we got nowhere. The Black people of Newark have got to wake up!

There are more cops at the Hospital than are watching the streets, crooks and gangsters. We demand that the cops be removed from the Hospital!

We demand that our Union be recognized!

We demand that the Mayor get off his --- and do something about it!

IF HE DOESN'T--- WE WILL!

WE ASK FOR YOUR HELP – COME OUT ON THE PICKET LINE, WE NEED THE HELP OF THE ENTIRE BLACK COMMUNITY IN NEWARK.

IF THE MAYOR AND THE MANAGEMENT OF ST. MICHAEL'S HOSPITAL WANT TO PROVOKE A FIGHT— LET'S GIVE IT TO THEM.

THE STRIKING COMMITTEE OF ST. MICHAEL'S HOSPITAL
MEMBERS OF LOCAL 1199, DRUG AND HOSPITAL UNION, AFL-CIO
1060 BROAD STREET, NEWARK, NEW JERSEY
TELEPHONE: 623-7952

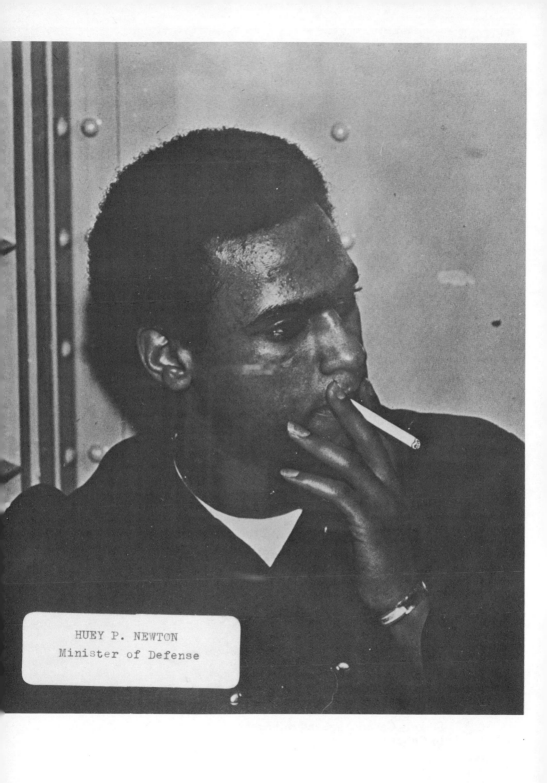

HUEY P. NEWTON
Minister of Defense

Stokely Carmichael and Bill Brendt (who later hijacked a plane to Cuba)

# The Crusader

## MONTHLY NEWSLETTER

**ROBERT F. WILLIAMS, Publisher — IN EXILE —**

**VOL. 6 — No. 2     OCTOBER SPECIAL EDITION 1964**

### CHAIRMAN MAO TSE-TUNG'S STATEMENT

Calling Upon the People of the World to Unite to Oppose Racial Discrimination by U.S. Imperialism and Support the American Negroes in Their Struggle Against Racial Discrimination

*August 8, 1963*

An American Negro leader now taking refuge in Cuba, Mr. Robert Williams, the former President of the Monroe, North Carolina Chapter of the National Association for the Advance-

Second Meeting: China's 15th Anniversary

## Robert Williams' newsletter from Cuba

## Rev. Albert Cleage, who "willed to be black."

Unidentified bodyguard and Milton Henry of the Republic of New Africa

Brother Imari (Richard Henry), one of the founders of the Malcolm X Society.

Panthers in front of Manhattan's Criminal Courts Building

Funeral of Little Bobby Hutton, first Panther "martyr."

# CHAPTER 6

# The Black Rebellion
# on Campus

## Storm Warnings

IT IS ONE OF THE CURIOUS PARADOXES OF OUR TIME THAT most white Americans know more about Europe and Asia than they do about Harlem and Watts, that they can name the leaders of far-off lands but would be hard-pressed to name more than two or three elected Negro officials in this country, that they are far more interested in world journalism than in the closeup firsthand reporting of the Negro press in the United States. Whites and Negroes live in the same cities, but not in quite the same world. They are strangers, and for all the artfully conceived campaigns exhorting them to brotherhood, they remain strangers. Americans can go to the moon, but still cannot navigate the gap between the ghetto and the rest of the city. Perhaps this is one of the prime reasons that white Americans find themselves continually in a state of surprise and bewilderment when news breaks of the latest "black blitzkrieg" (to quote the phrase of Dr. Nathan Hare). And yet almost without exception, there were loud and clear storm warnings of every twist and turn of black militancy, months and sometimes even years before, in the pages of the Negro press.

The appallingly inadequate preparation of many Negro high school graduates for college work was spotlighted in *Negro Digest* as early as September 1965, by Rayborn L. Zerby, Dean Emeritus of the Faculty of Bates College. The title of his article: "What Negroes Must Do To Close the Education Gap." At that time, based upon his observations as educational consultant at a Negro college in South Carolina, Zerby wrote: "The whole range of educational accomplishment, especially at the secondary level in Negro schools, is shockingly low. . . . Imagine one half of the entering class unable to write an intelligible paragraph. Add to this the inability to construct a simple sentence so that aggregations of words without subject and mismated verb forms must serve."[1] Zerby also noted:

> The Negro college has been attempting to meet the problem of poor preparation in one of two ways. The first is the establishment of adequate remedial courses with which the student by greater intensity of effort or by a longer time span is brought to the point of a legitimate bachelor's degree. The second method is the offering of a low grade curriculum of inferior courses and a low standard of grading that demands little effort, until the candidate is given a pseudo A.B. or B.S.[2]

Writing of this second group, Zerby observed:

> These colleges for nearly a century have been accepting candidates utterly unprepared for college work, giving them four years of undemanding curriculum and a purely gratuitous degree. Then the graduate most often has gone into teaching to continue the bad tradition. Such a college finds it hard to realize that the role it has been playing no longer serves any useful purpose.[3]

Today, some years after this article was written, some of the most illustrious Ivy League colleges in the country may be spending hundreds of thousands of dollars, and incalculable time and academic resources, merely to repeat the failures of the past—merely to offer a black student that which, in the real world, may be little more than "a pseudo A.B. or B.S." In effect, many Ivy League students, black and white, have been used as guinea pigs in hastily conceived educational experiments with fiasco virtually built in.

The reason? One could go back to the old truism that most white college administrators know little or nothing of the black experience in the urban ghettos. Bad enough. But worse still, given the vastness of their responsibilities in the academic community, they have evinced little or no knowledge of the prior experience with militants on Negro college campuses— experience that could have saved them, their faculty, and their students some of the most agonizing semesters in the history of higher education in this country. So many white colleges were either woefully uninformed about the lust for power—and the intoxication with violence of the new breed of black student militants on Negro campuses—or woefully arrogant enough to believe that white paternalism could succeed where Negro colleges had failed. How else explain the total lack of reaction to that chilling disclosure chronicled below by Negro college president Dr. James Cheek in early 1968? How else explain the attempt to escape from the inescapable conclusion that there was simply no reason in the world why the terrorism of student uprisings on the Negro campuses of Fisk, Central State, and Howard universities in 1967 could not be repeated—even more viciously—on Ivy League and state college campuses in 1968, 1969, 1970, and beyond.

It was in its issue of February 29, 1968, that *Jet* reported on an address by Dr. James E. Cheek, then president of Shaw University (and later named president of Howard University). His subject: "The Urban Crisis and the Negro College." Dr. Cheek said the nation was on the verge of racial war and that neither side could win. Cheek stated that at a recent meeting of Negro college presidents

we were informed that each of us, at that very moment, had students from our respective campuses being trained in Canada in riot and guerrilla tactics. About 18 months ago, I saw a secret Negro organization's "strategy paper" which outlined that secret society's plans to take over the Negro college campuses. This paper started out by saying that the only real power base for Negroes is the Negro college, but that most of these colleges are controlled by

Uncle Tom deans and trustees. This organization proposes to take over the colleges, to indoctrinate the students, and then to cause anarchy so as to bring the college presidents to their knees. I laughed when I saw this paper—we all laughed until the night the riot began at Fisk which is where the strategy paper said they would begin.[4]

Dr. Cheek named no names—nor did he identify the secret Negro organization. But "about 18 months ago" would have placed it around September 1966—a few months after Stokely Carmichael, then chairman of SNCC, had shouted five times to an audience in Greenwood, Mississippi, "We want Black Power!"

On April 9, 1967, Stokely Carmichael made a much protested appearance before a predominantly white audience at Vanderbilt University, in Nashville, Tennessee. A few hours later just across town Negro students at Fisk University hurled stones and fired pellet guns at riot policemen in a battle that went on into the early hours of the morning. Several hundred policemen had to be rushed to the scene to break up the crowd which grew to nearly 800.[5] The ostensible cause of the demonstration was the reported arrest of a Fisk Negro student by a white policeman at a Negro restaurant. The arrest took place at the request of the restaurant proprietor, himself a Negro.[6]

Captain John Sorace, intelligence chief for the police department, said, "All of those students who were with Carmichael at Vanderbilt were here tonight in the thick of things, and one girl volunteered that she was a Carmichael aide."[7] Carmichael himself had appeared on the Fisk campus but apparently left the university 30 minutes to an hour before the riots started.[8] Avon N. Williams, a Negro lawyer who led the civil rights movement in Tennessee for a decade, accused Carmichael of having created the "design" for the riot. Williams charged that Carmichael "didn't have to be present in town when this started. His bully boys were here and they knew what he wanted."[9] Carmichael noted that the *Nashville Banner* had accused him of coming to Nashville to "stir up" trouble. Carmichael stated, "They lie all the time, but this is one time they told the truth. There is going to be a change and a change soon in this community. If we don't get change, we are going to tear this country apart."[10]

Two of SNCC's field secretaries were charged with inciting to riot. In two days, the toll rose to more than 15 injuries and 40 arrests.[11]

In November 1967, James R. Lawson, president of Fisk University, in testimony before a Senate investigations subcommittee, expressed doubts that Carmichael's appearance on the Fisk campus could be tied in with the trouble that broke out. Nevertheless, Lawson testified that there were indications that the incident preceding the riot had been prearranged. Lawson testified that within three to five minutes after the Nashville policemen removed the Fisk student from the tavern, a group of students appeared, carrying signs, and set up a picket line. Lawson went on to state that about two hours later, after the disorder had spread, youths were throwing rocks from a pile that had been assembled nearby. The following day, he testified, students searching the campus under faculty supervision found about 60 soda bottles stuffed with rags in a girl's dormitory. Lawson said that there apparently had been plans to convert these bottles into Molotov cocktails.[12]

The black militant contagion spread to Central State University, a predominantly Negro state school in Ohio. On November 1, 1967, 50 to 70 student members of Unity for Unity, a small black nationalist group at Central State, led demonstrations to support non-academic employees at the school who were negotiating a labor agreement. About 200 to 300 Central State students blockaded a building entrance, trapping university president Dr. Harry Groves in his office for two hours.[13] At about this same time, organizers from Stokely Carmichael's SNCC appeared on the campus to help organize militant Negroes.[14]

The following day, student militants held a demonstration on the campus of Wilberforce University, another Negro school nearby. At that meeting, the president of Wilberforce, Dr. Rembert Stokes appeared and reprimanded students for their Black Power activities. At that time, Michael Warren, a Central State student, was said to have called Dr. Stokes an Uncle Tom. "When the revolution comes, I will kill you," Warren said.[15] Dr. Stokes complained to President Groves, and as a result Warren was expelled and warned that if he appeared again on the Central State campus he would be arrested for trespassing.[16]

Defying the expulsion, Warren appeared at Central State, and was surrounded by around 50 fellow students protecting him from arrest.[17]

Central State students barricaded a school building to keep police from arresting Warren. The university called the sheriff, who was squirted with liquid when he entered the building. The sheriff called for help from the police, the sheriff's deputy forces, and the National Guard.[18] Among those arrested were two men, not students, who identified themselves as SNCC workers.[19] David Smith, 21-year-old president of the Central State Student Government, said the students "saw 100 loaded patrol cars come on the campus. There was lots of fear. Some said, 'I guess we'd better fight now.' "[20] Dr. Groves had little or no choice; he read a proclamation declaring:

> By order of the Board of Trustees, Central State University is closed effective immediately for the safety and welfare for [sic] the student body. All students are advised to leave the dormitories and proceed directly to their homes at the earliest time.[21]

Sidney O. Davis, the head of the Greene County N.A.A.C.P., claimed that Dr. Groves had failed to "communicate" with some Negro students, particularly "poor ones." But in a statement supporting the administration, the school's faculty unanimously declared, "We hereby affirm our support of President Harry E. Groves and his administration in his attempts to develop and maintain a climate conducive to academic excellence for all who seriously seek such an experience. As a scholar in his own right, he has contributed greatly to the intellectual atmosphere of this university."[22]

During the thirteen days that Central State was closed to students, numerous threats were made on the life of Dr. Groves from anonymous sources. Groves submitted his resignation, effective in six months.[23] A university spokesman told the *Amsterdam News:* "There is an air of hostility here which seems stronger than before. And with our president resigning because of threats on his life, we believe we don't know if we can remain open for the remainder of the academic year."[24]

Possibly, with a great effort of will, the white academic powers-that-be could have loftily—if parochially—closed their eyes and ears to the terror tactics on the campuses of Fisk and Central State universities. But it was virtually impossible to ignore what was happening almost at the doorstep of the Congress— in Howard University, "the capstone of Negro education," often referred to as "the black Harvard."

The professional schools of Howard University have trained half of the nation's Negro physicians and dentists, a fourth of the Negro lawyers.[25] Howard has given the nation dozens of prominent Negro leaders. Among its graduates are Senator Edward Brooke of Massachusetts, Supreme Court Justice Thurgood Marshall, and Mrs. Patricia Roberts Harris, former ambassador to Luxembourg.[26] Howard's president, James M. Nabrit, Jr., was one of the attorneys in the 1954 suit to end segregated schools.[27]

As early as 1965, Nabrit detected the impending conflict at Howard. In 1965, a group called Students for Academic Freedom sponsored a demonstration to protest compulsory ROTC class attendance rules and the university's action in changing the status of a professor. About 350 students gathered for the demonstration. Nabrit noted that on one occasion he saw two known Communists on the picket line. Nabrit warned, "We must beware of some people who come to us like the Greeks bearing gifts. They do not believe in civil rights for anyone. . . . They are children of lawlessness and disciples of destruction. They are people who cloak themselves in the roles of civil-righters and plot and plan in secret to disrupt our fight for justice and full citizenship. They must be unmasked for the frauds they are. They must be fought in every arena and they must not be permitted to prevail."[28] In a day of double-think, double-talk, and vague generalities, Nabrit was refreshingly blunt and candid, for all to hear, including NBC-TV. In his words:

> I saw some Communists passing out throwaways. I saw some Communists helping deliver placards. . . . These are grown people, they're not students. . . . They have never denied that they were Communists, and they have been the leaders in the Communist group in Washington all the years I've been here. We had to put them out of the N.A.A.C.P.[29]

Nabrit felt that Howard University might have been designated as the target for the kind of outside agitation that stirred outbreaks at the University of California's Berkeley campus.[30]

It cannot be overstressed that these words were uttered by James M. Nabrit, Jr., for 32 years a leader in the struggle for Negro rights—for 24 of those 32 years, professor and dean of the law school that had trained many of the lawyers now active in civil rights. And yet in two years' time, with his back to the academic wall, James M. Nabrit, Jr., would be forced to announce his retirement as president of Howard University.

It happened in 1967. Ronald O. Ross and Leonard McCants, both Howard students and co-chairmen of "Project Awareness," invited Lieutenant General Lewis B. Hershey of the Selective Service to address a meeting. As the general began to speak, a youth at the rear of the auditorium stood and yelled, "Beast!" About 35 students rushed to the stage, waving signs saying, "America is the Black Man's Battleground," "Vietnam, Hell No!" and exhibiting pictures of two hanging, burned Negroes surrounded by a crowd of laughing whites.

Over 75 percent of the audience cheered and applauded the young militants on the stage at Howard.[31] Ross stated, "More of this type of reaction will occur until America solves its problem concerning the black man." The other co-sponsor was quoted as having said, ". . . as a black person myself, I found the entire affair repulsive."[32]

The following day, Ernest Goodman, Howard's public relations director, said that only one of the demonstrators who rushed onto the stage was identified as a student. President Nabrit sent General Hershey an official apology.

Fourteen student leaders presented a statement to the press: "We decry and deplore the irresponsible, premeditated, and unforgivable manner in which General Hershey was treated [and] would like for it to be known that the manner in which these persons conducted themselves is in no way representative of the student community."[33]

But in front of Cramton Auditorium, another press conference was being held to announce the formation of the "Black Power Committee." A prepared statement was read: "The Committee has as its goals the overthrow of the Negro college with white innards and to raise in its place a militant black university which will counteract the whitewashing black students now receive in Negro and white institutions." The statement was read, in turns, by Robin Gregory, the homecoming queen, Huey LaBrie, and Sociology Professor Nathan Hare.[34] We will hear more about Nathan Hare. For the moment, suffice it to say that he had been a mentor of Stokely Carmichael, and had written, "We foresee a black blitzkrieg . . . in which this country will either solve its problems or get the destruction it deserves."[35]

On April 19, 1967, four students, including Miss Gregory, were scheduled to appear before a university disciplinary committee on charges stemming from the "Hershey Demonstration." Some 400 or more students rallied and set fire to hanging effigies of General Hershey, President Nabrit, and Dean Frank M. Snowden of the College of Liberal Arts. After threatening to charge the committee room, the students regrouped on the campus and continued their rally. The hearings were postponed until a later date.[36]

All but lost in the furor was the telling and prophetic comment by the associate dean of students, Dr. Carl Anderson, who said, "If a speaker is not safe on a platform, next a teacher may not be safe in the classroom. There is no end to it unless it is stopped now."[37]

One week later, the Faculty Forum held a rally and charged the administration with denying students and faculty the use of campus institutions; an unjust firing of a philosophy instructor; and the "Kangaroo Court" trial of students over the Hershey affair.[38] The following day, about 50 students forced their way past three doors and down a corridor in order to halt the rescheduled disciplinary hearings. Encouraged by 200 students behind them, only the locked door of the conference room held them back. The students refused to move until Miss Gregory came out and pleaded with them to leave.[39]

A Howard official stated, "We had bomb threats almost daily. In one building we had four cases of arson in a six-hour period. Watchmen were shot at. Members of the faculty and students were threatened. Howard was almost like a combat zone. Some parents withdrew their children."[40]

On Saturday, April 23, with Dr. Nathan Hare presiding at a non-university-authorized rally of 2,000 or more people outside Douglass Hall, the guest speaker, Muhammad Ali (still known to some as Cassius Clay), proceeded to tell the sympathetic audience why he thought the "black man is still catching hell."[41]

The following week, Howard University issued a 10-point statement, which stated in summary:

1)   Protests must be confined outside the lecture hall, and limited to orderly picketing.

2)   A location shall be designated where students may conduct rallies at certain specified times.

3)   The university shall not allow itself to be converted into either a recruiting place or a regular forum for advocates of any particular ideology.

4)   Discourtesy or incivility to guests, visitors, or members of the university shall not be permitted.

5)   Students and faculty may exercise their rights as citizens, as individuals, and not as representatives of the faculty.

6)   A judiciary committee of students and faculty structured along the fundamentals of due process shall be maintained.

7)   All public announcements and news releases shall be cleared through the Public Relations Office. Arrangements to have representatives of the public communications media present on campus must be cleared by the Public Relations Office.

8)   All administrators, faculty, and students have a responsibility to abide by and support the above.

9)   Lawlessness and disorder shall not be permitted.

10)   The university is dedicated to all races. Violations of any of the 10 by the academic community shall be dealt with by the university.[42]

In an off-campus meeting, a group of students and faculty members decided to conduct a boycott. On May 8, militant law student Jeroyd W. (Jay) Greene told a gathering of some 500 students that the boycott was ". . . a movement to free us from bonds that do not allow us to act as adults and as individuals." At that time, Greene stated that the campus chapter of the American Association of University Professors (AAUP) went on record as supporting the student protests against the disciplinary proceedings emanating from the Hershey affair.[43] But then, it could hardly have been otherwise, considering that Nathan Hare was head of that chapter of the AAUP.[44]

The sponsors of the boycott drew up a list of demands, with

something for everyone—a list that had "been revamped and compromised many times in order to draw the widest possible support."[45] These were the final demands:

    1)   All charges against the four students allegedly taking part in the Hershey incident be dropped as the University has no written code of conduct which they have violated.

    2)   A guarantee in writing that no action retroactively or prospectively be taken against any student because of his or her political activities during the current academic year [1966–67].

    3)   Abolishment of all senior comprehensive examinations. . . .

    4)   That no faculty member be dismissed or denied promotion because of his political activism or non-conformity. . . .

    5)   That compulsory ROTC be abolished.

    6)   Immediate repeal of the recent policy statement on student protest. . . .[46]

With six turns at bat, it is little wonder that the boycott sponsors scored impressively in this grim game of militant brinkmanship. Howard University students who took a dim view of exams embraced demand number three. Students wanting to weaken ROTC (or simply humiliate the military) flocked to the support of demand number five. Students supporting the popular homecoming queen closed ranks behind number one. In the end, an estimated 80 percent of the student body—and possibly more—stayed away from classes.[47] In the next few weeks, all charges against Miss Gregory were dropped, and the three male students were merely given written reprimands.[48]

A few days later, fire department officials began investigating a series of suspicious blazes at Howard University. In one of the rooms, the pull-down maps were little more than charred remains, while that entire corner of the room was black. Every window in the room had cracked under the apparently intense heat. Splattered on the wall a few hundred feet away were the words, "Join the Black Guard."[49]

Late in June, Howard University announced that it had expelled fourteen students and five professors, among them Dr. Nathan Hare.[50] The American Civil Liberties Union requested

Howard to reinstate the ousted students and faculty until they could be given a hearing; legal action was threatened if the university refused.[51] The Howard Law Alumni Association of the Greater Washington Area went on record as condemning the university for dismissal without administrative due process.[52]

Those who opposed President Nabrit were louder and more strident than ever. Many who should have supported him stood silently on the sidelines or made an opportunistic alliance with the radicals. Faced with a hostile and divided campus, Nabrit announced his desire to retire "as soon as the Board of Trustees can find a successor."[53] (He remained at Howard for two more years, and was succeeded in the presidency by James Cheek of Shaw University). Nabrit was quoted as saying that he was deeply distressed by the events of the past year, as well as by the steps it became necessary for him to take in order to maintain law and order on the campus.[54] With the credentials of a lifetime of academic expertise documenting every word, Nabrit warned that a university must maintain order so that education can proceed. In fact, he added, a university needs even more order than other kinds of organizations.[55]

In September, the U.S. Court of Appeals ordered Howard University to reinstate the ousted students on the grounds that they were entitled to a hearing on specific charges. The court did not, however, order Howard to reinstate the five professors it had discharged.[56] Presumably the line of reasoning of the court ran parallel to that of a "prominent university professor" (not otherwise identified), who told *Jet:* "It is cowardly to dismiss these people a few months before school starts. The faculty members will have difficulty relocating and the students will have trouble entering another institution."[57] And yet the dismissals—which may have astonished the court and the "prominent university professor"—had been fully expected at Howard. The question was not whether these students and professors would be dismissed, but *when.* Writing in the December 1967 issue of *Negro Digest,* Robert A. Malson, a student at Howard, stated, *"As many students had been predicting all along,* the university had waited until the summer and then fired five professors and expelled 14 students"[58] (emphasis added). And Nathan Hare wrote, "I knew even then [in April] that probably I was passing through my last days at Howard, and perhaps as a college professor anywhere."[59]

But Dr. Hare was hardly a needy case. By the end of the year, Hare had already turned down two offers from larger, more richly endowed institutions[60]—an extraordinary demand for his services, considering his growing reputation as one of the intellectual kamikazes of the black militant movement. It was Hare who predicted a "hot Fall in which Howard's 'Toms' would be roasted and tenderized."[61] It was Hare who declared, "People will have to take over Howard and run it themselves to get a decent administration. The university might have to be brought to a halt, closed, wiped out, eliminated."[62]

The seething militant ferment in the Negro colleges found compelling expression in March 1968 when *Negro Digest* devoted virtually its entire issue to one of the most extraordinary collections of articles ever published. The subject: *The Black University.*

# CHAPTER 7

# The Black University

In March 1968, Hoyt W. Fuller, managing editor of *Negro Digest,* wrote, "The idea of a Black University—an institution designed to serve the *real* and *total* needs of the black community—has taken root, and there is every reason to believe that the idea will grow and eventually take concrete shape."[1]

In this same issue, J. Herman Blake, acting assistant professor of sociology at Cowell College, Santa Cruz, did not offer any specific definition of "the black community," but he noted estimates that black people comprised at least 25 percent or more of the population of 11 of the 30 largest cities in the country. Among them:

| | |
|---|---|
| Washington | 66% |
| Newark | 47% |
| Atlanta | 44% |
| New Orleans | 41% |
| Memphis | 40% |
| Baltimore | 38% |
| St. Louis | 36% |
| Cleveland | 34% |
| Detroit | 34% |

| | |
|---|---|
| Philadelphia | 31% |
| Chicago | 28%[2] |

But, of course, this was only the obvious outer layer of the concept of the black community. In essence, the black community was as much a state of mind as a state of being, existing wherever there was a gathering of a significant number of Negroes at the same time. In the same place, sharing roughly the same experience and the same reactions *vis-à-vis* the larger society.

This special issue of *Negro Digest* had developed through discussions with Gerald McWorter, a recent Ph.D. graduate of the University of Chicago, and now an assistant professor of sociology at Fisk University.[3] To McWorter, revolutionary power came out the barrel of a black militant textbook. More specifically, in his article he declared that "educational institutions are vital to a liberation movement, a fact of modern times in anti-colonial movements in the Third World." He believed: "As the pernicious oppression of racism is an organic part of the institutions, symbols, and values of Western industrial society, so it is firmly entrenched in the U.S.A. (as American as apple pie)." McWorter was therefore convinced that "an Afro-American liberation movement must subvert and/or supplant such a well-entrenched social system if it is to be a real source of radical change and not a false one." Viewed in this light, the black university was to have a prophetic social role, "for therein lies the fountainhead of revolutionary liberation." McWorter expressed the conviction that Afro-American nationalism, grounded in the black experience, and the Negro desire to get more out of society were the "general social sources of the cry for a Black University."

What was the black university? McWorter offered a three-pronged definition:

First, Blackness refers to the Afro-American community as the basic focus for the University . . . . A second, and more controversial point, considers the limits placed on participation in the University. Blackness does not categorically exclude all white people from the University . . . [but] the white participant must possess the sacrificial humility necessary for one historically and socially iden-

tified with the beast of Afro-American history and system
of oppression.

Last, Blackness is an affirmation of an identity independent of the historical human evils of modern nation states
and is closely tied to the emerging international identity
of man in his struggle for a better life.[4]

In a bit of phraseology that smacked of amateur theatrics,
McWorter asked:

Who are we? Afro-Americans, men of the world. Why are
we here? We were sent here to love. Where are we going?
Toward the community of love, and if stopped we will
continue "by any means necessary" because we must continue.[5]

Apparently, the McWorter concept of love did not exclude the
kiss of death for anyone daring to get in his way.

McWorter was appalled by the American ethic of individualism, considering it a *de facto* subversion of society. Denouncing
it as self-centeredness, he stressed that "the thrust of the Black
University must be to overcome this subtle social warlike-state
with the ethic of communalism. This means that instead of
hoping for social progress through the individual merits of its
students or faculty *qua* individuals, progress is to be viewed as
a social process through which the community is uplifted with
the aid of its contributing people."[6]

One could almost visualize a new Orwellian Big Black
Brother overseeing McWorter's black university. In his words:
"The values of the Black University must support the liberation
movement of Afro-Americans, oppressed people around the
world, and all that prevents man from leading the good life."
McWorter submitted this "unfinished design" for the black university:

## COLLEGE OF LIBERAL ARTS

UNIVERSITY LIBRARY
UNIVERSITY PRESS

COLLEGE OF                          COLLEGE OF
AFRO-AMERICAN STUDIES        COMMUNITY LIFE

1. Centers for International Study
   (Asia, Africa, Latin America)
2. International Conference Center

Under the McWorter plan, "even the student entering the College of Liberal Arts would have to work at least a year in one or more of the other two colleges in order to meet the requirements for graduation."[7] The centers for international study would presumably be devoted to third-world studies.

Vincent Harding, professor of history at Spelman College in Atlanta, discussed, "Some International Implications of the Black University." He began with the observation that "we are the largest single segment of the nation which holds within itself both East and West, both Africa and America, both developed and developing societies. . . . Any university which grew with integrity out of the ground of our black experience in America would have to reflect and bear the creative agony of that tension. . ." Consequently, Harding felt that "those of us who seek to build faithfully out of the materials of the Afro-American experience are called to other paths . . . our focus would be upon that segment of the non-West which has existed under Western domination for the relatively brief span of 400 years or less, and which now shakes the world with its efforts to wrench free." Of this group, the primary focus would of course be upon Africa. Harding visualized a black-oriented university that "could present a marvelous opportunity for the social sciences in America to break out of their nationalistic trap. Sociology might include such matters as urban development among black people in Nairobi, Chicago and Rio. Political Science could well analyze the forms of resistance to colonial domination in Harlem, Cuba, Mozambique and Vietnam." Practically a training school for rebellion, Harding's black university would give revolutionaries all manner of assistance by any academic means necessary. In his own words:

"Think Tanks" filled with the varied but constant experience of blackness might be established for the sole purpose of analyzing specific conflict situations from Detroit to Angola (and beyond) and suggesting directions of actions and ideology for those who are struggling to break away from the hegemony of the West.

And for any who, for some unaccountable reason, had still not yet grasped the Harding message:

> Representatives of the anti-colonial forces, members of Liberation Fronts, religious and educational leaders from the reborning nations would be invited and welcomed in order to give deeper meaning to the searching [for new ways of life free of imperialism]. Indeed, *such a university might well become a sanctuary of sorts for some of the world's revolutionaries.*[8] [Emphasis added]

In 1966, Stokely Carmichael was shouting, "Hell No! We Won't Go!" when asked about Negro soldiers serving in Vietnam. In March 1968 Harding put the matter much more genteelly:

> Conceivably a black-oriented Overseas Service Corps might develop, and this would not only provide excellent nation-building opportunities but it could become an alternative to action with the United States military forces. For it is likely that the international orientation of a Black University will create many dissenters to the foreign policy which our armed forces now enforce.[9]

Discussing the faculty, curriculum and research at the black university was Stephen E. Henderson, chairman of the Department of English at Morehouse College in Atlanta. Henderson wrote: "Although the Black University does not at present exist anywhere in toto, it does exist in part in that residue of blackness—social, cultural, and philosophical—which is found in the so-called predominantly Negro colleges; or to use another circumlocution, in the historically Negro colleges." Noting that the oft-cited purpose of many schools was to help the student discover his identity, Henderson declared, *"The single revolutionary concept that has emerged in recent years is that the black experience is not only relevant in such a search, it is fundamental and crucial."* In the last analysis, wrote Henderson, "one finally *wills* to be black. This is what the fuss is all about—Albert Cleage, Adam Powell, Walter White, Frank Silvera, *willed* in varying degrees to be black."

Convinced that "some of our [Negro college] presidents indicate their determination to die the white death," Henderson believed that the salvation of Negro colleges lay "in the will-to-blackness of the faculty and the students. When this will becomes strong enough, when it becomes *informed,* in all senses of the word, with SOUL, when it reaches the saturation point (or better still, when it reaches critical mass), it will demand institutional restructuring—in faculty, in general resources, and in acknowledged aims." Henderson predicted that some of these changes would take place rather rapidly in some institutions, not at all in others—that in some, the changes would be "harnessed for the good of all; in others, the result may well be destructive social explosion." What was not in doubt in Henderson's mind was that the change *would* come, and that those who opposed it "really have no business at all in the crucial task of educating this new black generation who may well be our last hope for sanity and decency in this country."

It was Henderson's belief that "we have to no inconsiderable extent Africanized this country. That time it was unconscious and passive. This time it must be otherwise, for unless the values inherent in "Soul" and "Negritude" are made to prevail in this country, we may yet find ourselves at Armageddon, across the seas, in our skies, and in our own city streets."[10]

A considerably more realistic and responsible tone was apparent in the article by Darwin T. Turner, dean of the graduate school at the Agricultural and Technical State University of North Carolina. In his article, "The Black University: A Practical Approach," Turner sought to "suggest ways of achieving the desired improvement within the present structure of higher education." Speaking of the Negro teacher in an integrated institution, Turner saw little hope for his advancement; and while there were rare exceptions, "most often, however, he rises to the lowly post of assistant or associate professor, and squirms there; the channels to prominence are damned for him, even though his intelligence and training may surpass those of men who rise beyond his rank." The picture Turner drew of a Negro teacher in a predominantly Negro college was even more bleak: "Even though the quality of instruction in individual classes may equal that observed in any college in the country, widely publicized reports by white men have proclaimed the innate inferiority of such institutions. Thus, as long as he remains attached to a predominantly Negro college, he too is adjudged inferior or, at best, an exception, a small-sized frog in a muddy cesspool."

Turner was only slightly more sanguine about the life of Negro students in integrated institutions. He conceced that some of them might be elected "homecoming queen or president of a club or even a class," if they were "exceptional in intelligence, athletic ability, charm or beauty," or if the school was "campaigning to prove its liberality." Academically, he saw some Negro students suffering from the prejudice "of instructors who believe Negroes incapable of swimming above 'C' level." And it may well be that he had in mind some of the more famous Ivy League schools when he charged that "still others, intelligent students, may suspect that they are being crippled by condescending tolerance." Turner described this grading, and degrading, paternalism:

> [Black students] answers are accepted too easily; their mistakes are forgiven too quickly. They fear that they are being hurried along, with good grades, by teachers willing to evaluate Negroes on lowered standards because after graduation, the Negroes will disappear into their own world where their ignorance will neither injure nor threaten the white world.

Noting that Negro students had complained they learned too little about themselves, and about ways to improve their community, Turner candidly stated, "Although I admit the justice of the charge, I cannot blame anyone except Negro faculty members—myself included. . . . Nothing—to my knowledge—prevents predominantly Negro colleges from offering any course that is desired. . . . The fact is that Negro educators—and I must include myself—have not conceived courses oriented to the Negro."[11]

As the title of his article indicated, Turner was interested in a *practical* approach to the building of a black university—and from that vantage point, practically ruled it out, for some years to come. "Negro teachers are needed," Turner readily agreed. "But the task of securing them is not as simple as might be presumed from listening to the bright young educators who demand a black university."

Hypothetically, Turner gave as an example the establishment of a university of 10,000 students, "small by standards of the prestige universities, colossal for a Negro institution." Assuming that there would be one teacher for every 20 students, that would amount to only 500 teachers, plus administrators and secretaries. "Only 500", Turner repeated. "But that number will not be found among Negroes who earn graduate degrees in 1968 . . . desire is not sufficient. Knowledge and teaching ability are required." It would be necessary to "raid" the facilities of already established institutions; but, "as anyone knows who has tried it, money does not always prove sufficiently strong to pry a teacher from an institution and a community where he has planted roots for himself and his family."[12] How long would it take for a new institution with sufficient money and satisfactory fringe benefits to build a satisfactory faculty? Turner thought "a decade may not be an unreasonable minimum."[13]

As a practical matter he deemed it evident that "it may be necessary to develop the program at an institution already established, for one may strengthen a competent faculty more quickly than create a new one."[14] However, Turner did not name which "institution already established" he envisioned as the black university. He urged that new curricula "prepare students for occupations previously closed to them." But in the very next sentence, he quickly added, "Many predominantly Negro colleges, starving financially, cannot afford the additional expense of new programs, no matter how desirable they may be." As for academic caliber, Turner noted, "Possibly experimentation will prove that many students cannot reach the required level of competence within four years. If so, the students must be retained longer."

Summarizing, Turner wrote that the final need of the black university was prestige. But he believed that in America "a black university will never earn national reputation as long as it uses only black teachers to instruct only black students. And I wonder how long Negro students will retain pride in their institutions unless that pride is respected by non-blacks."[15]

Of all those who wrote about the black university, it was clearly Darwin T. Turner who saw integration as the solution —the only really workable solution. He urged that the university secure teachers "black or white" who had the knowledge and ability to teach the courses, while accepting students "white or black" who wished this particular type of education. Turner freely acknowledged:

> What results will not be *the* Black University for it accepts white money, white faculty, and white students. But it should be the kind of institution best designed to provide adequate opportunity for black teachers and students to develop their capabilities fully, to serve the black community effectively to gain pride in and knowledge of their heritage and themselves, and to achieve recognition for their ability. And these, after all, are the major purposes for which a Black University is proposed.[16]

Gerald McWorter might indeed exhort "all of the brothers and sisters in 'other' colleges and university settings to come on home. And to those at home, let us get this thing together!"[17] However, the plain and simple fact was that even those Negro colleges most sympathetic to the cause didn't have the substantial sums needed to build, staff, and maintain the black university. But even if the physical edifice did not yet exist—and might not exist for some time to come—the *idea* of the black university was now very much alive, and very much a part of the thinking of young black militants who were being implored to attend Ivy League and other white schools.

With traditional academic requirements being shunted aside, with Ivy League talent scouts scouring the ghetto for those with some kind, any kind, of "potential," more and more back militants were now being enrolled at some of the most prestigious colleges in the country, and at a number of state and junior state colleges. Consciously or unconsciously, a number of these young blacks brought with them McWorter's evangelical zeal for an Afro-American liberation movement that would subvert or supplant a white "racist" society; Harding's Open Door Policy for International Revolutionary Doctrine; Henderson's determination to restructure the university and make the "values" inherent in *soul* prevail in this country; Turner's overriding emphasis upon black academic respect and prestige. Consciously or unconsciously, in their non-negotiable demands for black studies programs, some black militants sought to establish a beachhead for the black university—a center for revolutionary change—on the white campus. How? In the words of Malcolm X, "by any means necessary."

In the pages that follow, we will briefly visit some of these strife-torn campuses. Beginning, appropriately enough, at San Francisco State College, we will deal with one of the most controversial black studies programs ever demanded, headed by one of the black professors who had just recently been dismissed from Howard University—Dr. Nathan Hare.

# CHAPTER 8

# San Francisco State College

By any imaginable criteria, appointing Nathan Hare coordinator of black studies at San Francisco State was like dropping a Molotov cocktail down an incinerator. By now, Hare's activities at Howard, and his incendiary utterances both on and off campus, were a matter of public record. If more proof were needed, one had only to read his articles in *Negro Digest* over a four-year period. To be sure, some of his articles were thoughtful and perceptive social critiques—among them "How and Why Negroes Spend Their Money" and "The Frustrated Masculinity of the Negro Male."[1] Another of his articles—"Life Among White Liberals"—was as masterful and merciless a lobotomy of white liberalism as the author has ever read. In this article, Hare wrote, "While white liberals proved to be a rather mongrel breed, they did fall into discernible categories." Among the categories, he included "the Roving Inquirers," consisting "of two distinct divisions: those who know more about the Negro than the Negro knows about himself, and those who only recently discovered that Negroes actually exist." (Hare wrote this article shortly before the word *Negro* was placed on the militants' subversive list.) Hare wrote of the "Groovy liberal" who became,

> when in the company of Negroes, quite all-Negro or all-too-Negro. The moment, in fact, that they hear the sound of a jazz note or blues tune, or the gospel wail of Mahalia Jackson, they automatically close their eyes, snap their fingers and stomp their feet in superficial ecstasy. At the same time, they overwork themselves in the effort to acculturate to Negroes and expect, too often, that Negroes are obliged to return the compliment.

Hare told an anecdote, based upon his own experience with a "Two-Faced or Sneaky Liberal." Entering his apartment house one day, Hare was walking some distance behind a middle-aged white couple and their daughter. As Hare recalled it:

> The gentleman held the door somewhat unnecessarily (for it required a very long moment) until I rushed to reach the door in order to honor his exceeding courtesy. I thanked him and decided to check my mailbox which was soon discerned to be empty; and so I followed the threesome to the elevator, unbeknown to my liberal "doorman's" wife. "Wouldn't open the door for anybody else; what is this?" she joked seriously-humorously in contempt. The gentleman, noting my presence, tried desperately to inform her of the same while coyly brushing off her remark. Later, however, when we were alighting together from the elevator, the woman herself attempted to hold the door for me.

Hare told of "Lovelorn liberals [who] are given to masochistic rites. They gather with similarly-afflicted middle-class Negroes to engage in marathon testimonials, self-righteously confessing to bygone prejudices now turned to love. These guilt-ridden liberals place on Negro companions the burden of supplying free a sort of interracial psychiatric couch."[2] Ironically, this was published at a time when Negroes were celebrating the passage of one of the most sweeping pieces of civil rights legislation of all time—the Civil Rights Act of 1964, a law which would have had a quick burial in committee if white liberals had not pushed it through the Senate and the House of Representatives.

Six months later, Hare had passed even the point of caustic

satire, and made clear to the most obtuse white sycophant his loathing for whites in general, and white friends of the civil rights movement in particular. An article by Nathan Hare was published in January 1965 titled: "Why Negro 'Leaders' Lack Power." In this article, Hare quite obviously acted as an unabashed cheerleader for the riots "that leapfrogged through Northern cities last summer." Hare bemoaned the fact that "leftists, black nationalists and cultists were seized and raided, often on 'tips' from Negro bigwigs, on grounds that a couple of butcher knives, an old rusty pistol and, say, a couple of beer bottles were found in their headquarters. This, despite the fact that the rioters, even if organized, were largely unarmed except for bricks and such ready-made ammunition." Hare defended looting, because it was "selective, restricted on the whole to white stores." In his article, Hare discussed how Rex Hopper had divided social revolutions into four typical stages: The Preliminary Stage of Individual Excitement and Unrest; The Popular Stage of Crowd Excitement and Unrest; The Formal Stage; and The Institutional Stage. It was Hare's conviction that the Negro riots were part of the beginning of the second stage of an emerging revolution. As Hare put it:

> The second stage, which we may now be undergoing, is characterized by 1) the spread of discontent and the contagious extension of the several signs of unrest. . . ; 2) loss of faith in their leadership on the part of the repressed group; and 3) the emergence of conflict with the outgroup.

"In any case," Hare wrote, "many of the aspects present in the riots and public reaction were, as we said, apparent during the French Revolution. There was in both, selective looting; and the ruling groups and the rioters' own bourgeois allies similarly shouted bribery, resorted to name-calling and set about tracking down 'conspirators' instead of removing the social grievances."[3]

This would-be black Robespierre concluded: "It is only a conspiracy of silence and wishful thinking that lead white men of power and their colored henchmen to ignore the revolutionary aspects of the riots, while trying to shame Negroes back into complacency."[4]

Two years later, *U.S News & World Report* asked him: "As a

minority, don't you worry about hurting your chances by antagonizing the majority?"

Hare replied, "You know, there's always this hang-up on numbers—the idea that you need the whole world with you to do anything. I understand that only 30,000 persons were actively involved in the Russian Revolution. I don't know how many persons Castro had in the hills with him in Cuba, but not a great many. Some persons have all kinds of theories—such as, say, get a few pounds of this drug, LSD, and drop it in the water supply of each major city, and disorient the city."[5]

It bears repeating that all of this was a matter of public record *before* Nathan Hare received that coveted appointment to head the black studies department at San Francisco State.

Today, when one mentions San Francisco State, there are those who conjure up an image of mass repression—a sort of academic concentration camp. But probe ever so slightly below the surface and you find that for years this has been one of the most liberal of liberal arts institutions. You find that it is indeed true that San Francisco State operated "with fewer rules and regulations than 'most any institution of higher education."[6] At San Francisco State, the faculty had autonomy in hiring, retention, tenure, and promotion.[7] The president of the college could not even fire a faculty member; he could only recommend action to the chancellor.[8] At San Francisco State, the faculty senate was the first in the nation to seat student representatives as voting members.[9]

Nearly 60 academic departments offered a full array of bachelors' and masters' degrees.[10] The teaching load was 12 hours (nearly double the load at comparable institutions),[11] but at the same time, according to the American Association of University Professors, the average salary at San Francisco State was equal to, or greater than, the average salary paid at well over one-half of the state universities.[12]

It was at San Francisco State that the concept of a student-run experimental college within the regular college had its birth.[13] And San Francisco State was the first campus in America to have a Hyde Park–style speakers' stand erected.[14] But most of the students at San Francisco State had little time for great oratory. Most were married, with children, employed at full- or part-time jobs, and thinking about a career. With limited financial resources, they couldn't afford to lose course credits or school time.[15] At the more affluent Ivy League schools, a student strike might be a tiresome inconvenience; at San Francisco State, it was virtually a disaster.

Probably San Francisco State held the record for entering—and exiting—college presidents: five within seven years.[16] The chilling winds of black revolutionary change were lashing the San Francisco State campus as far back as July 22, 1966, when the *Golden Gator* (the campus newspaper) carried this choice item:

> [James] Garrett [president, Black Students Union of San Francisco State] said the present black nationalist movement is concerned only with the black people and that it does not strive for an integrated society. . . . The black nationalist movement wants a black society for black people, and Garrett said that he would do anything necessary to bring about such a society—from reading a book if that is necessary to killing, as the white man has done so often.[17]

It was Garrett who was picked to represent the student body on the faculty academic senate.[18] Garrett, along with other leaders of the BSU, received salaries totaling $3,244 through the Economic Opportunity Act of 1964.[19]

Out of some 600 Negro students at San Francisco State College, it was estimated that the Black Students Union had about 100 members.[20] The Black Students Union was financed from the Associated Students Fund, through compulsory contributions by students attending the college.[21] But not all students were blindly acquiescent in the granting of these funds. There was solid opposition—an opposition which had the rare courage to put it in writing in a 1967 report titled, " 'Black Power' at San Francisco State College." It was prepared by members of the Executive and Legislature of the Associated Students of San Francisco State,[22] and it was a grim indictment of the all but unconditional surrender to black militants on the campus:

> The student government's subsidies to the Black Students Union have been known and countenanced by the administration. A student majority of the legislature tried to express their concern by not funding the Black Communications Project. However, the motion was passed when the

two administration [members] and the one faculty member of the legislature voted together for the $4,420.00 figure. . . .[23]

Seven students voted in opposition to this program; four students (all members of the Black Students Union) voted for it. Supporting the four black students were two administrators and one faculty member, resulting in a tie vote. The Black Students Union and the administration members fought for the acceptance of two questionable proxy votes, and they won—over the protest of the majority of student members.[24]

This student report continued:

> The Black Students Union has become increasingly militant on the campus, packing meetings and threatening anyone who would oppose them. The administration's policy seems to be one of appeasement at every point. It is clear that the actions of the administration have ceased to be in the interests of the majority of students at San Francisco State. We [students] call for an immediate review by the Board of Trustees of the California State Colleges of the situation at San Francisco State College.[25]

To the members of the Black Students Union, the monies they received were due them, almost as a matter of birthright. They were more than content to repeat what LeRoi Jones had said about white Americans—"they owe us everything, including their lives."[26]

The Black Communications Project was to be the brainchild of LeRoi Jones, and it was made abundantly clear that those opposing the Jones program were living more dangerously than they realized. In the student report, Kay Tsenin, one of those voting against the program, stated:

> During the Associated Students Legislature meeting held on May 12, I expressed my objection to and voted against the appropriation of money for the Black Communications Project of LeRoi Jones. After the meeting, two members of the Black Students Union turned to me and one said, "Don't come on campus at night if you want to stay alive." I asked them to give me their names but they walked away. Several other people witnessed the incident.[27]

And from still another student, this statement:

> While I was walking away from the A.S. Legislature meet-
> ing of May 11, several Negroes approached me and asked
> how I was going to vote on the appropriation for LeRoi
> Jones. I replied that they would have to wait until the
> following day to find out. One of them then said, "If you
> boys don't vote the right way, some of you are going to get
> cut up."
>
> I certify this to be a true and correct statement.
>                                    Tony Volk, 5/17/67.[28]

LeRoi Jones was paid $1,600 by the Black Students Union for
what was supposed to have been two months of teaching. But
during that time, it is doubtful that he spent more than two
weeks on campus.[29]

The on-campus coordinator of the Black Students Union was
Jerry Varnardo. He said he did not hate white people—"you
don't *hate* a cancer. You cut it out."[30] In October 1967 Varnardo
made two trips to an Army surplus store, and acquired four
hand weapons. He returned within a week or ten days and
acquired five more. He paid cash for all of them.[31] On one
occasion, Varnardo attended one of his own meetings on campus wearing a .38 strapped to his hip.[32]

A month later the *Daily Gator* failed to run a photo of the
Black Students Union candidate for homecoming queen. On
November 6, 1967, a group of students, including members of
the Black Students Union, broke into the campus newspaper
office. They attacked the editor, who had to be hospitalized, and
injured other staff employees.[33] As the *San Francisco Examiner* reported it, ". . . as three others stood outside the main
office door, apparently to block exit or entrance, the other eight
men began beating other staff members, overturning tables and
scattering newspapers and typewriters."[34] It was all carried out
like a gangland vendetta, with invaders showing no interest in
the city editor's statement that the photo of the Black Students
Union candidate had arrived too late to run with the other
candidates' pictures (it was run in a subsequent edition as a
separate story).[35]

Ironically, at the time of the attack, the *Daily Gator* was running a series of articles very complimentary to the Black Students Union.[36]

Eventually, after considerable delay, formal complaints against the assailants were signed by Dr. John Summerskill,[37] who was then president and chief paper tiger—or tabby—at San Francisco State. There was an arrangement at that time that police would not go on campus. The students involved were to have surrendered through their attorney. But to avoid arrest, some of them were sleeping and living in the Black Students Union building, and refusing to leave the campus. Eventually it was necessary for the tactical squad of the police department to go in and arrest them.[38]

Under the Summerskill administration, nine students were suspended for participation in the attack. This was later reduced to four suspensions, and five were either put on probation or sent letters of warning.[39] The Academic Senate turned down a resolution recommending that the suspensions be rescinded.[40]

The Black Students Union attack on the newspaper office was no temporary racial aberration. It was not the exception, but the rule, the norm, the expected and demanded mode of conduct. Confirmation of this was readily obtained by listening to some of the members "doing their thing," at rallies and meetings. Like the speaker who told a Black Students Union rally:

> The ultimate responsibility . . . is to the black nation . . . in this Babylon called America. . . . We should be becoming warriors . . . [and] commit acts of war in the interest of people becoming a nation. [Contending that chemical warfare is developed on college campuses, he added] If you kill a chemistry professor, then you are preventing the death of maybe 20,000 black people.[41]

Like the member of the Black Students Union who said that " 'Uncle Toms' will now be designated as traitors." The member also added, "You realize you're a nation, and you deal with traitors accordingly."[42]

Like James Garrett, who made this statement:

> There will be reprisals. . . .There are certain brothers and certain sisters around this country who are slated to die.

That's very important if you can dig life. They're slated to be killed.[43]

In any event, San Francisco State had not heard the last of even the tepid suspensions, probations, and letters of warning that had been given to the students invading the offices of the *Daily Gator.* Now all of this was coupled with a new cause—the suspension of a writer and editor of another campus publication called *Open Process.* This paper had printed obscene material and an article on how to commit sabotage.[44]

Supporting both the black students and the writer and editor of *Open Process* was a new organization called MAPS (Movement Against Political Suspension). MAPS made five demands:

That Summerskill drop all suspensions and give the accused a "trial" by their peers.
That he reinstate *Open Process.*
That he drop "political harassment."
That he refuse to permit San Francisco police on the campus.
That he give assurance of student control of campus publications.[45]

James Garrett, off-campus coordinator of the Black Students Union, announced at the rally a plan for 1,000 or more of his members to appear at a demonstration (along with members of MAPS).[46]

Before the demonstration, President Summerskill had sent word that he was willing to meet with a 12-man delegation and discuss the demands with them. But the students refused; one yelled, "I don't think there's anything to talk about."[47]

On December 6, 1967, the demonstration took place. At first a joint protest by Negro and white students, it quickly degenerated into total chaos. One professor was heard to comment to another, "This is anarchy; complete anarchy." As the whites held back, Negro rioters were joined by a number of off-campus Negroes. At a given signal from James Garrett, there appeared outside the locked doors of the administration building about 60 Negroes, at least 50 of whom were not students, but who had been recruited from the Fillmore district for this specific demonstration.[48]

The mob first smashed through glass doors to invade the locked administration building and occupied it for almost two hours. Then it broke up and formed roving bands which broke into classrooms, the cafeteria, and the bookstore.[49] James Garrett told several hundred demonstrators, "We're going to close this place down now and tomorrow. Do you dig? The school is closed. You've got your assignments."[50]

The rioters threw dishes, silverware, and food around in the cafeteria. In the Associated Student Bookstore, windows were broken, cigarettes were stolen, and the cash register was looted. When photographers began taking pictures of looters emerging from the bookstore, the rioters chased and grabbed them. Several were beaten and injured. Some had the cameras torn from their hands and the film ripped out and exposed.[51]

To be sure, President Summerskill at least had the grace to protest that the violence "verges on civil insurrection."[52] But he failed to call the police, although 35 officers were in the vicinity and ready to move in on a moment's notice, if requested. The campus police also were conspicuous by their absence.[53] Summerskill congratulated himself on his "restraint"—presumably in not calling the police—and said, "We are grateful that a human catastrophe was avoided."[54] Apparently, as long as the buildings were still standing, Summerskill was willing to overlook—with a boys-will-be-boys indulgence—the dismissal of all classes, the cessation of normal activity on the 18,000-student campus, and the need to send home employees of the administration building before the violence broke out.[55]

State College Chancellor Glenn Dumke (a former president of San Francisco State) said he was "deeply shocked." Superintendent of Public Schools Max Rafferty said he would "like to go into those buildings and bounce those people out like ping-pong balls."[56]

One of the four Negro students under suspension in the *Daily Gator* incident, George Murray—instructor in English and also Black Panther minister of education—warned, "We will not tolerate racism on this campus any more and we'll move to destroy the institution before we will tolerate it."[57]

In 1968, Murray would come very close to making his threat of destruction a self-fulfilling prophecy.

LeRoi Jones, who by now had virtually become a patron saint

of the Black Students Union, once wrote, "Guerrilla Warfare is inevitable in the North and South. Every black is a potential revolutionist...you can't use nuclear weapons against us when we kill a few cops...there is no way of saving America."[58]

Those members of the Black Students Union who, like Jones, gave guerrilla warfare a resounding "R" for Relevance did not have to go very far afield to study it in grisly detail. They had only to enroll in the course in guerrilla warfare—"Theory and Tactic in Contemporary America"—being taught by Robert Kaffke at the Experimental College of San Francisco State College.[59]

Kaffke had a rather bizarre background. He had enlisted in the Army at the age of 15, and had separated from the service two and a half months later, with an honorable discharge. Later, he reenlisted, and, as a result of board action in the Army, was given an undesirable discharge. The board found the following: emotional instability, immature reaction with anti-social behavior. Thirteen years later, Kaffke petitioned for review of his undesirable discharge. The Military Review Board ruled that the certificate of discharge should be changed to honorable, with the provision that he was ineligible for future enlistment.[60]

And now—in 1968—Robert Kaffke was teaching a course in guerrilla warfare at the Experimental College of San Francisco State College. The Experimental College was run and operated by the students themselves, and funded by the Associated Students. The students could call in anyone they wanted to teach any course, and, somewhere along the way, the teacher would have the title "professor" gratuitously bestowed upon him. And so it was that Robert Kaffke, with no formal teaching credentials, became a "professor" at the Experimental College of San Francisco State College.[61]

Among the works Robert Kaffke recommended to his students as reading material in his course on guerrilla warfare were: *Guerrilla Warfare* by Che Guevara; *The Modoc War* by Murray; *War of the Flea* by Robert Taber; *The Protracted War* by Mao Tse-tung; Lenin's thesis, *Imperialism, Stalin* by Isaac Deutscher; *Revolution in the Revolution* by Regis Debray; *State and Revolution* by Lenin; *U.S. Army Guerrilla Warfare*

*Manual; How to Survive in the Wilderness, 101 Questions for the Guerrilla,* by Colonel Bayo; and *Second Declaration of Havana* by Fidel Castro.[62]

To Kaffke, his course in guerrilla warfare was not just merely academic, as witness this excerpt from an article in the *Berkeley Barb:* " 'Everyman's castle should have a shotgun,' Robert Kaffke told his class last Thursday. 'The Revolution is coming very fast to Latin America, and in another sense to the United States; if you don't believe that, I don't know what you're doing here.' "[63] And, in a letter to the editor of the *Golden Gator,* he had stated: "Perhaps better to die in the struggle than of old age and cancer in a bed that does not belong to one. Thus I say: To Hell with the Left; get out of our way or we will run you over."[64]

Early in January 1968 President Summerskill spoke at the Press Club. On that occasion, he was asked about the propriety of a course in guerrilla warfare where State College facilities were being used at the expense of the taxpayers. Summerskill replied that this was at the Experimental College, and not a course in the regular curriculum of the college itself. He said he could not find anything wrong with the course, and was not opposed to it. After all, he said, "there had been no shots fired on campus." He then was asked, "Dr. Summerskill, by the same precept, do you feel it would be all right if they taught a course in rape on the campus so long as no coeds were raped?" Summerskill laughed it off without a response.[65]

A month later, President Summerskill made Nathan Hare coordinator of the projected black studies program.[66]

In an article for the *Public Interest,* John H. Bunzel, chairman of the Political Science Department at San Francisco State, wrote that Summerskill had appointed Hare after he had already been chosen for the job by the Black Students Union. He emphasized, "It is also worth noting that the appointment of a Black Studies Coordinator was made by the president alone— that is to say, without the knowledge of, or consultation with, the Vice President for Academic Affairs, the Council of Academic Deans, or the faculty." The president, characteristically, was candid about what he had done: "this college is going to explode wide open if the blacks do not get what they want soon." Summerskill freely acknowledged that he had not spoken with anyone in the Sociology Department about the appointment of Nathan Hare, because he felt he had to move quickly "if we are going to keep the lid on this place."[67]

Bunzel was an *avis rara* at San Francisco State—a distinguished faculty member who was willing, frankly and openly, to criticize the choice of Nathan Hare as head of the black studies program. Since Hare would be in charge of the degree-granting department of black studies, Bunzel felt that Hare's "particular angle of vision, indeed his basic assumptions and attitudes, are especially pertinent."[68] And Bunzel provided these "especially pertinent" excerpts from a public speech Hare had made at Stanford University. On that occasion, Hare told his listeners:

> They say we are too few to fight. We should vote. But I can kill 20 [white] men. I can cut one's throat, shoot another, drop a hand grenade in the middle of a whole bunch. I get only a single vote, and that's between the lesser of two evils.

Bunzel cited other equally grim quotes from Nathan Hare's speech at Stanford:

> *On white historians:* It is anachronistic for white men to teach black history to black militant students. The white man is unqualified to teach black history because he does not understand it....
> *On the draft:* I was asked if I am an American first or a Negro first. I said I'm a black man first and not an American at all. Since most Americans do not consider me an American, I see no reason to fight for them. I said that before it was fashionable. I did serve six months in the Army, but that was in peacetime. And I said I couldn't fight for them, and if I did I would shoot as much as possible at the whites around me.

Addressing himself to the question of whether or not he was anti-white, Hare replied, "I don't believe in absolutes, so I do not categorically reject all white men, only 999 and 44/100ths of them."[69]

Bunzel felt that Hare's pronouncements provided "a backdrop against which his 'conceptual proposal' for a department of black studies can be more clearly understood and evaluated in terms of its basic rationale and philosophy." To Hare, the key component in the black studies program was "community involvement and collective stimulation."[70] To Hare, the community was the be-all and end-all, and individualism was not only irrelevant, but harmful to the communal concept. And, since the black community—not the individual—was the focal point of the Hare black studies program, white students were to be *personae non gratae.* Hare admitted as much, when he stated, "It may be necessary eventually to distinguish Black education for Blacks and Black education for whites."[71]

Academically speaking, San Francisco State was far from being a racial wasteland before Nathan Hare arrived on the scene. A year before, the first black studies were enacted, with a total of eleven classes for which 33 units of college credit were given. Several hundred students, black and white, enrolled in the courses.[72] And among the classes listed in the black studies program for the spring semester of 1968 were the following:

ANTHROPOLOGY: Historical Development of Afro-American Studies
DRAMATIC ARTS: Improvisations in Blackness
EDUCATION: Miseducation of the Negro
ENGLISH: Modern African Thought and Literature
HISTORY: Ancient Black History
PSYCHOLOGY: Workshop in the Psychology of, by, and for Black People
SOCIOLOGY: Sociology of Black Oppression[73]

Bunzel wrote, "By the end of the 1967–1968 academic year, it was taken for granted that there would be a black studies program. The question was no longer whether it would happen, but what direction it would take, and how the administration, faculty and students would choose to react."[74]

The direction it would take was toward "relevance"—with Hare reserving the right to define, or redefine, the word at will. In a section of the black studies proposal called "Redefinition of Standards," Hare noted that the two most "salient qualifications" for professorial rank today are a Ph.D. "and a string of 'scholarly' publications." Hare wanted the freedom "to depart from those criteria without risking the suspicion of 'lowering standards.' That the Ph.D. is not necessarily synonymous with teaching effectiveness is accepted by most persons confronted with the question."[75] What criteria would Hare utilize in recruiting a faculty for the black studies program? He would want to define a "qualified" professor "by honoring teaching effectiveness and enthusiasm more than qualities determined by degrees held and other quantifiable 'credentials.' "[76]

Hare's proposal for a department of black studies envisioned "collective stimulation"[77]—a program in which the black student no longer thought as an individual, but as part of a group, a collective entity, a community. Reduction of the role of the individual would become the *sine qua non* of the enlargement of the role of the community.

Not surprisingly, Bunzel had some searching questions about the entire program:

> Will those who teach in the Department of Black Studies be of the same political and ideological persuasion, or will efforts be made to recruit a black staff that purposely reflects different and opposing points of view? Would Black Studies hire a black undergraduate to teach one of its courses for credit: Will the Department of Black Studies mirror the views of the Black Students Union, thereby reinforcing the Union's political goals and purposes on campus?[78]

Perhaps most significant of all, Bunzel asked whether the "Department of Black Studies would substitute propaganda for omission, or, as some have said, new myths for old lies....Would Black Studies look on a course in African History as an opportunity simply to venerate the great achievements of cultural forebears, or would it also lay stress on, say, the historical fact that the more advanced African peoples and energetic leaders were often the very ones who sold other Africans to slave traders, thereby helping to bring about Negro slavery in America?"[79]

One of the sociologists Hare most admired was the late E. Franklin Frazier, member of the Howard faculty, and author of *The Black Bourgeoisie.* And yet, Bunzel observed, "Professor Troy Duster, a social scientist at the University of California

(Riverside), points out that much of E. Franklin Frazier's scholarly life was spent documenting the fact that the Negro in the United States was stripped of almost every vestige of his African culture, and that his primary substantive culture is an American one."[80] In direct reference to this position, Bunzel asked, "Would open and sharp disagreement over the nature and substance of an American Negro culture be encouraged?"[81]

Reaction to Bunzel's critique of Nathan Hare was not long in coming. Bunzel was informed by an officer of the administration at San Francisco State that black student leaders were furious with him.[82] About a month later, a bomb was found outside his office door.[83] Students began shouting him down while he was trying to conduct classes. Ernest Besig, a visiting official of the American Civil Liberties Union, said he was appalled at the classroom treatment accorded Dr. Bunzel. And Dr. Edwin Duerr, a college vice president who sat in on several classes, confirmed Bunzel's accounts of harassment.[84] But what Bunzel called the "real testing ground" came during his advance course for upper division students called, "Community Power and the Politics of Leadership." The course normally had an enrollment of 30 to 40 students. "But in preregistration," Bunzel related,

the first 50 slots were taken by black student leaders before formal registration began. They represented the first team of the Black Students Union, the Third World Liberation Front, the Students for a Democratic Society, and so on. I heard this on a Monday. This meant that on Tuesday, when the political science majors were to enroll, they would be closed out. So I opened up the registration to 100, and the first class had to move from my small lecture hall to an auditorium in the Creative Arts Building.[85] . . . I tried to explain in my opening sentences, at the orientation session, what the course was about. But I was drowned out in a flood of shouts and questions from 25 or 30 people.

He recounted how some of the disrupters called him "fascist pig Bunzel" and "shouted quotes from Chairman Mao and his little red book." He went on:

After about 25 minutes I dismissed the first class, telling them I intended to teach the course the way it's been taught. One shouted, "If we have to bring guns in here you won't teach it. We'll teach you about community power." I was interrupted by a student who spoke for 10 minutes and demanded, didn't power come out of the end of a gun? He wanted an answer "right now."[86]

By April 16, 1968, Nathan Hare submitted a formal proposal for a department of black studies to be established by September 1968. This was Hare's tentative Black Studies major:

| CORE COURSES | UNITS |
|---|---|
| Black History | 4 |
| Black Psychology | 4 |
| Survey of Sciences: Method & History | 4 |
| Black Arts and Humanities | 4 |
| | 16 units |

| BLACK ARTS CONCENTRATION | |
|---|---|
| The Literature of Blackness | 4 |
| Black Writers Workshop | 4 |
| Black Intellectuals | 4 |
| Black Fiction | 4 |
| Black Poetry | 4 |
| Black Drama | 4 |
| The Painting of Blackness | 4 |
| The Music of Blackness | 4 |
| Sculpture of Blackness | 4 |
| | 36 units |

| BEHAVIORAL AND SOCIAL SCIENCES CONCENTRATION | |
|---|---|
| Black Politics | 4 |
| Sociology of Blackness | 4 |
| Economics of the Black Community | 4 |
| The Geography of Blackness | 4 |
| Social Organization of Blackness | 4 |
| Development of Black Leadership | 4 |
| Demography of Blackness | 4 |
| Black Counseling | 4 |
| Black Consciousness and the International Community | 4 |
| | 32 units |
| | [sic][87] |

More than ever, it became pertinent to ask whether this would be education or indoctrination, fact or propaganda, with students toeing the line dogmatically drawn for them by Nathan Hare—on pain of poor, or even failing, grades if they insisted upon thinking for themselves.

On October 24, 1968, the Board of Trustees met in regular session. At this meeting, a black studies department for San Francisco State was authorized.[88] Nearby, George Murray, a member of both the Black Students Union and the Black Panthers, delivered a speech to assembled students about killing the "white oppressors."[89]

One of the black students accused of assaulting the editor of the campus newspaper at San Francisco State the year before, George Murray was still on probation.[90] Nevertheless, in September 1968 he had been rehired by the English Department to teach disadvantaged students at San Francisco State.[91] His rehiring came a month *after* the official publication of the Cuban Communist Party revealed that Murray had made an illegal trip to Havana. Murray had boasted to the Red press that black militants in the U.S. were "inspired by Che's example," and he stated that guerrilla warfare in America was tying up troops destined for Vietnam. Murray told the Cubans, "We are well aware that we will only be liberated if the peoples of Africa, Asia and Latin America are also free. And this will come about when the U.S. imperialists are dead."[92]

On September 26, 1968, the State College Board of Trustees voted 8 to 5 to ask the new president to remove Murray and assign him to non-teaching duties. But the new president—Robert R. Smith—refused, saying that Murray had been found qualified to teach by the English Department, and, further, was entitled to due process.[93]

Less than a month later, Murray made a speech in which he referred to the American flag as "toilet paper."[94] On October 28, Murray was standing on a table in the San Francisco State cafeteria, announcing a student strike on November 6 (the day after Election Day) to support demands by the Black Students Union. Murray said, "The only realistic way to deal with a cracker like Smith is to say we want 5,000 black people here in February, and if he won't give it to you, you chop his head off." Finally, he suggested Negroes bring guns to school, to protect themselves "against racist administrators."[95]

On October 31, Chancellor Glenn S. Dumke ordered Smith to suspend Murray temporarily. Smith reluctantly complied, but Murray was suspended with pay.[96] On November 4, the leadership of the Black Students Union held a press conference to issue ten demands and the formal strike call.

1) Immediate transfer of all Black Studies courses into the Black Studies Department, with full pay for their instructors
2) A full professorship for Hare
3) Creation of an autonomous Black Studies Department
4) Filling of all unused admissions in the special admissions program
5) Admission of all black applicants into the College, regardless of number
6) Twenty teaching positions for the Black Studies Department
7) Dismissal of the Student Financial Aid Officer, to be replaced by a black person
8) No disciplinary action against the strikers
9) Prohibition of Trustee dissolution of any Black Studies programs on or off campus
10) Reinstatement of George Murray[97]

The Black Students Union leaders said these demands were not negotiable.[98]

The black studies department demand was already in effect. The demands that Hare be automatically promoted, and the financial aid officer automatically dismissed were violations of due process. And any attempt to prohibit trustee dissolution of any Black Studies program was simply impossible to implement.

On November 6, the Black Students Union and the predominantly Mexican and Oriental Third World Liberation Front joined forces to strike at San Francisco State.[99] But the student body had wearied of this racial brinkmanship. During the morning, the vast majority of classes met as scheduled, and the deans reported that class sizes were "almost normal."[100]

Realizing that their strike was an utter failure, the Black Students Union and Third World Liberation Front met at 11:00 a.m. to plan strategy in the main auditorium.[101] Around noon, bands of non-whites ran to their assigned buildings and began disrupting classes. In one case, visiting lecturer Isidoro Mauleon was in the midst of teaching a Spanish class when, shortly before 1:00 p.m., there was a loud banging on the door. The door flew open, and a black student, followed by six orientals, Mexican Americans and other non-whites, came into the room. The black demanded, "Why are you holding class? Why aren't you honoring the strike?"

Mauleon answered, "We have spent some of the time today discussing the issues involved in the strike. Now we are learning Spanish."

The black ordered, "Well, break it up and get out of here."

Professor Mauleon demanded to know, "Who are you to give me orders? Those who wanted to leave and honor the strike left. The rest of us have a perfect right to be here. We all belong to the human race. Leave us alone."

The black grimly commented, "You should all leave now and honor the strike if you're smart."

The teacher and his students refused to move.

Finally, the black warned, "Either you get out of here now or some other people might come up here and tear this place up."

Dr. Mauleon and his students left[102]—and similar fear-filled confrontations were taking place by the dozen in many other classroom halls and buildings.[103]

Three students from another disrupted class banged on the locked door of the president's office. They shouted: "We came here for an education and we don't want our classes disrupted. We don't want them dismissed." Later, President Smith said they were right, and that "they deserve a chance to hold their classes in peace."[104]

There was a fire in the office of the Academic Senate. An American flag was burned on the back stage of the main auditorium. An Associated Press photographer, Sal Veder, was accosted by five black males and a white girl wearing a Red Cross arm band. One of the men punched him in the chest while others took away three rolls of film he had taken. The girl told Veder, "Give us your film. It's easier than having your skull broken in."[105]

President Smith called in the police. By the time they arrived —shortly after 1:00 p.m., most of the people in the buildings had left.[106] The police were met with cries, "Get the pigs off campus," and by 4:00 p.m. the campus was nearly deserted. Night classes were canceled.[107]

The ostensible cause of the strike, and the seething rampage that accompanied it, was the suspension of George Murray. But later, President Samuel Hayakawa would categorically state:

> The crisis was not triggered at all. It was planned very carefully over a long period of time. To illustrate, the strike started on the anniversary of the date in 1967— November 6—when nine black students attacked the campus newspaper editor and his staff in their offices. Many of those nine are the present student strike leaders.[108]

The following day there was a small explosion in the education building and a dozen scattered fires.[109] The day after, small groups wearing black stockings over their faces ransacked some offices.[110]

As if there was not quite enough chaos on the campus already, some 40 faculty members threatened to go out on strike if Murray were not restored to faculty status by November 12.[111] As sporadic arrests continued to be made on campus, black militants at San Francisco State refused to submit their strike to arbitration.[112]

On November 13, an ugly confrontation developed between students and the police department tactical squad. President Smith closed the college until the atmosphere became "more rational."[113] Governor Ronald Reagan denounced the action, and said it was "absolutely essential" that the campus be reopened. The governor stated, "For a school administration to deliberately abandon the leadership vested in it by the people of this state—at the expense of the vast majority of students intent on receiving an education—is an unprecedented act of irresponsibility."[114] On November 18, the Board of Trustees ordered that San Francisco State be reopened "immediately." The board further instructed President Smith that there was to be "no negotiation, arbitration or concession" to the dissident students.[115]

San Francisco State's Academic Senate presented the trustees with a recommendation that Chancellor Dumke rescind the suspension of George Murray and institute a program demanded by college protesters. But, at this same meeting, a representative of San Francisco State's 700 staff members relayed a demand for "a definite, realistic plan of protection that will insure its [the staff's] safety from vandals, ruffians, anarchists and amateur demolition squads."[116]After the trustees meeting, Chancellor Dumke said that classes would resume "no later than Wednesday [November 20]." He told newsmen, "Force will be used if necessary, but it will be avoided if possible."[117]

The following day, President Smith went before a crowd of 900, mostly faculty members, and in a "state of the campus" speech, asked for a reopening with police protection, and for a 90 day cooling-off period for all factions. But instead, the meeting overwhelmingly went along with a suggestion by the chairman of the college's Academic Senate, Dr. Leo McClatchy. He suggested that the faculty and the campus's students meet in "one big class" to discuss the "non-negotiable demands" of the Black Students Union. In effect, the "one big class" would be a continuation of that day's meeting, broadcast by closed-circuit television to other parts of the campus.[118]

Notwithstanding Smith's statement that "the faculty is asked to report for scheduled classes tomorrow," few classes met, and the convocation was held,[119] without any discernible success. A second convocation was held on November 25, and provided "one of the classic scenes of the confrontation." In the words of the *National Catholic Reporter:*

On one side of the auditorium sat a half-dozen middle-aged and elderly men . . . their faces lined with age, and showing the tensions of the previous two weeks. They spoke quietly and in wandering, diplomatic and confusing sentences.
On the other side sat a fierce and ragged collection of black students, hairy Latins and trim Chinese and Filipinos. They made impassioned speeches, shouted, waved their arms, used obscenities, spoke sometimes in low, cold voices.

Leroy Goodwin of the Black Students Union told the educators:

> The objective is seizure of power. Until we seize power—
> not visible power, but real, actual power—everything else
> is bull——. . . . Each day our demands are not met, our
> tactics will escalate. We have no illusions about using
> force, if armed strength is what we need to seize power to
> determine our own educational destiny, then that will be
> done. Peace and order are bull——. They are meaningless
> without justice."[120]

On November 26, at the end of a 15-hour session of the
trustees, Smith submitted his resignation as president of San
Francisco State College.[121] His request was unanimously accepted.[122] The trustees named as acting president of San Francisco State the internationally renowned semanticist Dr.
Samuel Hayakawa. Governor Reagan said that he was "very
excited and happy" about Dr. Hayakawa's appointment.[123] And
though he made no mention of it, the governor might have been
equally excited and happy that the terms of two trustees who
voted against the request to remove Murray would expire in
March.[124]

President Hayakawa had been a columnist from 1942 to 1947
for the *Chicago Defender,* a leading Negro newspaper, and he
had lived with Negroes on Chicago's South Side. He recalled, "I
traveled with them in the South, as non-whites, wondering
where the hell we were going to find a place to eat and sleep."
As for black militants, Hayakawa granted that they were an
important part of the black community, "but they're not the
whole black community."[125]

Nathan Hare's reaction to Hayakawa was summed up in two
contemptuous sentences: "Hayakawa will go out faster than
Smith. If he takes the hard line, we'll be ready for him."[126]

Hayakawa ordered San Francisco State reopened Monday,
December 2. Acknowledging that "we have been warned that
dangerous situations may arise," Hayakawa sounded a warning
of his own: "Police will be available to the fullest extent necessary to maintain and restore peace when school opens Monday."[127]

As promised, classes resumed on December 2, under police

protection. When he arrived at the campus that morning, Hayakawa was surrounded by demonstrators shouting, "On strike, shut it down." He climbed onto a truck parked just off the campus and tried to speak on a public address system mounted on the truck bed. The students shouted him down, and ripped out the microphone wires. Someone shoved him, and he shoved back.[128]

Hayakawa stated that faculty members who did not appear at their classes for five days straight would be considered to have resigned. Students who misbehaved would be suspended.[129]

But apparently, some regarded the new president as yet another paper tiger. George Murray told demonstrators, "It is an historic moment. The people are participating in an attempt to seize power. Hayakawa has no authority to come in and usurp the power of the people."[130]

Hayakawa's reply was concise and commendably relevant. At a news conference, he announced that because of Murray's activities, "I am taking action under provision of the law to suspend him for 30 days and I will institute new disciplinary action."[131]

The following day, policemen had to use clubs to keep student strikers from disrupting classes at San Francisco State College. One of the most violent confrontations came at about 1:45 p.m., after a rally held in violation of campus rules was turned into an attempt to invade a building where business and social science classes were being held. A student shouted, "We're going to close it down. It's the most racist building on campus." About a dozen stones were thrown through windows before the police arrived. The most violent clash was against some 300 students clustered on the library steps. Many of these were clubbed, and some were knocked down.[132]

Speaking over the campus public address system, Hayakawa said, "If you want police off the campus, please disperse. This is an unwarranted assembly. You will help your teachers, students, and yourself if you disperse. If some of you want to make trouble, stay right here. The police will see that you get it." A student shouted to a group, "Let's get Hayakawa," but the police broke up the charge.

Reporters watched the police beat dozens of demonstrators to the ground. Students broke up furniture and used the pieces as clubs against the police.[133] Throughout the strike, the recurring charge was made of police brutality (sometimes clothed in the more delicate phrase, "the police overreacted"). An interesting comment on this charge came from James McEvoy and Abraham Miller, both assistant professors of sociology, and co-authors of an article on San Francisco State appearing in *Trans-Action.* They wrote:

> We found it interesting that the brutality of the police increased some students' support for the strikers, but the brutality of the strikers toward the police did not diminish any students' support for the strikers. To the students, violence against the police is tolerable. Consequently, the administration was caught in the position of either turning the building over to the students, or calling in the police and swelling the strikers' ranks.[134]

And from his vantage point as coordinator of internal affairs at San Francisco State, Edwin C. Duerr brought his own particular insight to bear:

> There have been charges that the police on occasion over-reacted to the demonstrators. This is probably true, in some instances. In general, however, they were remarkably restrained in their behavior. The police had garbage, rocks, sticks, and pipes—as well as insults—thrown at them. In the early days of their presence on campus, one dissident came up behind a policeman and hit him with a pipe, breaking his collarbone. It was hardly a situation where everyone was likely to retain his composure at all times.[135]

The police arrested 31 persons that day, mostly on felony charges of aggravated assault, resisting arrest, and inciting to riot. An observer estimated that about 700 of the college's 18,000 students had participated in the demonstrations. He said that no more than 100 of these were Negroes, and he believed that many of the Negroes were not students.[136]

Hayakawa announced that he had suspended nine more students, and was planning to suspend even more. The leaders of the Associated Students of San Francisco State demanded that Hayakawa resign.[137]

On December 5, two busloads of off-campus Negroes appeared at Ecumenical House, across from the campus. After a short meeting, 150 Negroes led about 350 whites, Mexican Americans, and Orientals across to the campus. For more than an hour, various speakers, most of them Negro, spoke from a stand on the commons. Jerry Varnardo shouted, "Get the puppet, close it down," and led the marchers across the green to the administration building. Policemen with drawn guns used Chemical Mace to drive back some 400 demonstrators.

Speaking over the campus sound amplifier, Hayakawa told the crowd, "Police have been instructed to clear the campus. There are no innocent bystanders anymore." One of the "innocent bystanders" dropped an attaché case that popped open and spilled out a cocked and loaded .45-caliber automatic pistol. Twenty-five persons were reported arrested, among them Dr. Carlton Goodlett, publisher of the Negro-oriented *Sun-Reporter,* and former faculty member of a now-defunct Communist-front labor school in San Francisco.[138]

The following morning, Hayakawa announced he had a proposal that he hoped would be a breakthrough. He told a news conference that a black studies program was to begin immediately with 11 teaching positions assigned to it under the direction of Nathan Hare. Hayakawa also agreed to use 128 unused places in the 426 special admissions for educationally deprived students set up last fall. He said these places would be filled in the spring.[139]

But Hayakawa did not grant amnesty to those suspended for demonstration activities. He said the police would be kept on campus to maintain order. He promised that George Murray would have due process, but refused to give him amnesty.

Jerry Varnardo said the proposals were totally unacceptable. Nathan Hare said that "Hayakawa did an excellent job of whitewashing the black demands. It was nothing more than an exercise in semantics." The San Francisco State faculty senate, while praising Hayakawa's concessions to the strikers, voted to condemn his use of the police on the campus. In addition, they urged a rapid search for a prominent successor to Hayakawa.[140]

But what the faculty senate probably never really grasped was the fact that the black militants would accept nothing short of total capitulation by the administrators. "Understand what we are trying to do," said Jerry Varnardo. "What we are doing is revolutionary. We are going to have a black studies department that we control. Where we can hire and fire who we want. Do you understand what I am saying? Where we can say who teaches what. If we want Cleaver on here teaching, we can hire him. There's not a department like that in the country."[141] And for those who still could not bring themselves to understand, a rally leader told a throng of demonstrators, "This is war, man, and when we need them, we'll get us 14 more demands."[142]

On December 9, after a noon rally attended by about 2,000, the crowd was led in a march three times around the campus quadrangle before re-forming in front of the speakers platform. There, a raid was directed toward the classroom building serving the business and social science departments. Two demonstrators used a garbage can to break doorway windows. At that point, helmeted policemen with clubs came onto the campus and drove the demonstrators out. Notwithstanding the disruptions, most classes were being held.[143]

In a conciliatory move, Hayakawa temporarily lifted the suspension orders against 44 students (at the request of some faculty members who feared their defense in campus disciplinary hearings might jeopardize their defense against criminal charges).[144] And then, on December 13, it almost began to look as if Hayakawa might be going the way of Summerskill and Smith.

On December 13, Hayakawa stated that he was closing San Francisco State that day, and explained that he was starting the Christmas vacation a week early as a safety measure. High schools in the city were beginning their Christmas vacations, and he feared that high school students might come to the campus to watch the demonstrations or join them. He said, "The safety and welfare of the young people who might come to our campus during this period is of grave concern to the administration and faculty of the college." Leaders of the student strike regarded the announcement as a victory. Almost as ecstatic was the reaction of members of the American Federation of Teachers who had been ready to go out on strike the following Monday.[145]

But at the same time, Hayakawa overruled any student government role in future disciplinary courts, because of the "utterly irresponsible and rebellious body of student officers who now claim to represent the student body." He said he would "flatly refuse" to approve any plan that included the present leadership of the students. As for negotiations with the strike leaders, he declared, "I will not try to come to terms with anarchists, hooligans or yahoos."[146]

A week before San Francisco State was scheduled to reopen, Hayakawa announced what he called a "Christmas present" from Chancellor Glenn S. Dumke. The "present" amounted to $300,000 in surplus funds for the spring semester, which would prevent the layoff of about 120 faculty members and the cancellation of several courses. Hayakawa also disclosed that San Francisco State would start in January its first four-year program leading to a degree in Negro studies, one of the principal demands of the Black Students Union. Hayakawa said he was optimistic that the violence that ripped the campus in November and December would not be repeated in January, but added that the police would be called if there were any disruptions.[147]

Hayakawa was able to count on the wholehearted support of Governor Reagan—a point the governor emphasized as he dismissed suggestions that he "negotiate" with the rebels. Police would ring campuses throughout the state, "if that's what they must do" to keep the schools running, Reagan said.[148]

In a radio address, Governor Reagan stated:

> Academic freedom is one of the important freedoms to go in the new order envisioned by the New Left. There was no academic freedom in Hitler's Germany. There is no academic freedom in Mao's China or Castro's Cuba. And there is no academic freedom in the philosophies or the actions of the George Murrays, the Eldridge Cleavers, or the Jerry Rubins.
>
> It is therefore most imperative that we—the great and thoughtful majority of citizens of all races—keep our perspective. We must recognize the manipulations being carried out to frustrate our common interest in living together with dignity in one American society. And we must also recognize that those who exercise violence must be held accountable for their actions—and held equally accountable regardless of their color.
>
> The state college trustees and acting President Paul

Blomgren were appropriately color-blind—and correct—
when they took decisive action, regardless of who was
involved, against the militants at San Fernando State College last month, as were the trustees and Chancellor
Dumke, in their recent decision regarding the termination
of Mr. George Murray's relationship as a graduate student
and instructor at San Francisco State College.

. . . . Never can we capitulate, surrender to the vocal,
abusive minority of militants, thus completely closing
down an entire campus—depriving the majority of students of the education they seek and are entitled to and
depriving the vast majority of responsible faculty of their
rights to exercise true academic freedom. . . . Nationwide
experience has shown that prompt dealing with disturbances leads to peace, that hesitation, vacillation and appeasement lead to greater disorder.[149]

With all of these remarks of Governor Ronald Reagan, President Hayakawa could hardly have agreed more.

Now January was coming, and with it the reopening of San
Francisco State—and with it the problem of attempting to walk
backwards and forwards at one and the same time. As Wallace
Turner of the *New York Times* noted:

On the one hand, the school has tried to maintain itself in
about the same mold it has followed for the last 20 years;
on the other hand, it has admitted students and hired
faculty members that had shown by past actions they
would attempt violently to change the place.[150]

On Monday, January 6, classes were scheduled to resume.
Jerry Varnardo asserted that the students were prepared to
move "20 times as great as before the holidays."[151]

The three-week vacation in December had proved to be the
uneasy calm between the storms—a "cooling off" that never
was, as militant students used the time to pass out thousands
of leaflets, conduct rallies in halls and churches and on street
corners, and go from door to door to build support for their
cause.[152] Reiterating the obvious was the announcement by
Black Panther Chairman Bobby Seale: "There is no division
between the Black Panther party and the Black Students Union
—how could there be when George Murray is on the central
committees of both?"[153]

Leroy Goodwin, off-campus coordinator of the Black Students Union, was quoted by the underground press as saying, "After three years of negotiations, we hereby announce an official declaration of war. Under this state of war, all ad hoc rules and regulations set up by the acting president Hayakawa to hamper freedom of speech and freedom of assembly will be disregarded, and the battleground, tactics and time sequence will be determined by the central committee of our revolutionary people."[154]

Professor Gary Hawkins, president of the American Federation of Teachers Chapter at San Francisco State, chose this particular time to warn that "unless something big happens," its members would strike the school on January 6. But another professional group at the college called on the federation not to walk out.[155]

The year before, the AFT union had been specifically rejected, in a democratic, written secret ballot, as the faculty's bargaining agent.[156] Furthermore, it was readily determined from payroll figures (union dues were deducted from paychecks) that the AFT had only 163 members among the 900 regular faculty and 66 members among the 550 part-time faculty.[157] But this in no way inhibited AFT chapter president Gary Hawkins from announcing to faculty members on January 3: "Violating our picket line will be interpreted to mean that you have chosen to be with the Trustees and against us. . . . You will not have the luxury of nice distinctions or Byzantine excuses."[158] Ralph M. Goldman, professor of political science at San Francisco State, wrote in *Dissent:* "Many of the non-AFT faculty, with years of commitment to unionism and liberal causes, found themselves called 'fink' and 'scab' as they did what they never dreamed they would some day do, that is, cross a picket line."[159]

AFT chieftain Hawkins had stated, "He who observes our picket line is a friend—anyone who plans to cross will be subject to moral force." At times the pressure was more force than moral, as Dr. John Bunzel later testified. He told the House Subcommittee on Education and Labor that one night after he and his wife had gone to bed, someone slashed the tires of both his cars and painted all over them "fascist scab."[160]

Confronted now with the bleak prospect of two strikes instead of one, Hayakawa stressed that "only people with legiti-mate business" would be allowed on the campus when it opened. In addition, he also announced a ban on all student rallies, marches, parades, shivarees, and other events "likely to disturb the people who are here to teach and study."[161] (Within the week, he designated the athletic field, about half a block away, as an alternative place for rallies and loudspeakers. There, the noise was not likely to disturb the rest of the campus. But the athletic field was never used by the militants.)[162]

After meeting with newsmen, Hayakawa walked to the front of the campus, where he hammered into place a sign warning visitors to the campus. The sign read: "Persons who interfere with the peaceful conduct of the activities of San Francisco State College are subject to arrest." To secure the sign, he used a brick that had been thrown through the window of his office.[163] Hayakawa made it known that students would not be permitted to establish picket lines on opening day. And he also warned AFT faculty members that their threatened strike would not be tolerated. He acknowledged that the coming days "are likely to be difficult and trying" and that "there may be a real showdown of opposing forces."[164]

Opening day at San Francisco State came off on schedule, along with the renewed black students strike and the new AFT faculty strike. Besides union recognition, the AFT leaders were demanding more pay, smaller classes, and a larger voice in the administration.[165] With almost visible reluctance, the San Francisco Central Labor Council gave its official approval of the teachers strike. A statement issued by the council's secre-tary, George Johns, said, "We are granting strike sanction to the American Federation of Teachers Local 1352 in their fight against the Governor and the State Board of Trustees for wages, hours and working conditions, *with the clear under-standing that we do not regard student problems as labor strike issues.*"[166] (emphasis added). But the AFT pickets blithely ignored the last 15 words of that statement, and planned demonstrations with the students, picketed with them, and shared signs with them.[167] The two strikes virtually blended into one; indeed, in an ad in the *Harvard Crimson,* the AFT included in bold letters among the strike issues:

Amnesty for all faculty, students, and staff who have participated in the strike. . . .
Black Students Union and Third World Liberation Front grievances must be resolved and implementation assured.
. . .
Maintain the present faculty positions; gain new positions for a Black Studies Department and a School of Ethnic Studies. . . .
Approval of the Student Union plan presented by the Associated Students, and cancellation of proposed changes in Title 5 that would take away student control of student body funds.[168]

In terms of attendance, opening day at San Francisco State was a disaster. One unofficial estimate by a college staff member put attendance at 20 percent of normal.[169] Governor Reagan reiterated that striking faculty members who missed five days of instruction would be considered as having resigned, as stipulated in the state education code.[170]

The following day, members of the Black Students Union again joined the picket lines of the AFT faculty. In mid-afternoon, a commotion occurred after 200 students marching in a circle in front of the college administration building rejected a police order to stop chanting on campus grounds. Picketing faculty members obeyed the order and left the line when the students defied the police. About 50 policemen and 30 sheriff's deputies pushed the shouting rock-throwing students back.[171] "I want to make it clear to everyone," said Hayakawa, "that I will break up this reign of terror. This campus has been disrupted so damn long it is time things got back to normal."[172]

The phrase "reign of terror" did not even slightly overstate the case. During this period, an administrator who ordered demonstrators to disperse had his house firebombed. In one class, the intruders put a metal wastepaper basket over the instructor's head and beat on the basket with sticks.[173]

The crux of the struggle at San Francisco State was pinpointed in these words by *New York Times* education editor Fred M. Hechinger:

It was demanded at San Francisco State, at Cornell and elsewhere that "black studies" divisions be turned into autonomous enclaves run by black students. Some considered such enclaves as preludes to self-reliant participation by Negroes in a pluralistic society; others feared them as staging areas for guerrilla attacks on white or even integrated society.[174]

In superior court, Judge Edward O'Day signed a temporary restraining order prohibiting the teachers from striking. The order enjoined the union from "calling or inducing a strike against the Trustees and from picketing facilities or giving notice of a strike."[175] The following day, more than 200 striking faculty members picketed San Francisco State College in defiance of the court order. Accordingly, college authorities prepared to sever from the payroll all faculty members who had spent the week picketing instead of holding classes. However, 23 out of 57 department heads informed the deans of schools and divisions that they were refusing to turn in daily attendance reports as directed because this "tends to debase the faculty."[176] And keeping about one jump ahead of the applicable law, the AFT teachers managed to avoid automatic dismissal by teaching at least once in five days.[177]

College administrators announced results of a referendum on the teachers strike. Of 911 ballots mailed to the homes of full-time faculty members, 725 were returned. Of this number, 64 percent voted against the strike and 36 in favor. The referendum was sponsored by the Association of California State College Professors.[178]

Bunzel cited the blunt comment of an associate—"If the threat were white and right, instead of black and left, we on the faculty would always be close to unanimous."[179] Few doubted the validity of the statement.

Now Hayakawa wrote to faculty members, advising that all teachers must file signed weekly statements that they had performed their duties in the previous week, or face loss of their pay.[180] And the following day—whether or not it was cause-and-effect—a homemade time bomb was found in the lobby of the college administration building. Earlier that same day, a smoke bomb ignited inside a locker in the education building.[181]

Throughout this period, the non-striking students whose teachers were walking the picket line were bogged down in a morass of uncertainty. Would they receive proper credit in courses where their teachers were on strike?—credit some of them needed in order to graduate? One teacher airily replied, "They may get the credits anyway. My dean is scabbing on me." Earlier, the college had announced a system whereby a student could elect either to have a letter grade or to have the benefit of "pass-no record" grading. Under this device, the student got a passing mark if he had won one; if he failed, there was no record of his ever being in the course. Explained Dr. William Schuyler, assistant to the vice president for academic affairs, "The attitude is that we're going to protect the student, the striking student as well as any other."[182]

Unhappily, the attitude of the striking students was not nearly as benevolent. On January 23, another noisy rally was being held on the commons, in direct violation of President Hayakawa's order. In the words of the coordinator of internal affairs, Edwin Duerr, "The decision was made that the rallies and disruptions must be stopped if San Francisco State were to function as an educational institution." Two announcements were made over the loudspeaker, repeating the order that prohibited the rally, and reminding the militants that an alternate meeting place was available. The crowd was ordered to disperse. When it did not do so within ten minutes after the second reading of the order, the police moved in and arrested those around the speakers' platform. Students armed with rocks and with picket signpoles two inches square rushed to the attack, and at one point drove a dozen policemen into the library building, from which other policemen rescued them. The policemen used their clubs to quell the melee. In all, 454 persons were arrested, of whom 252 were students. In that one day, more arrests were made than had taken place in the preceding two and a half months. Duerr noted that this was the last confrontation and was convinced that because of the large number of arrests on January 23, "the cost of participating in the disruptive rallies suddenly became too high."[183]

Hayakawa was quoted as saying, "There is an all-out attempt on the part of outside radicals. It is the hope of these outsiders to close down [the college] because if they manage to close this one, they can close an awful lot more. Perhaps I'm working on the same theory from the other side in trying to keep the college open. If we can win this one, we can win an awful lot more, too, and protect an awful lot of American higher education."[184]

Hayakawa pledged that striking teachers who returned to class with the start of the spring term on February 17 would be reinstated, although their salary would be withheld for their time on strike. The offer was spurned by the AFT. The union president, Gary Hawkins, said the strike would continue unless "we get a negotiated settlement of our demands."[185] Accordingly, a superior court judge in San Francisco issued a preliminary injunction forbidding the teachers strike.[186]

At a news conference, Hayakawa disclosed that letters had gone to 199 teachers and nine non-faculty employees asking them whether they intended to work at the college in the spring term. Under state law, the 208 persons involved had been held to have resigned their jobs by being absent without leave for five consecutive days. Dr. Donald Garrity, the college academic vice president, explained: "The law is applied automatically in the personnel and payroll process. After an individual has been absent without leave five days or more, the controller is prohibited from issuing checks for any further work performed unless the person is either rehired or is reinstated by the California State Personnel Board."[187]

Hayakawa said he was assured that a black students program would be ready to begin when the strike ended.[188] But Jerry Varnardo of the Black Students Union brushed all such assurances aside like so many specks of lint. Compromise and negotiation were anathema to him—excommunicable sins, in his own weird liturgy of black rebellion. Further description would be superfluous. One has only to read Varnardo's own words:

> I am now a graduate student and a lecturer in the black-studies department. What we are involved in here at State is not a reform movement. That is what the civil rights movement was. This is a revolution. Reformists work within existing rules and regulations; revolutionists make their own rules and regulations.
>
> We will use any means necessary to uphold the principle that people of the third world have a right to determine what kind of human beings they want to be. Violence is the best means. It disrupts and terrorizes so that if people of the third world are not allowed to determine their own

kind of education, then nobody else on the campus can get any kind of education.

One course I teach is the sociology of black oppression. ... Once during class we were talking about what napalm was and how it was being used. I told them how it could get on the skin and burn a hole all the way through. And for all who didn't believe it, I put a formula for napalm on the board so they could make some. They could pour it on a piece of meat or on the police or somebody and see exactly how it works.[189]

Steeped in the doctrine of Che Guevara and Mao Tse-tung, Varnardo had been at San Francisco State for six years without accumulating enough credits to graduate.[190] "He scares me," said a white coed. "I know of several people that he has threatened, including some professors, if they didn't do what he wanted them to. They were so scared, they did it." A faculty member admitted, "I never wanted any trouble from the BSU, so I always did what I thought they wanted me to."[191] And what the BSU wanted was San Francisco State.

On February 16, a homemade bomb shook the administration building as the school prepared to reopen for the spring session. The predawn explosion shattered 18 windows. Hayakawa, standing where the bomb exploded, said he was "going to be firmly in control" when the school reopened. He said he expected more bombings, interruption of classes, and other "shameless behavior" when classes resumed. But he promised that students and teachers would be "protected by whatever means necessary."[192]

In a meeting that traditionally took place at the beginning of each semester, Hayakawa attempted to address the faculty on February 14. Only about a third of San Francisco State's faculty attended this meeting, a fact which some interpreted as a sign "of widespread faculty disaffection with Hayakawa."[193] Perhaps so. And then again perhaps it was one more tangible sign of the fear that pervaded the campus—of an atmosphere so contaminated by terror that a maintenance man was standing by, ready to drop the auditorium's asbestos curtain, should any attempt be made to set the stage on fire.[194]

About 20 black teachers and students sat directly in front of the stage, and allowed Hayakawa to speak only a few moments before beginning hostilities. "There are no easy times to look forward to, in the near future," he was saying, when the hecklers broke out in chants of "down with Hayakawa." He remarked, "This is a perfect example of their tactics to suppress freedom of speech."

Most of the audience burst into wild applause at his remark. Then Nathan Hare, Jerry Varnardo, and others climbed on stage, shouting slogans, and surrounding the podium. "Get the hell out of here," Hayakawa told Hare. A laughing Nathan Hare replied, "We're not going," and Jerry Varnardo said, "When the police are removed, we will leave." Most of the audience demanded that the hecklers keep quiet. Finally, Hare was arrested and, along with three others, was charged with disturbing the peace.[195]

Hayakawa commented, "Dr. Hare no longer has my backing to head the Black Studies Department." He suspended Hare and Professor Milton Stewart with pay, pending disciplinary hearings.[196]

After the faculty meeting, Hayakawa disclosed that San Francisco State was ready to go ahead with its own version of a black studies program. He said he had been in touch with black faculty members from other colleges in the United States, and that their idea was to "get first-class professors, from first-class institutions, to substitute for Hare." Pointedly, he emphasized that "we should put the program in the hands of those who really want it instead of in the hands of those who want to make a political football out of a reasonable demand."[197]

Hare had refused to submit his program proposal, pending settlement of the strike. He said that any attempt to bypass him would fail, and warned that an administration-sponsored black studies program "would amount to a declaration of war on the black race."[198] But Nathan Hare—a onetime Golden Gloves contender—was hopelessly outmatched by the scrappy bantamweight from British Columbia, Dr. S. I. Hayakawa.

Now came another blow aimed right at the Black Students Union moneybelt. On February 17, a judge ordered officers of the Associated Students at San Francisco State removed for mishandling funds. Superior Court Judge Edward O'Day, acting on a complaint by State's Attorney Thomas C. Lynch, named the Bank of America temporary receiver of more than $250,000 in student funds, plus a large reserve. Previously, Lynch had disclosed that the Associated Students had diverted $22,000 to the Black Students Union and $15,000 to the Third World Liberation Front.[199]

That same day, spring semester classes opened at San Francisco State with almost 100 percent attendance from both faculty and students. Enrollment was estimated at between 16,000 and 17,000, compared with about 18,000 for the previous fall semester. But it was all only a matter of tactical maneuver to the AFT, which explained that its members would return to their classrooms to meet "the first (and only the first) section of each course." Students and faculty each had to sign class cards at the initial course sections to complete registration. Once this formality was completed, it was expected that the strike would resume where it had left off.[200] This was soon confirmed by the college registrar John H. Sloane, who confided, "We're in a real mess. A lot of students had registered for classes taught by teachers who are still on strike. The teachers showed up the first day, asked the students to stay registered for the classes [so they wouldn't be canceled] and then went back to the picket line, telling the students, "see you when the strike is over."[201]

On February 28, Hayakawa announced that Dr. Nathan Hare —who was still under suspension—would not be rehired when his one-year appointment ended in June. Dr. Frank Dollard indicated that Hare was not being rehired because he had refused to submit a report on groundwork for implementing the black studies department. In reply, Hare accused Hayakawa of "trying to set himself up as a right-wing champion radical killer." He accused Hayakawa of trying to make a "black scab" of him by urging him to work while the faculty and Third World student strike was in progress.[202]

It was a classic case of reasoning in a circle—with Hare refusing to help set up the black studies department, and then joining a strike because, among other things, a black studies department had not yet been set up.

Hare charged that both Hayakawa and the State College Board of Trustees were "taking their orders from Governor Reagan." And Dr. Joseph White, dean of undergraduate studies, and Hare's superior in the projected black studies program, accused the college administration of "setting up black administrators one by one to be fired." White said that Hare would head the black studies department in spite of Hayakawa's announcement, and said his colleague "is still the only acceptable chairman for the program."[203]

Hare reiterated, "We are not accepting the fact I have been fired—not rehired—whatever you want to call it. I have the backing of the black community to head the black studies department. The black students have said they will not accept anyone else. It will take a way-out Uncle Tom to come here." Dean White stated that he thought it likely a job in the black studies department would be offered to Hare in the fall.[204]

On March 7, the *San Francisco Examiner* wrote:

> Black studies courses have quietly vanished from the curriculum at San Francisco State College, where the student strike for an autonomous School of Ethnic Studies enters its fifth month today . . . the Black Studies Program no longer exists.[205]

Dr. White said that "only two or three" of the classes remained in the spring catalog. One of those was canceled when the instructor, Malcolm Spence, was suspended.[206]

Meanwhile, the black militants were beginning to lose their AFT allies. The same day that Hayakawa announced that Hare would not be rehired, college administrators were giving striking faculty members an ultimatum to decide by that night whether they would accept a strike settlement. The college threatened to cancel the classes of striking teachers who did not return to work on March 3. Describing the strike as "in many ways extremely successful," the striking teachers accepted a peace pact and returned to their classes.[207]

Possibly the teachers saw the handwriting on the wall, written in large, clear letters by Governor Ronald Reagan. Two new appointees to eight-year terms on the Board of Trustees gave the governor an increasingly good chance to win close votes on major issues. The *New York Times* estimated that at this point, "Mr. Reagan can already count on roughly half the regents for support on crucial matters."[208]

In its accustomed box score on campus disturbances, the *San*

*Francisco Examiner* reported that on March 6 the number of estimated pickets at San Francisco State totaled just four.[209] The black militants were becoming more and more desperate, and attempted to make up in terror what they lacked in numbers. And it was at this time that the most gruesome event of the entire struggle burned and blasted and mutilated its way to page one. On March 6, a 19-year-old Negro student at San Francisco State, Tim Peebles, was hospitalized in critical condition —blinded, his hands torn, and chest crushed by a premature bomb blast while attempting to carry out what the police called an act of sabotage. A member of the Black Students Union, Peebles staggered bleeding and screaming through a dust-filled corridor minutes after the explosion occurred in a storage room of the Creative Arts Building. "I've got to get out of here," Peebles screamed as he stumbled into the hallway.[210]

Peebles was taken to San Francisco General Hospital for treatment. The doctors reported, "As of now the boy is blind because of the searing, burning action. We hope to be able to correct that with corneal transplants." However, the parts of his fingers that he lost from both hands in the explosion could never be replaced. This was not the only bomb in that building; in an adjoining room, investigators found two others, even more powerful devices. One of them contained six sticks of dynamite connected with a battery and an alarm clock set for 5:00 a.m. Had it gone off, officials said it would have reduced much of the building to rubble.[211]

"It was a terrible incident last night," Hayakawa told a news conference. But the Black Students Union chairman Benny Stewart offered his own analysis of the bomb explosion. He said that Peebles was "the innocent victim of the racist, oppressive society that is perpetuated at San Francisco State College." When newsmen reminded him that if Peebles was a victim, he was a victim of his own bomb, Stewart replied that the BSU didn't believe police or press accounts, and was conducting its own investigation.[212]

Two weeks later, Benny Stewart and Jerry Varnardo climbed atop chairs in the cafeteria and told more than a thousand students crowded around that the strike was over. The announcement came after days of growing rumors that an agreement was imminent between the students and a special Select

Committee of four faculty members and two administrators appointed by the college administration. But almost at the same moment the announcement was made, questions were raised about whether or not the administration had fully agreed to all its terms.

Frank Brann, attorney for the striking students, said the settlement provided for a maximum of a two-semester suspension for students convicted of bombing or setting fires on campus. For those students found guilty of physical disruption of classes, the penalty would be a suspension for the two-month balance of the semester. And for those students—comprising 95 percent of all disciplinary cases—who had been arrested for failure to disperse, unlawful assembly, and disturbing the peace, the penalty would be a written reprimand. Benny Stewart noted that no one would be expelled, and he told a press conference, "We view the agreed settlement as a foundation for revolutionary change in bringing together this college and various communities throughout the Bay Area." He stated, "The struggle to end institutionalized racism and the right of all people to seize power for determining their political, economic, educational and social destinies is not over, but will intensify."[213]

But doubts about the settlement still lingered, because some key administrators were obviously upset by terms of the strike agreement. Edwin Duerr said he was "not happy" with the agreement. One of the two administrators on the committee did not even attend the signing session, and the other did not sign the agreement. Bishop Mark Hurley, who had worked tirelessly to end the strike, declined comment when asked whether the strike was over.[214]

The following day it looked as if the BSU leaders might have climbed upon those cafeteria chairs a little too soon. Hayakawa said he would wait until the April 11 deadline agreed to by the students before deciding whether to follow the list of recommendations for disciplining students. In his words: "I think I should make clear that I have considered each of the seven recommendations with great care and can only say in reply that I cannot agree prior to any hearing what the limits of the penalty for a given offense will be."[215]

Attorney Brann called it "without question, a repudiation of the agreement." And Black Students Union member Jack Alexis commented, "We are just as confused as everybody else. We were under the impression when we signed the agreement that Hayakawa had agreed to the seven recommendations."[216] Alexis himself had a certain vested interest in the outcome of the recommendations. He had been placed on probation by Municipal Judge Albert A. Axelrod, who instructed him to stay away from future campus disturbances. And San Francisco State had directed that this 25-year-old student could go on campus only when he was attending classes.[217]

Hayakawa said that planning for a black studies department within a school of ethnic studies "shall be advanced as rapidly as possible." But he pointedly reiterated that "Dr. Hare's contract expires in June, as already announced," and that "George Murray's contract has already expired." As for the community board that would be formed to help run the school for ethnic studies, he made it clear that "ultimately I have the authority over any decisions made by the board."

Hayakawa refused to withdraw the police at this time. When asked if he considered the campus still in a state of emergency, he replied. "I certainly do." He noted that a section dealing with disciplinary hearings and penalties was in the form of seven recommendations. He would agree to none, he said, until April 11—one month after the major agreement lines had been drawn. The agreement, worked out with the Black Students Union and the Third World Liberation Front, stipulated that entrance requirements be waived for up to ten percent of the college's applicants, an increase from the then maximum level of four percent. Hayakawa promised to expand the college's special-admissions program, then including 428 below-average students, by at least 100 students. He also agreed to staff a black studies program with eleven professors, one fewer than the number demanded by the striking students[218]

Hayakawa was asked, "Did you win [the strike]?" With a grin, he replied, "I don't know."[219]

Roscoe and Geoffrey Drummond lauded the "two-edged backbone of Hayakawa," and believed that his effectiveness stemmed from the use of "firmness against violence and responsiveness to needed change without violence." They saw these as the component parts of Hayakawa's master plan:

&#35; Be thoroughly ready. Think through in advance what as
an administrator you will be willing to do and believe
you must do if violence arises. Dr. Hayakawa was himself ready when he was catapulted into the president's
chair. From the very beginning of the violent protest
which had turned the nearby Berkeley campus of the
University of California into a battleground, he began
to ponder what he would do if he were in charge. He did
make up his mind, though he never expected to be
called on to do it.

&#35; Don't let a little violence succeed when it is first tried.
That is when action can stop it in its tracks. This is the
warning of worse to come. If a little violence is re-
warded, then the process of escalating non-negotiable
demands, and the force to compel them, will mount.

&#35; Don't delay the use of force—adequate force—to put
down violence when that is the only means which can
do it.

&#35; Listen to the students. Provide clearly available means
so their views can be better heard and better heeded by
faculty and administrtion.

&#35; Have the backbone to remake the college curriculum
and restructure the faculty to make education more
meaningful to today's social needs.[220]

In testimony before Senate investigators, Hayakawa stated
his belief that wealthy white revolutionaries were deliberately
recruiting Negroes as "cannon fodder" for campus insurrections. Hayakawa added, "And when the crackdown on revolutionary activities comes, as I am afraid it must, it will be the
blacks who will go to prison, not the whites who fed them,
taught them their Marxism and egged them on." Asked by
Senator Charles Percy what evidence he had of a campus conspiracy, Hayakawa conceded that "all the evidence I have is
hearsay that would not hold up in a courtroom." He went on,
"But there is enough of this kind of hearsay about the rich
contributing to radical causes and bail bonds suddenly available for poor Negro kids, enough information which is also
passed on to me by federal authorities to make me sure this is
an area that really needs examination."[221]

Though Hayakawa cited no cases, he could have named such
a prime example of "cannon fodder" as Paul Okpokam, a 28-
year-old Nigerian graduate student at San Francisco State Col-

lege who was convicted for having a bomb on the campus. Okpokam, a drama student, was only six academic hours short of completing requirements for a master's degree when police arrested him in a campus building with a small explosive device in his pocket. Nigerian Consul General P. A. Afolabi told the court his government was prepared to "repatriate" Okpokam. But Superior Court Judge Harry J. Neubarth said, Okpokam "is a man who could maim, injure innocent people. This kind of violence has got to stop, and it's time someone does something about it." The judge sentenced Okpokam to a one-to-five-year prison term.[222]

On April 14, Dr. Hayakawa lifted emergency regulations banning meetings at San Francisco State. Now meetings could be held with permits, and the Free Speech Platform on the campus could again be used.[223]

But all was not yet quiet on the San Francisco State front. At the end of June, four of the college's six black administrators resigned their posts, charging that the school was attempting to prevent non-whites from enrolling there. Those resigning were: Ed Reaves, assistant dean of students; Elmer Cooper, dean of student activities; Dr. Joseph White, dean of undergraduate studies; and Reginald Major, director of the Educational Opportunities Program. In a prepared statement, they charged that Hayakawa had issued a June 19 directive cutting enrollment in the Educational Opportunities Program from 400 to 150. They charged that they were hired as "niggers in residence" and had no part in decision-making at the college. "We are expected to go along with every administrative decision," they said, "even if that decision adversely affects the educational lives of non-white students." They continued, "We refuse to condone racism in education by participating in this administration." Hayakawa emphatically denied their charges, and called their resignations "a shabby grandstand play." He revealed that "each had already planned to leave, and had a job set up. I'm glad to see them go. We can do without them." Now, said Hayakawa, "we'll get administrators who take an attitude of responsibility to the entire campus, not just black revolutionaries."[224]

That same day, a three-judge federal panel ruled that the mass arrests that took place at San Francisco State on January

23 were made under California laws that were constitutional. The panel's decision, written by District Judge Stanley A. Weigel, said, "There is no evidence in the record plainly establishing abusive invocation of State criminal laws to discourage free speech and assembly."[225]

All this time, Dr. Hayakawa had been functioning as acting president of San Francisco State. On July 9, 1969, his position was made permanent. By a 16-to-2 vote of the trustees of the California State Colleges, Hayakawa was named permanent president of San Francisco State College. With a wide smile, Hayakawa greeted a horde of television cameramen and reporters, and said, "The trustees' action represents, I hope, a vote of confidence in my policies in defense of academic freedom. I shall continue my defense of that essential freedom on behalf of all the people of California."[226]

Hayakawa conceded that the problems at San Francisco State are "far from solved, but I believe we are on the way. We have made significant progress in recent weeks—quietly, without fanfare or publicity—to build stability in the administration, faculty, and student body."[227] But perhaps Professor John Bunzel expressed it as well as anyone. "I don't think I can claim a victory," he said; "there are no victories at San Francisco—but maybe we've got a tie."[228]

# CHAPTER 9

# *Federal City College*

As THE TIDE OF CAMPUS REBELLION THREATENED TO engulf higher education, the federal government moved into the controversy only long enough to test the temperature, shudder fastidiously, and then wash its hands of the entire affair. The excuse was that campus disruptions were essentially state and city problems, and could best be handled at the local level. It was a most ingenious and serviceable argument—satisfying those liberals who opposed any federal intervention on campus anyway, and those conservatives who eagerly grasped at any word or gesture that acknowledged the doctrine of states' rights.

There was always the hint—implicit in the rousing rhetoric of the federal government—that somehow, some way, the Nixon administration, given the opportunity, would have solved the problems tormenting the campus. Those readers holding such a view are hereby warned in advance that the story of Federal City College may come as a shock.

If any college in the United States is quite literally the creation of contemporary federal government, it is Federal City College. A report from a blue-ribbon committee established by President Kennedy in 1962 to study higher education in the District of Columbia led to the Morse-Green Bill in Congress.[1]

This led to the establishment of a board of higher education in 1967, and finally to the starting of the first class at Federal City College on September 9, 1968.[2]

Federal City College was Washington's first four-year public college of arts and sciences. It was the nation's first urban college to be given land-grant status by Congress.[3] It "temporarily" occupied a building about five blocks from the Capitol, and was a very short distance from neighborhoods where every fourth structure burned in the riots that followed the murder of Martin Luther King.[4] For its first year, Congress gave it an operating budget of $ 4.3 million.[5]

Federal City College (often referred to as FCC) had an open-door admission policy, which meant that anyone with a high school diploma or its equivalent was eligible to attend. Because of this, and because of its low annual tuition charge of just $ 75, applications were so numerous the first term that students were chosen by lottery.[6]

As originally planned, Federal City College was to become the liberal academician's dream institution. In the words of David Dickson, the Negro provost of FCC:

> Instead of technically limited and routine freshman courses, a core curriculum was fashioned to stress the topical, the urban, the permanently relevant, the concrete and the philosophical to allure the student to the more recondite academic joys of the distant and the abstract. Instead of freshman English, there would be reading, writing and speaking discipline to all courses and in small fifteen-man freshman seminars; instead of hasty "Cook's Tours" of Western culture and history, the student would select an interdisciplinary humanities course in the theory of revolutions, in the concepts of the good life, or in the search for identity . . . a media center would bring the student into McLuhan's world of multisensory impression as well as preserve the joys of the linear verbal world by providing each student with a fifty-book basic paperback library of his own. . . . Democratic idealism brightened these golden days. . . . Healing the wounds of interracial strife by practicing social democracy within and beyond its walls, Federal City College would be a catalyst to urban renewal and the midwife of a more truly pluralistic America.[7]

This was the dream. In a tragically short time, what some lauded as the Great Challenge became the Great Nightmare of Federal City College.

Unlike San Francisco State, the student body at Federal City College nurtured few fire-eating militants. It would have been ludicrous to mount a campaign at FCC for an increased number of ghetto residents; 94 percent of the student body was black. It would have been carrying the proverbial coals to Newcastle to hold up picket signs urging more lenient consideration of lackluster grades; there were flexible deadlines for completing courses, and students might prolong their studies until they achieved success.[8]

Unlike the political dilettantes of the SDS and the fire-eating militants of the Black Students Unions, most of the students at FCC were in college for the most practical of reasons; they sought a bachelor's degree as a means to advance economically. They especially wanted job-related training. Ninety percent of them were employed; 40 percent were evening students. About 66 percent carried a full academic load. The majors they preferred were business, sociology, teacher education, and physical education.[9]

What, then, was the problem at Federal City College? David Dickson offered the answer, in a disturbing speech that went, curiously, unreported by much of the nation's press. "Our profoundest problem," Dickson made clear, was not with the student body, but with the faculty and staff:

> Our biggest problem is the great problem of this nation, race. Racial tension, racial suspicion and racial polarization have almost blasted our lovely spring buds. . . . Some of our counter-punching blacks are blatantly and boisterously separatist and some of our whites are too missionary-minded, proud and so guilt-ridden that they have lost common sense in their pusillanimous response to unjust black pressures. . . . Our meetings display passion quite as much as reason, intimidation rather than discussion. The black or white moderates shocked at the flight of sweet reason are supine while the well-disciplined and intense cadre of black separatists neglect academic principles for revolutionary ends.[10]

FCC's white president, Dr. Frank Farner, denied the charges, and said that Dr. Dickson had "overstated the case in almost every regard."[11] But as we will soon see, the gravity of the crisis could in no way have been overstated.

Among those possessing even the slightest knowledge of the situation, there could be little doubt that Dickson had aimed much of his verbal artillery at the acting director of Federal City College's black studies program, James Garrett. The *Washington Post* found Garrett "soft-spoken in conversation,"[12] a description that would have evoked utter amazement at San Francisco State. For this was the same James Garrett who had helped found the Black Students Union at San Francisco State; the same James Garrett who had said he would do anything necessary to bring about a black society for black people, from reading a book, if that was necessary, to killing; the same James Garrett who had threatened, "There are certain brothers and certain sisters around this country who are slated to die."[13] And this was the man who had been appointed director of FCC's black studies program, after first having been foisted on the students as "a teacher of creative writing."[14]

In the writing about the aims and objectives of the Black Studies Program, Garrett emphasized that "Nation building, then, must be the end product of black studies and the beginning of a lasting and meaningful black peoplehood. Whether that nation is to be a collection of enclaves or a geographical location, existing within or without the United States, is a question we must ultimately answer as a people."[15]

Helping Garrett were Andress Taylor, assistant professor of English, and Samuel F. Carcione, a mathematics instructor. Both had been compelled to leave Howard University after the campus turmoil of 1967.[16]

In the student paper at Federal City College, Garrett further expounded his "philosophy":

> Black teachers must fascinate black children with visions structured in their images. They must drop George Washington and Benjamin Franklin and Thomas Jefferson— those—— ——. They must make Malcolm X, Elijah Muhammad, Huey Newton and LeRoi Jones real heroes, or they have failed. . . . How can we blame a child for getting

bored with listening to omnipotent white stuff all day
when he knows he can whip any white boy around?[17]

In the February 1969 issue of *Focus*—a periodic report on
FCC activities from the College Information Office—James
Garrett's projected black studies program was outlined in some
detail. Like Nathan Hare at San Francisco State, Garrett's program at FCC all but stripped the individual of his personal
identity and personal freedom. In the inventory of black nationalism, each individual was a social automaton—little more
than another pair of willing arms and legs, another malleable
mind, unquestioningly at the beck and call of "the community"
(or those who professed to speak for it). Thus, in *Focus,* we find
these comments about the FCC black studies program:

> Community involvement and dedication will be the means
> for achieving the goal of love among black people. Accord-
> ingly, the Program will seek to develop a relationship
> among black people that manifests itself to the black com-
> munity. It will advocate an African cooperative family
> concept of dedication to the black community, as opposed
> to the individual concept of "me first." For example, a
> black doctor would go into the black community that most
> desperately needs his talent. He would seek *only to make
> a living* and not accumulate great amounts of wealth. In
> time the black community would support him and he
> would serve that black community.[18]

The large and varied choice of courses that students have
demanded in hundreds of colleges would simply not have existed in Garrett's FCC black studies program. The program was
to take "total responsibility for the academic pursuit of students enrolled in Black Studies." All courses in the degree program were to be mandatory.[19]

The first year of study included the Pan African World—the
study of the historical, social, and cultural development of African communities in the Caribbean, on the Continent, and in the
Americas; African Peoples and World Reality; Physical Development, which included Akikdo, Karate, and the African Hunt
and Dance.

The second year of study featured Interpretation of the African Experience; Cultural Concepts of African Peoples; and
World's Great Men of Color.[20]

As for the staff, the black studies program looked for those with "thorough knowledge of the area of specialty—*not necessarily expressed in the form of degrees*" [21] (emphasis added).

Coming from the pen of a black militant, the implications of the black studies program were staggering—and were soon to send a tremor or two through the nation's capital, and even the halls of Congress itself.

It was a disenchanted *Washington Post* that read between the lines of the proposed black studies program, and broke the story with this blunt lead paragraph:

> Federal City College more than halfway through its first year, is bitterly divided over a black studies program explicitly working toward an emerging—and wholly separate—"black nation." [22]

The *Washington Post* noted that "last year, black studies were planned as merely a group of courses in the humanities and social sciences divisions," but that "next year, after a series of bruising internal political fights over recent months, black studies will be the second largest division of instruction at Federal City and will approach the status of being a separate college."

The newspaper revealed that the proposed curriculum would devote the first two years to the "decolonization of the mind" —the systematic eradication of "white values" held by entering students. The last two or three years of the program were to concentrate on training an elite for what was believed to be the coming "black nation" including Negroes worldwide.

A paragraph was devoted to James Garrett's message of "revolution" and "nation building," noting that he had lectured students at the University of Oregon on techniques of making firebombs and hand grenades on the anniversary of the assassination of Malcolm X. [23]

The greatest irony of all was that "separatism has been almost exclusively a faculty issue." It was *not* black studies, but business and science courses that were always the first to fill up a quarterly registration. [24]

Nevertheless the black studies department was to get 40 out of the 172 new faculty posts open for the following year, for a total of 54 teaching positions. By contrast there would be 51 instructors in the natural sciences and only 41 in the professional division, which included teacher training and business administration.[25]

The immediate issue that forced the crisis out into the open was hiring standards, if any, for the incoming members of the faculty. Recruitment for the black studies program was almost entirely in the hands of James Garrett. And Garrett and his allies were pressing the college administration to discount traditional academic credentials like doctoral degrees, and give weight to experience with black political and social action organizations. One black radical said that "five minutes of working for SNCC is more important than a Ph.D. for teaching at Federal City."[26]

Already, some young Negroes without doctorates had been made department heads, while senior, more traditionally minded faculty had, in several instances, been relegated to positions of little influence.[27] To be sure, the system had its defenders. "Isn't it conceivable," asked William Couch, Negro chairman of the humanities division, "that [activists] would have something to offer that Ph.D's would not?" But another Negro faculty member at FCC, Margaret Just Butcher, a former professor at Howard, complained that FCC had brought in many instructors of "dubious quality and competence" and was recruiting more. Mrs. Butcher said, "I'm a little tired of this nonsense of black, black, black." And a senior professor who preferred to remain anonymous said Federal City College was in danger of becoming a "glorified high school."[28]

It was not without humor that among the most avid supporters of black studies were the Black Muslims, and even they refused to practice what James Garrett preached. FCC might debate whether a degree was relevant for teaching, but the Black Muslims insisted that "applicants must have a college or university degree" to teach at their University of Islam.[29]

In a special report, the American Council on Education critically scrutinized several black studies programs, the Federal City College program among them. On the surface, at least, the American Council on Education granted that the FCC curriculum "might be thought of as a four-year preparation for Peace Corps work in the areas inhabited by black Africans and by their relatives in the New World. It does not exclude white students; in fact, no distinction between white and black is made in the program."

The A.C.E. Special Report went on:

> However, if one looks at the proposal apart from the program details, one may doubt the appropriateness of the program for a white student. For example, the "focus" of the first-year program is given as "Decolonization of the mind. Development of the ways of looking at the world (Interpretative Skills)." In the introduction, we find these statements: "If education is to be relevant to Black people, it must have a two-fold purpose: revolution and nation-building. If the education of Black students is to be meaningful, it must direct these students toward the destruction of the forces of racism, colonialism and oppression that continue to drain Black people all over the world; and it must develop in them the skills which will allow them to conceptualize and structure the projections of future Black existence."

Calmly and devastatingly, the report continued to quote from the introduction to the proposed FCC black studies program, including this chilling paragraph:

> The main emphasis of Black Studies will be toward the liberation of the African world. Since education should serve to expand the minds and spheres of action of the people involved in it, Black Studies must prepare Black people for the most complete self-expression, which must, in fact, be liberation and self-determination. Black studies will take the position that the total liberation of a people necessarily means that those people separate themselves in values, attitudes, social structure and technology, from the forces which oppress them. Concurrent, then, with the liberation of African people must be the construction of a durable, productive and self-sufficient nation. The building of a lasting and meaningful African nation must be the end-product of the Black Studies Program.

The American Council on Education report concluded: "The burden of the Federal City College proposal is that the Black student must become himself a member in full of the 'African nation' before he can render service. . . . Thus programs like the

Federal City College proposal will unquestionably raise serious doubts about their propriety in an academic setting."[30]

Concerned that FCC might not become accredited because of a faculty recruitment policy that gave greater weight to social activism than academic degrees, about 20 Federal City College students met with President Farner and urged him to exercise more administrative power. Speaking for the representatives of the FCC Veterans Club and a new group of business administration students, Marvin Jordan said, "A whole lot of things have been going on around the school that aren't right. We feel the right hand has not been placed." He told Farner, "You as the top man should give guidelines. If no one takes authority, who's going to do it?"

Farner replied, "I never wanted to run this place like a high school." But the problem was that Farner wasn't running "this place" at all.

Most of the students at the meeting said they held part-time jobs and had previously not had the opportunity or time to participate in student-faculty policy-making committees. Some said they took time off from jobs to attend the meeting.

Said Ozema Moore, chairman of the Veterans Club (and one who had served 11 years in the Navy), "This school means a lot to us. One of the main things that I was looking forward to when I was overseas was getting out and getting an education. I don't want anyone standing in my way."

Sandra Johnson, who said she would major in marketing, added, "We are out in the working world. We know what it is to struggle without an education."[31]

Farner stated that his style of administration was to let faculty and student committees initiate new policy, which he then reviewed. He told the students that he felt qualified faculty members were being hired.[32]

Not long after, President Farner underwent an agonizing reappraisal of his "style." In an interview, he admitted, "I have not made any policy decisions on my own. That's probably the wrong style of administration for this situation."[33]

Paradoxically, after sifting through the sound and fury for the cold facts and figures, one found that only about 20 percent of Federal City College's students were enrolled in at least one of the black studies classes.[34]

All of which served amply to confirm the conviction of FCC's associate director of media services that "most FCC students have shown a preference for the traditional types and styles of subjects and of teaching. They strenuously object to what they regard as overemphasis on Black Studies. They do *not* want guerrilla warfare. They do want to earn a diploma which will be highly respected in the career market."[35]

Irene Tinker, assistant provost at Federal City College, came to very much the same conclusion: "Our students think very much like the second-generation immigrant groups you read about, who see education as the fastest way up the ladder. They are not here for a liberal education, but for a passport to a better job."[36]

When the school first opened, the faculty deliberately didn't offer any special writing courses, but instead planned to deal with composition skills in other courses. However, these measures proved inadequate to meet the students' writing problems, and soon both students and faculty requested English composition courses. About 18 sections were planned in January 1969, but when more than twice the expected number of students registered, the FCC wound up with 40 sections, and writing was given high priority in future planning.[37]

It cannot be overstressed that the furor over black studies went on unabated, *in spite of* the great majority of FCC students, *not because of them*—most of them had not evinced any fervent desire to take these courses. In his "Capital Education" column in the *Washington Post*, Peter Milius summarized it in this succinct paragraph:

> Faculty moderates have been distressed, but so far not distressed enough to organize and fight back. Some are leaving. Farner has not interposed. The debate has gone on over the students' heads, and seemingly beneath the trustees' notice. The faculty militants have won.[38]

One of the few members of the faculty who would confirm this grim state of affairs for publication was Kenneth S. Lynn, who had left a professorship at Harvard to join the faculty at Federal City College. One of the most highly regarded members of the faculty, Lynn was quitting FCC, convinced that a radical coalition of black and white faculty members was ruining the college. Lynn said simply, "The militants have won. That's really it. I just don't see that people with academic interests have much of a chance here." He added that his teaching had gone very well, and that "none of the trouble here has come from the students. It's all come from the faculty." Of the 100-member faculty (which was quite evenly integrated), Lynn estimated that radicals comprised about two thirds of the faculty, and said that many of the remaining third, black and white, were planning to leave the college.[39] Reported to be the highest-paid faculty member, Lynn left FCC to become professor of intellectual history at Johns Hopkins.[40]

Another noted academician, Arthur H. Webb, chairman of the division of natural sciences at FCC, incurred the wrath of the radicals when he gave only one-year appointments to members of his faculty who lacked doctorates. Attacked by the radicals in an open faculty meeting, Webb resigned. But his resignation was rejected by the provost when a poll of students and faculty in his division showed that nearly all wanted him to stay on.[41]

For some time, the Board of Higher Education had been doggedly pursuing a policy of See-no-controversy, hear-no-controversy, mouth-no-controversy. But the outcry was simply becoming too clamorous to be ignored. And so it was that the board finally faced the grim facts of academic life at Federal City College. After acknowledging the situation, on February 4, 1969, the Board of Higher Education gave its tentative approval to a statement entitled, "The Purpose of Federal City College." The board cautioned: "That statement of purpose, it now appears, has not been adequately understood by persons within the College and within the community. This further statement, it is hoped, will correct misunderstandings and elaborate some of the policies heretofore stated only in more general terms."

The board considered it "highly appropriate" that black studies be made a "major field of academic credit." But at the same time it devoted some time and space to the complexity of the matter, in the sense that this was a new and evolving field. Zeroing in on the black studies controversy at FCC, the board carefully stressed, "No program for a course of study in this field has been presented to the Board and no program has been approved by the Board, tentatively or otherwise."

With an eleventh-hour fervor surpassed only by its procrasti-
nation, the Board of Higher Education declared:

> The Board will not approve a program which is designed
> to encourage separation between the black and white
> races, or which would increase rather than seek to elimi-
> nate racial antagonism and conflict, or which would en-
> courage or condone violence as a means of resolving
> issues.

The black studies course the board would approve was to be
a program of the college, and neither in form nor in substance
a separate school, and would be related to and integrated with
the other programs of the college.[42]

On May 9, 1969, Senator Joseph D. Tydings (D., Md.), chairman of the Senate District Committee, sent a letter to Charles
Horsky, chairman of the trustees (another name for the Board
of Higher Education), expressing "concern that grave problems
exist in the administration of Federal City College that may
threaten not only the effective education of its students but also
the very existence of the college itself."

Tydings said,

> All the evidence that has reached me indicates that
> there has been a substantial abdication of leadership on
> the part of the administration of the college. As I have
> previously indicated to you, I hold the Board responsible.
> . . . I expect the Board to take whatever action is necessary
> to provide effective, efficient and balanced leadership
> within the college. I also expect the Board to replace any
> officer or faculty member . . . whose attitude or role in the
> college is inconsistent with this goal.[43]

Two days later, the trustees had a long, private, previously
scheduled meeting in Horsky's law offices. Much of the discussion centered about the effectiveness—or lack of it— of FCC
President Frank Farner.[44]

The trustees froze further hiring of black studies faculty
members for the coming academic year. Chairman Horsky told
James Garrett that the freeze was ordered until the trustees
could make up their minds about "the nature and scope of an
appropriate black studies program."[45]

The following day the FCC faculty adopted a resolution censuring the trustees for what it termed "discriminatory practices against the black studies program." The resolution stated that "it is the responsibility of the faculty, not the Board of Higher Education to structure . . . the various curriculums." Finally, the faculty warned the board not to interfere in what was being taught in the college's classrooms.[46]

The Board of Higher Education lost little time in backtracking on its position. The following weekend, it agreed to "move toward removal" of the ban on black studies hiring, and the faculty agreed to "move toward presentation of its full curriculum" to the board. In the wary manner of an ambassadorial communiqué, both agreed that "a mutually acceptable definition of . . . roles . . . is needed."[47]

In the midst of this recital of platitudes, it was revealed that President Frank Farner had resigned—at the express request of the board—and that David Dickson had resigned as well.[48] Harshly criticized for speaking his mind too frankly and publicly on the black studies program, "Dickson had felt for some time that his usefulness at Federal City had ended."[49] In one of the last memorandums to Farner two weeks before the ax fell, Dickson reiterated his outspoken opposition to James Garrett's proposals. He wrote, "The methods employed by the black studies program stress ideological conversion rather than reasoned commitment. It is clearly outside the role of a public university to provide a course of indoctrination for True Believers."[50]

Perhaps the High Priest of True Believers, James Garrett took umbrage at the board's fainthearted attempts to brake his "course of indoctrination." Or perhaps he sensed vague rumblings of discontent on Capitol Hill. In any case, it was the Black Muslim newspaper *Muhammad Speaks* that broke the news to the brothers and sisters, in the story, "New Trends Coming in Black Studies." And to no one's surprise, it was Garrett who would be setting that trend. The article asked, "Can a truly effective Black Studies Program be established on the campus grounds of a white-dominated institution?" The "unequivocal no" that followed was almost a formality. The article continued, "The framers of this program [at FCC] . . . have decided to quit their campus grounds altogether in a move to establish a Black educational program which will become 'The foundation of an independent education institution in the community for which it is designed, the Black community.' " It was James Garrett who explained to *Muhammad Speaks,* "It has become necessary for us to establish educational institutions independent of white control."

Garrett added, "A lot of us do a lot of talking about 'independence,' but are afraid to practice it." He disclosed that the move was decided upon more than three weeks before, after efforts to establish "a truly workable campus-based community-related program" proved futile. He stated that 14 faculty members and several students in the current black studies program had agreed with this decision.

Garrett asserted that government officials had tried to persuade the FCC black studies faculty "to change or modify their rhetoric," and then their program would be "acceptable." But the militants had rejected the attempts because "our rhetoric is what we believe. It is basic and critical to believe in the establishing of a new nation. We refuse to smooth off the rough edges for a few thousand dollars."

Asked why the faculty members had decided to pull out while there was still a chance of approval for the four-year black studies program, Garrett replied, "Any victory would be a hollow one. Our program, though developed here at FCC, was not exclusively designed for FCC."

Garrett was adamant in his position that black studies programs must be removed from conditions where black people were studied from a white perspective.

Garrett's public declaration was made just a few days prior to the renewal of contracts for the next year at FCC, but he maintained that the entire black studies faculty had prepared for any contingency that might require a loss of position or salary. And as he saw it, the Board of Higher Education was impaled on the horns of a much more pointed dilemma: "The board of education is committed to establish a Black Studies program, and we have advised the students that they should not accept any white-oriented program which would be the only alternative to the present program."[51]

But if enrollments were any criteria, most of the students could not have cared less, one way or the other. After almost a year of proselytizing, only about 20 percent of the students at

Federal City College were interested enough in the black studies program to take even one of its courses. This was the humiliating truth—to most of the career-oriented student body at Federal City College, James Garrett's black studies program and James Garrett himself were almost totally irrelevant.

# CHAPTER 10

# Cornell University

IN TRYING TO UNEARTH THE FACTS ABOUT CORNELL, and "The Guns of April,"[1] it is necessary to feel one's way warily if only to keep one's head above the quicksand of verbiage that covers the entire subject. Ironically, the 14-year-old son of the editor of the *Cornell Alumni News* cut through the miasma of rhetoric as succinctly as anyone: "I didn't know the university could fall to pieces so fast."[2]

But did Cornell University "fall to pieces" in 48 or 72 anarchic hours, or had the academic mortar started to loosen, brick by brick, stone by stone, rule by rule, regulation by regulation, over a considerably longer period of time? To find the answer, we would do well to begin some 3,000 miles from Ithaca—at San Jose State College in California.

In 1967, California's San Jose State College, with an enrollment of some 22,700, had a national reputation for its fine athletic teams. Unfortunately, San Jose State also had an assistant professor of sociology named Harry Edwards, a black leader who would soon have a national reputation for a militancy bordering on fanaticism. Edwards and his newly organized United Black Students for Action threatened to demonstrate at a football game unless this state-supported college ended alleged discrimination in housing and athletic recruiting. Edwards told the college president that anonymous "soul brothers" had threatened to burn the 18,156-seat wooden stadium to the ground if the season's opening game—with the University of Texas—were held.[3] President Robert D. Clark quickly beat an inglorious retreat, canceled the game, and placed all of the college's 27 fraternities and sororities on probation until they submitted proposals to end "discrimination."[4]

Edwards later stated that if that football game had been played, it could have marked "the onset of the second American revolution." He told a Foothill College audience, "I'm talking about guerrilla warfare with snipers in buildings."[5]

Edwards said, "We're going to be rational so long as rationality works," but added that "if it comes down to an animal to animal confrontation, then that's what it's going to be." He asserted that if the group of Negroes had been attacked while demonstrating at the football game, he could not have controlled them. But for that matter, he could hardly have controlled himself:

> I made it extremely clear to the administration and to the racist dogs that I am non-violent. But if anybody throws garbage on me or spits in my face, I am going to try to send him to the cemetery.[6]

The cancellation of the game was condemned by Governor Reagan, who considered it "appeasement ... yielding to a threat of force." And State Superintendent of Instruction Max Rafferty labeled it "blackmail," and vowed, "If I had to call out the Marine Corps, the game would have been played."[7]

A month and a half later, Harry Edwards warned the police that guerrilla warfare was rapidly approaching. In a letter mailed to all Northern California police departments, Edwards called for an emergency conference:

> In place of lines of communication, battle lines are being drawn. A condition of open warfare between the police and the black communities and certain white allies is developing. Let there be no mistake, gentlemen. We are no longer talking about bricks and bottles. We are talking about a state of total, hostile and aggressive guerrilla war-

fare carried out on streets and highways of our communities and cities. We are talking about the development of a situation in which no one will be the victor. There are nonetheless those of us who are willing to pay the price.

In an interview, Edwards spelled it out even more bluntly. If minority groups wanted to retaliate, he said, the police were "out in the open in marked cars, perfect targets, and they will be picked off."[8]

Six months later—on April 11, 1968—Edwards announced that he had decided to become a member of the Black Panther Party. He urged Negro doctors and lawyers to join, thereby helping to serve society with a notice that "you can no longer ignore the Black Panthers." Decked out for the occasion with "the Panther Look," including a black beret and large black sunglasses, he said he felt black people had "an obligation to participate even if they didn't agree with all the goals" of the Panthers.[9]

Edwards declared, "I personally encourage violence, until somebody shows me a better way. Non-violence essentially has not worked."[10]

Possibly it was in pursuit of that "better way" that Harry Edwards aimed his sights on Mexico City, which was playing host to the 1968 Olympics. It was there that he used his very considerable influence with Tommie Smith, the listed world recordholder for the 200-meter and 220-yard dashes, and with John Carlos, who had a pending application for a world record for the 200 meters of 19.7 seconds. Both Smith and Carlos were students at San Jose State, and knew Edwards well. It was Harry Edwards who, in the words of the *New York Times,* "inspired the black-gloved salute at Mexico City that catapulted Tommie Smith and John Carlos onto the world's front pages." Smith wore a black glove on his right hand to receive a gold medal. Carlos wore a black glove on his left hand, to receive a bronze medal. While the "Star Spangled Banner" was played, they bowed their heads and raised their black-gloved hands high. The U. S. Olympic Committee suspended Smith and Carlos for using the victory ceremony for a Black Power demonstration. Their credentials were taken away, thus making it mandatory for them to leave Mexico within 48 hours.[11]

Edwards emerged unscathed and untouched by the entire controversy. Shaking the dust of San Jose and Mexico City off his feet, he calmly resumed his studies for a Ph. D. at the same university where he had done his thesis for his master's degree on phases of the Black Muslim movement. As if nothing untoward had occurred, Harry Edwards was back at Cornell University.[12]

One picture of this embittered Black Panther supporter, allowed to return to Cornell *after* doing everything possible to humiliate his country before the world, was worth more than a thousand words about the dry rot of permissiveness that was sapping the integrity of the university.

In the frantic drive to recruit and keep black students in Cornell—by virtually any means necessary—permissiveness twisted the rules, or discarded them at will. Permissiveness pushed the regulations into some remote corner until such time as it was convenient to obey them. And if one were so rash as to inquire why the administration did not intervene, the somber response was that the president of Cornell University, James Perkins, was the worst offender of all.

Ernest Dunbar, senior editor of *Look* magazine, wrote, "Ironically, the Cornell black revolt is linked to Perkins' arrival at the university's helm."[13] Perkins recalled that when he came to Cornell in 1963,

> there was an average of six or seven black students per class, or only about 25 out of a total enrollment of 11,000. That had been going on for decades, and I suspected it was not an accident—that there was a quiet quota. I later discovered there was no quota, but neither was there an affirmative interest in increasing that number; and in this area, where there are few Negroes without a special recruiting effort that's the kind of situation you get.[14]

Perkins' idea of "a special recruiting effort"—with the aid of a $250,000 grant from the Rockefeller Foundation—was to bring to Cornell disadvantaged black students whose SAT (Scholastic Aptitude Test) scores averaged only 450 to 550. The average scores for white students at Cornell were between 600 and 700. Perkins attempted to justify the procedure by stating, "It wasn't that we didn't substitute anything for these deficiencies. We put great reliance on personal interviews and visits with these students, as well as on what their principals and teachers said the students were capable of doing."[15] Of course, no matter how he and his academic allies rationalized the process—including the now-hoary chestnut about intelligence and aptitude tests conforming to "white middle-class values"—the fact still remained that whites were compelled to score some 150 to 200 points higher than ghetto students in order to be admitted to Cornell. Many black students were admitted under the Committee on Special Educational Projects (COSEP), an expanded recruiting guidance and counseling program administered by Dr. Gloria Joseph, a black sociologist who was a Cornell assistant dean of student affairs. By September 1968 there were 240 blacks at Cornell. "In about five years' time," predicted Perkins, "we will have gone from a total enrollment of 25 Black students to somewhere around 400,"[16] and it soon became evident that the same program that served as an open door to bring some blacks in became a wall to keep some whites out.

Alumni, and particularly alumni secondary school interviewers, became infuriated when good white students from their local schools were not offered admission to Cornell but black students with much less impressive records were.[17] One dean conceded that "there's no doubt we're bending things for the blacks"—but they were obviously not "bending things" for blacks of proven scholastic ability. Quite the contrary. The trustees were told more than once that "middle-class blacks do not belong at Cornell."[18]

Of the thirty-seven blacks who enrolled in 1965 as the first COSEP group, only two had left for academic reasons. Twenty-five graduated in June 1969, and as of that date, six others were still in good standing at Cornell.[19] But the trustees were told "by some" that these reports were suspect for two reasons:

1) Some professors, for whatever reason, had tended to mark black students easier than they did whites;
2) Some blacks with poor academic performances were being kept in Cornell longer than whites with similar records would have been.[20]

The trustees found "no official evidence to prove these charges,"[21] leading one to wonder if they had found some *unofficial* evidence proving the charges valid.

But a number of black students saw it all quite differently, through rage-colored glasses. More than simply unwilling to regard Perkins as the Great White Father, they regarded themselves as liberal window dressing. As one Negro Cornellian remarked, "They brought us here for their benefit—to integrate the place. This is Cornell, the great liberal campus in the East. And you can't be liberal without Negroes."[22]

As early as April 4, 1968, there were storm warnings of the racial tornado hovering over the campus. On that date, 60 students, most of them Negro, seized control of the Economics Department office and held the department chairman virtually captive for seven hours to protest "racist" remarks by a visiting professor. They charged that the Reverend Michael McPhelin, a Jesuit priest, had stressed the achievements of white, Western peoples, and downgraded non-whites. They were particularly incensed by his statement in a lecture that slum youths "play sickly and perverted games stressing cunning and survival as in the jungle." Father McPhelin insisted he had intended no racial slur.[23]

It was of course quite possible to question the appropriateness of Father McPhelin's remarks on grounds of relevancy and academic soundness, and still condemn the tactics of harassment and intimidation used by black militants after they had wearied of less martial forms of protest.

Blacks were threatened by whites. Soon certain white fraternities were getting threats from blacks. Blacks who associated with whites on campus were being subjected to strong pressure to separate into an all-black life with others in the Afro-American Society. Several blacks dropped out of school.[24]

As for those 60 black students who had held the chairman of the Economics Department captive in his own office, there was no punishment, no penalty, no reprimand. Given the rampant permissiveness of Cornell University, it was not terribly difficult to predict the outcome. All 60 black students were granted amnesty[25]—a none too subtle way of guaranteeing that white guilt and paternalism in high places would always come groveling to the rescue of black militants, even if it meant accepting the most flagrant indignities.

In 1967, Cornell University's Board of Trustees approved a series of sweeping resolutions banning racial and religious discrimination in sororities and fraternities on campus. In 1968, a group of black women were demanding the right to ban racial integration—demanding the establishment of a black women's cooperative to house some 10 to 15 black students.[26] The cooperative, which was to include a black cultural center, was endorsed by the Faculty Committee on Student Affairs on April 19, 1968, at the request of the Afro-American Society (AAS).[27] Members of the all-Negro student society contended that the atmosphere in the dormitories was "hostile" and "threatening."[28] Of course, one scarcely has to ponder for long what the decision of the Faculty Committee on Student Affairs would have been if other students had demanded a *white* women's cooperative.

Cornell officials explained that the black co-op would be open to any disadvantaged students admitted to the university through COSEP. The Cornell student chapter of the American Civil Liberties Union felt that the legality of the co-op was "open to considerable question," and might be challenged by an individual or the New York Civil Liberties Union if such action seemed appropriate. As Ira Glasser, the associate director of the New York Civil Liberties Union, saw it, if the black cooperative was formed "on behalf of the pressure of a black student group, it could be done tomorrow on the pressure of the K.K.K. or a German-speaking group or anyone else, and it would be no more unjustified."[29]

Equally "open to considerable question" were the black studies courses that the Afro-American Society urged be open only to black students, "because in this field we're so far ahead of whites they'd only hold us back."[30]

In September 1968 Cornell set up a committee of eight faculty members and seven students from the Afro-American Society to outline a black studies program. The university pledged to initiate an Afro-American studies course by the fall of 1969, and in what was then an unprecedented move, Cornell accepted nominations by the black students for the post of program director.[31]

Two months later, "the brothers" had a falling-out. In a dis-

pute within the Afro-American Society, one faction headed by
Earl Armstrong (then the group's president) was challenged by
the society's vice president, Marshall John Garner. The Garner
group charged that the Armstrong faction was too much in the
pocket of the college administration, and argued that the only
meaningful black studies program was one entirely under the
control of blacks.[32]

In December 1968 a student-faculty committee meeting was
convened to interview a candidate for the directorship of the
Afro-American studies program. Suddenly, 40 or more members of the Afro-American Society entered the room and announced that the blacks on the committee were no longer
authorized to represent their group, and that the committee
itself no longer had the sanction of the society. Marshall John
Garner told Professor Bradford Morse, acting director of the
program, that the invading students were the newly elected
operating committee of the studies program, "the Afro-American Institute." The black studies program, they said, was to be
an autonomous program, run entirely by blacks. Garner led the
black students in a vote on whether they wanted any white
representation in their group. They unanimously voted no.[33]

That same day, six black students entered a Cornell-owned
building that had been requested by the Afro-American studies
program. The blacks told the three persons in the building at
the time that they had "three minutes to leave." The three, all
of them white, left. Thereupon, the six black students placed on
the door a note proclaiming that, as of noon Saturday (the following day), the building was to be restricted to members of the
Afro-American Institute. Among those meekly acquiescing in
the decision were faculty members with offices in the building;
they cleared out their records and equipment in the building
Saturday morning.[34]

A group of black students came to President Perkins' office
for a session that Perkins described as "semi-polite." In Perkins' words: "I just explained to them that the setting up of an
autonomous black college granting its own degrees was impossible. The Afro-American studies program, the headquarters
for it, the taking on of a black director for it, the hiring of more
black professors [there were then fewer than a dozen blacks
among Cornell's 2,200 faculty members], the employment of a

black psychiatrist—which some students wanted—were all things we *were* willing to do, but an autonomous black college was out of the question."[35]

In December 1968, groups of blacks marched around the quadrangles playing bongo drums, while another contingent entered the president's office with water pistols. There was a wild melee in a dining hall, as blacks walked on the tables during a meal. They pushed white students away from several tables in the student union and claimed them for themselves as "black tables." A group of blacks carried hundreds of books from the library shelves to the checkout counters, and dumped them there as "irrelevant."[36] One thousand white students signed a letter of protest, but no immediate disciplinary action was taken.[37]

The "demonstrations" were in support of demands that included the establishment of an autonomous college of Afro-American studies at Cornell. The proposed college was to be run by a committee of black students who would have total power to hire and dismiss faculty members, allocate its budget, devise courses for credit, and control admissions. Asked his personal opinion of the black proposal, Perkins replied that he was "unable to feel it's a good thing for Cornell to have a college exclusively for members of one race. I've fought too hard on the other side of that game."[38]

In January 1969 Cornell agreed to establish an Afro-American studies center, and set aside $175,000 for it. But there were two sharply differing schools of thought about what the center would be. The black students wanted the center to be a degree-granting institution with a director able to choose his own staff independent of the university's department heads. On the other hand, the university administration specified that the center would *not* be a degree-granting unit. Its students would continue to be enrolled in one of the schools or colleges of Cornell, and while the center could offer courses for credit, it would be up to the divisions of the university to determine whether the credits were acceptable.[39]

In February, the relatively moderate president of the Afro-American Society, Earl Armstrong, was replaced by a much more militant "chairman," Ed Whitfield.[40] That same month, some 500 students and faculty members attended a meeting to discuss Cornell's investments in banks that provided money for South Africa. Dr. Perkins began to address the group about this issue, saying, "I doubt if I'll satisfy you, but I'll do my best." While the president was saying that the Board of Trustees' investment policies used to be carried out "without any reference to campus or social policies," a black student, Gary Patton, standing on the stage several feet behind him, advanced, and gripped Perkins' shoulder. Perkins turned, a look of surprise on his face. The audience gasped while half a dozen Negroes, sitting in a group of about 30 in a front row, began beating on drums.

As quickly as he had grabbed Perkins, Patton released him. Without a word, the university president turned and walked out. The administration said it would discipline Patton, but he left Cornell before any action was taken.[41]

Dr. Donald Kagan, professor of ancient history at Cornell, was critical of the administration "for not being honest and above board" in its handling of the whole affair. Kagan recalled a meeting where

> we were asked to approve two courses in which we all understood the students would be black. It was not spelled out, but we all understood what we were being asked to agree to. I opposed [it] but was outvoted 5 to 1, and the black students went away thinking that the courses would be segregated. Later, the university backed out on that one and when the classes were actually held, they were not all-black. The black students felt, understandably, that they had been double-crossed. I felt they should have been told in the beginning, "No, we are not going to do it."

At first, Kagan had opposed a black co-op for girls,

> but I've changed my position on that. I now feel that some blacks will feel so uncomfortable and so alienated in communities so different from what they've ever known as to interfere with their education possibilities. I'm prepared to bend all kinds of feelings to avoid that. . . . There's a Young Israel House, and all these Jewish kids observing the same dietary laws live together. . . . It also seems necessary for some people to live in these stupid fraternities. We aren't moving on *that,* so a black co-op is understandable in view of all the other stupid things we do.[42]

Kagan's analysis was not terribly convincing. The fraternities, at that point in Cornellian history, were under orders to integrate, and most of them did: most, in fact, have one or two Negro members. As for the Young Israel House, it was simply exercising the same freedom of association allowed other religious groups. Only a black group, it seemed, had the right to segregate *qua* blacks—a right, which, quite expressly and emphatically, would have been forbidden a white group *qua* whites.

Kagan was on much firmer ground, in his critique of Perkins' performance as president. Kagan said of Perkins:

> I think he is handicapped in the same way that most whites are handicapped—they have never known any black people *as people*. I consider myself less handicapped than my colleagues. I grew up in a ghetto, in Brooklyn's Brownsville, and I went to a junior high school that was 55 percent black. I was in classes with black kids. I played basketball with black kids, and although blacks and whites rarely get to the point where they can call each other *friends*, by God, I had daily contact with black people up until the time I was 18 years old. And I happen to know things that my colleagues here don't know. I know black people are *people*, which implies that they can be bastards too. They can be smart and dumb, they can be pushing improperly or they can have a legitimate demand. I don't think Perkins has that kind of experience. He's flawed, like most whites, in his capacity to understand these things.[43]

A month before the "guns of April," the Cornell police began working extra hours to strengthen campus patrols, following an assault on a student. Joel H. Klotz remained in serious condition at Arnot-Ogden Memorial Hospital in Elmira, New York, with head injuries suffered in a beating on the campus. Klotz was one of three white students attacked in a single weekend. Two of the youths said their assailants were Negroes.[44] After the beating of the three white students, threatening phone calls increased against both blacks and whites.[45] One of the twelve black women living at the housing co-op (Wari House) was Muriel Hall, who claimed that there were constant, almost daily, phoned bomb threats and insults, as well as rocks that were hurled through the windows.[46]

Dr. Gloria Joseph, black assistant dean of student affairs, was quoted in *Life* as saying:

> Black girls are constantly being harassed and taunted. Last week several of our girls were chased across campus by white male pranksters. The girls live in fear and I don't think it's an exaggeration. Sometimes when I step out of my car—and I'm no young girl—a car of whites will pull over, act real brave and yell something at me like "nigger gal."[47]

Even if every single allegation of white threats against blacks were true, it was exceptionally difficult to find cases that went beyond verbal mutterings into the area of physical assault. Harry Edwards and other militants swore that black women had been attacked, but the police said the attacks were never verified.[48] About the worst that could be said was that there were some bigots on the Cornell campus—just as there are some bigots in the larger society—but who they were, what they had specifically done, and whether they represented more than a tiny percentage of the Cornell undergraduate body, were questions that remained unanswered. And like the ancient saw about the chicken and the egg, it would have been most instructive trying to determine which came first: the fierce, contemptuous hostility—if not hatred—of a small number of violence-prone black students, or the name-calling and telephoned threats of a small number of whites.

About three weeks before the racial avalanche, one member of the Afro-American Society bought $50 worth of ammunition in Ithaca—about the same time the trustees were voting to create a center for Afro-American studies at Cornell to open in the fall of 1969.[49]

On April 13, a week *before* the building seizure, the Cornell trustees agreed to most of the black demands for an autonomous program of black studies. Specifically, the Board of Trustees established a center for Afro-American studies, and allocated $240,000 for its first year of operation. Slated to move into full operation in the fall, the center was expected to develop an undergraduate major in Afro-American studies and a program of graduate study and research.[50]

Also about this time, 60 offers of admission to the Cornell Graduate School had been sent to black applicants—representing three times the number of black graduate students then enrolled. W. Donald Cooke, dean of the graduate school, said, "We didn't have the number of [black] applicants we would like," and acknowledged that "currently enrolled black graduate students were very helpful in increasing applications." The black recruiters made it very clear that to get the number of applications *they* would like, Cornell would have to "bend" considerably on graduate record exam scores and grades as criteria for acceptance. Condemning what he called "the implicit racism in this school," one of these recruiters, black grad Cleveland Donald Jr., suggested "interviews [of applicants] by blacks who have this awareness of the black community" as a possible means of seeking the students who want to make "some contribution to the black community."[51]

How did white students feel about all this? Quite obviously, the university didn't know, and didn't want to know. Stan Chess, then the editor of the campus newspaper, the *Cornell Daily Sun,* said, "A lot of people here feel that the university is disregarding white students in its dealings with the blacks, and that much of what the administration does is being done under an implicit threat by the black students."[52]

Equally damning, the university was disregarding black moderates, and their urgent storm warnings, as well. Before the black militant blitzkrieg, moderate blacks were privately complaining to faculty members that they were under increasing pressure from 30 to 40 activists in the Afro-American Society. One black student said in the presence of three professors that he had attended meetings of the society where blacks were told to "prepare for the great black revolution." Black coeds, he said, were instructed to harbor wounded blacks, dress their wounds, and hide the fugitives from police.

The moderate black student said, "I was told that the only way I could be a good black was to be a flaming revolutionary, and that violence was essential to our survival."

At first, the moderate student dismissed all the talk of violence as revolutionary rhetoric. He added that he "didn't realize its full impact until the seizure of Willard Straight Hall."[53]

Every seizure must have a pretext, and one of the pretexts for seizure of Willard Straight Hall was the "trial" of six members of the Afro-American Society before the student-faculty conduct board. The word *trial* is enclosed in quotes, because the defendants refused two requests to appear. The proceedings grew out of the raucous black militant demonstrations of the preceding December. On one occasion, the blacks were verbally threatened with suspension if they didn't appear. When they didn't show up, letters were sent. The blacks challenged the board's composition, because it was all-white;[54] in reply, university spokesmen pointed out that extensive efforts to get black students to serve on it were rebuffed.[55] The black militants claimed that the December demonstrations had been political acts for which the entire AAS organization should be held responsible, and that singling out six members for trial represented victimization[56] (this may have been a valid plea to put more of the guilty on trial, but was hardly justification for letting some of the guilty go free). Further, the black militants argued that the university was not only the aggrieved party but the judge and jury as well—a somewhat specious argument, in view of the fact that the conduct board was dominated by faculty and students, rather than by the administration hierarchy.[57]

On April 18, 1969, the Cornell Student-Faculty Board on Student Conduct decided to give reprimands to three black students charged with Student Code violations, and no penalties to two other students. The sixth student was on a leave of absence from the university. About the mildest conceivable punishment, a reprimand merely involved letters to one's parents and dean.[58]

Less than an hour after the student-faculty board meted out the reprimands, a cross was burned on the doorstep of Wari House, the black women's cooperative at Cornell. In all, some eleven false alarms were set off in various campus buildings. Five campus call boxes were pulled and there were two telephoned bomb threats. In one incident, an alarm box in University Hall, a men's dormitory, was ripped out of the wall. Eugene J. Dymek, director of the university's Division of Safety and Security, said that he had put some members of his 30-man police force on extra duty and that the Ithaca Police Department was also patrolling the campus.[59]

Charisse Kannady, a black senior living in Wari House, gave this account of the cross-burning:

> I looked out of the window and saw a glow on the front porch. I went to the front door of the house and saw a burning cross on the front steps. Because of this we were afraid to go outside and I told the girls to go into the kitchen and lie on the floor.

Miss Kannady pulled the fire alarm and telephoned the campus police. The campus police and Ithaca Detective Edward Traynor arrived within minutes. Traynor kicked over the smoldering cross. But then the police left, without questioning the occupants of Wari House. Miss Kannady recalled, "We were considerably upset, because they had not . . . left protection at the building, which we felt was necessary." She called the dean of students' office and about an hour later she was informed that a campus patrolman was stationed at Wari House.[60] Evidently, Miss Kannady could not, or would not, accept the explanation that eleven false alarms on campus between 1:43 and 5:08 a.m. could conceivably delay police inquiries and protection.

To this day, no one knows who burned that cross in front of Wari House. Most outsiders seemed positive it was the work of whites, but could anyone really be that certain? If white students were involved, why would they have turned in almost a dozen false alarms as well? Why would they have ripped an alarm box out of a men's dormitory in University Hall having no connection with the Afro-American Society? Why would white students have set a false alarm that drove several hundred people into a chilly rain from Willard Straight Hall—including some of the parents gathered there for parents' weekend?[61]

Why, after the last false alarm, were half a dozen black students picked up for questioning, albeit released?[62] There were just too many questions, and few, if any, answers. Rowland Evans and Robert Novak reported from Cornell that "the burning cross which supposedly forced black militants into armed insurrection is widely believed here to have been set by Negroes themselves."[63]

The embattled blacks projected to the campus and black community—if not the country—the image of a university almost brutally insensitive to the fears of the coeds after the cross-burning outside Wari House. The Afro-American Society stated, "The campus authorities left the scene of the crime after having examined the evidence, but did not return until 1½ hours later. They made no effort to secure protection of these 12 Black women despite the very serious nature of such a threat. At this point we became very aware of the level of concern and respect that the University held for Black lives on this campus."[64]

This is the image–and a little thing like the truth is hard put to shatter it. But a report of the Special Trustee Committee on Campus Unrest gave it the good old college try. These were the facts, taken from the official records:

> [At Wari House] Miss Charisse Kannady, a senior and head resident there, was awakened by a brick thrown at a window in her bedroom on the ground floor of this frame house. She quickly went to the window and saw a burning cross on the front porch steps. At 2:53 A.M. she pulled the fire alarm in that building. . . . Police from three sources were promptly at the scene: City of Ithaca, Cornell Safety Division, and Cayuga Heights. A city detective who was patrolling nearby reached the scene almost immediately, found the cross burning on the steps, and removed it to the front yard. He and a Cornell Campus patrolman smothered the fire. *This police action took only about four minutes from the time Miss Kannady turned in the alarm at 2:53 A.M.*[65] [Emphasis added]

A response time of four minutes is hardly the author's idea of administration apathy or police brutality.

How long did it take to have a policeman stationed outside Wari House? Again, quoting from the report of the special trustee committee:

> According to the Safety Division Records, at 3:30 A.M., *less than a half hour after the cross burning was first discovered,* a campus patrolman returned to 208 Dearborn Place (Wari House) and remained there until 3:40 A.M., when he was relieved by another campus patrolman who policed the premises until morning.[66]

Nor were the campus policemen slow to investigate the cross-burning. In the words of the report of the special trustee committee,

> At approximately 5:30 A.M., with the first light of day, two men from the Safety and Security Division went to 208 Dearborn Place (Wari House) and took pictures of the window which had been broken, of the steps where the cross had been burning, and of some footprints which were found outside. The cross itself was about 6 feet long and 3 feet wide and had been wrapped in white cloth, which had not been completely burned. It was later determined that the wood came from the Campus Store, being sold there frequently for use in art courses.

This paragraph in the report (dated September 5, 1969) ends with a most intriguing sentence: "There is no *official* knowledge of who may have been responsible for the cross-burning"[67] (emphasis added). This curious phraseology can only leave one wondering whether this is an oblique intimation that there is some unofficial knowledge—some informal indications—of the person or persons, black or white, who set this fire.

What happened next? According to the statement of the Afro-American Society's chairman, Edward Whitfield, the black invaders who seized Willard Straight Hall were so many doves of peace, occupying the building with an Old World Alphonse and Gaston courtesy. To quote from the Afro-American Society statement in *Muhammad Speaks:*

> On Saturday, April 19th, the Afro-American Society (subsequently renamed the Black Liberation Front) began its occupation of Willard Straight Hall, the Student Union building at Cornell University. We entered the building at approximately 5:30 A.M., and proceeded to secure our position there. This action included asking the workers and parents (there for the annual parents' weekend) to leave. They responded quite agreeably and left the building a few minutes later. There was absolutely no form of physical coercion employed. The atmosphere in which the parents and workers left was a peaceful one.[68]

But the *New York Times* had quite a different story to tell:

About 100 black students at Cornell University staged a surprise raid on the student union building at dawn today. They ran through the halls, shouting "Fire!" and pounding on doors, and ousted 30 sleeping parents from guest rooms.[69]

The *New York Times* reported that the black invaders ordered the parents and about 40 university employees to leave the building—that after hurriedly throwing on clothes, the parents and employees were herded into a basement room, and then out on a loading platform.[70]

And the *Cornell Alumni News* reported:

[The black students] walked into Willard Straight Hall shortly before 6 a.m. Saturday, April 19, and gave its occupants ten minutes to leave. . . . Eleven of seventeen doors were broken through when occupants were slow in responding.[71]

That cold Saturday morning, Les Hutchinson, a black disc jockey on WVBR, the Willard Straight–based campus radio station, handed over the microphone to AAS Chairman Whitfield for "a message of political relevance." Whitfield announced that the Afro-American Society had occupied Willard Straight Hall. He said they were demanding a nullification of the reprimands given the three black students, and amnesty for those participating in the seizure. Whitfield then signed off.[72]

The black students vowed not to leave the student union building until the university declared the judicial proceedings against the black student demonstrators "null and void," reopened negotiations on a disputed urban renewal project in Ithaca, and started a "full and thorough" investigation of the cross-burning at Wari House.[73]

Afro-American Society Chairman Ed Whitfield stated, *"The immediate issue which crystallized Black student action was the cross-burning incident"* (emphasis added).

And yet, in the very same article in *Muhammad Speaks,* the Afro-American Society categorically declared that in seizing the building,

*our only intention* was (1) to re-raise the issues of the
illegitimacy of the faculty-student judicial board and (2) to
leave the building when the University had admitted its
mistake and changed its position regarding this judicial
issue.[74] [Emphasis added]

Here no mention is made of the cross-burning at all.

The point is of considerable interest because it sheds some
light on the question: was the black seizure of Willard Straight
Hall a spontaneous act of students goaded by the cross-burning
and the desire to protect black women, or had this seizure been
planned well in advance? The burning cross was discovered
less than three hours before the takeover of Willard Straight
Hall and some members of the administration simply did not
believe that this incident was motivation for the seizure, which
they believed had been planned long before.[75] Strong corrobora-
tion for this view came from Howard Rodman, a member of the
editorial board of the *Cornell Daily Sun:*

> The occupation of Straight by 100-odd blacks had immedi-
> ate repercussions. The first group to react was SDS, whose
> leaders had met with AAS representatives *the preceding
> week when the action was planned. Armed with this fore-
> sight,* SDS had scheduled a meeting for 6 A.M. Saturday.[76]
> [Emphasis added]

Among those originally entering the building, a group of
blacks carried a large supply of wire, chains, and rope with
which to secure the entrances to the building.[77] Quite obviously,
these were scarcely the type of items one secured on the spur
of the moment, at 4:30 or 5:00 in the morning. The extensive
preparations of the blacks even included intercom equipment,
enabling them to talk to observers outside, whom they had
placed in strategic locations on the campus.[78]

About a dozen white students, led by members of the DU
(Delta Upsilon Fraternity), attempted a counterinvasion of
Willard Straight Hall later in the morning. What happened?
Here is Whitfield's version of the incident:

> ... about 12 fraternity boys from Delta Upsilon broke into
> the building through the campus radio station office and
> proceeded upstairs at which point they were asked to

leave the building. They refused and proceeded to assault several people (including some Black women). They were armed with sticks and crowbars. After the scuffle, one brother had been wounded.[79]

In a separate reply, a letter to the *Cornell Daily Sun* from a member of Delta Upsilon (the writer's name was withheld by request) stated that the white students "did *not* come armed or with any intention of assaulting or harassing blacks." With the white students outnumbered about 4 to 1, the fraternity member went on, "it is absurd to suggest that a handful of whites seriously considered taking on a multitude of blacks." The writer also insisted that *"no* assault on a black woman was made."[80]

But perhaps for the final word about who were the assailants, and who were the assaulted, one found the most definitive answer in the campus hospital, where four students were treated for minor injuries sustained in the fighting. Of this group, three were whites and one was black.[81]

A fact that was little known at the time was that by now, with administration approval, Willard Straight Hall had become a no-man's land for white students. Shortly after the seizure, Eugene Dymek, Cornell's director of safety and security, made a shocking decision: the blacks were to be free to enter and leave Willard Straight Hall at will, but whites were to be barred from entry.[82] His decision was based upon an experience that had occurred almost a year before, when two campus policemen were knocked to the floor by blacks after trying to prevent some of them from entering an office already occupied by black students.[83] And now in 1969, Dymek was, in effect, *guaranteeing* black occupancy of Willard Straight Hall, *protecting* the black militants from a counterinvasion, and putting any and all white students daring to enter the building in the category of trespassers. Whether or not he realized the consequences of his decision, Dymek had made himself and his staff *de facto* allies of the black militant invaders, for no other reason than fear of a confrontation with the Afro-American Society and its supporters. An even more fateful consequence was that his decision made it possible for black militants to bring guns into the building, without even the formality of a challenge.

The black seizure of the building forced President Perkins to cancel a convocation speech he had scheduled for 9:00 a.m. The topic was to have been, "The Stability of the University."[84]

An angry meeting of fraternity men took place in the freshmen student union building. "We're getting tired of them getting everything they want and doing everything they damn please," shouted one student during the meeting. After several university officials urged calm, the meeting voted to ask the administration to seek a court injunction against the occupation of Willard Straight Hall.[85]

Shortly after noon, Elmer Meyer, Jr., dean of students, came to the rear door of the occupied building to tell the black students that a sizable group of white students was gathering to try to force them out of Straight, but that the administration could prevent any such attempt. Meyer recalled, "I said to Ed [Whitfield] that we've got the hotheads under control."[86]

This single sentence spoke volumes about the paralysis of will at Cornell University; to the administration, the villains of the piece—the hotheads—were those students who wanted to oust the black invaders from a building they had no legal right to occupy. And few administrators seemed discomfited by the black invader who shouted through a window, "If any more whites come in . . . you're gonna die here." If others entered, the black militant promised "a reign of terror like you've never seen."[87]

Whitfield stated that the Afro-American Society received reports that Delta Upsilon had organized over 100 armed fraternity boys to evict the black invaders forcibly from the building. He added, "We later learned that 8 carloads of fraternity boys were armed with rifles and shotguns and were on their way over to the building."[88] Presumably, all eight cars simultaneously broke down along the way. In any event, none of these cars, if any existed, was ever seen near Willard Straight Hall; the safety division confirmed that there was such a rumor but could find no substance behind it.[89]

Using the rumors, gossip, and "reports" as their justification, the black militants asked that arms be brought in for their protection. The decision was made at a meeting of the "tactics committee" shortly after 8:30 p.m. "That decision didn't take long," said Whitfield. "What else could we do?"[90] What they could have done, of course, was to leave the building they had illegally seized.

Cornell's vice president for public affairs, Steven Muller, said the campus policemen were *ordered* to allow the arms to enter Willard Straight Hall, because if they had attempted to stop the arms, "we would have found ourselves in a position where we would have been open to the possibility of scuffling or incidents around the periphery."[91]

Why didn't Cornell University seek an injunction against those blacks who had seized the building? The report of the special trustee committee offered this analysis:

> If, on Saturday, the University had applied for a court injunction, and if that order made by a Justice of the Supreme Court of the State of New York was not sufficient to move the blacks from the building, then the students would be in contempt and the court would be forced to act. Control of the situation would have moved into the hands of the law and completely out of the hands of the Administration. It would be up to the court to order the city police and deputy sheriffs to move in and arrest the blacks.
>
> With strong sympathy for the blacks being clearly demonstrated outside by the SDS members, as well as by hundreds of concerned moderates, the group outside and the blacks inside would make a formidable foe. The prospects of serious injury on both sides would be real.
>
> The Administration chose to have the blacks remain inside Saturday night rather than face the potential of violence. Hopefully, if the campus calmed down on Sunday, they might be able to talk them out of the building that day without any large concessions.
>
> Unfortunately the growing fear of the blacks waiting inside Willard Straight drove them on Saturday to bring in arms for their own protection. A court injunction on Sunday, not honored by the blacks, would force the judge to use police and deputies to try to dislodge the blacks. This would have to be a last resort, knowing that those inside were armed with guns and ammunition. Certainly no man in a position of responsibility wanted bloodshed on the Cornell campus.[92]

In tones of sweet reasonableness, the trustees report reaffirmed that violence works, and that the mere threat of violence would be enough to bring a once-great university to its knees. Certainly, the trustees report could scarcely have made a more absurd assertion than the statement, "Control of the situation would have moved into the hands of the law and completely out of the hands of the Administration." The tragedy was that the administration had never had the slightest control of the situation at all.

Playing both ends against the middle, President Perkins rejected the idea of an injunction, fearing it would lead to violence, but later pooh-poohed student and faculty fears that the black militants might have used those guns. Perkins categorically stated, "At no time did the black students threaten to use their weapons against either the negotiators or others on campus."[93] And yet Whitfield told *Muhammad Speaks:* "The truth was that we were very serious about why we had guns in there. People keep asking us silly questions like 'would we have used them?' We didn't bring them in to play with them. I don't like to play with guns. If we had to pull the trigger, I'm sure we would have."[94] And during their occupation of Willard Straight, some blacks had written on the walls, "Kill the fraternity honkies."[95]

Mike Thelwell, a militant black writer who joined the faculty as a resident fellow, commented, "This is hunting country. There have always been guns on this campus, guns in the hands of the ROTC, guns in the hands of the white police, guns in the hands of the fraternity boys. Guns on campus is nothing new; what was new, and shocking to the whites, was the sight of guns in the hands of black students."[96]

Possibly some whites reacted as Professor Thelwell suggested, for just the reasons he indicated. But it seems much more probable that many whites were shocked, not simply because blacks possessed guns, but because these black militants threatened to use them on their fellow students.

To anyone who had followed his unsavory record at San Jose State, it was not surprising that Harry Edwards was among those who advised the black students to arm themselves. At one point, Edwards said to the blacks in Willard Straight Hall, "If the University tries to use force, you go home and arm yourselves and we'll come back and take this place over."[97]

Vice Provost Keith Kennedy tried to persuade the blacks to leave the building and offered to bring buses around to take them home. The offer was refused. He then asked Whitfield to bring the guns out and put them in the trunk of Kennedy's car. This, too was rejected.[98]

At a Sunday meeting with President Perkins and some members of his executive staff, the dean of the faculty, Robert D. Miller, suggested that he call a meeting of the Cornell faculty on Monday and recommend nullifications of the judiciary decisions against the blacks, provided the blacks left Willard Straight Hall immediately. In a phone conversation with Whitfield, Miller stated that if the faculty refused to nullify the reprimands, he would resign as dean.[99]

At 12:00 noon, Steven Muller and Keith Kennedy left for Willard Straight. After 30 to 40 minutes of discussion with the blacks, they left, and Muller had the main points of agreement typed up. They returned to Willard Straight Hall shortly after 3:00 p.m. and brought up the subject of the guns. Muller and Kennedy asked that the guns be left behind, but Whifield insisted that they were needed for protection. After considerable discussion it was agreed that the blacks were to leave with their guns, unloaded, and breeches open.[100]

About an hour later, Supervisor of Public Safety Lowell T. George directed the eleven uniformed campus patrolmen and two plainclothesmen to clear a path in front of Straight. They were aided by SDS members who took up positions on the front lines.

The policemen then re-formed in two lines in front of Straight. Then around 4:10 p.m., like a conquering army, 110 blacks left the building, led by two Afro-American Society members, Edward Whitfield and Eric Evans, who were armed with rifles. The rest of the group filed out of the building, followed by Kennedy and Muller.[101]

Fifteen Black students with rifles were deployed throughout the group, and two carried homemade spears. One of the rifles was equipped with a telescopic sight. Although the breeches were open in the rifles, two of the students wore bandoliers with live ammunition. Reporters said they saw bullets in several of the blacks' guns.[102]

The evacuation was a success—but that day part of Cornell died.

The blacks marched to 320 Wait Avenue, headquarters of the

Afro-American Society. Kennedy and Muller spoke briefly with Whitfield at the bottom of the steps, and then continued the discussion inside. Then the three came down to the bottom of the steps where they signed the agreement that ended the occupation of Willard Straight.[103]

This was the pact that they signed:

### AGREEMENT BETWEEN THE AAS AND CORNELL RELATING TO BLACK STUDENT DEPARTURE FROM WILLARD STRAIGHT HALL

PART I      In a meeting to be held 21 April 1969 the Dean of the Cornell Faculty, Robert D. Miller, will recommend to the full faculty that the judicial procedures taken against the five students as a result of incidents last December and January be nullified by action of the full faculty.

PART II      The University promises best efforts to secure legal assistance to defend against any civil actions arising out of the occupation of Willard Straight by the AAS. Such efforts will be made on behalf of individuals or the group.

PART III      The University will press no civil or criminal charges, or take any measure to punish by means of expulsion or otherwise activities of the AAS involved in occupation of WSH. The University will assume all responsibility for damages to WSH. [Damage to Willard Straight Hall was later estimated at approximately $10,800.]

PART IV      The University will provide 24 hour protection for 208 Dearborn Place (Women's Co-op) and 320 Wait, with men assigned this task at all times.

PART V      The University undertakes to investigate thoroughly police activities related to both the burning of the cross incident and the attack on Willard Straight Hall by unknown individuals. A detailed report will be issued to the AAS and made public *including identities of those involved.* [Emphasis added]

PART VI      The AAS has discontinued the occupation of Willard Straight Hall.

PART VII      The AAS undertakes to cooperate in devising a new judiciary system to promote justice on

Cornell's campus for all members of the student body.

Signed on 20 April 1969

For the AAS                               For the University

Ed Whitfield                              Steven Muller
Chairman                                  Vice President

Zachary W. Carter                         W. K. Kennedy
Vice Chairman                             Vice Provost[104]

Later, Muller said, "It was a choice of surrender or extinction," adding that "all other solutions took time. We didn't have any time, not days, not hours, but minutes, only minutes."[105] But the statement came with ill grace from an administration that from the very first had rebuffed all efforts to use the police or the courts, and now bemoaned the fact that it was defenseless.

A statement by the Afro-American Society emphasized that in evacuating Willard Straight Hall, "we only leave now with the understanding that the University will move fairly to carry out its part of the agreement that was reached. Failure on the part of the University to do so may force us to again confront the University in some manner."[106]

It was fear that signed the agreement with the blacks—just as it was fear that wrote the editorial in the *Cornell Daily Sun* urging that the faculty nullify the judicial proceedings against the black students. To be sure, attempts were made to coat it all over with a veneer of reasoned analysis and lofty discussion. But the last paragraph of the editorial gave it all away.

Acceptance of the proposal will hopefully lead to the construction of a viable judicial structure as well as serve as a gesture of good faith that may mollify the suspicions of black students. Rejection of the proposal may lead to bloodshed, and the judicial system, frankly, is not worth anyone's dying over.[107]

The grim equation could hardly have been clearer, and could hardly fail to be used time and time again, whenever and wherever needed, on countless campuses: black militants + threat of bloodshed = capitulation by university. Or as Malcolm X had so often exhorted his followers: by any means necessary!

But not everyone caved in before the threat of black militant aggression. Writing in the *Cornell Daily Sun,* Paul A. Rahe, Jr., delivered this scathing critique:

> Little need be said about yesterday. In short, Cornell's administration in the face of a violent takeover of a University building, the harassment of the University's guests, and implicit threats in the form of firearms of a hitherto unimaginable degree of violence, accepted the tyranny of a small minority enraged over slaps on the wrist given to a few members of that minority for intimidating members of this community. In short, Cornell's administration implicitly agreed that violence is a legitimate method of seeking change in this community and has proceeded to encourage the use of such violence.

Rahe was equally incensed about the administration's agreement to reveal to the Afro-American Society the names of the white athletes who had attempted to gain entrance to Willard Straight Hall, *"an act which is a breach of University policy concerning identifying those involved in student conduct proceedings, an act which may spell great danger for the individuals involved."*

Rahe entertained no illusions about the outcome of the faculty vote:

> The results of a rejection of the black demands are all too clear. Violence would return immediately to the Cornell campus; but reason, not violence would rule. The results of an acceptance of the demands is also all too clear. Violence would not return immediately; but it would return— and return soon.

There was not the slightest question in Rahe's mind that acceptance was, by far, the greater of the two evils:

> Faculty acceptance of that agreement would be a betrayal of this community; a betrayal of those black students unwilling to cooperate with the militants, of those black students who have been the object of substantial in-

timidation; a betrayal of those professors teaching politically sensitive material who since last year's economics office sit-in have grown more and more afraid to speak out; a betrayal of the entire concept of academic freedom and integrity; and an unforgettable betrayal of this student body.[108]

For one brief, dizzying moment, Perkins acted firmly and decisively. The headline in the *Cornell Daily Sun* read, "PERKINS TAKES ACTION FOR CAMPUS SECURITY." Declaring "a situation of emergency" on the campus, President Perkins said that effective immediately, students with firearms in their possession outside of their own rooms would face automatic suspension. He added that non-students who brought firearms onto the campus would be arrested. He also announced that students who participated in future building takeovers would be automatically suspended, with non-students being arrested. As for any campus organization involved in occupying a building "for coercive purposes," Perkins declared it would be liable to disbanding. "I am taking these emergency actions", said Perkins, "in the hope and expectation that more drastic action may be avoided."[109]

Harry Edwards was not noticeably impressed. He said that Perkins "can make all the rules he wants. That stuff doesn't mean anything to us till he moves. What this university's community has to understand is that our existence is going to be as good as that of the whites, or theirs is going to be as bad as ours."[110]

Professor Clinton Rossiter, one of Cornell's best-known academicians, took the initiative in drawing up a statement signed by about 40 members of the history and government departments, warning that if the agreement was affirmed by the faculty, they would "undertake a review of our relationship to the university in the light of this intolerable, and one would have thought, unthinkable situation." To Rossiter, the basic point was simply that "a man can't teach at a place that is in a condition of turmoil . . . where every change that is made is a result of confrontation."[111]

Ordinarily, a Cornell faculty meeting drew fewer than 300 members. But the Monday faculty meeting was attended by over 1,100 members. What was decided that day? The *New York*

*Times* headline read: "CORNELL FACULTY VOTES DOWN PACT ENDING TAKE-OVER."[112] Unfortunately, it was not nearly that simple, and not nearly that categorical.

At the meeting, Dean Miller repeated the promise he had made to the AAS that he would resign if the reprimands were not nullified. He recalled, "I was anxious to do anything to avoid a tragedy. Let's face it, this was an armed camp." But by a hand vote of more than 1,000 members of the faculty, a proposal by Dean Miller to dismiss the reprimands was decisively defeated. Miller resigned on the spot.[113]

By a vote of 726–281, the Cornell University faculty approved this resolution:

> 1. The Faculty expresses its sympathy for the problems of the black students in adjusting themselves to life at Cornell;
> 2. The Faculty condemns the seizure of Willard Straight Hall;
> 3. The Faculty condemns the carrying and use of weapons by anyone except those officially responsible for maintaining law and order on the campus;
> 4. The presence of arms and the seizure of Willard Straight Hall makes it impossible for the Faculty to agree at this meeting to dismiss the penalties imposed on the three students;
> 5. The Faculty is prepared under secure and non-pressurized circumstances to review the political issues behind the Afro-American complaints; and
> 6. Therefore, the Faculty directs the Faculty council to meet with representatives of the Afro-American Society tomorrow and to report to the Faculty by Friday at 4 p.m.
> 7. The Faculty supports, in principle, the President's action taken today to preserve law and order on the campus.[114]

Re-read section four and you find the faculty did not absolutely reject the motion to dismiss the reprimands. It merely postponed a decision—preferring not to agree "at this meeting."

This motion was offered by a professor who read from a sheet of paper. At one point, finding the handwriting illegible, he handed the resolution to its author for clarification. The author was President James Perkins![115] In the words of Howard Rodman, of the *Cornell Daily Sun* editorial board:

The faculty meeting's outcome left many deeply disturbed. In the persons of Steven Muller and Robert Miller, the administration had agreed to the AAS demands: in the person of James Perkins, it had rejected those same demands and imposed what had come to be considered a state of martial law. Faced with this contradiction, groups as disparate as SDS and the conservative History Department united in struggle against the man they called Diamond Jim.[116]

The ad hoc "Committee for the Silent Center" placed announcements on the campus radio station WVBR at five-minute intervals saying, "Jim Perkins must go."[117]

At a cheering rally of 1,500 white supporters, Zachary Carter of the AAS, and one of the signers of the agreement, declared that in seizing Willard Straight Hall, "we made the initial move which sort of limits our next move. I feel pretty shaky about going into another building, police just might not see it my way. The die is cast. I hope in making that move you don't let us outdo you. You know what I mean."[118] Citing the new regulations providing for automatic suspension of students who seized university buildings, Charles Marshall of the SDS noted that "it is impossible for them to suspend 500 students who say they are going to stand up and fight. It's impossible and they won't do it."[119]

Eighty deputy sheriffs from surrounding counties were stationed in Ithaca, ready for possible use if requested by Cornell University. Tompkins County Sheriff Robert Howard was pleased "with the speed with which they assembled. We had 50 men here in less than an hour and we could have had twice this number in about half the time."[120]

One of the most highly respected and independent-minded members of the black community, Dr. Kenneth Clark, a psychologist, teacher, and member of the New York State Board of Regents, compared the gun-wielding black militants with "the Birmingham police use of cattle prods on human beings and the recent hysterical sadism exhibited by Chicago police." Clark spoke about the "unfinished business of democracy," "the unfulfilled promises," and "flagrant injustices," but underscored the point that attacks on basic liberties could not be justified by citing the "high moral or ethical ideals" of those who sought to disrupt or destroy institutions. He reminded his listeners: "In the tortuous struggles and turbulence of human history, all forms of tyranny are introduced initially under the guise of moral indignation and are justified by some higher moral ends."[121]

On Tuesday, April 22, President Perkins announced the cancellation of all Wednesday afternoon classes, so that all students might attend a massive teach-in at Barton Hall. The teach-in had the backing of Perkins, the Afro-American Society, the president of the Inter-Fraternity Council, and at least one member of the judiciary system. In a large ad in the *Cornell Daily Sun,* the meeting was described as "a non-political informational means to acquaint all Cornellians with the background and current status of the situation at Cornell." Arthur Walsh, one of the organizers of the teach-in took pains to emphasize that "this teach-in is purely non-political. We are trying to give all interested parties representation on the platform so that we may once and for all clear up all the rumors and misinformation which has [sic] been floating around this campus."[122]

It was then, and is now, impossible even to hazard a guess as to how many of the thousands of students who attended the meeting at Barton Hall did so to "clear up all the rumors and misinformation" and how many were there primarily to cheer on black militants like Tom Jones, a leader of the Afro-American Society.

Others spoke that night but it was Jones who dominated the meeting and the campus. It was Jones who told the audience he was ready for a confrontation with local policemen and sheriff's deputies. "It's been the black people that have died," he said. "Now the time has come when the pigs are going to die too. We are going to move."[123]

That night, in an interview on Cornell-owned radio station WHCU, Jones warned, "Cornell has three hours to live." Jones charged that black students had been attacked by members of the Delta Upsilon Fraternity, and labeled several members of the university administration, Perkins included, as "racists." He said that Perkins and members of the faculty were "going to be dealt with." Jones declared, "We will stand up. We're going to demonstrate that we will die in the process, but by God, we won't die alone."[124]

Some of the faculty members branded as "racists" were forced to evacuate their homes for the night. One black student who had openly opposed the resort to force was spirited by friends across the border into Canada for safekeeping.[125]

Among the spectators at the meeting was a sociology professor, Gordon Streib. The professor watched as many students leaped to their feet and shook their fists in the air to show their solidarity with Jones. Asked what he thought of the demonstration, Professor Streib replied, "Heil Hitler!" Later, Streib recalled, "The Hitler movement is the only thing I have ever seen that resembled that meeting. I was terrified."[126]

At this point, with an ineffectuality so obvious as to come over almost as a spot of comic relief, President Perkins, in a radio broadcast, again reminded students of his prohibition on arms and explosives, and his ban on the seizure of buildings.[127]

An anonymous phone call threatened a takeover of Day Hall, the building in which Perkins' own office was located. Secretaries carried out huge armloads of files, as the building was quickly emptied of its occupants. Perkins was one of the first to leave the building.[128]

How many students were at that meeting in Barton Hall? Estimates ranged from 6,000 to 8,000, and even 10,000. Whatever the exact number, it was a very large assemblage, comprising a considerable percentage of the student body of Cornell University. An article co-authored by Harry Edwards said of the meeting: "That such an incredible outpouring of students could take place showed that student sentiment had shifted to the blacks, *although it was less clear whether the shift had occurred for substantive reasons or because of the fear of violence*" [129] (emphasis added). Howard Rodman of the *Cornell Daily Sun* felt that those "in the 'silent center' as well as those who were admittedly right wing, flocked to the meeting in hopes of dissuading SDS from militant action."[130]

One of the SDS speakers at that meeting, Charles Marshall, seemed to acknowledge these mixed feelings in the audience. "The most important thing people have to do now is to stick together even though they take different action," Marshall said. "There is no way they [the administration] can ignore this many people, if this many people stand up in their different ways and move."[131] At another meeting, 26 faculty members had voted to commit themselves to the seizure of buildings; a larger number, 49, said they were ready to strike until the black student demands were met.[132]

At Barton Hall, SDS leader David Burak was scaling monumental new heights in hypocrisy. Months before, Burak had helped create the judiciary system;[133] now, he was among those leading the attack on it. Making a split-second decision, Burak invited all who supported the black demands but were unwilling to occupy a building, to remain in Barton Hall until the faculty reconsidered its decision.[134] Over 40 professors and 3,-000 students bedded down for the night.[135] "Well," said a speaker from the podium, "I guess this is a seizure"[136]—a direct violation of Perkins' edict against occupying any more buildings. There were cheers from the audience.

Later, President Perkins, ignoring his own edict, called the action at Barton Hall "the most constructive gathering in Cornell's history."[137] But his remark, far from "cooling it at Cornell," simply added a few more degrees Fahrenheit to AAS leader Tom Jones' already volcanic fury.

In Jones' words:

> If there were three to four thousand black students here, Perkins would have his pigs here, and they would all be in Tompkins County Jail.
>
> When five thousand white people decide to spend the night in Barton Hall, Perkins decides to change the law that he made yesterday for the black people. Boy does that turn my guts.
>
> Now do you see the racism in this institution we are fighting about for the last four months.[138]

Clearly, Jones had a point, insofar as he was denouncing the transparent hypocrisy by which Perkins flouted his own rules. But at that particular time, it was wildly improbable that anything short of a declaration of war would have induced Perkins to send the city police on the Cornell campus, whether the Barton Hall gathering was moderate or militant black—white, brown, yellow, or chartreuse.

At Barton Hall, the study-in, with a touch of the chameleon, had changed its colors to a sit-in, and now a sleep-in. Some sped home, and returned with blankets, sleeping bags, or air mattresses. Shoes and boots were passed around, and some $800 was collected to buy 583 hamburgers, 40 cases of soda, and 70 dozen doughnuts in downtown Ithaca. Many students brought in their own personal provisions, and some bought gallons of wine or six-packs of beer. At least one student was passing out apples gratis.[139] And though it appeared nowhere on the bill of fare, a rather substantial portion of humble pie was being reserved for the president of Cornell University.

Later, Perkins was to comment, "Those who asked—even some trustees—why I didn't take disciplinary action against some student violators never bothered to find out that I have no power to do so." That power, he said, rested with the faculty under Cornell's bylaws.[140] That was true enough. Yet Perkins used his considerable persuasive powers to lobby for the militants. Evans and Novak noted that behind the scenes, Perkins' aides were prodding the faculty to nullify the disciplinary proceedings.[141] And it was Perkins who, at the outset of the Wednesday faculty meeting, said the good faith and integrity of Cornell were involved in the agreement under which Dean Miller had persuaded the AAS to vacate Willard Straight Hall.[142]

The faculty meeting that day was not open to the press, but a few newsmen managed to slip into Bailey Hall where the emergency meeting was taking place. One of these newsmen, Read Kingsbury, city editor for plans and training at the *Rochester Times-Union,* filed a most illuminating report.

Kingsbury told of a faculty ripped by fear and dissension. He wrote about Professor Ernest F. Roberts, acting dean of the faculty, who presented the faculty council's resolution for nullificaton of the judicial decisions against the black students and for creation of a judicial system "that all of our students will consider fair." He realized that "people are going to say we're doing it out of fear. I'm doing it because it is just. . . . We must announce to the world the courage of Cornell."

Vance A. Christian, professor of hotel administration, asked, "What did we ever do for the ghetto?" He stated that Perkins had called the cross-burning at Wari House "a little incident . . . a prank." His voice rising with passion, Roberts declared, "To a black man, a cross-burning is not a prank. It's a hell of an issue."

Professor Robert S. Pasley of the Cornell Law School defended the university's judicial system, and said there had been a "barrage of propaganda" against it. He added, "We are still under an ultimatum . . . there are still guns on this campus. . . . Do we leave this hall as free men or as cowards?"

Professor James John called the faculty council's resolution a "short-sighted ill-conceived measure." Referring to Tom Jones' threats against Cornell, Professor John picked up the gauntlet and said, "If Mr. Jones says he and his accomplices are going to destroy this university, I say let him try it."

Another academician remarked, "If Clinton Rossiter is a racist I am one too. . . . I want to know what is the consequence [of making such threats as Jones made]."

After about an hour and a half of discussion, the vote was taken. Those favoring nullification of the reprimands against the black militants won by a margin of at least 3 to 1.[143]

Professor Roberts might contrive to paint roseate pictures of "the courage of Cornell," but Cushing Strout, professor of English, bluntly admitted, "Basically we couldn't conceive of watching troops and students battling in conflict. We felt we had to draw back from the abyss of chaos."[144] And with similar frankness, William Keeton, professor of biology, had told the crowd in Barton Hall just before the faculty meeting, "I will vote for nullification from fear [for the university]. I will lose some self-respect doing so; I want you to know I terribly resent this."[145]

Dean Miller withdrew his resignation. He said he wanted to stay at Cornell, now that the faculty had reversed itself. A motion asking Miller to remain as dean of faculty was adopted unanimously.[146]

The government department faculty had been almost solidly in support of Monday's decision, postponing action on the demand for nullification, but Wednesday the faculty suffered a key defection when Clinton Rossiter changed his vote. Rossiter said, "I feel not only that we corrected what was a doubtful action Monday, but we moved immediately to restore peace and harmony on campus."[147] Discussing his change of position, he explained, "I feel the campus had put before me a number of arguments I had not heard before that led me to seriously question the faculty's action last Monday. Moreover, I now feel assured that an atmosphere of peace and mutual respect will prevail on campus."[148]

Rossiter expected some of his fellow professors to accuse him of being "a Judas."[149] The response of Professor Allan P. Sindler, chairman of the government department, was to submit his resignation to President Perkins. Sindler gave this as his reason: "I do not believe I can perform effectively my teaching, scholarly and institutional duties in the changed context at Cornell."[150] Another government professor, Allan Bloom, charged that "the resemblance on all levels to the first stages of a totalitarian take-over are almost unbelievable."[151] Bloom told the *Cornell Daily Sun:* "Happily, I shall be on sabbatic leave next year and will be spared the further acts of this desperate comedy which has left academic freedom at Cornell in a shambles and degraded the faculty. In such an atmosphere, I could not have conceived of teaching."[152]

Walter Berns, professor of government, and 1969 recipient of the distinguished teaching award of the College of Arts and Sciences, called the faculty reversal "abject surrender." Berns added, "And anyone who claims he voted one way on Monday but then, having had an opportunity for rational discussion in an atmosphere free of coercion, changed his mind, is simply not telling the truth."[153]

President Perkins conceded that the campus had been filled with threats and counterthreats and that a number of professors had received anonymous phone threats. When asked if some professors had not, in fact, been driven from their homes by anonymous threats, Perkins insisted, "It's not true."[154] Later, however, a senior professor told a reporter, "I had to get my family out of the house yesterday and take them to a motel. I've been threatened." Other faculty members were forced to take the same desperate measures.[155] The *Cornell Daily Sun* demanded "a strong statement from the administration that the days of fear are gone forever, and their return will not be allowed." In the same editorial it was realistic enough to admit, "The Faculty reversed its Monday vote on Wednesday partly out of fear—fear of violence."[156]

Arch Dotson, a professor of government, agreed. He called the faculty vote "capitulation" and "a surrender to intimidation."[157]

In Barton Hall, Afro-American Society leader Ed Whitfield recounted the parable of the mule who would move if you just talked to him, but first you had to hit him on the nose to catch his attention. His conclusion: "Now we know we have the university's attention. . . . It is time the university as a whole should stop and take a look at itself and its role in society."[158]

In the midst of a speech by Tom Jones, President Perkins appeared at the rear of the stage and sat down near AAS leaders Whitfield and Eric Evans. When Evans got up to speak, Perkins walked up beside him, shaking his hand, and bent over to talk with him. With a laugh, Evans told the crowd that Perkins "put a grandfatherly arm around my shoulder and then said: 'Sit down, I want to talk.'" In this context, "grandfatherly" denoted a kind of superpaternalism. Perkins, visibly nervous, sat behind the podium, drinking from a can of soda. When Evans finished, he called Perkins to the microphone and asked, "Sir, are we still in a state of martial law and a state of emergency and are all the proclamations, orders, and directives you issued still in effect?" Perkins replied that the campus was still in a "modified state of martial law." He added that police mobilized earlier this week were being reduced by one third. As for other emergency regulations, Perkins said, "There is nothing I have said or will say which will not be modified by changing circumstances."[159] With an Alice-in-Wonderland naiveté, Perkins stated, "We cannot prevent acts of violence from occurring unless we believe in each other."[160]

Tom Jones said of the faculty decision to nullify the reprimands, "Let's not miss the point. That decision was made right here. They didn't make any decision; they were told from this room what to do."[161]

The nightmare needed only this crowning touch: President Perkins invited Ed Whitfield to become a member of an emergency advisory board on campus stability.[162] Under the circumstances, it was like inviting a pornographer to join the vice squad.

Professor George Hildebrand attributed much of the university's troubles to the COSEP program and other Perkins policies. It was his firm belief that "there has been a preference for activist Negro students, apparently on the same premise that the administration has also expressed a preference for SDS students and for faculty sympathetic to some of the SDS goals."[163]

Some of these activist Negro students were being called to account for their activities in Tompkins County Court at the time their brothers seized Willard Straight. Larry Dickson, a former Cornell student and member of the Afro-American Society, was accused of harassment by a *Cornell Daily Sun* reporter. The reporter (who subsequently became managing editor of the *Sun*) charged that Dickson had struck him in the face and knocked him to the ground during a threatened sit-in on December 7, 1968. Dickson pleaded guilty, and was given a suspended sentence of 15 days in the Tompkins County Jail.[164]

A week before, Gary Patton, Cornell student and another AAS member, was sentenced to one year each on two misdemeanor counts in connection with a burglary (the two terms to be served concurrently). The judge noted that the terms were the maximum allowable under the law, and then suspended the sentence on the condition that Patton leave New York State and not return.[165]

Still another Negro undergraduate, Mark Walker, was jailed after he had allegedly held up and robbed at gunpoint a white graduate student on the Cornell campus. The Ithaca police stated that a detective sergeant came upon Walker as he allegedly stood holding a gun at the head of the white student. The sergeant drew his own pistol and ordered Walker to drop his weapon. The black youth complied. The policeman said he found in Walker's possession a wallet that had been taken from the victim.

President Perkins came under pressure from the Concerned Faculty, "an ad hoc group of young professors usually identified with liberal and leftist causes," to lift Walker's suspension. They did so despite the pleas of one professor who said he thought the eyewitness testimony that Walker pointed a gun at the head of a white student seemed "unusually strong." Perkins was also visited by representatives of group of senior professors who asked him to ignore the pressure.

The following day, the grand jury returned an indictment charging Mark Walker with first-degree robbery and possession of a deadly weapon.[166]

All this was, of course, a matter of public knowledge—the

fact that inside or outside Willard Straight, on or off campus, black militants at Cornell were fully capable of assault and violence. And it is perhaps in this context that one should consider an article by Milton R. Konvitz, professor of law and industrial and labor relations. His article was titled, "Why One Professor Changed His Vote," and was written the day after he changed his vote and supported nullification of the reprimands. In a kind of torment, he wrote:

> For, tragically and unbelievably, the campus had suddenly, in a matter of hours, reverted to a state of nature. As we sat in the auditorium thinking, feeling, suffering and halfheartedly engaging in some sort of uninspired debate, we knew, from the expressed and implied threats, from the temper of thousands of our students and perhaps threescore members of the faculty, that in a matter of minutes the campus might become an armed camp.

Konvitz readily acknowledged that "on the surface, it seemed as if we were being asked to declare on Wednesday that $1 + 1 = 3$, though on Monday we had said, firmly and decisively, that $1 + 1 = 2$. Were we wrong on Monday? What new facts had been presented to persuade us that we were wrong only two days before?"

These were the "new facts" that "persuaded" Konvitz, and others, to change their votes:

> Since Monday's faculty action, the two days and the hours and minutes had been used by leaders of the Afro-American Society and the leaders of SDS to heat up the students, with the result that anywhere from 2,000 to 4,000 students (I think this is a fair estimate) were ready to throw the campus into utter turmoil if the faculty did not nullify the penalties against the three students. They, and some faculty members as well, stood ready to seize buildings, and after that there probably would have followed acts of harassment against many professors and administrators.

Konvitz wrote of Tom Jones' threats, including his warning that the AAS would seek to achieve its aims "by whatever means." As he sat through that Wednesday meeting, Konvitz wrote, "The message of the students came through to me very clearly. . . . The faculty *must* nullify the reprimands or else. . . ."

Konvitz feared that if the police had been called on the campus, it would have turned thousands of moderate students into militants. He wrote: "Possibly hundreds would be injured, many perhaps seriously, some might get killed, fires would be set, and worst of all it might take years, as at San Francisco State College or at Berkeley, to reinstitute peace and order and mutual trust and respect. A society can be destroyed in hours, but it takes years to build one." But surely it was the quintessence of self-delusion to believe that any society could endure —or deserved to endure—which stolidly watched its foundations being eaten away by brute force and brute terror.

Konvitz conceded, "To our students, and to the outside world, the faculty action must look like a faculty capitulation." When he voted for the resolution, "I could barely myself hear my 'Aye.' It was almost as if I would gag on the word. It was a very bitter pill to swallow. For I know how eager students will be to interpret the vote of the faculty as an admission of weakness, cowardice. . . ."[167]

Now Professor Walter Berns joined Professor Allan Sindler in resigning from the faculty. In an emotion-choked voice, Berns told an audience of 450 government students, as well as 15 government department faculty members, "I am speaking to assure you this is a very sad moment for me. I love Cornell University. My best friends in the world are here." He explained that he was resigning because he felt his academic freedom had been jeopardized. "It was too much," Berns concluded. "We had too good a world. It couldn't last."[168]

Professor Andrew Milnor said that although he would be forced to "edit" some aspects of his courses, he would continue teaching, because he felt a commitment to his students. Would he be able to keep that commitment? "If there are some questions you cannot ask," said Milnor, "why have a mind, why live?"[169]

Professor Allan Bloom predicted, "Within the next few days many more departures will come to your attention. Maybe morality was on the other side, but it is quite striking that our moral sympathies go only to those who have the guns in their hands."[170]

Professor Myron Rusk said, "An atmosphere of menace has now been established, so that it has become difficult for a professor to profess what he really believes. If this trend continues, students will hear in the classrooms not what the professors truly believe but what the professors believe the class will accept. That's not what students come to a university for."[171]

Professor Walter LaFeber, the chairman of the history department, bluntly gave this reason for resigning: "I don't want to associate myself with a bunch of cowards."[172] And Professor Fred Somkin grimly predicted, "Cornell is going to become just like a Latin American university. The students can march, demonstrate and tear the place down. But there hasn't been one decent scholar from Latin America since they gave the universities to the student thugs."[173]

Denouncing the administration's reasoning during the past week as "double-think," Professor Donald Kagan said, "George Orwell could have written the script." After he canceled a course and walked out, one student was heard to say, "Well, that's one down."[174]

While professors of this stature were resigning, Harry Edwards was announcing he would be back at Cornell in the fall, teaching sociology, and building a firm base for a black studies department.[175]

A black alumnus' view was offered by Bedford T. Bentley, Jr., Class of '67, in a thought-provoking letter to the *Cornell Daily Sun*. Bentley's sole concern was "in demolishing the insane logic which leads sixteen (a figure quoted from the media) American university students to introduce firearms and knives as agents of persuasion into the academic community." Bentley wrote:

> Any time the tools of murder are a common commodity in the community, there exists a profound threat to every individual which is independent of his political, moral or any other human stance. It is based simply on the fact of the fragility of human flesh. I contend that nothing can justify the existence of such a threat in the Cornell University Community.

Writing "firstly as a human being and secondly, as a black alumnus," Bentley reminded the weapon-wielding black militants that "the revolutionary murderer has his hour of lucidity —an hour of remorse."[176]

By now, a growing number of teachers were refusing to teach until they had written assurance from President Perkins that the campus was disarmed. At one point, at least a dozen professors signed a pledge to stop teaching unless the guns and rifles in the hands of persons and groups on the campus were surrendered.[177] Perkins had warned students that guns were forbidden on campus, but he was apparently unwilling to demand that the Afro-American Society hand over the 17 rifles and shotguns its members and supporters had carried out of Willard Straight Hall.[178]

The first weapons to be surrendered to the Cornell safety division were handed in by Otis Sprow, the Negro president of Chi Psi Fraternity. Sprow said he was not a member of the AAS but had attended some meetings. He said he was not among those who seized Willard Straight Hall. In handing over two rifles and a shotgun that belonged to his fraternity members, Sprow said, "We are doing this as an act of good faith toward the community as a whole. We feel we can trust the community. We don't need the weapons." But Tom Jones of the AAS repeated that his group would not yet disarm. "As long as a state of racist oppression exists, we cannot afford to disarm," Jones said.[179]

After Perkins issued regulations directing that all firearms on campus be surrendered, fourteen firearms were turned in, including one shotgun owned by a faculty member.[180] On April 26, Perkins said that he had received the following message from Ed Whitfield:

> I want to tell you, as chairman of the Afro-American Society that there are no guns of any kind or description in 320 Wait Avenue [headquarters of the AAS], or in the two co-ops [Wari House, and the dormitory for black men].[181]

Perkins still could not bring himself to inspect the AAS buildings. Asked whether Whitfield had implied any threat if the university carried out its announced plan to inspect dormitories and buildings on the campus, Perkins replied: "He would be—he didn't say 'insulted'—he said, 'We want the community to believe I'm speaking the truth.'" Perkins added, "This is almost identically the language used by some of the white fraternities."[182] Thus, still one more of Perkins' grandiose pronouncements withered on the rhetorical vine, because he lacked the willpower to enforce it. He was something less than persuasive as he plaintively asserted, "I find it hard to believe there's a gun on the campus."[183]

Perkins went on, "We will continue in what we call step one —using every means available voluntarily to assure us and the community that the campus is in fact disarmed. Then, if I cannot honestly say I believe the campus is disarmed, more severe measures will be taken." He indicated that the next step would be inspection; this would require civil authority because "we don't have police power."[184] But, considering the manner in which Perkins had kept the police at arm's length all through the Willard Straight seizure, it seemed hard to believe that Perkins ever would have taken that next step. Luckily, the black militants bailed Perkins out. Eric Evans, a spokesman for the group (which had abruptly changed its name from Afro-American Society to Black Liberation Front), graciously agreed to allow Cornell to search its headquarters, provided an hour's notice was given. Eugene Dymek accepted the invitation and announced that the Black Liberation Front's headquarters had been voluntarily inspected and found to be in compliance with firearms regulations.[185] But, given the threats of death and violence to which the campus had been subjected, it was fair to inquire whether their firearms were off the campus or merely out of the building.

Certainly, Tom Jones had not suddenly become a dove of peace. His glowering pronouncements still bristled with hostility for white America, and with a mania for things revolutionary. Jones cited what he called a "state of both overt and covert racist oppression" at Cornell, which condition prevented the AAS (or Black Liberation Front) from joining a "university community." Criticizing the "existence of oppressive institutions at Cornell," Jones lashed out at the Center for International Studies, ROTC, and Defense Department contracts.

The CIS, Jones said, "is deeply involved in developing counter-revolutionary tactics and anti-guerrilla tactics which are at this time being used primarily against colored peoples in the third world who are striving for their freedom—specifically, the Vietcong." ROTC was unacceptable to the AAS as the supplier of a military machine that "obviously controls the entire world" and that was, in the process, "suppressing black, yellow and brown people throughout the world."

Jones, who had been one of the student developers of the Afro-American Studies Center, described the current black courses at Cornell as "traditionally structured. There are seminars and much reading, and papers to write. The reading, however, is not totally of traditional material." Sometimes, he said, students conducted the twice-weekly classes. Among the textbooks for the courses, Jones cited *The Myth of the Negro Past, Essentials of Nkrumahism* (no doubt based upon the dogma of Kwame Nkrumah, the deposed pro-Marxist dictator of Ghana), *Before the Mayflower,* and *"African Socialism."* A course in black ideology was taught by Cleveland Sellers.[186]

The black militants declared that the purpose of black studies was "to enable black people to use the knowledge gained in the classroom and the community to formulate new ideologies and philosophies which will contribute to the development of the black nation." As part of the black studies program, the black militants demanded Course 300c, Physical Education: "Theory and practice in the use of small arms and hand to hand combat. Discussion sessions in the proper use of force."[187]

Forty-one Cornell faculty members placed an ad in the *Daily Sun* declaring:

> We recognize the need for many substantial changes. There are, however, essential conditions for preserving our integrity as teachers and fulfilling our responsibilities to students. For the sake of both teachers and students, we must have freedom to inquire, to teach and to learn without intimidation. We must maintain standards of professional judgment and scholarly achievement. If these conditions are no longer met, a decision to stop teaching or leave Cornell will be a necessity. At such a time, which may be dangerously near, we propose to act together.

Among the signers of this statement were Clinton Rossiter and Milton Konvitz.[188]

Some professors suspected that their lectures were being monitored by black militants for any suggestion of "racism." Perkins called for "the fullest possible investigation of any infringement" of freedom to teach. In a letter to Dean Miller, Perkins said he had received no reports of any such infringement from either the dean or the faculty committee on academic freedom.[189] But Perkins did not have to go very far for such a report. He had only to pick up the May 2 issue of the *Cornell Daily Sun,* turn to page four, and read this paragraph from a guest column by Walter Berns and Allan Sindler:

> Would the Perkins' administration do as our students have pledged themselves to do when, for example, monitors from the Black Liberation Front and SDS complain of the readings we assign, the questions we raise, the examples we use, or the doubts we cast on what is now the orthodoxy around here? What will be its response to the Government Department's refusal to be guided by the Black Liberation Front's instructions regarding curriculum and new staff? When the Government Department refuses to grant course credit for Harlem summer projects sponsored by the Center for Afro-American Studies (or whatever it will now be called)? When it refuses to accede to every demand respecting the admission of new graduate students? When it refuses to offer a course taught by a series of lecturers drawn from the ranks of the national SDS staff? These questions are not drawn out of thin air, and enough has happened around here—and not merely last week—to indicate the answers to them.[190]

Letters and statements from the faculty, some supporting, and more denouncing, President Perkins, proliferated in the *Cornell Daily Sun* and the *New York Times.* But it may well be that the most devastating criticism of the Perkins administration was delivered by Professor Thomas Sowell, one of Cornell's few Negro faculty members.

Professor Sowell disclosed that he had resigned, and charged that "paternalism" at Cornell had hurt black students. Sowell counted himself among those who favored the departure of Perkins, whose administration, he said, had been "a veritable weathervane, following the shifting crosscurrents of campus politics." Sowell said that Cornell had been "interested in its image—anything to keep the black students happy." He was convinced that "some members of the white faculty give grades more easily to blacks. Of course, many blacks resent this type of thing, and would rather have a truer grade." Sowell insisted that "paternalism" would result in the graduation of "inadequate" black students.[191]

An investigating committee of trustees was told by six senior members of the faculty that a "crisis of confidence" existed on the campus, and that not only Perkins but also several of his aides should go. The investigators were told that, of the administration leaders, only Dale Corson, the provost, retained the trust and respect of most faculty members.[192]

On May 31, Dr. Perkins asked the Board of Trustees to start looking for his successor.[193] A week later, Cornell's Board of Trustees assigned the duties of the president to Dale Corson.[194]

What could President Perkins have done in April when the black militants seized Willard Straight Hall? Exactly what he did in May when white members of the SDS played fun and games with ROTC. At about the time a trustees meeting in New York City was directing Perkins to deal firmly with further disruptive tactics on the campus, members of the Cornell SDS taunted ROTC cadets at drill, and then broke into a restricted area to paint peace slogans on a three-inch Navy destroyer deck gun. Some leaders of SDS visited the offices of the *Cornell Daily Sun,* trying to persuade the editors to withhold any photos of the incident. However, that student paper published a picture on page one, showing the SDS members involved.

The following day, the regional director and five other members of SDS were arrested and charged with criminal trespass. Among those arrested was Jeffrey Dowd, son of Douglas Dowd, an economics professor who acted as faculty adviser to the Cornell SDS. These arrests marked the first and only time that Perkins summoned city policemen to the campus.

Professor Harrop A. Freeman of the Cornell Law School, who was defense counsel for the arrested SDS students, said he would present motions contending that Cornell handled discipline in a discriminatory manner. Freeman reminded newsmen that Cornell took no action against the armed black students, but now apparently was singling out members of SDS for punishment on a relatively trivial charge.[195]

It was certainly possible to concede, and deplore, the existence of this double disciplinary standard without condoning, in any way, the retrogressive infantilism of the SDS actions. Of equal importance, the incident went a long way toward proving that Perkins could have called police on the campus to arrest the black militants without Cornell or Ithaca coming to an end, and without the emergence of some sort of academic Armageddon.

In the closing days of Perkins' administration, Cornell named James Turner director of the proposed Center for Afro-American Studies—a center with a first-year budget of $240,000.[196] It was a choice that aroused considerable controversy among some members of the faculty—a choice which, quite frankly, left the author stunned when the announcement was first made. Based upon Turner's activities and writings, Cornell could hardly have made a worse choice, as the following facts unfortunately will demonstrate.

As far as the general public was concerned, James Turner made his activist debut as a student at Northwestern University. On April 22, 1968, the administration at Northwestern received the following lists of demands from members of the black student community. The demands were:

1) a statement by the administration deploring "white racism"
2) assurance that Negroes would compose 10 to 12 percent of each new freshman class and that half the students come from urban ghettos
3) increase in financial aid
4) provision for a black student housing unit
5) new courses in Negro history, literature and art, and a voice in approving professors who would teach these courses
6) approval by the black student community of personnel hired to counsel black students
7) a place that black students could use for social and recreational activities
8) desegregation by Northwestern of all its real estate holdings.[197]

The demands were presented by two chief spokesmen for the black students. One of these spokesmen was James Turner, then a graduate student member of the Afro-American Student Union.[198]

After a considerable amount of jockeying back and forth for about a week and a half, during which time the black students rejected the administration's reply, the black students seized the bursar's office and locked themselves in. Of 124 black students at Northwestern, 90 were in the occupied building.[199]

Of the eight demands that the black students made, four were granted, one was partially granted, and three were denied. On the demand for a policy statement on the matter of "racism," Northwestern said that although the university had worked to right racial wrongs, "the fact remains that the University, in its overwhelming character, has been a white institution." Northwestern accepted the basic "sentiments expressed in the black students' demands."[200] All of which seemed to say that, regarding the accusation of white racism, Northwestern was pleading guilty as charged.

While Northwestern declined to set up any quota for Negro students, the agreement noted that Northwestern had been committed to increasing the number of Negro students at Northwestern as rapidly as possible, and to seeking at least fifty percent from inner-city schools.[201]

On the demand for special living units, Northwestern said that by the fall quarter of 1968 it would reserve sections of existing living units for Negro students who wished to live together.[202]

Three hours after the agreement was signed, the black students evacuated the bursar's office, leaving the building as they found it. They had occupied the building for 38 hours.[203]

Less than a month later, the federal government told Northwestern that its officials violated the Civil Rights Act of 1964 by promising to provide separate living quarters for black students.[204]

It was this same James Turner who had helped formulate and present these demands to Northwestern officials; it was this same James Turner who championed a quota system for black students, black veto power over the hiring of certain personnel, and separate housing for black students, who was now invited to head the Afro-American Studies Center at Cornell.

All of this was, of course, a matter of public knowledge long before his appointment was announced—as was the incredible interview of James Turner in *Muhammad Speaks* on February 14, 1969. In this issue, Turner said, "There is only one way for a captive nation like ours to develop . . . we must control our land, and communities, and chart our destiny and relationships with other groups."

This interview was so highly regarded by the Black Muslim newspaper that it was continued in its February 21 issue. Here, Turner's views and thoughts were presented in exhaustive if incredible detail, as witness these Turnerisms, which were proudly featured in a specially bordered insert under the heading, "Student Leader Warns: Extermination If We Remain A Colony":

The greedy few have caused all human devastation of the past—done in the guise of individual achievement and free enterprise.

But the progressive and independent "Third World" knows there must be a new system based on mutual sharing, cooperation and collectivity. We will go beyond Marx to say that this development will be based on the unity of our blood, instead of the class struggle alone. The blood I mean is the blood spilt by all oppressed people.

Our blood flows through wide stretches of history of the oppressed, colored peoples of the world. The new world will be a new world of humanism between the great peoples of Asia, Latin America, the Indies, the Pacific Islands, the Caribbean and, of course, Africa.

United as a great and irresistible force for human change, we will overcome the European descendants if they continue to block us with military arms. And of course the African-American, with his long and first-hand knowledge of the Euro-American, must use his education and all of the technical and military skills he has to help build this new world.

We are among the best-suited peoples to help provide independence for the colonized world and then to help build the new world with our brothers.[205]

These were the articles of militant faith for James Turner, and perhaps with this in mind, some faculty members expressed deep concern about the autonomy they thought Cornell was willing to confer upon the proposed Center for Afro-American Studies. They sought some assurance that the center, under Turner's directorship, would not merely become a training ground for black militants.[206]

The press releases announcing his appointment had barely gone out of the media, when Turner named John F. Hatchett as a man he wanted on the black studies faculty at Cornell. Hatchett, accused of anti-Semitic views, had been ousted from a position at New York University in 1968. In one of his last acts before resigning, Perkins told Turner that Hatchett was definitely not acceptable at Cornell.[207]

Hatchett was a former New York City school teacher who, while teaching at P.S. 68, had written a lead article in *Forum,* the official publication of the African-American Teachers Association. In this article, Hatchett asserted that Jewish "domination" of the public school system was responsible for black children "being educationally castrated, individually and socially devastated" to the point where they were no longer capable of participating in "meaningful educational experience." Describing "the phenomenon that spells death for the minds and souls of our black children," Hatchett called it "the coming of age of the Jews, who control and dominate the educational bureaucracy of the New York City Public School system."[208]

Evans and Novak recounted how, in a campus speech on June 29, black militant leader Tom Jones denounced Cornell's refusal to hire John Hatchett on the black studies center faculty. Jones blamed Allan Sindler for the university's decision. "Yeah, I'm going to be brutal with you now," said Jones. "Allan Sindler is Jewish. . . . Some of the faculty members, like Allan Sindler, got on the phone, called over to the Administration, told them over there that if John Hatchett was hired, they were resigning."[209]

Hatchett's anti-Semitism, said Jones, was irrelevant. "I might think if he's right or if he's wrong [*sic*] . . . but that has nothing to do with his academic expertise and his competence to teach African history and African culture."[210] Jones' position was exactly the reverse side of the coin that black militants had hurled at the administration the year before, when outraged members of the Afro-American Society forced an economics professor—accused of "racist" remarks—to leave Cornell University. On that occasion, the professor's academic expertise was considered wholly irrelevant; his unpopular remarks were all that mattered.

Jones warned his audience, "We're waiting for the fall. John Hatchett's going to be the issue in the fall. Now you tell me— you tell me, do you think we're going to back down over John Hatchett?"[211]

In a letter to the *New York Post,* Cornell administration official Dale Corson protested that "the statements by Evans and Novak contain a mixture of truth and falsehood," with "the factual inaccuracies . . . particularly blatant and damaging."[212] But nowhere in his letter did Corson deny that Jones had made the statements quoted in the Evans and Novak column.

Cornell asked Vice President Muller to request a retraction from the columnists. Novak replied that he and his colleague had rechecked their sources "and stand by the column as written, without exception."[213]

Throughout the black militant uprising at Cornell in April, pleas from concerned citizens that the state do something— anything—to cope with the crisis were countered by the response that Cornell was, after all, a private university. But in July, very suddenly, Cornell became considerably less private. It was in July, for what a state official said was the first time in New York history, that 52 private non-sectarian colleges were declared eligible for financial support from the state. Among those receiving the biggest allocations was Cornell University, recipient of $1,260,400 in state funds.[214] With public funds going to this private university, New York State would now, like it or not, have a clear-cut obligation to make certain that these tax monies would not be expended to foster black racism at Cornell.

And what of the future? Where, if anywhere, would Cornell go from here? Inevitably, one's thoughts returned to that evening in Barton Hall, when a leader of the Afro-American Society stated:

The old Cornell died at 9 o'clock last night when 6,000 of you stood up for black people. The old order has ended.[215]

And now came the New Order. And now came the New Cornell. And with it the New Racism.

# CHAPTER 11

# The City College of New York (CCNY)

IF THERE IS A SINGLE IDEA THAT TIES TOGETHER the black militant campus outbreaks from coast to coast, it is the dogma that labels it all a "class struggle"—a fight between the haves and have-nots. In one corner, there are the "underprivileged," "disadvantaged," "poverty-stricken" black militants. In the other corner—the affluent, overprivileged White Anglo-Saxon Protestant sons of the power structure. Of course the match is over before it's begun. Because with white guilt feelings, paternalism, and self-flagellation calling the shots, the judges' decision is in before the antagonists even enter the ring.

This is the stereotype and it is all but invincible. It is a rare college that breaks the mold—a college as rare as the City College of New York (or as most New Yorkers call it, CCNY). At CCNY, the struggle was not between privilege and under-privilege, affluence and want. Here it was have-not *confronting* have-not, minority *challenging* minority. It is vitally important to understand this fact at the very outset, if indeed we hope to understand anything about the CCNY conflagration at all.

*Saturday Review* wrote of CCNY:

City College has long been the brightest academic light in
New York City's famed system of higher education. Admission has always been highly competitive, and the
school has produced many of the city's business, political
and professional leaders.[1]

At the height of the campus disruptions, Louis L. Snyder,
professor of history at City College, reminded the city and indeed, the country

This is the college that produced Bernard Baruch, Morris
Raphael Cohen and Jonas Salk. The whole fabric of New
York City's professional structure—from judges to physicians to engineers—owes much to this institution.
City College men staff colleges and universities throughout the country. They make up a large proportion of the
Federal, state and city civil service. To strike down a top
institution like CCNY would be the kind of blow from
which the country would find it difficult to recover.[2]

According to a survey released early in 1968, most freshmen
at City College came from families whose incomes were *below*
what the federal government said was needed to maintain a
"moderate" living standard.[3]

Many, if not most, CCNY students looked on a college degree
as the passport to a more promising future, a future with
greater opportunity than they and their families had ever
known. For some of them, attendance at CCNY entailed considerable financial hardships, requiring some belt-tightening sac-
rifices for a number of years. To them, a CCNY degree was a
coveted possession that could boost their earning power, en-
hance their status, propel them up the ladder three or four
rungs at a time. Competing against thousands of others, they
had been required to prove themselves to enter CCNY; once
admitted, they had to keep proving themselves to remain there.
But they knew it was precisely this selectivity that had given
a CCNY degree its inestimable prestige and value in the academic and business marketplace. And it was for this reason
that some were resentful or hostile, and many of them were
concerned, when new programs were instituted admitting
black students to CCNY with little or no regard for their grades.
The fact that CCNY was located in the center of Harlem hardly

seemed to them sufficient justification for having one set of rules for whites and another set of more lenient rules for blacks.

Almost from the start, there was discernible friction between black and white students at City College. One of the earliest incidents involved the Onyx Society, a black student group founded because "we wanted an organization of our own on campus where we could feel comfortable."[4] Officers of the Onyx Society denied that any racial split on campus existed between black, Puerto Rican, and white students,[5] but it was rather a difficult stance to maintain in view of the charge that the society had discriminated against white students wanting to attend a meeting addressed by Rap Brown of SNCC. The president of the Onyx Society said that only members and their friends were admitted, and "we can't help it if our members' friends aren't white."[6]

The incident took place in October 1967 and CCNY's student council attempted to punish the Negro group for the alleged discrimination. A motion was introduced to restrict some of the Onyx Society's activities. The motion failed after several hundred shouting and jeering members of the Onyx Society produced what one council member called "an atmosphere of violence." Joseph Korn, then president of the student council, said, "The council was clearly intimidated and afraid to do what they should have, whether they were afraid of riots or of alienating the black kids on campus. Whatever their reasons, they were wrong."

Allan Milner, the council member who had brought the charge, said the council had not acted because it was "physically intimidated by the size of the [crowd] and its support for its leaders." Milner charged, "I was told by members of Onyx, and Negroes not members of Onyx that if Onyx was even censured, there would be 'hot trouble'."

The chairman of the Onyx Society's education committee called the proceedings a "lynching, City College–style," and warned the council that "there are an awful lot of us here and you aren't going anywhere."[7] The black student who sounded this warning was Serge Mullery—the same firebrand who in 1969 would help lead those manning the barricades at CCNY's South Gate.

Notwithstanding Mullery's none-too-veiled threat, a few days later the student council—meeting in an atmosphere of calm—voted 13 to 7 to "strongly censure" the Onyx Society. In reply, the society president called the student council "a racist body" and said his group "will continue to function in a greater capacity than it has before."[8]

The black-white tension grew, along with the increased admission of "disadvantaged" black students to CCNY. As part of the City University of New York, CCNY was one of seven colleges participating in the SEEK program (Search for Education, Elevation and Knowledge). SEEK was a program "for high school graduates who have the desire and potential ability for college but may not have the required courses or grades and who also cannot afford college."[9] Thus, by its very definition, low-income students who *did* have the required courses or grades did not qualify for the SEEK program.

In an article in the fall 1968 issue of *Educational Record,* Leslie Berger, associate university dean of SEEK, discussed the rationale behind the program. Berger wrote that "good high school averages are usually indicative of intellectual ability, appropriate motivation for academic success, adequate study skills and a supportive environment," but low grades "can be caused by any or all of these variables being deficient." Berger wrote that all the dimensions were potentially changeable, "with the exception of intelligence," which he then quickly brushed aside. He believed that "such factors as quality and method of instruction, exposure to different kinds and amounts of remedial teaching, counseling, financial assistance, medical care and living arrangements, all interact with the characteristics of the individual to determine what is learned." Though such a construction was obviously the farthest thing from Berger's mind, a hypersensitive black militant could have interpreted this as a kind of test-tube paternalism.

In his article, Berger noted that none of the SEEK students "met the requirements for admission into any of the colleges of the City University as regular matriculated students." This was still the case in 1969; the application for admission to Special Programs plainly stated that to be a SEEK student, "you cannot qualify for regular admission to a program which leads to graduation. If you have applied to the City University for matriculation, but are not accepted, you will still be considered for SEEK. . . ." All of which was a way of saying you had to be ineligible to be eligible for SEEK.

Berger wrote: "The policy of SEEK is to accept—provided that space is available—all applicants with an average of 70 or better in academic subjects, regardless of the type of their diploma, and all who pass with a score of 50 percent or better on the examination for an equivalency diploma." The 1969 Application for Admission stated, "The type of diploma does not matter."

By contrast, on April 5, 1968, the *New York Times* noted that students applying for regular full-time freshman admission at CCNY were finding it more difficult to gain acceptance; the academic qualifications needed for entry into CCNY and other member colleges of the City University had risen "because students with better records had applied and because most of the colleges lacked extra space to accommodate students with the same grade averages or test scores as last year."

The SEEK program provided for counseling, tutoring, books, and supplies, "and, if necessary, an allowance for living expenses." (Of course no such allowance was forthcoming for needy students with good grades who had entered CCNY on the basis of ability.) To provide conditions "conducive to studying," the SEEK program even opened a residence hall for 100 students—a first in the City University's history.

Dean Berger wrote, "If a [SEEK] student is not doing satisfactorily, the teachers are expected to question *themselves,* and explore different approaches" (emphasis added). He conceded that:

> not all the faculty believe that these students are educable; or if they do, they somehow fail to communicate their belief in the students. Some instructors start out with great enthusiasm and become discouraged when student response falls short of their expectations. On occasion, teachers may react with hostility when subjected to considerable testing by a student. Other teachers tend to be overprotective, overly concerned about whether or not the students are going to like them.

Berger disclosed that of the 190 SEEK students who started at City College of New York in September 1966, 148 (or 78 percent) enrolled for a fourth term. They had taken an average of 21 credits and 88 percent of the students averaged C or better in their credit courses for the fall 1967 term.[10]

In August 1968, the City University's governing board granted matriculated, or degree-candidate, status to the students enrolled in the SEEK program. Although the SEEK students would now be regarded as university degree-candidates they would continue to receive special counseling, tutoring, and other help.[11]

At the same time, the Board of Higher Education was announcing "revolutionary" measures that were expected to bring a dramatic increase in the number of Negro and Puerto Rican students attending the City University. A new citywide admissions program would make it possible for some students who had high school averages as low as 68 percent to be admitted in the fall to CCNY and other senior colleges of the university; the regular requirement was an average of 82 percent.[12]

Under the new citywide admission policy, the City University would guarantee senior college admission to the top 100 graduates annually at each of the city's 60 academic high schools, *regardless of grades.* This meant that some ghetto youngsters with averages in the high 60's or low 70's would be admitted to CCNY and other senior colleges, because even with these poor averages, they placed among the top 100 in their graduating class.[13] Just as obviously, this meant that some white students with grades in the 80's, in more competitive high schools, would be denied admission to CCNY because they were not in the top 100.

Dr. Albert H. Bowker, chancellor of the City University, said that these and other new measures would give the university in the fall of 1969 an entering freshman class that would be 26 percent Negro and Puerto Rican—the same ethnic distribution as among the city's high school graduates. Bowker rhapsodized, "This is the most revolutionary thing the University has done since I became chancellor," and unconvincingly asserted that these new policies would not affect "the traditional academic excellence of the colleges."[14]

At a meeting with a black dean at CCNY, Leonard Kriegel, an

assistant professor of English, expressed fears that a special-admissions program for blacks, without a financial cutoff point, might penalize white students from the lower-middle-class families. The black dean replied, "I really don't give a damn about what happens to the white students." Looking back on the incident, Kriegel commented, "Neither I nor any of the other twenty or so white professors opened his mouth to protest."[15]

But far from being even vaguely satisfied, the black militants were, if anything, more furious than ever. In February 1969 a self-styled Black and Puerto Rican Student Community group made the following demands of CCNY President Buell Gallagher:

# A separate School of Black and Puerto Rican Studies.
# Separate orientation for black and Puerto Rican freshmen.
# A voice for students in the SEEK program; this would mean setting all guidelines, including the hiring and dismissing of all personnel.
# A racial composition for all entering classes to reflect the city high schools' black and Puerto Rican population—about 50 percent.
# A requirement that all students majoring in education be required to take black and Puerto Rican history and the Spanish language.[16]

The militants asserted that they were "wholly dissatisfied with racist conditions currently existing on the City College campus," and heckled President Gallagher as he responded to their demands. Gallagher invited the militants to plan "programs of African, Afro-American and Hispanic Studies" to be offered in September 1969, and he noted that Professor Wilfred Cartey, a Negro, had joined the City College of New York faculty on February 1 to prepare the program. He asked the dean of students, G. Nicholas ("Nik") Paster, to reexamine orientation programs "in consultation with student and faculty groups" in order to meet "the particular needs of black and Puerto Rican students." Gallagher stated he welcomed "greater participation" by the SEEK students, and looked toward an elected student council. As for the racial composition of the entering classes, Gallagher said that City University's admissions the previous September were "in full proportion" to high school graduates[17] (here it must be stressed that the percentage of black and Puerto Rican high school *graduates* was considerably smaller than the percentage of black and Puerto Rican students *in attendance* at the high schools). Finally Gallagher agreed that familiarity with black and Puerto Rican history was "essential for all teachers" in the city's schools and that proficiency in Spanish was essential for many.[18]

Rejecting Gallagher's replies, about 100 of the black and Puerto Rican students invaded City College's administration building. No attempt was made to stop the takeover of, first, the lobby, and then, half an hour later, the second and third floors, including the president's office. College officials and their staffs —about two dozen persons—left the building. The invaders left after occupying the building for four hours—and after news photographers had snapped a picture of a handwritten sign, the militants' handiwork, which read, "Free Huey—by order of BPRC. Malcolm X–Che Guevara University."[19]

Gallagher said he did not think there would be any disciplinary action.[20]

CCNY's president said that he agreed with the demonstrators demands, but could not give an unqualified yes to all of them. In a manner suggestive of the Melancholy Dane at Elsinore Castle, Gallagher commented, "I have refused to say no on each point, and I have found it difficult to say yes."[21]

A student spokesman warned "If our demands are not met, the black and Puerto Rican student committee will have no choice but to move into the next stage of our struggles."[22]

A few days later, small groups of Negroes and Puerto Ricans raced through City College classrooms and offices, splattering paint and milk on blackboards and floors, overturning chairs and desks, releasing stink bombs, and setting three small fires. No one was arrested in any of these several dozen incidents. Gallagher had warned that any student caught committing an act of vandalism would be prosecuted. But a spokesman for the president said that the vandals could not be identified for prosecution.[23] In any event, college officials had decided not to call the police on the campus. Dean of Students Nicholas Paster explained, "The kind of action the police might bring would be an escalation of the type of thing we want to avoid. The police also don't want to go inside of buildings to protect material."[24]

No one was arrested. No policemen were called. No disciplinary action was taken. The encouragement to commit more aggressive, if not violent, actions in the future, without the slightest risk of punishment, was readily apparent to all the militants; indeed, it was all but spelled out in neon signs.

Dean Robert Young, director of the City College SEEK program, asserted, "These are not actions by SEEK students. I feel very certain of this."[25] And yet black students told the *Amsterdam News* their actions were prompted by Gallagher's refusal to give an unqualified yes to the militants' five demands.[26]

Dean Young said that CCNY was willing to let students have more say in the running of the college through an elected student council and that the administration was willing to involve students in setting up guidelines for operating the school. But the dean drew the line at students having the power to select the faculty. "We cannot," said Dean Young, "and no society can, afford to have students sitting in judgment of professional educators who have studied for more years than the students have been living."[27]

On April 17, a resolution by faculty members at CCNY called for maintaining the current percentage of black and Puerto Rican freshmen in the fall 1969 entering class. With Dr. Gallagher approving, the faculty council of the College of Liberal Arts and Sciences voted, in effect, that even if the freshmen class were cut in half because of budget reductions, the percentage of black and Puerto Rican freshmen for the fall would still equal the percentage of those two ethnic groups in city high school graduating classes.[28] The black and Puerto Rican admissions would come first; then whatever freshmen places were left would be offered to white students with superior grades and records.

If the CCNY powers-that-be expected this incredible concession to act as a campus tranquilizer, they sadly underestimated the non-negotiable fury churning in militant ranks. Less than a week later, almost a thousand singing and chanting college and high school students marched through the campus in support of a boycott of classes to dramatize demands for a separate school of third-world studies and still more changes in the admissions policy of the City College.

At the administration building, "racism" was indicted and

prosecuted in a mock trial. Among the charges brought against "racism" were: 1) it hinders the development of a separate school of third-world studies; 2) "it has infiltrated our ranks with a bunch of mechanical niggers"; and 3) it stops blacks from going to school—"everybody should be allowed to go to school, even the ones who get 30's in class."

Leaders at the open-air court poured kerosene on a life-sized, stuffed-sheet dummy, labeled "Racism," and set it afire. Students marched noisily through the halls of the college building, chanting, "On strike, shut it down" and "Who will survive America/Very few Negroes, no pigs at all/Black Power for black people." At a rally, Rick Reed, a spokesman for the Black and Puerto Rican Community (BPRSC), said the question was not simply the black studies program, but rather, "are we going to have control of it?" The procession ended, after three hours of marching. The strike and boycott were estimated to be 30 percent effective.[29]

The week before, President Gallagher's Policy Council had voted to recommend the use of court injunctions and/or "Notre Dame tactics" to deal with student sit-ins.[30] Specifically, this referred to the actions taken by Father Hesburgh of Notre Dame during a period of disruptions. At that time, Notre Dame students were given a specific amount of time to evacuate the buildings. Those who did not comply were automatically suspended.[31]

Gallagher said that he would "wait and see" before acting on the recommendations at CCNY, according to student Policy Council members Bill Andermann and Laslo Varadi.[32] The council was split over another motion, either to close City College or to use massive police force in the event of "guerrilla tactics," and delayed action until a future meeting.[33]

The delay was very nearly fatal to CCNY. Gallagher's "wait and see" evasions struck just the note of timidity in high places that the militants needed to hear. Less than 24 hours later, Gallagher ordered City College closed for the day, after more than 150 Negro and Puerto Rican students locked themselves inside the gates to the South Campus. Their blitzkrieg tactics blocked access to eight of CCNY's 22 buildings.[34]

This was the first time during his 17 years as president that Gallagher had ordered the school closed. He did not recall that any of his predecessors had ever done this.[35] The demonstrators, who remained behind the gates during a day of heavy rain, were demanding that a much larger percentage of Negroes and Puerto Ricans be admitted to City College.[36]

Gallagher said that he would ask the demonstrators to "evacuate" the campus, but the black and Puerto Rican students proceeded to make arrangements to remain overnight. The militants' action closed off classes of about half the more than 11,000 students who attended day classes. The police had cut a chain on one of the gates and then left. But the demonstrators remained and kept the gates closed.[37]

Gallagher indicated that, barring an emergency, he would not call the police before a faculty meeting took place. He refused to commit himself on whether or not he would ask for a court injunction.[38]

The *New York Post* revealed:

> Reportedly the dissidents original plan for their CCNY demonstration was a modest one—to chain the South Gate as a "symbolic confrontation" and then leave peacefully after police were called.
> But ... Gallagher was out of town at the time, and although police were summoned to cut the chains, college authorities did not let them enter the grounds. As a result, the dissidents suddenly found themselves in effective control of the entire South campus, grounds and buildings as well.

Once the militants realized what they had accomplished, they "escalated their demands," the *Post* was told.[39]

Asked why the police were kept off the campus, Gallagher replied, "I was on a plane at the time. Dean [of Students] Paster was giving the orders until I got back. By the time I got to the campus, it [the occupation] was an accomplished fact."[40]

Dean Paster stated that he did not ask police onto the campus "because it is the university policy not to call the police, and to try and solve our problems internally. Dr. Gallagher was as involved in that policy as anyone."[41] And yet six months before, CCNY had indeed called the police when *white* students disrupted the campus, in a far less serious incident. More than that, Paster had written a letter to the *New York Times*, in which he praised the conduct of the police. In Paster's words:

At a recent City College action involving sincerely disturbing activity by a few students, the police acted to remove them efficiently and—yes—gently under somewhat trying circumstances. I want to publicly thank them for this service.[42]

It all seemed part and parcel of the New Racism—feel free to call in the police when the student disrupters were white, and keep the police off the campus when the disrupters were black. And as we will see, Gallagher was just as shackled to this policy as was Paster. Indeed, at one point, Gallagher declared, "If I were required by the courts to use police to clear the South Campus under present circumstances, I would submit to the rule of law by going to jail."[43]

Repeating the five demands they had made in February, a Negro leader of the demonstrators vowed, "This school will stay shut until all of these issues have been resolved. None of these demands are negotiable. They are fair, just, long overdue and we will not wait any longer."[44]

Some professors, including Nathan Susskind of the German department, warned against "yielding to a minority of terrorists"; others, like Cliff Adelman of the history department, said, "What is truly moral in America today is on the South Campus at this moment." Many professors were especially concerned about admission quotas based on race.[45]

President Gallagher said that "no police will be called to South Campus tonight or tomorrow and no injunctive processes will be instigated in this interval." He announced that the demonstrators "are ready for a small group of their leaders to talk with me tomorrow at noon," and ordered City College closed again for another day.[46]

The following day, Gallagher again ordered CCNY closed, and again promised that the police would not be called to remove the 200 protesters while negotiations were in process. By a narrow vote of 115 to 103, faculty members deplored the cessation of classes but opposed bringing police on campus. By a slightly larger margin, faculty members voted to endorse the closing of the college "in all its parts."[47]

Despite all this, faculty and students of the engineering school on the North Campus said they would hold informal classes. A spokesman for them, Ara Barsamian, said that "a small neo-Nazi minority is depriving us of our education." Some professors feared opposing students would clash if engineering undergraduates carried out their plans to have classes. Nevertheless, Dr. William Allen, dean of the engineering school, expected many of the 2,200 engineering students to be in class, conducting "a teach-in."[48]

As Dr. Allen had indicated, seven hundred engineering students at City College ignored President Gallagher's order closing the school, and went to class on Friday. Gallagher insisted that "if regular classes are held on the campus Monday, the negotiations will be seriously delayed" and could create "the possibility of igniting the kind of conflict we all wish to avoid." Some City College professors urged Gallagher to prefer charges against Dr. Allen unless the engineering school were closed.[49]

No more grotesque Theater of the Absurd ever existed. Those wanting to go to class were to be censured; while almost a few hundred militants sealing off the campus to thousands of students were to be met by groveling appeasement.

Shortly before 8:00 p.m., a spokesman for Gallagher reported that the dean of the engineering school had concurred with his "request," and that the engineering division would be closed on Monday.[50]

At this time, between 40 and 50 Negro and Puerto Rican members of the City College faculty, made up of part-time as well as tenured teachers, announced the formation of the Black and Puerto Rican Faculty of the City College of the City University. The group issued a statement supporting the demands of the militants, and asked that CCNY remain closed, pending continued negotiations. The group declared that the issues were of "immediate concern to the whole black and Puerto Rican community" and expressed "continuing determination to participate in decisions affecting our people."[51]

About a week after the lock-in had begun, President Gallagher, with the backing of the Board of Higher Education, announced an agreement to keep the school closed as long as negotiations continued with the black and Puerto Rican students who had seized the South Campus. A key paragraph in the agreement to keep City College closed said in part: "All parties involved will commit themselves to maintain the status quo until the Board of Higher Education and any others whose approval may be necessary to implement the settlement, concur with the settlement." Some high City College officials noted that it could take the Board of Higher Education and other required agencies many weeks to work out some of the complex demands. They feared that the "status quo" provision would mean keeping the college closed for the rest of the academic year.[52]

President Gallagher was asked point-blank whether CCNY would be forced to remain shut for the rest of the academic year by extended negotiations with the blacks and Puerto Ricans. He replied this was not so, but added, "It will be if there is interference from other students." Presumably, his comments were aimed at the engineering students, and others, who had the audacity to want to go to school. He said he could not predict when a settlement would be reached, and stated, "Don't ask me to set a time limit. We are concerned here with the survival of the college."[53]

Ironically, that survival was being threatened by only 75 to 300 militants holding the South Campus; only a small percentage of some 3,000 black and Puerto Rican students[54]—and even smaller than that, when one considered the total enrollment of 20,000 at CCNY.

On May 1, two show-cause orders were served upon Dr. Gallagher in an effort to force him to reopen City College. Gallagher, the Board of Higher Education, and Albert H. Bowker, chancellor of the City University were asked to show in state supreme court why they should not reopen City College "to all duly enrolled students and to immediately commence the conduct of collegiate instruction, as provided for by the Education Law."

One of the writs was obtained by Congressman Mario Biaggi, and the other by the Jewish Defense League. They represented individual students.

In a statement about the show-cause order, Congressman Biaggi said:

> The officials who govern the college have capitulated to the rebellious students by closing the college. As a result, the students who want to get an education have been

locked out of the college of their choice. This is basically
the issue, and it is a matter of deep principle. For that
reason, we are handling this case without a fee.[55]

Meanwhile, the invaders holding the South Campus were
becoming more and more solidly entrenched.

The main gates of the South Campus bore a sign reading,
"Harlem University." Black and Puerto Rican community residents, including youngsters, freely entered with shopping bags
of food. One occupier asked for chicken, and when a youngster
said, "I've got bologna," the militant replied, "I'm tired of that.
I've got to have some chicken." Black faculty members visited
the South Campus frequently. The Negro and Puerto Rican
students occupying the South Campus called a neighborhood
rally at which Finley Hall would be renamed Che Guevara
Hall. Other buildings were to be renamed Malcolm X Library,
H. Rap Brown Political Science Building, Pedro Albizu Campos
Hall, and Huey Newton Hall.[56]

On the South Campus lawn at the first "Open House at the
University of Harlem," Emory Douglas, minister of culture of
the Black Panther Party, called for the restructuring of society
and spoke of the need for college students to relate to the problems of society. Another speaker, Mrs. Eldridge Cleaver, hailed
the takeover as "beautiful" and called for a similar takeover of
Central Park.[57]

On May 4, the Board of Higher Education directed that City
College be reopened to comply with court orders. The board also
asked that the black and Puerto Rican students occupying the
South Campus "voluntarily vacate [it] in an orderly manner,"
and pledged "mediatory negotiations" following such a withdrawal. Porter Chandler, chairman of the board, said, "The
board itself will not negotiate while any campus is seized."

The board noted that no violence or destruction had occurred
since the student occupation began, and asked the occupiers to
vacate "in an orderly manner consistent with their conduct up
to this time."[58] Faculty sources at the board meeting said the
board was "very concerned" about avoiding any action that
might provoke a violent response in Harlem, and were, at this
time, unwilling to call for police help to clear the South Campus.[59]

Gallagher told 350 faculty members and students that he was reluctant to call in the police to end the occupation of the South Campus because such action might provoke racial disorders in the city. On the other hand, if he failed to comply with court orders to reopen the college, "I will be in contempt of court."[60]

By now, the militant occupation of the South Campus was well into its second week.

Gallagher said that eleven days of negotiations between the college and the black and Puerto Rican student militants had failed so far to produce agreement on two key demands: an admissions policy that would reflect the racial composition of the city schools, and a separate school of black and third-world studies (involving the underdeveloped nations).[61]

One professor said the settlement proposals were "worse than my worst expectations," and denounced them as "a complete capitulation" that would "help to destroy the City College as an effective educational institution." At the same time, the demands were supported by 140 faculty members, most of them junior teachers. The partial settlement, worked out by Gallagher, three faculty negotiators, and seven representatives of the protesters, would have called for a separate orientation program for black and Puerto Rican freshmen to be headed by a director nominated by black and Puerto Rican students and approved by the college's departmental appointments committee. This director would be given autonomous powers to deal with the freshman orientation program, just as any other director had within his department.[62]

The agreement would have transformed the SEEK program into a full-fledged department of City College. SEEK students also would have been given representation on the new department's curriculum committee and on a committee that would establish criteria for hiring and reappointing faculty members. Some faculty members denounced this as separation, and warned that it had grave implications for the future of CCNY. Gallagher, in response, took some faculty members to task for "their condescension and paternalism and inability to understand." He was met by shouts of "shame, shame."[63]

Professor Stanley Feingold of the political science department said, "I am offended by this proposal for singling out one group." He suggested that any group of 100 students who wanted their own orientation program the following fall should be provided with it upon petition to the college. Professor Stanley W. Page of the history department charged that the proposals were developed "in an aura of terror," and constituted "complete capitulation" to the demands of a small group of black and Puerto Rican students.[64]

At 7:40 p.m., on Monday, May 5, an assistant corporation counsel read a writ sworn out by the Board of Higher Education, which enjoined the barricaded black and Puerto Rican students from congregating or assembling on the campus or in the buildings. Two hours later, about 250 of the militants marched peacefully out of the South Campus. They were accompanied by about 50 members of the SDS. The black and Puerto Rican protesters left, chanting "Power to the People" to the beat of drums, and singing civil rights hymns. One of them was accompanied by a Doberman pinscher on a leash. Other youths were carrying black nationalist and Puerto Rican flags, and a sign reading "University of Harlem."[65]

The demonstrators refused to talk to newsmen, but one of them commented, "This phase is over."[66]

The following day, City College reopened in its entirety for the first time in two weeks, but the state of siege had still not been completely lifted. Now white radical students staged a series of disruptive hit-and-run forays into classroom buildings in support of black student demands. Fire alarms were set off, and glass in at least two doors was broken as 200 white radicals marched through the corridors, shouting, "On strike! Shut it down!" Seven or eight of the Negro girls who had helped occupy the South Campus set fire to some bathing suits in a girls' gymnasium. There were also several fist fights between black and white students. College officials said that there were at least two incidents in which white students were attacked by black students. In one of these cases, a white student was robbed of $30 and his companion was struck on the head.[67]

At this point, the Board of Higher Education decided to replace the team that had negotiated with the black and Puerto Rican students, and replace it with a team of two faculty members, two students, and a chairman to be selected by these four.[68]

All that had happened up until now was a mere skirmish.

Now came the war, and CCNY suddenly became a raging battlefield. And it was the *New York Post* that detailed the terror
in a chilling article titled, "Violence at City College—Hour by
Hour."[69] What you are about to read took place within a period
of four hours, on a single morning in May.

At 8:30 a.m., Israel Levine, CCNY's publicity chief, got word
"of sporadic vandalism. We heard some students had been
punched as they walked to the campus." At 9:00 a.m., a white
girl was trapped in a bathroom by four black girls. One held her
at knifepoint as they robbed her. On the South Campus, the
bookstore opened. Minutes later, a group of dissidents invaded
the store, taking books and other items and refusing to pay. In
the cafeteria, a cash register was looted.

One of the major incidents erupted at Steinman Hall. Morris
Ettenberg, an electrical engineering professor, stated, "There
were a fairly large number of people inside the lobby. I'd come
there about 10 o'clock. They told me some people had been at
the doorway earlier and were coming back. About 10:15 they
did, there were perhaps 6 or 8 or 10, it's hard to say, young
people. They were armed. One had a golf club, another a kind
of tree trunk. They came toward the hall and wanted to get into
the building."

Professor Michael Plummer, walking toward Steinman, got
in the way and was punched in the mouth. His lip was split.

The intruders were black and Puerto Rican. Some were
recognized by instructors as students. Others were "people who
looked like they were from the outside community," another
professor said. "By 10 o'clock," said Israel Levine, "President
Gallagher called the police." Subsequently, "we got calls from
others saying they were calling police and we said we'd already
done this. We instructed the police to guard the campus, particularly the South Campus."

Professor Louis Heller, a teacher of Hebrew and classical
languages, was in Mott Hall and recalled,

A large contingent—I don't know what to call them, certainly black militants and SDS members, came into the
building about 10 o'clock and entered most of the rooms.
Then they went into Professor Nathan Berall's class—he
teaches English—and a group of about a dozen ordered the
students out. They started throwing chairs into the center

of the room. When Berall tried to get his notes together, they threw them around, too, and broke his glasses. Prof. Robert Hennion, who was in a nearby room, came to help Berall. One intruder tried to stop him but Hennion wasn't going to be stopped. There was a clash. He was thrown to the floor and six of them jumped on him until someone rescued him. His face was cut and he had bumps and bruises.

The invaders raced upstairs and broke into Room 313, where Professor Lottie Kohler was teaching second-term German to ten students. "About 10:20 the door burst open and five of them came into my room," she said. "They said immediately: 'This class is over. Everybody out.' Before I could say OK, OK, they pointed a fire extinguisher at my students. They sprayed it; they wet my students, their books and me. Because I wear glasses I could hardly see. Fortunately, it was water and not that foam spray."

On the second floor, said Professor Kohler, "some white students barricaded themselves inside a room so the blacks could not get in. I sought refuge on the fourth floor, where there were steel doors."

In Wagner Hall, Slavic languages Professor Michael Rywkin locked his door to bar militants. They smashed the glass in the door's window. Elsewhere in Wagner Hall, the invaders—some black, some Puerto Rican, some white sympathizers wearing red arm bands—disrupted classes, smashed windows, overturned chairs, often dumping students still in them. Soon afterward, a fire alarm sounded, and the building was evacuated.

It was 10:30. By this time, the word had gotten out that the college was closed for the day.

Outside, hundreds of milling students grew to thousands, in varying moods of bewilderment, resentment, and cold fury. At about 10:45, a Burns guard car, driven by a Negro guard, drove to the gate, and the guard tried to lock it. Some of the white students demanded to know, "What's going on here? Why are you locking the gate?" Trying to pass it off with a quip, the guard replied, "I want a little privacy." The white students were not amused. "This is our school," one shouted, "We want it open." Repeating those words—defiantly, desperately—they began an impromptu march toward the library. Near the library steps, the red-banded sympathizers, hearing the commotion and seeing the crowd coming toward them, joined arms to form a barricade between the black students, who were clustered behind them, and the oncoming whites.

A press photographer who had climbed a stone wall to take pictures saw a young boy climb alongside him. "He couldn't be more than 12," the cameraman said. "I felt a tug on my other camera, and when I looked at it, he'd smeared black ink on my lens. I was astounded. I couldn't believe it."

And few could believe what was now to happen.

The whites started to march toward the radical sympathizers, shouting, "Open the gates, open the gates." A student in a lumber jacket raised his arm and shouted to the marchers, "Come on, back in," and they surged through the gate the Burns guard had never succeeded in closing. Some 400 marchers reached the steps of the library and talked about "getting the revolutionists." Thinking that the library had been captured by dissidents, they shouted, "Let's get them out of the buildings and get them the hell out of there."

The radical sympathizers with the red bands meekly gave up their placards, which were destroyed and tossed in wastebaskets. Now the white students headed for the South Campus.

It was 11:15. The group, now numbering about 300, headed for the Finley Student Center. "Open it up," they chanted, and rushed to the center, forced the windows open, and climbed into the building. (In the rush of events, they hadn't taken time to determine that the door was unlocked.)

Now it was 11:30 a.m., and the eye of the hurricane was just minutes away.

The white crowd decided to unlock the St. Nicholas Terrace gate as a symbolic gesture that the campus was still open. As they neared the gate, they saw a black youth sitting high in a tree, holding a red flag. A white youth climbed the wall and went up the tree after the banner. The counter-demonstrators urged, "Rip the thing down," as he reached for the flagpole. Suddenly, the white student looked down and saw, massed outside the gate, some 40 to 50 blacks and Puerto Ricans. The white student retreated, and quickly three of the dissidents appeared atop the gate, armed with tree branches and broken bottles.

They climbed to the top of the fence and shouted to the whites, "Go home, the campus is closed."

Soon, about 25 of the dissidents were lined up on the grass, facing the 200 whites. The blacks carried weapons including sticks, clubs, and a radio antenna. Some of the whites fell back, but a few stayed to face down the invaders. After a shouting match, the blacks insisted, "Go home," and the whites, equally insistent, replied, "I won't." Then a black youth struck a white youth in the face, and the battle was joined.

The blacks lashed out with their weapons. The white students fell back in panic. "Come on back," pleaded one white youth. "Help us. There's only a few of them and many of us." Some whites ripped off boughs of a tree, which they used as weapons. But not all the whites stayed. "I'm not getting my head split for this," one shouted as he ran. The remaining whites were routed. Seven were seriously hurt; one of them was hit in the face with a golf club. Chatting with a Negro and Puerto Rican group, a girl exulted, "That's power, real power, when 10 guys can come across a fence and chase 200 white guys. Black power—Puerto Rican power."

Several squad cars came rushing down St. Nicholas Terrace, and a contingent of police marched across the South Campus to the cheers of the defeated white students. "We want cops," they chanted to the suddenly popular police. The blacks warned their group: "The pigs are coming. Come on, get out." They swiftly scaled the fence, and the rest of their group broke into two groups and quickly scattered. By the time the police arrived, there were no invaders left. It was now 11:45 a.m.

Gallagher himself had gone to the West 100th Street police station to complete "the arrangements to bring the police on the campus." He explained, "To request police on the campus, one must sign the forms. And I did so." Asked why he had finally decided to call the police, Gallagher replied, "The violence was between blacks and whites, and it was a case of stopping an incipient race riot."[70]

Later, the police reported that they had found bottles and a flammable fluid that appeared to be intended for the manufacture of Molotov cocktails. The police stated that the materials were found hidden behind a security shack at the 133rd Street gate to the South Campus.[71]

302 THE NEW RACISM

Five blocks away, at the administration building, Ira Bloom, executive assistant to the dean of students, used a bullhorn to announce: "The college will be open tomorrow, with adequate police protection on campus." The white students cheered.[72]

A policeman ordered, "Please leave, please leave. I want everyone off campus." A bearded white youth asked a police sergeant, "Are you going to stay on campus?" The sergeant replied, "As far as I know, yes." The crowd burst into loud applause, and the bearded youth shook hands with the sergeant. "I'll tell you a secret," the student said. "I never thought I'd shake a policeman's hand." The policeman shrugged and said, "We're not all bad guys, you know."[73]

On the North Campus, two white radicals talked as they strolled along Convent Avenue. Said one, "When I saw those pigs standing outside the South Campus, it burned me up. I hope these black students burn the school down to the ground." His friend nodded in agreement.[74]

Afterwards, faculty members supporting the black and Puerto Rican students claimed that white students had threatened to attack four black girls, and that this was the reason for the melee in which seven white students were injured. The faculty members—most of them black and Puerto Rican— spoke of threatening acts by whites, some armed with sticks and clubs; they said that white students converged on the black girls and in effect trapped them at the locked east gate of the South Campus. It was only then, the instructors said, that some 25 Negro and Puerto Rican youths climbed the fence and started fighting with the white youths, three of whom were hospitalized. But a *New York Times* reporter at the scene observed that some 300 white counter-protesters had poured over the campus, tearing up a poster and taking down a red flag hanging at the East Gate. The reporter stated: "Two black girls caught between the gate and the white crowd tried to climb the 10-foot gate but failed. They escaped from the crowd, frightened but unharmed."[75]

The black and Puerto Rican students did not fight unaided; they had help from their friends in Harlem. The *Amsterdam News* noted, "Residents in the neighborhood went on the campus and participated in the skirmishes."[76]

During this period, the press came under sharp attack by

black and Puerto Rican faculty and students. Their spokes-woman, Betty Rawls, complained, "The coverage of the press wasn't fair at all. Every time the press refers to the black and Puerto Rican students at the College, they call them dissidents. They referred to a white faculty member and called him by his right title, assistant professor. But when they referred to Professor Cartey [appointed to develop a curriculum of black and Puerto Rican studies] they don't use his title."

Agreeing with her was Professor Addison Gayle, Jr., who con-tended, "The best coverage we have gotten has been in *Muham-mad Speaks.*"[77] Professor Gayle's admiration for *Muhammad Speaks* was clearly consistent with the strident militance of his own writings, as witness this excerpt from an article Gayle had written for *Liberator:*

> Were Black Power an actuality, Adam Clayton Powell would have his seniority in Congress; John Hatchett would be directing the Martin Luther King Center at N.Y.U.; John Carlos would not have been dismissed from the Olympic Team; and the Mayor of the City of New York would not be cowtowing [sic] to the racist-oriented United Federa-tion of Teachers. Therefore, despite the fact that there are Blacks who are hindrances to the movement, no organiza-tion has accomplished enough to warrant the right *to as-sign such men to the wall.*[78] [Emphasis added]

Actually—as the Black Muslim newspaper readily admitted —the reporter for *Muhammad Speaks* "was one of the few newspapermen allowed and welcomed behind the blockaded South Campus gates."[79] When Sylvan Fox, the *New York Times* reporter who had been covering events at CCNY, tried to inter-view black students inside the South Campus during the sei-zure, he was told, "Go away, pig."[80]

There were times when the white students could have regis-tered some complaints of their own about press coverage. Cer-tainly, some protest would have been in order about the *New York Times* statement, "In the end, the college had to be kept open, with the help of heavy police guards. One officer, startled by the white backlash, said, 'They even cheered us.' "[81] This was probably the first time that students eager to get on with their studies and education were castigated as members of "the white backlash."

Some of these white students carried Malraux and mathematics books, and some carried the *Partisan Review* and physics papers. Some wore their hair shaggy and some short. Some were quiet, others were shouting. But all had one simple, basic, non-negotiable demand: "Open it up." At a rally before the guarded administration building, one youth in a khaki jacket shouted, "I want to graduate next month." Tom Taldone, a mathematics major, said, "We don't want terror. We want classes, that's all, just classes." Eighteen-year-old John Bohn, a 200-pound English major, sat with a bleeding forehead in the emergency room of Knickerbocker Hospital and commented, "Look, I think a lot of the black demands are just. But there was this fantastic tension—it was all bound to happen. We've had enough, though, of a shut-down school. We want this place open."[82]

For two tortuous weeks, many of them—working their way through college—had been worried about job interviewers not appearing on campus, about canceled examinations, possibly even a delayed graduation. But the black students could not have cared less. "So you lose a day, a week or a semester," a tall Negro shouted to a white student. "We've lost generations, and damn it, this is what we intend to stop." The white student argued, "It's not the way to do it. This will only turn people against you." The black youth just swore.[83]

When white students tried to get black and Puerto Rican youths to admit that the use of violence was wrong, the blacks simply insisted it was "not a question of violence, but of justice." A Puerto Rican girl put it more bluntly: violence "was the only language the [white] man understands."[84]

On May 8, City College was nominally open, but few classes were held because of the continuing tension and turmoil. At 1:20 p.m., there was a clash between protesters and policemen, during a rally of white radical students supporting the black and Puerto Rican militants. Their speakers called for a new closing of City College. As the radicals' rally progressed, 400 counter-demonstrators held a rally of their own to demand that the college be kept open. Some of them heckled and booed the radicals. Suddenly, some of the radicals threw eggs at the hecklers. The counter-demonstrators responded by throwing bottles and rocks. Luckily, no one was injured. About 25 policemen, carrying nightsticks, marched to the North Campus area (known as the Quadrangle) and some of them swung their clubs. The radicals retreated as black students denounced the police action in advancing only on the radicals. A black girl was seized by some policemen. As she was being apprehended, a black youth started swinging at the police. He was clubbed to the ground, and then taken into custody.[85]

The police said another black youth was arrested with a knife and one was seized with a vial of fluid. Policemen pursued the Negro and white radical youths up 138th Street into Amsterdam Avenue, swinging their clubs as they went. At least eight persons were taken into custody.[86] A campus building was severely damaged by a suspicious fire, and ten smaller fires were set by student protesters. One fire was set in Eisner Hall by a group of black students who slashed a 6-by-15-foot abstract painting and set it ablaze. The painting was the work of two City College student artists who had spent six weeks working on it before the Easter vacation.[87]

Throughout the day, there were fist fights between black and white students. One of the blacks warned a white youth, "The police won't be here forever. We'll remember you."[88]

President Gallagher released a statement in which he expressed hope "that the black and Puerto Rican student community will decide to resume negotiations." In the same statement Gallagher deplored "these adventurers in guerrilla tactics who, it would seem, prefer anarchy to justice."[89]

Mayor Lindsay said that he would unilaterally send police onto the troubled campuses of the City University, regardless of the wishes of the college presidents, "when Chancellor Bowker and the Board of Higher Education in my judgment have completely abdicated their responsibility." He quickly added, "We are not at that point." Lindsay said that the failure to send in police in no way condoned the student disrupters. He said that the police had to be used with great care, because "the very presence of uniformed police can have a galvanizing effect" on a campus disorder. Lindsay went on, "It can have the effect of turning something which is controllable and relatively quiet—relatively mild—into something that's far more dangerous."[90] What Lindsay seemed to be saying was that if the black and Puerto Rican students mildly and quietly kept the campus closed—and mildly and quietly deprived other students of their right to an education—the police would be kept off the campus.

A box score of openings and closings at CCNY would have read something like this:

> closed by Gallagher after the student occupation started; opened by the Board of Higher Education in response to a court injunction; closed again by Gallagher after racial clashes among students; reopened again by the Board of Higher Education and all within a period of just 2½ weeks.

Even more incredible was the total cost of student disorders at CCNY—$348,000.[91]

On May 9, Dr. Gallagher asked the Board of Higher Education to relieve him of his "duties and responsibilities" at CCNY. Gallagher said he had hoped to remain until the end of the semester, but

> when the forces of angry rebellion and stern repression clash, the irrepressible conflict is joined. A man of peace, a reconciler, a man of compassion must stand aside for a time and await the moment when sanity returns and brotherhood based on justice becomes a possibility.[92]

Among those noticeably unmoved by Gallagher's exit was Jeffrey Ira Zuckerman, a columnist for the City College under-graduate paper, *The Campus.* In a "thirty column," Zuckerman expressed regret that he was unable to write about the usual "beautiful memories," but he felt "it would be irresponsible for any graduating student to make believe that the College of the past four years (or five, or six) is the College that he is leaving behind." Zuckerman continued:

> That College disappeared at the moment on the morning of April 22, 1969, when Dr. Gallagher decided that black students were to be treated differently than white students —white students who had sat-in only on Site 6 and just blocked construction of a hut had been arrested, but blacks who occupied the entire South Campus and forced the cancellation of all classes were not to be.[93]

A week after Zuckerman's column appeared, one of those white activists, Ron McGuire, was expelled from City College, on recommendation of the Student-Faculty Disciplinary Committee.[94]

Zuckerman dismissed the notion that a desire for dialogue had been the real motive for the black seizure of the South Campus. In Zuckerman's words:

> The real motive was not dialogue but destruction—the destruction of the City College as an institution of Higher Education. The main thrust of the occupation was to replace the laws of the university with the laws of the streets—in a university it is the stronger reasoning which should prevail; in the streets it is the stronger bodies. The ultimate irony was that the BPRSC [Black and Puerto Rican Student Community] couldn't win, whether the struggle was intellectual or physical. The only chance they had was if the University backed down from confrontation on either level. This is what Dr. Gallagher did, and this is what has now forced the resumption of the confrontation on a purely physical level—the triumph of the gutter over the university.

Zuckerman pointed out that City College could have secured a court injunction "and then proceeded to have overwhelmed them on the intellectual level." But since it had refused to do this, "the college is now paying the price that falls due on all those who try appeasement in the face of extortion."

Zuckerman supported the black demand that "Black and Puerto Rican History and the Spanish Language be Required for all Education Majors"—a demand, he noted, that the School of Education had agreed to, *before* April 22. He also felt there was something to be said for: "A Separate Orientation Program for Black and Puerto Rican Students." As for the others:

> Consider the third [black demand]: "A Voice for SEEK Students in the Setting of Guidelines for the SEEK Program, Including the Hiring and Firing of Personnel." Beautiful. Since the SEEK program should be geared to the needs of the SEEK students, and since SEEK students know their own needs best, they should control the program. Bull——. The SEEK program is precisely for students who went through twelve or more years of primary and second-

ary education without realizing their own needs for a good education. When they enter the program, it is a sign that they have begun to recognize this need, but it is just a beginning. If they know what the program should cover, they should be teaching it, not studying in it.[95]

The debate went on and on—but without Gallagher as prime target and participant. The speedy exit of Gallagher from the CCNY presidency was equalled only by the speedy entrance of his replacement, Professor Joseph J. Copeland of the City College Department of Biology. Copeland was named acting president of City College, following a three-hour meeting of the Board of Higher Education. He was one of the three faculty members who had been involved in recent negotiations with the dissident Negro and Puerto Rican students.[96]

Copeland stated, "I am basically sympathetic to the demands of the black and Puerto Rican students. I became even more so during the recent negotiations and, while I do not regard illegal action as either proper or efficient, I am convinced that this is an issue that cannot be dodged by tokenism or solved by brute power."[97] Two weeks earlier, in an address to members of the faculty, he had said of the black and Puerto Rican students, "We are not giving these people a fair break, and before God we will do it."[98]

In the age of stereotypes, Dr. Joseph Copeland defied all the conventional categories. A self-described "philosophical pacifist," he twice interrupted his teaching career to serve in the armed forces, during World War II and the Korean conflict. The Copelands had five wards ranging in age from 8 to 27, whose education they had been supporting. Three were American Indians, one was black and one was white. Copeland was considered a conservative by many of his colleagues, some of whom said he had "learned a lot" as one of the negotiators with the black and Puerto Rican students.[99]

In assuming the office of acting president of City College, Professor Copeland called for "law, order, peace, harmony," while pledging to "rectify the shortcomings" at the college. The black and Puerto Rican dissidents still insisted the school be shut, while negotiations were held, but Copeland was equally insistent in stating, "I fully expect the talks to take place while the college is open. I expect the college to remain open."

Asked how long police would remain at the college, Copeland replied, "They will remain here until we have an atmosphere of peace and order. The police are here at my invitation and request."[100]

City College was scheduled to open the morning of May 12, under heavy police guard. But Copeland agreed to a plan proposed by the college's Faculty Senate, under which conferences and workshops would be held in place of regular classes for the next three days.[101] The new acting president rejected a Faculty Senate resolution that police be removed from the campus. In a stern speech to the 87-member Faculty Senate, Copeland declared that the police would be kept on the campus as long as there existed a "real and substantial danger of disorders and maltreatment of property, vandalism, arson and the like."[102]

Furthermore, Copeland said normal classes would be held at the 20,000-student college for the rest of the week, unless Negro and Puerto Rican student militants agreed to resume negotiations while the police remained on campus. He also made it clear there was to be a limited—rather than general—convocation in place of some classes.

Copeland said the workshops had to be planned, "meaningful, serious discussions" of college problems and that normal classes had to continue to function in the graduate and evening divisions of the college, which were not directly affected. In addition, he insisted, students and teachers not participating in the convocations and workshops had to be able to attend normal classes if they wished.[103]

Referring to his insistence that the police remain on campus, and that at least some regular classes be held during this period, Copeland told the Faculty Senate, "These are non-negotiable conditions. You will in fact live with them and so will I." He maintained, "This college and all colleges must remain in operation and not allow pressure, duress and threats of destruction to force us to retreat time after time after time." Conceding that he was overriding the Faculty Senate, Copeland added, "For that I do not apologize." He pledged that he would be "firm, blunt, direct and, I hope, helpful, in guiding the college through these difficult days."[104]

Black and Puerto Rican students and faculty members distributed copies of a letter written three weeks before, in which the CCNY negotiators had agreed that "as long as negotiations are progressing, the college is to remain closed." One of the signers of this letter was Dr. Copeland. Copeland acknowledged that he had signed the letter because he had agreed with the policy of then-President Gallagher to close the school while negotiations were going forth. "I was not then the president," Copeland commented. "Now I am."[105]

A few days later, in yet another on-again, off-again flip-flop that had become all too dismally familiar on the campus scene, the police were withdrawn, and several hours later, negotiations resumed on the demands of the black and Puerto Rican dissidents.[106] These were the conditions for the start of negotiations:

# That the city police remain off the campus.
# That the college administration, Faculty Senate, black, and Puerto Rican students and faculty organizations "call upon all parties both within and without the college to refrain from engaging in any activity injurious to the continuation of the negotiations."
# That a convocation of students and faculty instead of regular classes be held for the next 2 days. If negotiations had not been satisfactorily concluded by then, "the parties to the negotiations shall assess the state of affairs and determine the conditions under which negotiations will continue."
# That all students "involved in the negotiations in any capacity shall receive no academic penalty."[107]

College sources said Copeland had changed his position after getting assurances from black and Puerto Rican students and from their white radical allies that the campus would remain peaceful during the negotiations. Said one faculty member, "I think that he made tremendous concessions in the interest of getting the negotiations started again."[108]

One of the black militant leaders, Serge Mullery, stated that his group condemned violence and the setting of fires at the college. He said, "We have set up security forces to make sure this will not happen; that there will be no destruction and no looting." Mullery said there was no need for police on campus, and stressed, "We will not participate in any function as long as this is an armed camp." [109] His indigniation might have been a bit more persuasive if his group's tactics had not made "an armed camp" absolutely necessary.

Dr. Kenneth Clark, a Negro faculty member at CCNY, and also a member of the New York State Board of Regents, condemned student protests that prevented the majority of an institution's students from attending classes. Clark emphasized that "no minority students, and I mean minority in this sense —numerical minority—should have the right to interfere with the right to an education of other students." Clark felt that black and Puerto Rican students at City College and elsewhere should demand not that admissions policies be changed but that colleges and universities become involved in improving the quality of primary and secondary education so that black and Puerto Rican students could "compete seriously in a college setting."[110]

The black and Puerto Rican protesters' demand that education students be required to take courses in Spanish and black and Puerto Rican history and culture had readily been granted by the Board of Higher Education and was due to go into effect in the fall.[111] But an impasse remained over one key demand of the dissidents: a sharp increase in the number of black and Puerto Rican high school graduates to reflect their percentage in the city's high schools.[112] It was estimated that this would have amounted to about 40 percent of future freshman classes.[113] Many teachers feared that in yielding to this demand, scholastic standards would be sacrificed. Many students were equally concerned about the pressure for "open admissions" in which minority groups would not have to meet the same scholastic admission standards as other high school students. This feeling was particularly strong among students at the engineering school and among those majoring in science or mathematics.[114]

The negotiations continued, and, along with them, the convocations and workshops that were being used as makeshift substitutes for regular classes. A professor, Louis Heller, said that at one of the afternoon workshops, he and a colleague were threatened by a black student. Professor Heller, who was in the classical languages and Hebrew department, said a black girl came up to him after a heated discussion of the protesters' demands, and asked him, "Aren't you afraid?" The professor said he was not, and he quoted the girl as having said, "Well you ought to be because we're going to get you." Professor Heller went on, "She then said something to the effect that 'we're going to kill you,'" and then pointing to a colleague, Professor Nathan Susskind of the German and Slavic languages department, added, "Your friend, too."[115] Another professor, Joseph Wohlberg of the classical languages and Hebrew department, said his wife received a threatening telephone call from a man the preceding afternoon, while he was out.[116]

On May 21, classes at City College resumed, as black and Puerto Rican student protesters won a concession under which no undergraduates in the school could fail any courses that term. In what went under the euphemism "a show of good faith," the college administration agreed to make drastic changes in its grading system for that term. Undergraduate students were to be given grades of p, representing Pass, or J, indicating that course was dropped before completion. No one was to be failed, or given a grade of D. Unlike a failure, which reduced a student's total college grade point average, the J or incomplete grade had no effect on the student's academic average. If, but only if, students requested it, they would get a letter grade of A,B,C.[117]

This grading plan for the term was formally endorsed by Acting President Copeland.[118] Senator John Marchi denounced the plan as "thoroughly objectionable" and "probably unconstitutional."[119]

Now, students, faculty, and administration negotiators were meeting around the clock in a frenetic effort to produce a settlement. For the second day in a row (probably to the mild astonishment of many, both inside and outside CCNY), classes were conducted normally.

The negotiators had labored wearily to remove a landmine, and now they practically detonated a bombshell. After a month of turmoil at City College, the school and the black and Puerto Rican dissidents reached a tentative agreement to set up a dual system of admissions. Under the terms of the 14-page document, by the fall of 1970, half the freshmen were to be admitted on the basis of grades, as always. But the other half, from poverty areas, would be permitted to enter City College "without regard to grades."[120] In other words, half of the freshmen spaces from 1970 onward would be filled through competition based on marks and test scores, and the other half would be filled by intensive recruitment in poverty areas without regard to conventional college admissions credentials, "averages" and "college boards" (the scholastic achievement tests taken in the senior year). These students would be chosen on the vague basis of "potential, motivation, interest level and desire to attend college." The agreement stated: "The expressed goal of this dual admission policy is the matriculation of a City College freshman class which more adequately meets the needs of all the disadvantaged segments in the city's public schools."[121]

Another part of the agreement proposed establishment of a school of urban and third-world studies by September for "the study of the culture and history of Blacks, Puerto Ricans, Latin Americans and Asians.[122]

Of scant concern to those signing the agreement was the protest of a small group representing the Student Senate—the student governing body—that white students had been barred from the negotiations. According to Copeland, this had been done at the desire of the black and Puerto Rican dissidents, with his consent.[123]

Quickly, a storm of opposition began to center around the "open admission policy" for half of each year's freshman class —a policy that would waive traditional admissions and grade criteria for poverty-area high school students. City University sources said the faculty of City College was "bitterly divided" on the measure, and there was widespread talk of many resignations and early retirements if this policy went into effect.[124] Some of those threatening to resign were full professors.[125] Influential alumni besieged City College with protests.[126]

City University sources told the *New York Post* that such a policy would totally transform City College:

# If the City College budget was not sharply increased, those students coming into the 1970 freshman class by the competitive route would probably have to compile a composite average of "87, 88, or maybe even higher." Up until now, the highest grade requirement for City College admission had been 86, and that was back in 1965. Thus, grade competition among middle-class students would be heightened to an unprecedented peak to

make room for poverty-area students whose marks were virtually irrelevant.

# City College would become "Two colleges," in the words of one official. There would be one school (probably with one set of teachers and one group of courses) for those coming in with high marks, and another school for academically handicapped students needing remedial work. In effect, C.C.N.Y. would become "a separatist institution."

# The total number of incoming freshmen would probably go into significant decline, if the budget remained at the present level, because it was far more expensive to educate the "disadvantaged" student than one who did not need intensive makeup work. Citing just one example—because of additional individualized instruction, special tutors, guidance counselors and other services—it cost about twice as much per student to run the SEEK program than it did to operate the regular college program.[127]

In an attack on the proposal, Arleigh B. Williamson of the Board of Higher Education said, "I'm heartbroken. This is like jumping from the frying pan into the fire. It put me in a state of shock. There is bound to be opposition by some members of the board. What are the implications for the future in keeping qualified faculty and getting a new president? The whole fabric of the university will deteriorate."[128]

One of the faculty negotiators who had participated in the secret sessions that produced the agreement, Professor Stanley Feingold of the Department of Political Science, resigned about two days before the pact was produced.[129]

The American Jewish Congress, in a telegram to Porter Chandler, president of the Board of Higher Education, and to other officials, urged the board to reject the agreement:

Acceptance of the tentative agreement means substitution of group standards based on race and economic condition for individual achievement and promise. It means discrimination against numbers of students whose individual accomplishments and promise qualify them for admission.[130]

There was deep division in the City College faculty over the whole question of dual admissions—a conflict that rippled through the interviews the *New York Times* conducted with ten professors of associate and full professorial rank.

Arthur Waldhorn, professor of English, said:

> I support the dual-track admissions proposal. I have no doubts about the problems that attend its acceptance, problems involving funding facilities, and recruitment of personnel. I have no doubt either—and that is why I shall vote for the proposal—that the stop-gap and piecemeal measures currently operative are unfair, unrealistic and uneconomical. What lies ahead is not separatism but a remedial program that will tap a vast reservoir of black and Puerto Rican students who, when judged academically ready, will be channeled into the mainstream of academic competition.[131]

Leo Hamalian, associate professor of English, commented:

> I think it's workable. It ought to be understood that no one who qualifies for City College by present standards of admission is likely to be deprived from attending City College in the future. . . . It does not seem to me a quota system.[132]

Alfred H. Conrad, chairman of the economics department, felt the proposed admissions policy was aimed at correcting a failure of opportunity. He stated:

> It does not impose any quota system. It seeks, rather, to offer a place in the college, to public high school graduates whose potential has been masked by frustration and hopelessness in the high schools. The new policy would make City College a more exciting place, with an intellectually richer student body, ready to come more directly to grips with the most serious problems of our society.[133]

But Howard L. Adelson, professor of history, voiced vigorous opposition. In his words:

> I'm opposed to the dual-admissions system on a number of grounds. It involves a concealed quota system, and having seen the text of the agreement, any amendments passed to

that agreement will only serve to obscure the quota arrangements involved. The proposal does necessitate a decrease in the number of merited admissions and a variety of racism which must be abhorrent to any rational human being. It will result in a sharp decline in the standards of the college, or in setting up two colleges, neither of which will function effectively. We would be well advised to replace our present proposal for the disadvantaged with one that trained them adequately, so that they could enter our regular programs and compete effectively.[134]

Agreeing with him was Marnin Feinstein, associate professor in the classical languages and Hebrew department, who stated:

At City College not a single student was ever rejected on the basis of race, religion, color or ethnic grouping. Scholarship has always been the sole criterion. . . . To introduce a policy of brazen discrimination would be to deny college education to thousands of proven students whose parents for the most part are in the low-middle-income grouping and unable to send their children to private colleges.[135]

And Hubert Park Beck, associate professor of education, was even more outspoken:

The negotiations were conducted like a kidnap gang's negotiations, with the so-called representatives of the faculty and of the administration fearful that the college would be invaded from Harlem and destroyed. On the other side of the table were 19-year-olds whose concept of how the world operates is hardly adequate to their demands. City College has no special magic by which student shortcomings—18 years in the making—can be quickly overcome. A year's study commission is what is needed to effect a constructive outcome and prevent more gangster-like acts on the part of impatient students.[136]

In a letter to the editor of the *New York Times,* Leo Klauber, Class of '23, stated that the contemplated changes at City College would mean that the college would be "reduced to a level at which only the mediocre will be admitted." Again taking up the cudgels for dual admissions, Professor Hamalian replied:

When Mr. Klauber entered City College, a high school diploma alone was sufficient to obtain admission. All secondary school graduates who desired entrance were
allowed to enter. . . . As late as 1955, a student with a high
school average in the low 70's could matriculate at City
College (if his college-entrance score was 79%). At the
Baruch school, standards were even lower.[137]

A most cogent rebuttal to Hamalian's views was speedily
offered by Herman Arthur in still another letter to the editor.
Mr. Arthur wrote:

In the early 1920's, when the college admitted all high
school graduates, the high schools were themselves highly
selective, with a most rigorous academic course of study
patterned on the European gymnasium. Only a handful of
public school students completed high school, with the
vast majority leaving school at the end of the eighth grade
or earlier. In the 1950's, the seventy plus averages which
he cites as qualifying for admission were based on an academic course of study which included a minimum of two
years each in mathematics, science and foreign language
and at least three years in one of the above subjects. It was
normal practice at the time (no longer followed) that no
student could pass these courses without passing state Regents examinations as well. Even today a student would,
for practical purposes, have to pass state Regents to attain
the minimum 82 average, because teachers will give low
passing grades to students who fail the Regents, assuming
they pass them at all.

Mr. Arthur also noted:

Under the proposed City College admissions system, white
students with academic averages of less than 82 would go
to [two-year] community colleges, [while] black and Puerto
Rican students with general diplomas and any average on
an academic diploma would be admitted to four-year colleges. Perhaps Lewis Carroll could justify such a proposal.[138]

In defense of the dual-admissions proposal, Betty Rawls,
counselor of the SEEK program, stated, "The political comments have shown a lack of real examination of the document.
They are inflating an issue which we had hoped would be ap-

proached with calm and reason. This is not a quota system. If it is, then the one we've had until now is even more a quota system. The testing system we've had until now has been geared to middle-class society."[139]

Miss Rawls' contentions might have had some slight semblance of validity if members of the middle class had automatically waltzed through the admissions office and into CCNY. But the whole point was that the individual student's grade average —and *not* his bankbook, status or family—was *the* determining factor in whether or not he entered CCNY. Such a student could have been bulging with middle-class credentials, and still be denied admission to City College if his grades were not high enough. And here, too, we might well recall that survey showing that many freshmen at City College came from families whose incomes were *below* what the federal government said was needed to maintain a "moderate" living standard.

Miss Rawls said that elaborate methods would be evolved for remedial education for the students who were admitted without regard to scholastic standards. She indicated that some students might take five or six years to get a degree. Then, not very convincingly, she concluded, "The scholastic standards of the school will not decline."[140]

Even less convincing was the analogy drawn by Negro Assemblyman Charles B. Rangel. He told the *Amsterdam News* that preferential treatment "is not a new idea in the system and in our educational system. I have been the beneficiary of preferential treatment, one: because I was a veteran and two: because I was a Korean veteran. Therefore, if some individual similarly situated as I was—a high school dropout who did not serve in the service, he did not receive the benefits or the preferential treatment that I received. The same can be said of the veterans of World War II."[141]

There of course was a great difference between awarding educational benefits to a veteran for services rendered to his country (a veteran who still would have to meet normal college entrance requirements), and pushing college-entrance rules aside to enroll some academically unqualified black and Puerto Rican students. There was an equally great difference between awarding financial benefits to veterans and instituting a plan that deliberately rejected some students with high averages in order to admit some other students with low averages.

Mayor Lindsay attacked the proposal for dual admission to City College as a "quota system" and urged its rejection by the college's Faculty Senate and the Board of Higher Education.[142] In addition, controller Procaccino delivered to the mayor's office a petition he said was signed by 1,456 City College students urging that "only students capable of meeting the academic standards should be admitted." Procaccino said some students taking this position had been beaten up and others had been threatened.[143]

On May 28, the *New York Post* reported a poll it had taken indicated that the Board of Higher Education would reject the dual-admissions policy. David Ashe, a labor lawyer, expressing the majority sentiment on the board, declared, "I am unalterably opposed to a quota system, which is what this is." He denounced it as "a sham and a fraud." Ashe said that he believed "the proposal for a 'Third World School' is much more dangerous than the question of open enrollment. We certainly want open enrollment, but we won't be able to afford it until 1975." He insisted, "We have got to maintain the worth of the degree. If we give in to this plan so that anyone who goes to college gets a degree, then the degree will be meaningless. We have got to stand up as responsible members of the community."[144]

Was dual admissions the only answer to the educational problems of these black and Puerto Rican students? Was there no other way that they could secure a college education? Actually, there were many roads to a college education in New York City. Black and Puerto Rican students with high enough grades could qualify for admission to CCNY, or one of the other four-year senior colleges. Those whose marks did not qualify them for one of these colleges could apply for one of the places in a two-year community college. Those with inadequate grades, who had to work full-time, could apply for a place in the City College Evening Session which offered students the opportunity to take courses until they could be raised to full senior college standing.[145] The choice was there, the options were open, well before the first dual-admissions proposal saw the light of day.

All of this was conveniently ignored by the champions of dual admissions—notably the black and Puerto Rican dissidents at

City College. The *New York Post* revealed that some of the student leaders involved in the negotiations about dual admissions had had contacts with the Black Panther movement. One source said that at least two and possibly four of the dozen or so negotiators had been seen at Black Panther Party meetings. The police said that at least four of the student negotiators were known to them, and that two had been observed at Panther meetings by undercover plainclothesmen. At the time it was not known whether the students were there as sympathizers or as members of the party.[146]

Other sources told the *New York Post* that the negotiators linked to the Panthers had kept the association hidden from their fellow black and Puerto Rican students, to keep it from discrediting their activity on the campus.[147]

Sources said a blueprint for the CCNY disruptions was prepared as part of a Panther program to create a "separate school" there, intended to be an East Coast Panther base. The proposed school to teach black and Puerto Rican studies and the "Third World Institute" outlined in the negotiated settlement were to be this "separate school." It was to be a "politically oriented" institute, with elements of "community control," and chosen for its proximity to Harlem.[148]

During the New York City mayoralty campaign, a former high-ranking police official, Sanford Garelik, was running for City Council President on the Lindsay ticket. (He was subsequently elected.) In an interview, Garelik said he had strong reason to believe that campus dissidents had received aid from Communist China and Cuba.[149]

Richard Aurelio—at that time Lindsay's campaign manager —issued a hurried "clarification" in Garelik's name, purporting to quote him as saying, "I want to correct an erroneous impression—I want to make clear that I know of no hard evidence" of Communist involvement in the campus dissent. In private, Garelik strenuously objected to the unauthorized statement.[150]

At City College, Acting President Copeland was arousing just as much controversy in a plain two-fisted speech that turned the criticism upon the campus critics. About 60 graduating students walked out of the City College commencement exercises, as Copeland was delivering a stern attack on campus dissidents and black separatists. The walkout came as Copeland was about two-thirds through his speech—a speech in which he declared that "there are those in the New Left and the old left who are dedicated not to the reform of American colleges, the American Government and American society, but to their destruction." Copeland denounced "racial extremists, both white and black, who seek to impose a new apartheid or separatism on American society at a moment when for the first time in three centuries the promise and possibility of racial reconciliation have at last appeared on the horizon." The acting president called for expansion of college recruitment programs in the slums, but emphasized that "to insure the maintenance of high standards, we must continue to admit a preponderance of our students through the traditional and successful competitive achievement basis. We must not decrease the number of freshmen entering in the usual manner. We will not use racial quotas in admission."[151]

With one eye on the black campus revolutionaries, the Board of Higher Education "approved an historic resolution advancing the target date for Open Admissions from 1975 . . . to September 1970, subject to the provision of sufficient funds by the City and State governments to finance this major move."[152] And anyone who doubted that violence had won the day—and won the campus—simply did not understand the political facts of life in New York City.

Certainly, Open Admissions was not wildly popular with the CCNY student body. Of a thousand students replying to an administration poll in October, 53.8 percent registered an unfavorable response to Open Admissions, while some 39.2 percent were favorable.[153]

At about this time, a 37-member City University commission recommended that admission to specific units of the university be based on a student's class ranking in high school rather than on his grade average, as in the past. But Mayor Lindsay, running hard for reelection, demanded that "every student who can now get into a senior college must be guaranteed a seat in a senior college. And therefore class rank cannot be used to govern admission to senior colleges."[154]

The response of the Board of Higher Education was to do an academic juggling act with both criteria, and hope it didn't all come tumbling down before the board members had finished taking their bows. Under this plan, students with averages of 80 percent or higher, or students in the top half of their graduating class, would have "opportunities for senior college admission if they so desire. . . ."[155]

According to the projections of the City University's Task Force on Open Admissions, the September freshman class was estimated at about 35,000. This figure included some 8,500 high school graduates from the city's poverty areas who would be admitted to the senior and community colleges *regardless of their grades and class ranking.* The task force said it could be assumed that from 25 percent to 45 percent of the entering freshman class would require some measure of counseling, remedial work, and financial aid.[156]

The *Jewish Press* wrote:

> City College and Brooklyn College have traditionally been schools where the highest intellectuals, many Jewish students, have attended. As a result of the new ethnic balance program, students with excellent grade averages may be forced to leave the city and have to borrow money to obtain an education that their parents, as taxpayers, have been paying for throughout their lifetimes.[157]

That same newspaper noted, "The leading educators in the City University have begun to search elsewhere for teaching posts. One Professor declared, 'It is no longer a matter of dollars and cents. I am an educator—if I want to lecture to stone I can visit a museum.' " Some professors pointed out that they had been told to reduce pressure in their courses—"Make it so every student can obtain some accomplishment."[158]

A department chairman said that "anyone who expresses concern about the quality of education is cast in the role of a reactionary."[159]

The *Jewish Press* felt that under the new admissions policy, "a student with a grade average of 70% or even less, *who might have a high class standing,* stands a better chance of entering a City college than a student with a 90 average" (emphasis added). It asked, "What value will a City University diploma have outside New York City in the years to come? To start with, it automatically tells a prospective employer you are not superior, but closer to the bottom of the academic ladder."[160]

The *Jewish Press* readily conceded the good intentions of the efforts to increase the ethnic balance at the City University, but it all reminded them

> of the two men in a boat, one of whom drilled a hole in his part of the boat. "After all, it's my side of the boat!" that man exclaims, as the boat sinks lower into the water.[161]

# CHAPTER 12

# The "Impossible" Revolution

AS ONE WATCHED THE BLACK MILITANTS ON ONE BELEAGUERED campus after another and read their incendiary handbills and statements, one could almost see the black university looming large in the background—not the physical edifice, as yet, but the thought of it, the motive power of it, the omnipresence of its symbolism searing the minds of the campus kamikazes.

Certainly, Dr. Vincent Harding, who had contributed one of the most controversial articles about the black university to *Negro Digest,* could hardly have been more laudatory of the new raging crescendo of black student militance. Dr. Harding —now director of the Institute of the Black World, in Atlanta— gave "an educator's view" in a two-part *Ebony* series titled, "Black Students and the 'Impossible' Revolution." He recalled the graffiti scrawled on a city wall, "Be realistic. Demand the Impossible," and made clear that those words were to be taken quite literally.

He pointed out that in the colleges "the demand has been for the transformation of normal admissions procedures to allow 'impossible' numbers of black young people to enter the campus. . . . Again and again, the demand which has troubled the campus authorities—and others—has been the student demand for black power and autonomy to control and direct experiments with new forms of education on and off the campus."[1] Harding wrote:

> They are demanding that the long neglect of black children, that the years of wasted black talent, be overcome with a speed and a disrespect for "traditional procedures" which can only be called revolutionary. That is why they take over admissions offices, why they demand transformation of and control over the policies which determine who shall enter the college. They reject the elitism they were expected to affirm. This is the meaning of one of the central struggles at City College in New York and in other places.[2]

Once on campus, the next struggle of the black students was "for a total reassessment of the curriculum," and again, Harding showed that he must be taken literally in what he said. Black students demanded no less than "the total reorganization of university knowledge and curriculum *from a black perspective.* . . . They insist that the university either provide the black faculty members who have the 'credentials' or allow them to experiment with paraprofessionals from the black side"[3] (emphasis added). A paraprofessional could be anyone from the black community—from a dedicated social worker to a Black Panther—anyone whose "credentials" the students, or black studies director, decided to accept.

Quite obviously, whoever taught the black studies courses would have to teach "from a black perspective" that slavishly followed the dogma of the black militants. To Dr. Vincent Harding:

> The "Founding Fathers" must then be viewed also as the masters of our black forefathers; the Constitution must be understood as condoning our slavery when it was written; the abolitionists and transcendentalists, the Jacksonians and the Republicans must all be seen anew through black eyes. Lincoln must be known as a white man of the white men and not as a lover of blacks. The Progressives must be questioned for their insensitivity to black suffering; great American literary masters must be asked about their failure to deal with the nation's deepest tragedies.[4]

What Vincent Harding envisioned was not a dialogue, but a monologue—a long, droning litany of alleged abuses of the black man dating back to the dawn of the New World, with little, if any, margin for dissent, rebuttal, or even the mild suggestion that it is most unrealistic to judge 17th- and 18th-century individuals—black or white—by the standards of the 20th century.

There was still more to come—more of the Black Gospel according to St. Vincent:

> The "winning" of the West, the rise of industrialism, the dropping of the atom bomb and the expansion of American imperialism and power all look very different when viewed by black students bearing deep wells of self-love and affirmation, and beginning to sense their profound levels of community with the other oppressed victims of the West.[5]

Harding saw the black surge in academic matters as "a demand for a new definition of America and its institutions, a total re-evaluation from a Black perspective." Ultimately, this approach would question "America as a civilization, and by implication all of Western life and culture."[6] Once the black militant jury found America guilty as charged, a country imbued with "profound tragedy, oppressive reality," there would be no need to ask why "the students increasingly refuse to fight for it."[7] He cited one group of black students, former students in Atlanta, who proclaimed themselves "colonized Africans" in America, and on those grounds, refused to fight in America's wars.[8]

Another demand was that black people "from every stratum of American society be brought into the life of the key institutions of the nation at rates now considered impossible." To Harding, a logical concomitant of this demand was that black student militants would act as gatekeepers, determining "how many black people shall enter and what their qualifications shall be."[9] It was understood, without Harding's having to say it, that the militants would also determine *who* these black people would be.

The bitterest scorn was reserved for integration:

If black students are taken seriously, then black people all over America would have to begin to examine the possibility that we are being called to imitate a dying society. If we hear black students, we might understand their question: "Why integrate with cancer?" If black students are right, then the demand that we adapt our life-style, our education, our political and economic beliefs, our religion, to America as it is can only be interpreted as an invitation to moral—and eventually physical—destruction.[10]

There seemed not the slightest question in Harding's mind that the black students were right.

If the entire text of Harding's articles had not been so compellingly intense, and so deeply felt, one would have been tempted to dismiss the following sentences as a momentary rhetorical aberration, an intoxication with the sonorousness of his own prose. But Harding was in grim earnest:

America has no ultimate hope without a renewed surge of black men and women, transforming now what must be transformed totally if we ourselves are to live in health and truth. *The call is now to take over.* For white America —and, sadly, for most blacks—this is surely the impossible thought, to believe that radical, life-affirming change in America may have to follow black leadership, black directions. . . . Perhaps the Age of Blackness is here, perhaps its moment has come, perhaps the impossible is upon us, ready to be received.[11] [Emphasis supplied]

With obvious approval, Harding quoted a black scholar who had recently written, "Today's black students are in a race to build a sense of Black community before a racial Armageddon overtakes them. This sense of urgency must be grasped if one is to understand the powerful forces which are motivating them. There is little doubt but that they will have a permanent effect on the future of black people in America."[12]

There was even less doubt that the black student struggle was to forge new Afro-American alliances with the Third World. As Harding expressed it, "Blackness meant, too, an increasing sense of solidarity with colonized and broken colored peoples across the globe whose movement for new life and new control had quickened black Americans and in turn been strengthened by our struggle."[13]

Though the phrase may not have appeared in his articles, Harding quite evidently supported students' pursuit of their goals "by any means necessary," even if it meant trampling law and order. Obviously ready to improvise the most convenient definitions, Harding declared, "The campus experience strongly indicates that in a society where law and order support exploitation, justice may demand disorder."[14] These articles were published a few months after the turmoil at CCNY, and Cornell, and the timing of their appearance—in one of America's most influential Negro publications—could hardly have been lost upon its readers.

Harding's contempt for law and order was second only to his denunciation of "America's sudden love affair with 'integration'—defined nowadays as anything which prevents the building of black solidarity and a new black sense of direction." Integration, in his mind, became "one of the most obvious and immediate dangers to the impetus of revolutionary directions," draining off possible support for "the impossible revolution."[15] Evidently, Harding was most fearful of integration's impact upon the friends and families of the black student militants, for if "those of us who are the brothers and sisters, the mothers and the fathers of the students . . . do not support their struggle, they will fail; and their failure will be our own."[16]

The last paragraph of Harding's second article said it all:

> The only time we have is now. So now we must demand the impossible. Now we must struggle for the impossible. Now we must live for the impossible. Now we must die for the impossible. Only then will it burst into the realm of the possible. Only then will our bright and morning star replace the rocket's red glare. Only then will our children—and our fathers—be free. Right on, brothers. Right on.[17]

Traversing the full circle, Dr. Vincent Harding had come back to the pseudo-aphorism, "Be realistic. Demand the impossible." And in so doing, this champion of the black university—and now of "The Impossible Revolution"—was demanding no less than the impossibility of true academic freedom in America's colleges and universities.

# CHAPTER 13

# Black Anti-Semitism and the New York Mayoralty

THERE IS AN ANECDOTE TO THE EFFECT THAT THREE JEWS WERE once shipwrecked on a desert island, and proceeded to form four political parties. At that, it may be only a slight exaggeration. Jews have long been noted for independent and individual thinking and often have found their greatest success in those fields requiring analytical reasoning and a probing turn of mind. This rugged intellectual independence extends even into their religious practices—divided into Orthodox, Conservative and Reformed services, with varying degrees of emphasis on ritual and observances.

One of the very few subjects on which Jews in America have shown nearly absolute unity is the subject of anti-Semitism. As a matter of deeply felt principle, and survival, rich and poor Jews, suburban and urban Jews, immigrant and native-born Jews, young and old Jews, have firmly closed ranks to oppose anti-Semitism in all its works and forms. The point has been reached where anti-Semitism in America is no longer acceptable in public life, in national government, and in the major cities where most Jews live and work and raise their families.

Until now.

In the days when practically all anti-Semites were white, the battle lines were clearly drawn, with no quarter given or asked by Jews, and no respite until the bigots were vanquished.

But now, anti-Semitism has publicly crossed the color line. Now there are a few black anti-Semites who, by virtue of their color, exercise an impact and influence far out of proportion to their numbers, an influence which may be almost as great in the white as in the black community. And now there is the New Racism, which condones in Negroes what it would condemn in whites—the New Racism, which usually murmurs only the faintest reproach of black anti-Semites, although it would emit a stentorian roar if whites uttered the same calumnies.

The dilemma poses all the intellectual tortures of the rack for the Jewish liberal—how to put one arm around the shoulder of a black militant, while his other arm is being twisted, if not broken, by the very black man he is trying to befriend; how to "give a damn" about the ghetto, while black Jew-haters are damning their would-be benefactors in some of the ugliest language ever heard in this country.

The Jewish dilemma is hardly resolved by playing the numbers game. It is true that, numerically, black anti-Semites represent only a tiny fraction of the community—thus far. But the problem is not, "How Many Black Anti-Semites Are There?" but, "Who Are They?" "What Is Their Standing in the Black Community?" "Are They in Positions Where They Can Transmit the Anti-Semitic Virus to Students?" Most important of all, "Are Their Views Repudiated by the Leaders of the Black Community?"

It is difficult to resist a lingering suspicion that some who urge Jews not to *overreact* to black anti-Semitism would really prefer Jews not to react at all. These superpaternalists think of black anti-Jewish feeling as, at most, a regrettable display of bad manners, a childish temper tantrum. Caught in a very real identity crisis—torn between their liberalism and their Jewishness—they occasionally forget themselves, and criticize the few Jew-baiters in the ghetto, but then quickly recover, and exude all manner of excuses for the most infamous outbursts of black bigots.

Probably never before has the Jewish community been as hopelessly divided as it is today. To call it a conflict between young and old is to strip it of full meaning. It would be much

more accurate to call it a cascade of conflicts: a conflict between Jews in changing neighborhoods and Jews in affluent,
lily-white areas; conflict between Jews with relatives who died
in Hitler's ovens, and Jews who were spared this tragic experience; conflict between Jews with beards and yarmulkes and
black hats—all the trappings of high Jewish visibility—and
Jews who have anglicized their names, who are less likely to go
to shul, and who would probably have a great deal of difficulty
reading a prayerbook in Hebrew; conflict between Jews who
sacrificed to achieve a position of renown and Jews who never
personally knew want or deprivation or poverty; conflict between Jews whose businesses and livelihoods are threatened by
black militant encroachments and Jews who are relatively secure from such fears.

Obviously, these descriptions are not, and cannot be, all-
inclusive. There are overlappings and exceptions, and possibly
some cases that are in a ruggedly individualistic class by themselves. But, "exceptions excepted," the author believes these
basic descriptions will serve as a useful frame of reference for
the pages that lie ahead.

At one point, the cascade of conflicts found its greatest outpouring in the pages of the *Jewish Press* (an orthodox-oriented
weekly newspaper published in Brooklyn) and in the activities
of the Jewish Defense League. Formally, the two were quite
separate and distinct. But for all practical purposes, the link
between the two was in the person of Rabbi-lawyer-journal-
ist Meir Kahane, associate editor of the *Jewish Press* and national director of the Jewish Defense League. Kahane quickly
became the most eloquent champion of Jewish protest and
defense, and the most vociferous Jewish opponent of Mayor
Lindsay.

In an age of Black Panthers, in an age when black extremists
sometimes threatened, sometimes practiced anti-white—and
more specifically, anti-Jewish—violence, the emergence of a
group like the Jewish Defense League was all but inevitable.
Haunted by the genocide of the Nazi slaughterhouses, the Jewish Defense League's creed was a starkly simple "Never
Again." Ridiculed by its opponents for thinking in terms of
some imminent American pogrom, the Jewish Defense League
replied that it opposed *all* attacks on Jews, Jewish property,

and Jewish rights—whether from right or left, or from black or white.

For a time, criticism of the Jewish Defense League was fairly muted, as its members went to court to force college authorities to reopen CCNY, demonstrated against the "outrageous racism" of the African-American Teachers Association, and guarded the polling places to protect Jews voting in an election for seats on the Crown Heights Community Council (the local body which allocated funds for the anti-poverty program).[1] And then one day, the Jewish Defense League suddenly found itself famous—or infamous—the subject of both impassioned defense and outraged denunciation.

It happened a month after a revolutionary faction seized control of the Black Economic Development Conference, and approved a "black manifesto" presented to the conference by James Forman, director of international affairs of the Student Non-Violent Coordinating Committee. The manifesto outlined a plan to seize "white Christian churches and Jewish synagogues" across the nation, until these bodies paid $500,000,000 in reparations to black people.[2]

The introduction to James Forman's black manifesto read in part:

> Racism in the United States is so pervasive in the mentality of the Whites that only an armed, well disciplined, black-controlled government can insure the stamping out of racism in this country. And that is why we plead with black people not to be talking about a few crumbs, a few thousand dollars . . .
>
> We think in terms of total control of the U.S. Prepare ourselves to seize state power. Do not hedge, for time is short, and all around the world the forces of liberation are directing their attacks against the U.S.
>
> It is a powerful country, but that power is not greater than that of black people. We work the chief industries of this country and we could cripple the economy of those while the brothers fought guerrilla warfare in the street. . . .[3]

Forman did, in fact, disrupt some church services, generally brushing aside elderly ushers to mount the platform and to demand reparations, while the ministers made a pathetic show of welcoming the interruptions. Then Forman announced his intention to disrupt services at Temple Emanu-el,[4] one of the largest and most prestigious Reformed Jewish temples in the country, and it was at this point that the Jewish Defense League decided to challenge Forman in the only language he was capable of understanding.

On the Friday that Forman had threatened to disrupt the service, a group of 175 Jewish Defense League members stood at attention in front of Temple Emanu-el. Many of them were openly armed with bats, iron pipes, and chains. Asked the reason for the weapons, a JDL spokesman declared, "After CCNY [when students had been beaten by armed extremists] we are not prepared to be unarmed again."[5]

Rabbi Nathan Perlman of Temple Emanu-el opposed the JDL presence, deploring the fact that it had come. Rabbi Perlman stated that if Forman appeared, he was welcome to the use of the pulpit to state his demands.[6]

Perlman had phoned the JDL office earlier in the day, asking that the group stay away. Questioned as to why the JDL had ignored the rabbi's request, a spokesman answered, "This is not an affair between Emanu-el and Forman. This is a symbolic assault on all Jewish synagogues and if Forman wins here, each and every other synagogue will be affected. Forman will not walk in here this afternoon." The Jewish Defense League spurned Forman's demands for reparations with the statement, "We Jews came to America as oppressed people and we had no hand in the oppression of the black man. Forman is an extortionist. We Jews owe him nothing, and that is what he will get."[7] Possibly acting on the principle that absence was the better part of valor, Forman failed to appear.[8]

As a Jew, the author had mixed feelings about the incident. He considered it self-evident that, in standing outside the temple uninvited, and indeed, against the expressed wishes of the rabbi, the JDL members were clearly committing a trespass. And yet he would be the first to admit that the generation gap is small compared with the gap that separates the thinking of most Orthodox and Reformed Jews. For the most part, JDL members were Orthodox Jews, who loved their religion with a passionate intensity that survived the concentration camps of Europe, and the gentle and subtle assimilationist pressures of religious ecumenism.

One of the few newspaper stories that really depicted the depth of religious feeling of Orthodox Jewry was carried in the December 9, 1968, edition of the *New York Times*. It recounted how the charred remains of seven Torahs—the sacred scrolls of Judaism—that were destroyed in a fire set by vandals in a Brooklyn Yeshiva were buried in a plain pine box. The burial took place in Beth David Cemetery at Elmont, Long Island, as fifteen hundred mourners chanted the 79th Psalm, beginning with, "O God, pagans have defiled your Holy Sanctuary." To devout Jews, the burning of a scroll was considered as much a tragedy as the loss of an immediate member of the family. The same prayers were recited at the grave, and eulogies were said beforehand at synagogue services.[9]

In the author's opinion, it was this kind of deep and abiding commitment to its faith—this kind of revulsion at what seemed to it a desecration of the Sabbath and a religious service—that motivated the Orthodox-oriented Jewish Defense League to take the determined and controversial stand it did that Friday in front of Temple Emanu-el.

Virtually every major Jewish organization whirled on the Jewish Defense League with a fury that had once been reserved almost exclusively for neo-Nazi organizations. The Anti-Defamation League defamed the JDL as "a self-appointed group of vigilantes. . . ."[10] Rabbi Maurice N. Eisendrath, president of the Union of American Hebrew Congregations, asserted, "The so-called Jewish Defense League violates every ethic and tradition of Judaism and every concept of civil liberties and democratic process in American life. Jews carrying baseball bats and chains, standing in phalanxes, like goon squads in front of synagogues, are no less offensive and, in essence, no different from whites wearing robes and hoods, led by self-styled ministers of the gospel standing in front of burning crosses."[11]

But all too few read the eloquent reply to Rabbi Eisendrath by Dr. Theodore N. Lewis, rabbi of the Progressive Synagogue in Brooklyn. Rabbi Lewis stated:

> Rabbi Eisendrath, and many other liberals, Jewish and Christian, suffer from a sense of guilt when they approach Negro problems. It is this which compels them to follow a

double standard—one for the white community, and a totally different one for the black. . . . Rabbi Eisendrath and many others find it impossible to denounce, condemn or rebuke blacks, even when their behavior is fiercely immoral and wicked, detrimental not only to society but to *them.* It is this double standard which has led many white liberals astray, to the permanent injury of the black masses.[12]

About the only Jewish organization publicly to endorse the JDL was the Council of Jewish Civil Service, headed by Dr. Herman Mantell.[13]

Even the Jewish War Veterans (Department of New York) blasted the JDL in an internal release, which leaked out to the press. The release stated, in part:

The Department of New York considers the Jewish Defense League to be extremist in its attitude and irresponsible. We believe that it has failed to make a positive contribution to the Jewish community or the community at large. In an era of social change, its tactics are both dangerous and divisive, and no less abhorrent than those of other extremist groups. Despite the difficulties that some segments of the Jewish population have had during this urban crisis, we condemn the use of baseball bats and chains for the purpose of protecting our good name, our worldly goods, or our existence. By the same token, we fail to see the need to brush up on our marksmanship or to learn the use of karate in order to feel like men, capable of handling a difficult situation.[14]

At its summer camps, the Jewish Defense League taught karate, the firing of weapons, and hand-to-hand combat.[15] Its interest in marksmanship was unusual, but not unprecedented among New York City Jews, as a letter to the *Jewish Press* made quite clear. The letter was from Rabbi Arnold Pessin, director of the Brooklyn Palmach. Rabbi Pessin described Club Palmach as

. . . a long established New York area rifle and pistol club. The club has recently been expanding in Brooklyn, Manhattan and Queens. Many Yeshiva students, seminarians, and even rabbis have joined the Palmach. These new members have already entered matches. For example, a

team of seminarians and rabbis shot in a match at Peek-
skill, New York, on April 27, 1969, and scored 186 x 200.
. . . The Brooklyn Palmach branch has members from the
following seminaries: Tefereth Jerusalem and Rabbi
Jacob Joseph (Manhattan) and Mirrer Yeshiva and Torah
Vodaath (Brooklyn). The Palmach welcomes all those interested in shooting. . . . State in which borough or county
you want to shoot.[16]

Later, an official of Club Palmach wrote to the *Jewish Press,*
"In the past two days we have had a record heavy mail in
response to Rabbi Pessin's letter to your paper. Several of the
writers were Rabbis; almost all wanted to join Palmach. Many
honestly stated they never owned a firearm, but wanted to
learn."[17]

So, the Jewish War Veterans Department of New York notwithstanding, there *were* Jews who wanted to brush up on their
marksmanship—and those even included some of the Jewish
War Veterans' own members.

The commander of a Brooklyn post of the Jewish War Veterans assured the *Jewish Press:*

Not this post Rabbi, not any post that I know of was consulted by the Department [State] Leadership before a
statement condemning JDL was issued. . . . The leadership
and the rank and file membership apparently dwell in
separate worlds; the higher ranks are concerned with not
making waves and the rank and file are trying to stay
afloat. This post feels that it is very relevant to brush up
on marksmanship. This post has its own rifle and pistol
club, a first in JWV. . . . It is the peculiar type of Jewish
thinking that have [sic] blessed us with senators like Jack
Javits and mayors of the ilk of J. V. Lindsay. It is the type
of thinking, exemplified by the Department [State] leadership, that have [sic] kept the Jewish people as vassals of
the ultra-liberal wing of the Democratic and, most recently, the Republican parties.[18]

Was black extremism a valid cause for Jewish concern? As a
small, new group, it was easy to brush off JDL protestations,
activities, and press releases. But it was considerably more
difficult to assail the January 1969 report of the Anti-Defamation League of B'nai B'rith.

Picture a man who suffers from acrophobia walking a tight-rope while carrying two hand grenades, and you have some idea of the agonizingly painful reluctance with which the Anti-Defamation League released its Preliminary Report of "Anti-Semitism in the New York City School Controversy." In an extraordinary action, its national chairman, Dore Schary, wrote of the "sadness" and "concern" with which the report was issued, and cautioned, "It is a time neither for panic nor Jewish anti-Negro backlash."

The Anti-Defamation League stressed that the black anti-Semitic activities "are not representative of the attitudes or actions of the majority of the Negro community," and said the ADL's task was threefold:

> to expose the obvious bias against Jews posed by Negro extremists; to combat the insensitivity to that peril by non-Jews; to clear the blurring of the complicated issues in the overall need for equitable reform and change, not only in the New York City public schools, but in our society as a whole. We would be deluding ourselves if we said the task will be easy, but we would be denying our responsibilities and long-time purposes if we did not accept the challenge.

The ADL report met the challenge head-on, confirming the worst fears of some, and jolting the torpid complacency of others, as it bluntly stated:

> The use of anti-Semitism—raw, undisguised—has distorted the fundamental character of the controversy surrounding the public schools of New York City. The anti-Semitism has gone unchecked by public authorities for two and a half years, reaching a peak during the school strike of September–November 1968 and in the post-strike period. It is still going on.
>
> Five major circumstances can be defined in which clear anti-Semitism has become commonplace in the school dispute:
> \# attempts to drive Jewish teachers and principals—as Jews—out of schools in several areas of the city;
> \# vicious anti-Semitic statements at Board of Education hearings on decentralization and other issues during the two-and-a-half-year period;

\# anti-Semitic remarks and threats in thrusts for control of local school districts;

\# anti-Jewish incidents during and connected with the 1968 school strike; and

\# anti-Semitic activities in the controversy over makeup time that followed settlement of the strike.

ADL's continuing investigation into the anti-Semitism in and around New York City schools points to the following initial conclusions:

1. It has been perpetrated largely by black extremists.

2. Its growth has been aided by the failure of city and state public officials to condemn it swiftly and strongly enough, and to remove from positions of authority those who have utilized anti-Semitism. These include, among others, representatives of the Council Against Poverty, the city's official antipoverty agency.

3. Anti-Semitic material has been produced, in at least one instance, by a publicly funded antipoverty unit.

4. There is a clear and present danger that schoolchildren in the city have been infected by the anti-Semitic preachings of Negro extremists who, in some cases, are teachers and to whom these youngsters increasingly look for leadership. Such infection is not contained when members of the Establishment . . . either fail to see the anti-Semitism or attempt to explain or condone it on one ground or the other.[19]

One of the most authoritative critiques of the Anti-Defamation League report came from Leonard Fein, associate director and director of research for the Harvard–MIT Joint Center for Urban Studies and also chairman of the Commission on Community Interrelations of the American Jewish Congress. Fein complained that the ADL report "fails to distinguish between gutter anti-Semitism—epithets and obscenities from the mouths of a mob . . . and the statements of public men; it equates vulgar imprecation and sophisticated if specious reasoning; it neglects entirely the counter-provocations which, though they can never justify anti-Semitism, at least help to explain it."[20] Another criticism of the ADL report was written by Henry Schwarzchild, a Fellow at the Metropolitan Applied Research Center and a member of the Commission on Religion and Race of the Synagogue Council of America. Schwarzchild called the ADL report an "anti-Semitic herring," and wrote:

The ADL report should have comforted everyone who was concerned with an apparent rise in the noise level of Negro anti-Semitism. To find forty anti-Semitic incidents in two and a half years in a city of 1.2 million Negroes and almost 2 million Jews, beset with a multitude of social, racial and class problems that make for some inevitable friction between ethnic groups, that is a surprising datum of relative tranquility.[21]

But the ADL report was not so much concerned with noise level or a nose count as it was with the tendency of too many in high places to rationalize black anti-Semitism or "explain or condone it on one ground or another." And, clearly, the ADL was also concerned with "the failure of city and state public officials . . . to remove from positions of authority those who have utilized anti-Semitism." And neither Leonard Fein nor Henry Schwarzchild faulted the ADL for denouncing the essay in the official catalog for "Harlem on my Mind," the *African-American Teachers Forum,* John Hatchett, and Leslie Campbell.

In January 1969, the Metropolitan Museum of Art featured an exhibit called "Harlem on my Mind." The official catalog for the exhibit carried an introduction by an eighteen-year-old Negro student, Candice Van Ellison, who had written it two years before when she was a student at Theodore Roosevelt High School in The Bronx. Miss Van Ellison wrote:

Behind every hurdle that the Afro-American has yet to jump stands the Jew who has already cleared it. Jewish shopkeepers are the only remaining "survivors" in the expanding Black ghettos. . . . Another major area of contact involves the Jewish landlord and the Black tenant. A large portion of Harlem's Black women serve as domestics in middle-class Jewish homes. Perhaps this would explain the higher rate of anti-Semitism among Black women than men. . . . Psychologically, Blacks may find that anti-Jewish sentiments place them, for once, within a majority. Thus, our contempt for the Jew makes us feel more completely American in sharing a national prejudice.[22]

Thomas Hoving, director of the Metropolitan Museum, saw "nothing inflammatory" about Miss Van Ellison's essay, and said it represented "a statement of the facts." He commented,

"If the truth hurts, so be it."[23] William Booth, then New York City Human Rights Commissioner, said that Miss Van Ellison was a "product of her society." While critical of her for generalizing about groups, Commissioner Booth said "there was no racial intent in the young lady's mind or on the part of the museum."[24]

The Anti-Defamation League commented:

> Curious in connection with the City Commission on Human Rights has been its sustained silence on the subject of anti-Semitism in and around the New York City schools for the entire two-and-a-half-year period discussed in this report. Much of the material set forth in the previous pages has had sufficient dissemination for the Commission at least to have heard of it. Its failure to take appropriate investigative action awaits explanation.[25]

This was not the first time the charge of indifference to anti-Semitism had been made. Two years before, Rabbi Julius G. Neumann resigned from the city's Commission on Human Rights, charging that Booth was "whipping up animosity among people," ignoring discrimination against Jews, and investigating only the complaints of Negroes.[26] In December 1968 —before a gathering of rabbis and synagogue officials—Lindsay himself conceded that Booth "could have done" a "better" job of looking into the anti-Semitism that "certainly surfaced during the school strike. . . ." But the mayor attributed Booth's failure to human error.[27]

Booth's term as New York City's Human Rights Commissioner expired on December 26, but he remained at the post in January on a holdover basis.[28] The New York Board of Rabbis asked Lindsay not to reappoint Booth, charging him with a "singular insensitivity to anti-Semitic incidents."[29] In early February, Booth was replaced as Human Rights Commissioner, and appointed a judge of the criminal court by Lindsay.[30]

Apparently 1967 was a vintage year for black anti-Semitic writings—the year Candice Van Ellison penned her essay, and the year John F. Hatchett wrote "The Phenomenon of the Anti-Black Jews and the Black Anglo-Saxon; A Study in Educational Perfidy" for the November–December issue of the *African-American Teachers Forum*. Hatchett, at the time, was a substitute teacher in P.S. 68 in the I.S. 201 complex, in Harlem. His article read in part:

> We are witnessing today in New York City a phenomenon that spells death for the minds and souls of our Black children. It is the systematic coming of age of the Jews who dominate and control the educational bureaucracy of the New York public School system and their power-starved imitators, the Black Anglo-Saxons. . . . In short, our children are being mentally poisoned by a group of educators who are actively and persistently bringing about a certain self-fulfilling prophecy to its logical conclusion.[31]

In a joint statement, the American Jewish Congress, the Catholic Interracial Council, and the Protestant Council of the City of New York called it "black Nazism" and "a naked appeal to racial and religious hatred."[32] Hatchett's teaching license was revoked a few months later, but not because of the article; the charge was that he had taken a group of pupils to the Malcolm X program at I.S. 201, despite an order from the Superintendent of Schools barring these pupils from attending.[33]

With his teacher's license revoked, Hatchett could no longer teach in the city's public schools—but, apparently he was just what New York University had been looking for. In July 1968 Hatchett was appointed director of New York University's new Martin Luther King Jr. Afro-American Student Center.[34] Later, Dr. Allan Cartter, chancellor of NYU, said that college officials had known about Hatchett's dismissal from the city school system, but not about the article he had written. He indicated that NYU would look into the matter.[35]

The Anti-Defamation League assailed the appointment of Hatchett as "an affront not only to Jews, but to the memory of Dr. King."[36] But, in a letter to NYU President James M. Hester, former Supreme Court Justice Arthur Goldberg wrote:

> As a result of my frank and candid talk with Mr. Hatchett, I believe he now understands the injustice and dangers inherent in the kind of criticism he voices in the article. Mr. Hatchett strongly denies that he is anti-Semitic although the expressions in the article can be so regarded.[37]

Goldberg added that Hatchett's references to Jewish educators "are completely unfounded and cannot be condoned."[38] But Hatchett, in a statement of his own, insisted, "My criticism of the New York City public school system remains valid. Our children are dying, and it behooves us all to work to end it."[39]

Largely as a result of the Goldberg letter, New York University announced that it would keep Hatchett as director of its Afro-American Student Center. Hatchett said he would "welcome the opportunity to be judged on the merits of what I will do at NYU."[40]

The university did not have to wait very long to see what Hatchett would do. Two months later, Hatchett told an audience of 700 NYU students that Richard Nixon, Hubert Humphrey, and United Federation of Teachers President Albert Shanker "all have something in common—they are racist bastards."[41] Within 48 hours, NYU dismissed John Hatchett from his position.[42]

Hatchett's article was not the only anti-Semitic diatribe to appear in the *African-American Teachers Forum*. The *Forum* was the official organ of the African-American Teachers Association, headed by Albert Vann, then acting assistant principal of J.H.S 271 in Ocean Hill-Brownsville. The November 1968 *Forum* featured an editorial titled "Needed: A Responsible Jewish Voice." The editorial stated:

> How long shall the Black and Puerto Rican communities of New York City sit back and allow the Jewish dominated United Federation of Teachers to destroy every effort to rescue our children from those incompetent teachers whose only goal—aside from receiving fat paychecks—is stifling our children's intellectual growth? . . . And the Jew, our great liberal friend of yesterday, whose cries of anguish still resound from the steppes of Russia to the tennis courts of Forest Hills, is now our exploiter! He keeps our men and women from becoming teachers and principals and he keeps our children ignorant.[43]

At about this same time, Leslie Campbell, another teacher in Ocean Hill-Brownsville, appeared as a guest on radio station WBAI-FM and read a flagrantly anti-Semitic poem which he characterized as both beautiful and true. The poem was dedicated to the United Federation of Teachers' president, Albert Shanker, and, according to Campbell, it had been written by a fifteen-year-old student:[44]

Hey, Jew boy, with that yarmulke on your head
You pale-faced Jew boy—I wish you were dead;
I can see you, Jew boy—no, you can't hide,
I got a scoop on you—yeh, you gonna die.
I'm sick of your stuff; every time I run 'round,
You pushin' my head deeper into the ground;
I'm sick of hearing about your suffering in Germany,
I'm sick about your escape from tyrrany,
I'm sick of seeing in everything I do
About the murder of six million Jews;
Hitler's reign lasted for only fifteen years—
For that period of time you shed crocodile tears,
My suffering lasted for over 400 years, Jew boy,
And the white man only let me play with his toys.
Jew boy, you took my religion and adopted it for you,
But you know that black people were the original Hebrews.
When the UN made Israel a free independent state
Little 4- and 5-year-old boys threw hand grenades.
They hated the black Arabs with all their might,
And you, Jew boy, said it was all right.
Then you came to America, land of the free,
And took over the school system to perpetuate white supremacy.
Guess you know, Jew boy, there's only one reason you made it—
You had a clean, white face, colorless and faded,
I hated you, Jew boy, because your hang-up was the Torah,
And my only hang-up was my color.[45]

Mayor Lindsay called for an investigation of Campbell's reading of "an obviously anti-Semitic poem" on the radio. Albert Vann charged that the mayor "in his hurry to appease the powerful Jewish financiers of the city" had "played fast and loose" with Campbell's rights.[46] A few days later, speaking before an audience in a Bayside, Queens, synagogue, Lindsay said that Vann and Campbell did not have "any place teaching" in the city's schools and that he had asked the Board of Education to "take appropriate action."[47] His remarks drew loud applause from the audience of seven hundred people, but drew a listless response from the Board of Education, whose most militant members were Lindsay appointees. And the most apathetic response of all came from Rhody McCoy, unit administrator of the Ocean Hill–Brownsville Community School District—a district Lindsay had worked as hard as anyone to establish and support.

If the United Federation of Teachers had been too quick to link almost every adverse action in Ocean Hill–Brownsville to anti-Semitism, Rhody McCoy had been just as quick to hurl the charge of "racist" at almost every one of his white opponents. McCoy himself had not engaged in any anti-Semitic actions or uttered any anti-Semitic remarks. On the contrary, he had issued a memo, "The Meaning of Rosh Hashanah—The Jewish New Year," which could have served as a model of racial and religious amity.[48] And the Ocean-Hill–Brownsville Governing Board had gone on record as opposing anti-Semitism.[49] Furthermore, there were many Jewish teachers conducting classes in Ocean Hill–Brownsville. "How far do we go?" asked McCoy.[50]

The answer was self-evident. McCoy should have gone as far as he most assuredly would have if Campbell and Vann had been white, and made equally bigoted remarks about Negroes. It was just not nearly enough for McCoy to wash his hands of the matter by telling School Superintendent Donovan, "I know of no power that either you or I have to discipline any teacher for an expression of opinion outside of the school system, and I doubt that such power could be exercised consistent with the Constitution."[51] *New York Times* education editor Fred Hechinger felt that if Campbell did nothing to answer his pupil's hate-filled views, "if the teacher thus acted to reinforce the hatred and the racism, then he did not exercise the right to teach; he was instead engaged in indoctrination and distortion. At the very least, he was either incompetent or derelict in his duty."[52]

It was not until three weeks after Election Day that Rhody McCoy announced that Campbell had "resigned" his position.[53] It had taken McCoy and the governing board almost a year to get Campbell out of Ocean Hill–Brownsville after reading that wretched poem on WBAI—an incredibly snail-like pace that, like Booth, seemed to indicate "a singular insensitivity to anti-Semitic incidents."

Albert Vann, Leslie Campbell, the *African-American Teach-*

*ers Forum,* John Hatchett, and "Harlem on my Mind" were all very much on the minds of Jewish voters during the mayoral campaign in New York City. The earliest indication of Jewish resentment came in the June primary that saw the most conservative Democratic candidate, Mario Procaccino, defeat all other contenders, including a once highly popular ex-mayor, while the Republican primary gave the victory to conservative John Marchi over John Lindsay. The *New York Post* took a survey of voting in the city's 58 assembly districts, and concluded, "The Mayoral candidates of the Democratic and Republican parties are the candidates of the city's Italian and Irish party members, plus a sizable minority of Jewish voters. . . ."[54] On the Republican side of the primary, the *New York Post* found that "Mayor Lindsay rolled up a 3½-1 margin in the largely Jewish 65th A.D. around Lincoln Center—but Marchi registered 2-1 margins among Jewish voters in Queens (the 19th) and 3-1 in Brooklyn (the 41st, Crown Heights)."[55]

Lindsay headquarters called them "The Swingables," and defined the average swingable as "a middle-aged Jewish Democrat raising a family in Queens on maybe $12,000 a year. He voted for Lyndon Johnson and Hubert Humphrey, and if he voted in the Mayoral Primary last month, he was probably for Robert F. Wagner, although there's a chance that he voted for Mario A. Procaccino, the Democratic winner."[56] Lindsay strategists felt that many of the swingables could be persuaded to swing over to the mayor on Election Day.[57] Indeed, their votes were considered indispensable, since some analysts predicted that Jews would cast just about fifty percent of the 2.5 million votes expected in the mayoral election.[58]

It was generally conceded that Jews were the swing voters who would decide the election.[59] In 1965, they gave Lindsay 33 to 40 percent of their votes, depending on the analyst. This year, Lindsay had to get 40 percent of the Jewish vote to have a chance, and 60 percent to guarantee victory.[60] Compounding the problem was the fact that private polls classified 20 percent of city voters as "undecided," with the highest proportion of undecided voters in predominantly Jewish neighborhoods.[61] An important Lindsay strategist flatly declared, "The Jewish vote is the ball game."[62] And a Procaccino strategist agreed, saying, "What we're really talking about this year is the Jewish vote.

Most of the other vote is locked in."[63] At Lindsay and Procaccino headquarters, the candidates and their advisers weighed almost every decision in terms of what impact it would have in Jewish neighborhoods.[64]

No fair damsel was ever wooed more ardently than the Jewish voter in New York City during the mayoral campaign. *New York Times* political reporter Richard Reeves wrote of

> classic New York ethnic politics with its delightful little cynicisms: Lindsay and his people moving with the precision of a drill team to block other candidates trying to get into photographs with Israeli Premier Golda Meir; Procaccino reaching into the glove compartment of his limousine to choose among three yarmulkes while his people remind everyone in whispershot that their man's nickname at City College was "moishe."[65]

The headlines in the *New York Times, New York Post, Daily News,* and *Village Voice* said even more:

PROCACCINO CHARGES LINDSAY SPURS ANTI-SEMITISM
GOLDBERG BACKS LINDSAY IN RACE
PROCACCINO GETS THE WORD "MAZEL." (Jewish Vacationers Warm to Mayoral Candidate)
MARCHI JOINS HASIDIC JEWS IN MARKING A FESTIVAL
LINDSAY GETS BIG WELCOME IN FLATBUSH
MARCHI GETS A BIG HELLO ON THE LOWER EAST SIDE
PROCACCINO SEEKS MANHATTAN VOTES (Tours East Side and Wins Brooklyn Jews' Cheers)
MARCHI SAYS JEWISH VOTE IS TURNING TOWARD HIM
MARIO ATTACKS THE MAYOR IN TALKS TO JEWS
LINDSAY VS. THE JEWISH VOTER (When in Brooklyn, Play Gimpel The Fool)
LINDSAY SPEECH SETS OFF RUCKUS (Pro and Anti Forces Clash at Brooklyn Temple)[66]

During the mayoral campaign, the three major candidates were practically doing a 50-yard dash to any Jewish temple that would allow them to speak. Some rabbis preferred to keep politicking out of their temples altogether; others heard one or two of the candidates; still others decided, as a matter of courtesy and fairness, that all three candidates should be offered the opportunity to speak to their congregations.

The Ocean Parkway Jewish Center in Brooklyn announced that its congregants would have a chance to "meet your mayoral candidates." Marchi would appear at the temple on October 19 at 7:00 p.m.; Procaccino would speak on October 21 at 8:00 p.m.; and Lindsay would address the congregation October 29 at 8:00 p.m. The author decided to see and hear all three candidates at this temple.

The very timing of Marchi's appearance was one more proof of his positive genius for political ineptness. A debate featuring all three candidates had already been scheduled for six o'clock on TV Channel 7, that same day. This TV confrontation would end at seven o'clock—the exact time Marchi was to address the congregation of the Ocean Parkway Jewish Center. In other words, Marchi would be competing with himself—and those wishing to hear both the TV debate and Marchi's speech at the temple would either have to leave their homes halfway through the TV program, or watch the debate in its entirety and arrive at the temple a half-hour or more after the Marchi speech was scheduled to begin.

The author left his home midway during the TV debate, and arrived at the temple shortly after 7:00 p.m. Marchi had not yet arrived. The audience, patiently waiting for him in the temple, was primarily comprised of the middle-aged and elderly, with some teenagers and a very few in their twenties and thirties. An elderly gentleman at the door kept a watchful eye to make sure all the men in the audience were wearing yarmulkes.

No campaign worker was standing outside handing out Marchi buttons or Marchi campaign literature. No loudspeaker on a truck exhorted voters to meet Marchi at the Ocean Parkway Jewish Center. As far as any political efforts by Marchi headquarters were concerned, the entire meeting could have come under the heading of "classified information." The crowd good-naturedly waited for Marchi to arrive; he did—about an hour late. The author, counting as best he could, estimated there were about two hundred people in the audience.

Probably the most notable feature of Marchi's speech in the temple was not so much what he said as the way in which he said it. The contrast was all the more pronounced after watching him in the three-way TV debate. There, Marchi's demeanor was that of a political *bon vivant,* limiting himself to gentle jibes and wry irony, almost overshadowed by mumbling dissertations on whatever struck his fancy. But at the temple, he came out of his corner fighting—loud, strident, and sometimes almost shrill.

The main thrust of Marchi's speech was the subject of crime, and here, to his credit, he reeled off some frightening statistics —every ten hours someone was murdered in New York; there were fifty thousand more assaults; at least twenty houses had been burglarized during the hour the audience had waited for him to arrive.

Marchi shouted, "This city is dying, inch by inch," and few in the audience cared to dispute him. He asked, "If Procaccino won't debate the issues, how will he face up to Jesse Gray?" The audience was sympathetic—there was applause, some of it spirited—but there seemed no great groundswell of enthusiasm for his candidacy, and little evidence that he had won over any of the waverers. The question-and-answer period was brief and uneventful, and Marchi seemed to sense that his appearance had been something less than a smashing success. Which may have been why he commented, "If you think I'm wrong, work against me. But don't be indifferent." Before the meeting ended, with a wide grin he told the audience, "Win, lose, or draw, I love you." As if on cue, the audience applauded, and undoubtedly came away convinced that John Marchi was a "nice guy." But soon the election results would confirm the truth of that cynical dictum, "Nice guys finish last."

October 21 was a very different night. That night, one heard the blaring of loudspeakers advertising the appearance of Mario Procaccino at the Jewish Center. At the entrance to the temple, there was a man wearing a saucer-sized Procaccino button, and offering passersby their choice of any of a plateful of buttons he was holding. There was a rash of Procaccino posters outside. Mario Procaccino may have been stone-cold-dead in the land of the "Limousine Liberals," but apparently he was alive and well in this middle-class Brooklyn neighborhood.

The audience for Procaccino was almost double the size of the audience that turned out for Marchi. Again, the author donned his yarmulke, and went through the now-familiar ritual of waiting for the candidate. For the most part, the audience accepted the waiting period with equanimity, using the time to wave at acquaintances, to finish conversations they had started while trudging up the temple steps, and just to look around to see who was there.

At least fifteen people were wearing Procaccino buttons, in an audience that was mostly elderly, with some who were middle-aged. A few eventually tired of waiting and left.

"I'm afraid a lot of our Jewish people are going to vote for Lindsay," an elderly man said. "He makes a nice appearance, and fools a lot of people." His friend was just as disenchanted with the mayor. "All of a sudden, he has lots of projects. The last few years—nothing!"

All things come to him who waits, and eventually Mario Procaccino came to those who were waiting for him at the temple. He finally arrived one and a half hours late; some stood, some whistled, and many cheered as he entered the Ocean Parkway Jewish Center.

That night, Procaccino had already spoken at Temple Emanu-el, and at the National Council of Young Israel, and now he was here in the temple, giving a speech that pretty well summarized what he had been saying all through the campaign —that he came to America in 1921, and never remembered such chaos, dissension, and confusion as existed today, with "race against race, group against group, teacher against parent." He declared, "The greatest mistake this city ever made was electing John Lindsay," and here there was great applause. Procaccino went on, "He pretends to be a great liberal, but ran on the Republican ticket. He wanted the Republican endorsement this year. When he lost in the Republican Primary, he said those who voted against him were bigots, and prejudiced"—a line that John Marchi might have used to considerable advantage during his own speech two nights earlier. In a *j'accuse* posture, Procaccino stated, "Lindsay supported Nixon. Lindsay supported Spiro Agnew. He can't answer that, can he?" Procaccino's words may have rallied the party faithful, but only incensed those moderates and conservatives who were disillusioned with Marchi, and might have voted for him.

Procaccino asserted, "I've been told by newsmen that I have

been the subject of the greatest smear of the century. Is it because I don't belong to the 'limousine liberals' who don't know what it is to work with your back or your hands? I walked around Jerusalem—Athens—Rome—at three in the morning. We weren't mugged. I didn't see gates on store windows. Am I committing a crime when I say I want safety in the streets and at home, and want to enjoy the safety they have in other parts of the world?" His audience responded with obviously heartfelt applause.

It was a week for contrasts. The highly emotional Procaccino of past campaign encounters was supplanted by a Procaccino whose delivery was quiet, and who raised his voice only occasionally.

The audience response was positive, enthusiastic, almost fervent, when Procaccino pledged that, as mayor, "the hands of the police will be untied," and when he promised, "I'll enforce the law." He repeated what he had earlier described as the "hidden issue" of the campaign—"the next Mayor will make two appointments to the Board of Education. Will we have appointees like Galamison or Haddad, or those who believe as I do, in tranquility in the classroom?" And the audience loudly applauded his firm declaration that "there is no right to burn, destroy, or damage property in Higher Education." But his greatest rapport with this audience of parents and grandparents came when he reminded his listeners that when militants shut down CCNY, "I went to court—and it was the proudest moment of my life when I reopened City College!" And he all but brought the audience to its feet when he said, "I'm against the quota system, and the lowering of standards [at CCNY]." He later added, "If a black, Puerto Rican, or other student hasn't enjoyed quality education, he should have special tutoring, special classes. But we will not sacrifice the future of a bright young man to put through a quota system."

Acknowledging that he had been described as emotional, Procaccino commented, "I get emotional when an old man is stabbed in the back—and an old lady is robbed—and I get emotional about what happened last week, when a seven-year-old girl was raped in class. If that's being emotional, I'm proud to be emotional."

During the brief question-and-answer period that followed,

Procaccino was asked, "Why do Robert Wagner and Arthur Goldberg refuse to support you?" At the mention of Goldberg's name, there was a vigorous chorus of "boos" from the audience. Procaccino, in reply, doubted that Goldberg's selection of mayoral candidates was any wiser than "his selection of Hatchett at NYU."

It was the ultimate blasphemy for a young Lindsay supporter. In a dazed tone—as if he couldn't quite trust his own vocal cords —the Jewish youth gasped to his equally distraught girl friend, "They booed *Goldberg!*"

A week later, on October 29, it was John Lindsay's turn at the Ocean Parkway Jewish Center. Outside the temple, members of the Jewish Defense League were distributing anti-Lindsay leaflets. Another JDL member was holding up a sign which read, "Brethren, don't embarrass the mayor. Don't ask him about his appointments of anti-Semites."

Inside, a large audience had already gathered. There were quite a few Lindsay button-wearers in the crowd, but there were some vociferous critics of the mayor, as well. Debates were going on in the audience, and some angry voices were being raised, with one man protesting, "It's not nice in the shul to heckle anyone."

The audience that was waiting for Lindsay was different in many ways from the audiences that had gathered for Marchi and Procaccino. About forty percent of this Lindsay audience was young people—there were some Orthodox Jews with black coats and hats; some rather intense-looking WASP's were there; and, for the first time, there was a Negro couple sitting in the audience.

Undoubtedly, of the three candidates, the largest turnout was for Lindsay—but it bears repeating that not everyone in the audience was among his admirers.

While waiting for the mayor, the audience was well entertained by a group of talented youngsters, who went from place to place doing "Lindsay shows." There was a sing-along of an Israeli folk song, a musical trio played some most agreeable melodies, a guitarist held forth, and all received a rousing hand of non-partisan applause.

It was a smooth operation run with computerlike efficiency. One had the feeling that the whole well-packaged affair—

smiles, songs, patter, and all—had come off some beautifully oiled political assembly line. The entertainment stopped just long enough for speeches by Lindsay's running mates, Perotta and Garelik. Perotta told the audience, "I am proud to be on the John Lindsay ticket," a statement which some greeted with vigorous applause, while a few others derisively turned thumbs down.

Looking about him, the president of the temple, in a brief address, drily commented, "I wish all of you here tonight were really our members. I wish all of you here tonight were really our worshippers." He urged those in the audience "to respect the house you are in. We have given an equal opportunity for all the candidates to be heard. I expect you to conduct yourselves in the spirit that this is a house of worship."

Outside the temple, there was some commotion as members of the Jewish Defense League chimed in with this baleful refrain:

"Who hires criminals?"
"Lindsay!"
"Who hires anti-Semites?"
"Lindsay!"

They were countered by some, with pro-Lindsay signs, who chanted:

"Who's F.D.R., Jr. for?"
"Lindsay!"
"Who's Frank Hogan for?"
"Lindsay!"

Undaunted, some JDL pickets started chanting, "Lindsay must go!"

Inside the temple, the singers and musicians were still providing excellent entertainment, but more and more necks were craned toward the entrance, waiting for the mayor. When Lindsay finally did arrive, he was two hours late.

As Lindsay strode into the temple, there was a tremendous burst of applause, along with some who booed, and a few who turned thumbs down. Some others sat quite still, and did not react at all. The applause was sustained, and Lindsay took it all quietly, as some of his supporters flashed V for victory signs. Two people in the audience almost came to blows, and had to be separated.

A knowledgeable friend of the author, who has worked on a major newspaper for many years, once said that politics has become a branch of show business. If so, of all three candidates, John V. Lindsay most clearly looked the part. He acted the role with consummate skill—here a touch of humility, there a bit of toothy charm, here a touch of "point with pride," there a bit of "view with alarm." Lindsay had become letter-perfect in his role, and gave a flawless performance. The problem was that a sizable number of his listeners seemed to be aware that it was *only* a performance.

In his speech, Lindsay disclosed that this was the sixth time he had run for office, and that now "I've learned so much." He said that he welcomed the campaigning because "this has given me a chance to speak to as many New Yorkers as possible, to listen, and to take the pulse of New Yorkers." He asserted, "New Yorkers do not easily abandon the liberal faith," but his supporters, somehow missing their cue, failed to applaud. Lindsay swept on, "New Yorkers don't scare easily, and they won't be stampeded. . . . They want someone who will build bridges between groups. If I should be elected Mayor (here someone in the audience shouted out, "God forbid!") I will help all New Yorkers."

Again and again, Lindsay pounded out the theme of reconciliation, which he subdivided into protection against unfair rents, action against crime, protection of workers and housewives from frauds. Lindsay mentioned Procaccino, and smiled wanly at the great applause that followed. His most tumultuous ovation came when he said, "We want peace in Vietnam." He contended that "through our tax dollars, New Yorkers are the chief supporters of the war." He went on, "New York is the most heavily taxed city (here someone shouted out, "welfare!" and Lindsay had to wait until the shouts subsided). We send twenty-two billion dollars to Washington, all of which goes to the military." He insisted, "Our city has held together because it has adhered to the liberal tradition." At this point, the cue was picked up, and there was a generous round of applause. With just the right little catch in his voice, Lindsay stated, "It is with great humility that I again seek this office."

His speech had been punctuated by sporadic shouting from the audience. When he had finished, there was heavy applause, with some standing, while others booed. A fist fight that broke out was only the most obvious surfacing of a pent-up tension that was incredible and indescribable. There were furious arguments, with one old man being protected from a youth who was trying to accost him. One young man—probably a teacher—asked, "Why is Al Vann still in the New York City school system?" Asked whom he would vote for, he shrugged helplessly, "I don't know, but it won't be Lindsay."

The Jewish Defense League dogged Lindsay's footsteps, from one synagogue to another, throughout the campaign. In Brooklyn, The Bronx, and Queens, its members were there handing out anti-Lindsay literature, holding up signs, and heckling, almost every time the mayor put on a yarmulke.

One piece of JDL campaign literature showed the face of John Lindsay on a dollar bill, issued by "The United Stupes of America."[67] The author saw more than one truck carrying a JDL poster with a soulful-looking photo of Lindsay, along with the caption, "New York City's Greatest Mistake." And a large ad by the JDL appeared in the *New York Times,* and virtually gave Lindsay partisans political apoplexy. The ad read, in part:

> We have deliberated.
> We have searched our souls.
> We have patiently and agonizingly considered.
> The stark tragic reality remains unchanged.
> THE JEWS OF NEW YORK CITY CANNOT AFFORD
> FOUR MORE YEARS OF JOHN LINDSAY.
> ... John Lindsay desperately needs the Jewish vote in New York. He is frantically attempting to woo it, promising much, and hoping that the Jewish community has forgotten—forgotten the record—but we have not! In the nearly four years of John Lindsay's catastrophic administration we have seen the following blows to the survival of the Jewish community: ... a violent outpouring of anti-Jewish hate during the needlessly prolonged school strike. This vicious anti-Semitism was featured by physical assaults on and vicious threats to Jewish school personnel. ... the growth of a reign of terror against Jewish merchants in so-called ghetto areas. They have been murdered, extorted, burned out and daily harassed. They "go under"

economically with depressing regularity. It is an un-
dramatic story that seldom makes the headlines. John
Lindsay's silence on the nightmare is deafening. . . .
Crime in every neighborhood in the city has reached
intolerable levels but in the Jewish areas it has an added
thrust of anti-Semitism. Women live in terror; children
are beaten and shaken down; synagogues are vandalized;
organizations fear to call meetings at night and residents
are prisoners in their own "castles." Mayor Lindsay's instructions to the police have much to do with the nightmare. . . .
A de-facto quota system has been put into effect in many
of our schools. It blatantly excludes meritorious students
. . . in great part, Jewish . . . from both undergraduate and
graduate schools. This same illegality is being used in city
government. Such a policy will have a disastrous economic, social, and political effect on the Jewish community and is a direct result of the philosophy of
Lindsayism.[68]

Probably the most widely quoted anti-Lindsay literature to
appear in the campaign was the reprint of an article by JDL
leader Meir Kahane, which had appeared in his weekly column
in the *Jewish Press*. Rabbi Kahane's column was titled "Twenty
Questions"—questions which called for "polite but firm demand for specific answers" from Lindsay. Among the questions:

3– Why did the mayor not open his mouth when John
Hatchette [*sic*], a teacher, wrote his infamous anti-Jewish
garbage in the December, 1967 edition of the African
American Teachers (ATA) publication, Forum?
4– Why did the mayor—WHY DOES THE MAYOR—not
demand the immediate firing of the staff of Forum (all of
whom are teachers) and the dismissal from the public
schools of the ATA officials and the de-certification of that
group as the spokesmen for black teachers in the public
school system? . . .
6– Where was the mayor's slightest criticism of Commissioner Booth during all the years of the latter's incredible and planned failure to investigate any black racist
hate?[69]

The political activities of the Jewish Defense League aroused
tremendous controversy in the Jewish community. Some lib-

eral Jews became practically incoherent on the subject of JDL transgressions; some Orthodox Jews felt the JDL had gone too far; and the *Jewish Press* was evincing ever greater reluctance to be held personally responsible for the superactivist Rabbi Kahane.

The whispers, the rumors, the gossip, the word of mouth—all meshed into cold print a week before Election Day. In a front-page story in the October 24 issue, Rabbi Sholom Klass, publisher of the paper, announced that the *Jewish Press* had disassociated itself "from the leaders of the Jewish Defense League." Rabbi Klass accused the Jewish Defense League of using vilification during the campaign, "the very tactics the JDL has always condemned and which are contrary to our Torah." The publisher denounced rumors that the *Jewish Press* had "sold out" to Lindsay as "a libel as stupid as it is false." He denied that Kahane had been fired, but said that he had "resigned in favor of the JDL. . . ."[70] Thus, Meir Kahane, the most vigorous Jewish critic of Mayor Lindsay, was dropped from the staff of the *Jewish Press* during the closing days of the campaign—a signal victory for the Lindsay forces.

It was one of many in a string of triumphs for the Lindsay candidacy. Lindsay was outspending his rivals 4 to 1.[71] He had received the endorsements of the *New York Times, New York Post,* three radio stations, and one TV station,[72] not to mention a dazzling array of the beautiful people. Many influential Democrats were practically standing in line to endorse him.

Probably John Lindsay's greatest assets were the glaring liabilities of his opponents. At a very early stage in the campaign, Mario Procaccino had been dubbed Mr. Malaprop, with diction that reminded some political reporters of an old Edward G. Robinson movie. To make matters just a little worse, he easily blew his cool—a factor his opponents used to advantage during the rough and bruising days ahead. John Marchi was almost completely the opposite—cool to the point of boredom, given to rambling philosophical dissertions that left some voters bewildered and others openly disenchanted. A Republican district leader told the author that he sat in front of his TV set watching Marchi in debate engaging in an almost interminable introduction to his remarks. The district leader, in sheer exasperation, snapped, "Spit it out, John, spit it out!" By the

time Marchi did "spit it out," his time had expired, and it was
time to hear from one of his opponents.

The *Daily News* Straw Poll had picked the winners in New
York mayoral elections seven times in a row.[73] In each of four
Straw Polls, the *Daily News* gave Lindsay a commanding lead
in the three-way race, with Procaccino running from 11 to 18
percentage points behind in second place. The fourth Straw
Poll was taken from October 27 to 29 inclusive, and the results
(below) were published just a few days before the election:

|              | Straws | %       |
|--------------|-------:|--------:|
| MARCHI       | 602    | 20      |
| PROCACCINO   | 871    | 29      |
| LINDSAY      | 1,405  | 47      |
| UNDECIDED    | 110    | 4       |
| TOTALS       | 2,988  | 100[74] |

The *News* wrote that in its poll, Lindsay "has attracted more
than one of two Jewish votes . . . the poll this year shows him
getting about 52% of the Jews."[75]

Procaccino went to court to claim that the *Daily News* Straw
Poll might be inaccurate and unfairly helping to reelect Mayor
Lindsay.[76] The *News* announced that it was inviting the mayoral candidates or their representatives "to review the polling
methods we are using," and offered to pay $10,000 to charity "if
any of the candidates can prove that the poll results have been
manipulated in any way."[77] Procaccino's campaign manager,
Jacob Fuchsberg, said *News* representatives revealed that
about 20 percent of those approached by the pollsters declined
to participate. He contended that this cast doubt on the poll's
accuracy.[78]

The *Daily News* Straw Poll left the anti-Lindsay voter in an
agony of indecision. Should he vote for Marchi, who had consis-
tently lagged behind in third place in poll after poll, or for
Procaccino, who, according to the fourth poll, was only nine
points ahead of Marchi? The earliest conservative defection
came in September, when the Conservative Party leader of the
50th Assembly District in the Bay Ridge section of Brooklyn
announced that his local club would support Procaccino because Marchi "obviously cannot defeat Mayor Lindsay."[79] At
the end of October, a Conservative candidate for the City Coun-

cil in Queens said he was backing Procaccino,[80] as did the General Douglas MacArthur Republican Club in Manhattan.[81] The *Daily News* wrote, "The strong possibility of an informal coalition between some supporters of Controller Mario A. Procaccino and State Sen. John J. Marchi to form a Stop Lindsay movement loomed yesterday in Democratic, Republican, and Conservative circles."[82]

But it was just so much political shadowboxing. The anti-Lindsay vote was split two ways and in a state of almost total demoralization—the highly respected *Daily News* Straw Poll had predicted a decisive Lindsay win, and it seemed as if voters would be trooping to the polls more for the exercise than for anything else.

"One of the wisest prognosticators in the city" told Joseph Alsop, "If the Democrats had only nominated Marchi instead of Procaccino, they'd still be well ahead. And if the Democrats had found a guy like Stenvig (the brisk policeman who was elected mayor of Minneapolis) they could count on a big win on election day. As it stands, Lindsay is getting re-elected by default."[83]

Election Day came, and these were the complete results of the balloting:

| | |
|---|---|
| Lindsay | 981,900 |
| Procaccino | 821,924 |
| Marchi | 545,088[84] |

Marchi's total was dismayingly low, in view of his aides' predictions, a few months before, that his vote would reach or surpass a million.[85]

Lindsay's proportion of the total vote—less than 42 percent—was the lowest in the past 40 years of New York mayoral elections(except for the 39.4 percent that elected LaGuardia as mayor in 1933.)[86] An analysis circulated by the Center for New York City Affairs of the New School for Social Research found that the total vote for the mayoral candidates had declined by about 200,000 below the 1965 level, yet the third-party candidate won. The analysis thought these might be the reasons for the turnabout:

   (1) The *News* poll discouraged some Procaccino or Marchi voters from voting and caused some Lindsay supporters to think their vote was not necessary. (2) Democratic

precinct captains were less energetic than usual in urging enrolled Democrats to go to the polls and (3) a larger than usual number of voters were not attracted by any of the mayoral candidates and decided not to vote.[87]

The *Daily News* candidly conceded that its Straw Poll

forecast that Mayor John Lindsay would win with a larger margin than he actually polled on Tuesday. . . . The poll predicted that Lindsay would carry all four big boroughs, but Procaccino captured the Bronx and Brooklyn. Election results showed that the *News* had overpolled Lindsay in The Bronx and Brooklyn, while it had underpolled Procaccino in those two boroughs. . . . Indications are that the poll erred in predicting that Lindsay would capture 55% of the Jewish vote, which amounts to 30% of the citywide total. *Apparently, Procaccino took a slim majority here. . . .* [Emphasis added] In Brooklyn, final elections results showed that the poll underestimated Procaccino's strength in five of the heavily Jewish areas and overestimated Lindsay in three of them. Procaccino ran better than the poll showed in two Bronx Jewish areas and Lindsay did better than predicted in another.[88]

The *New York Times* found that:

The balance in the mayoral race may have been held by the city's Jewish voters, normally more likely to vote Democratic. This year, analyses of Assembly District counts indicated upper-income and apartment-dwelling Jewish areas voted to re-elect Mayor Lindsay while middle-income and home-owning Jewish areas tended to favor Mr. Procaccino.[89]
The two mayoral candidates considered more conservative—Controller Mario A. Procaccino, the Democratic and Non-Partisan parties' choice, and State Senator John J. Marchi, Republican and Conservative—together polled 58.2 per cent of the vote, or 1,366,682 of the 2,348,492 ballots tallied for the three major choices.[90]

That newspaper came to the reluctant conclusion that

analyses of returns from Tuesday's election suggested yesterday that the city might have moved toward the ideological right since the June 17 primary.[91]

# CHAPTER 14

# Black Help Wanted

PERHAPS ONLY EDWARD LEAR could really have done justice to the Nixon Administration's civil rights policy in the field of employment—a policy that makes job discrimination illegal except where it is legal—void except where it is valid—forbidden except where it is mandatory. Perhaps *only* a nonsense limerick could have described it:

> It's illegal to discriminate
> in the city, the county, or state
> But you must hire black
> or come under attack
> And the white workers? They're out of date!

Unfortunately, there was neither rhyme nor reason in the Nixon Administration's civil rights policy—a policy that made the New Racism the cornerstone of its job program.

Ironically, even at the height of the rioting and burning in the ghettos there was never really an unemployment problem, in the sense that there were not enough jobs to go around. On the contrary, *Nation's Business,* in its January 1967 issue, emphatically declared, "We can get anybody a job." This was their offer, in cool, brisk, no-nonsense prose:

The editors of *Nation's Business* guarantee that there is a job available for every person in this country who is willing and able to work. This claim is backed by the 1,500-member National Employment Assn., the country-wide organization for private employment agencies. "We can find a job for any person who is able and willing to work," states A. G. Hayes, NEA's president. "By able we mean any person of integrity who is physically capable of working. By willing we mean any person who has enough desire to work that he will, if necessary, take some training, move to another location and settle for a job reasonably consistent with his qualifications.[1]

The magazine quoted Max Mosner, a New York employment agency operator who felt "the government has made a tremendous mistake in taking initiative away from people. Everybody now wants to start at the top. They don't believe that some of the best chefs were once dishwashers."[2]

And Dr. Simon Ramo, a Cleveland employment operator, put it this way, "It's not socially acceptable to do unskilled work any more. It is much more socially acceptable to do nothing at all."[3]

The magazine concluded its article by repeating its sweeping offer:

*Nation's Business,* with the support of the nation's private employment agencies, throws out the challenge: We can get anybody a job who is willing and able to work. Write the Editor, Nation's Business, 1615 H. St., N.W., Washington, D. C. 20006.[4]

So the problem for the Negro was not a job, per se, but a job that he considered sufficiently dignified, sufficiently well-paying, and carrying sufficient prestige. There were enough jobs, but it came down to these questions: Would the unemployed Negroes accept one of the jobs that might be offered? And if the answer was "no", was it the obligation of government—and business—to find them jobs they did like—even if it meant substituting one form of discrimination for another—even if it meant excluding whites from some jobs *because* they were white—and including blacks in some jobs *because* they were black?

In March 1968 Senator Paul Fannin (R., Arizona), a member

of the Senate Labor and Public Welfare Committee, wrote an article titled, "Does Washington Force Racial Bias?" The subject of Fannin's article was a power-hungry federal bureau with the noble if misleading title of The Equal Employment Opportunity Commission (EEOC). Formed as an outgrowth of Title VII of the Civil Rights Act of 1964, the EEOC proved to be fervently devoted to reverse discrimination in employment at almost every opportunity.

Senator Fannin told how, during its first year of operation, the EEOC singled out the Newport News Shipbuilding and Drydock Company as a likely target. A defense contractor, the company became a sitting duck for the EEOC. Representatives of the EEOC started knocking on doors, soliciting complaints about Newport News. Out of 22,000 employees, they found 41 who were willing to complain. Later, the list narrowed down to only four complainants,[5] but that was all the EEOC needed to notify the company it was in violation of the Civil Rights Act. As a defense supplier, Newport News had already signed an agreement to take "affirmative action" in eliminating discrimination. But in rapid-fire formation, all the federal bureaucratic heavy artillery was turned on this Southern company. The Department of Justice notified Newport News that it was holding up a pending case awaiting the outcome of the negotiations with EEOC. The Office of Federal Contract Compliance under the Department of Labor notified the company all its defense contracts would be suspended pending the outcome of its talks with an EEOC "conciliator."[6] In Senator Fannin's words, "Small wonder that Newport News Shipbuilding 'voluntarily' agreed to the compact which Commission spokesmen called a 'landmark' case and a 'model' for future agreements."[7]

Under this agreement with EEOC, a preferential promotion list was created at Newport News, with 100 Negroes on it. This list had to be exhausted before a white worker could be promoted. Any exceptions to the order of placement had to be cleared with the commission. The EEOC agreement provided that in the apprentice school, "the ratio of Negro to white apprentices in any given year should approach the ratio . . . of Negro to whites in the labor area." As for promotions, "Vacancies will be filled by qualified Negro employees,"[8] meaning that qualified white employees need not bother to apply.

It was hardly surprising that in an extraordinary action, a union at Newport News filed a "document of protest" with the Equal Employment Opportunity Commission. The union complained that instead of evening things up between Negroes and whites, the agreement actually created "discrimination by giving some employees rights that others do not have."[9]

Newport News was only the beginning. An excellent series of articles by Shirly Scheibla in *Barron's* amply confirmed that in 1968 the Equal Employment Opportunity Commission was uprooting labor-management collective-bargaining agreements with all the fury of a tornado in a Kansas wheatfield. One worried executive, dependent for most of his business on federal contracting agencies, stated:

> If I don't sign a commitment to hire a certain number of non-whites in each job category the government threatens to deal me out. I face formal complaints by the Equal Employment Opportunity Commission and possible lawsuits by the Justice Department. I stand to lose millions of dollars in contracts—which means that dozens or even hundreds of workers' jobs are placed in jeopardy too, affecting blacks and whites alike. Yet I have no way to guarantee that I can find the people to meet these quotas, particularly in high-skill classifications. And the irony of it is, if I do go all-out with such "reverse discrimination" in my hiring and firing, I run the very real risk of all-out trouble with organized labor.[10]

Under the National Labor Relations Act, collective bargaining on seniority was mandatory where the NLRB had certified a union to represent workers. But how could an employer bargain, when still another agency—the Labor Department's Office of Federal Contract Compliance (OFCC)—had ordered his company to make specific changes? Asked that question, the OFCC seemed to give the employer a choice between slashing his wrists and cutting his throat. The OFCC planned to use its influence to help, but "if differences on a seniority contract cannot be resolved, a contractor may have to decide whether to take a strike or lose a [federal] contract."[11]

W. Willard Wirtz, then Secretary of Labor, told the AFL-CIO's Building & Construction convention, "I think it is an error to approach this problem . . . in terms that mean a number of . . .

Negroes or whites or anybody else, as being required on every single situation. . . . [That] involves quotas in one form or another, and as far as I am concerned . . . that is simply the wrong approach to that problem, and we have got to find a better one."[12] But apparently some of Wirtz's own departments had not gotten—and had no intention of getting—the message.

By early 1969, Miss Scheibla reported, "Roadbuilders from all over the country warned the Senate Public Works Committee in January that the federal aid highway program is coming to a virtual standstill because of the impossibility of their complying with equal employment opportunity (EEO) regulations."[13]

The trouble had really come to a head a year before, when it became evident that if any more federal highways were to be built at all, they would be built over the EEOC's prostrate regulatory body. The *cause célèbre* was that of the Carl M. Geupel Construction Company of Columbus, Ohio. On February 21, 1968, that company was declared low bidder and awarded a federal contract to build 3.3 miles of Interstate Highway Project No. 25 in Ohio's Summit County near Akron, part of a $125-million beltway program planned for that year.[14]

Just five days earlier, however, the Office of Federal Contract Compliance had issued a new regulation saying that each federal aid construction contract of $500,000 or more must have its approval before going into effect. As the contracting agency, the Department of Transportation and its Bureau of Public Roads, as well as OFCC, set out to determine if Geupel was really an equal-opportunity employer.[15]

The federal officials told John Geupel (the company's president) that he would have to be creative and come up with an affirmative action program to preclude discrimination. Geupel said he could not come up with a program without knowing exactly what they wanted. By mid-March, under instructions from both the Department of Transportation and the OFCC, the Bureau of Public Roads told the director of highways for Ohio that Geupel would have to supply "manning" tables by race for his own firm and for his subcontractors (essentially, this would have been a contractual commitment to employ specific numbers of Negroes in each craft).[16] Geupel said he could make no guarantees because he obtained his workers through a union hiring hall, nor did he know how he could go outside it to reach minorities.[17] To the federal regulators, this constituted failure to take appropriate affirmative action.[18]

On April 12, the Bureau of Public Roads said the Geupel bid should be rejected and the job re-advertised.[19] But P. E. Masheter, director of the Ohio Department of Highways, insisted that the job had already been awarded to the Geupel company:

> It is a matter of grave concern when the duly authorized representatives of the U. S. and the state of Ohio enter into a seriously considered written agreement, and other representatives of the U.S. then order that agreement to be breached. . . . It is not my intention at present to take bids on any of the projects in the Cleveland Operation Plan area which are scheduled to be let in contract this year, totaling $125 million . . . until this problem is solved.[20]

On May 22, Assistant Controller General Weitzel ruled that no post-award obligation that had not been spelled out in federal advertisements for the bids could be imposed on road contractors.[21] But in spite of this ruling, the federal contract with Geupel remained unexecuted.[22]

In the summer, Congress passed an amendment to the Highway Act of 1968, saying essentially what the assistant controller general had said. By late summer, Geupel finally got his contract, at the same price he had bid in February.[23] Geupel told *Barron's:* "There is no question but what we will lose money on it." He estimated that the delay would cost him between $200,000 and $300,000 in wage rates alone, to say nothing of higher costs of materials. Moreover, the project itself would be about a year late.[24]

The amendment to the Highway Act provided that the Secretary of Transportation must receive assurances from each state that employment in connection with proposed projects would be without regard to race, color, creed, or national origin. The Federal Highway Administration apparently interpreted this to mean that if it couldn't require a roadbuilder to come up with his own affirmative action program *after* bidding, it could do so *beforehand.* Accordingly, on October 1, the Federal Highway Administration issued Order 7-2, establishing vague "prequalification procedures," and said that all roadbuilders should be prequalified by December 1.[25]

Among other things, Order 7-2 said that no bid would be accepted unless the bidder submitted an EEO "Prequalification Statement" acceptable to the state highway department and concurred in by the Bureau of Public Roads. The approved statement was then to be made part of the contract.[26] But the guidelines for approval were so unclear that no two states interpreted them alike; what was accepted by one FHA official frequently was turned down by another.[27]

At the time Miss Scheibla's article was written, New York State had prequalified nobody, and all Federal highway work was being delayed. In Virginia, only 10 percent of 500 contractors had been prequalified, and that state decided to hold up all federal highway construction until most of those who normally bidded were able to do so. California had been unable to start the $700-million federal aid highway program it planned for 1969 because only two of its 300 contractors had been prequalified.[28]

Based in large part upon the articles in *Barron's*—which appeared at the time the Nixon Administration was taking over the reins of the federal government—Senator Dirksen believed a Senate subcommittee "should give the OFCC and EEOC a good looking over. It is my strong impression that the orders and requirements flowing out of these offices exceed the authority granted to them by Congress and are beyond any reasonable interpretation which can be given to the intent of Congress in the enabling Legislation."[29]

At the end of March, Clifford Alexander, Jr., then chairman of the Equal Employment Opportunity Commission, testified before a Senate subcommittee, of which Dirksen was a member. In a denunciation that made national headlines, Dirksen protested to the EEOC chairman that "businessmen are streaming into Washington every day to complain they've been harassed by your operation." Dirksen warned Alexander: "Either this punitive harassment is going to stop, or somebody is going to lose his job or I'm going to the highest authority in this government and get somebody fired."[30] The following day, the White House indicated that President Nixon would replace Alexander as chairman of the Equal Employment Opportunity Commission. A week and a half later, Alexander resigned his chairmanship, attributing his decision to "a crippling lack of Administration support."[31]

There was a faint glimmering of hope that the Nixon Administration would end the double standard in employment that made it legal to discriminate against whites and illegal to discriminate against blacks. The hope was encouraged by the statement of the new Secretary of Labor, George Shultz, that the administration was prepared to take "strong action" to bar discrimination in hiring practices by government contractors, but would emphasize "mediation and persuasion." But it soon became clear that the new Secretary of Labor's idea of "mediation and persuasion"[32] was a bludgeon tipped with velvet.

A new federal effort to increase Negro employment in the construction trades—the Philadelphia Plan—was scheduled to go into effect on July 18, 1969, barring an adverse last-minute ruling from the controller general.[33] Under the Philadelphia Plan, federal contractors bidding on construction jobs would be required to agree to employ given numbers of minority workers, before they could get a contract, *even if they put in the lowest bid for the work.* The Philadelphia Plan was to apply to ironworkers, plumbers, pipefitters, steamfitters, sheet-metal workers, electrical workers, roofers, waterproofers, and elevator construction workers.[34]

From the very outset, the Philadelphia Plan, devised by the Labor Department as part of its equal-employment program, was praised by Whitney Young of the Urban League—which was hardly surprising since Young had once made the same proposal himself, a few years back.[35] The plan, however, was opposed by Senator Dirksen and Senator McClellan; a Dirksen aide said the senator might introduce legislation to block the effort if the Labor Department went ahead with the plan. Dirksen and McClellan contended that requiring a contractor to employ a certain number of minority workers was the same as imposing a quota, and that quotas were prohibited by the Civil Rights Act of 1964.[36] A slight modification of the plan was made by Secretary of Labor Shultz. He inserted a clause saying a contractor would not be held to the employment figure in the bid, if he could prove he had made a "good faith" effort to hire minority workers and could not do so.[37]

Controller General Elmer B. Staats threw up a temporary roadblock after holding that the Civil Rights Act prohibited contractors from considering race or national origin in their hiring practices.[38] In rebuttal, Secretary of Labor Shultz told a news conference, "The Controller General is the agency of Congress, not a part of the executive branch. His opinion was not solicited by the Labor Department." He added, "The Department of Justice has approved the Philadelphia Plan as consistent with the Civil Rights Act."[39]

Shultz's news conference hardly quelled Congressional criticism of the Philadelphia Plan, and hardly rebutted the statement of Controller General Staats:

> There is a material difference between the situation in those cases, where enforcement of the rights of the minority individuals to vote or to have unsegregated educational or housing facilities does not deprive any member of a majority group of its rights and the situation in the employment field, where the hiring of a minority worker as one of a group whose number is limited by the employer's needs, in preference to one of the majority group precludes the employment of the latter.[40]

A.F.L.-C.I.O. President George Meany expressed strong doubts about the workability of the Philadelphia Plan. He said that the number of non-whites qualified in the seven most highly skilled building-trades unions was not sufficient to make possible the hiring of non-whites in the Philadelphia area[41]—a contention which was vigorously challenged by various Negro spokesmen. Meany asserted, "The plan is presenting contractors with an impossible situation."[42]

At the request of Senator Dirksen—who questioned its legality—the Phildelphia Plan was temporarily held up by the Labor Department.[43]

The Philadelphia Plan required bidders for contracts on federally aided construction projects above $500,000 to pledge "specific goals" in the hiring of minority groups. At the start, the plan covered only about half a dozen construction crafts in five counties in the Philadelphia area. If the plan was fulfilled, it was estimated that minority group members would constitute 19 percent of the membership of the unions by 1973, and that by then, the plan would add 1,000 non-white workers to these unions.[44]

Attorney General Mitchell threw the full weight of the Justice Department behind the plan, declaring that, contrary to Controller General Staats' ruling, it was perfectly legal, and did not violate the Civil Rights Act of 1964. In a 20-page ruling that obviously grasped at every conceivable legal straw, Mitchell argued that the plan was legal because it required affirmative action to meet goals rather than established firm quotas.[45] Asked to explain the difference between goals and quotas, Secretary of Labor Shultz said that a "quota is a system which keeps people out. What we are seeking are objectives to get people in."[46] One can only wonder how Shultz failed to understand that to the extent he got Negroes in jobs—because they were Negroes—he was keeping whites out of those jobs—because they were white.

On September 23, Shultz formally ordered the Philadelphia Plan into effect[47]—two weeks after the death of its most influential opponent, Senator Dirksen. Later it was announced that the Department of Labor planned to extend the plan to New York, Seattle, Boston, Los Angeles, San Francisco, St. Louis, Detroit, Pittsburgh, and Chicago.[48]

Opposition started building in Congress, and Nixon Administration officials had to keep telling the lawmakers that the Philadelphia Plan did not require an employer to increase minority employment on Federal construction projects, but only called on the employer to make a "good faith" effort to do so.[49] But Senator Sam Ervin, Democrat of North Carolina, flatly declared, "The Philadelphia Plan requires quotas that are based on race in violation of Title VII of the Civil Rights Act of 1964. That is as clear as the noonday sun on a cloudless day." Ervin quoted the language of Title VII that "nothing contained in this title shall be interpreted to require" employment on account of "race, color, religion, sex or national origin."

Senator Ervin summarized:

That says as plain as any language can that no person on account of race is to be given preferential treatment. Yet the Philadelphia plan amounts to legislation to do this. I can't find any authority for the Secretary of Labor to enact statutes.[50]

In November, Controller General Staats reiterated his intention to block payment to the first contractor who agreed to the minority quota hiring arrangement under the Philadelphia Plan. A spokesman for the controller general's office said that Staats would send letters to heads of executive departments, chairmen of Congressional appropriations committees, and others, informing them of his decision.[51]

By law, the controller general paid the bills of the federal government and might refuse to make any payments he considered to be illegal. Staats said he would not honor contracts signed under the plan because he believed it was unconstitutional.[52]

Meanwhile, one of the highest-ranking black officials in Washington, Arthur Fletcher, Assistant Secretary of Labor, said that nine bids had been made in Philadelphia on the first construction project awarded under the plan—an addition to Children's Hospital. The $4-million contract was awarded to the Bristol Iron and Steel Company of Tennessee. Fletcher said the company had agreed to increase its minority work force in Philadelphia to 20 percent over a three-year period. He said there had been no protest about the stipulations from other contractors.[53]

But a protest had begun groundswelling on Capitol Hill. Now the fight against the plan centered around a supplemental appropriations bill that ordinarily would have glided right through the Congress. A rider was attached to the bill and approved by the Senate specifying that no funds could be spent on any program or contract that the controller general held to contravene a federal law.[54]

The Secretary of Labor pleaded with the House of Representatives to defeat the rider. Shultz called the upcoming House vote "the most important civil rights vote in a long, long time." He said he hoped the administration could mount a successful campaign against the rider and charged that the measure had been passed only because of the support given it by the A.F.L.-C.I.O.[55]

President Nixon was said to have told top federal officials, "I want the action reversed."[56] His special consultant on civil rights, Leonard Garment, reached key people in civil rights, and enlisted the support of Roy Wilkins, Whitney Young, and

Joseph Rauh, Jr., vice chairman for civil rights of the Americans for Democratic Action, who agreed to call his friends on Capitol Hill.[57] Rauh and Garment watched the House voting from the gallery. When a prominent liberal would vote for the Philadelphia Plan, Garment would nod appreciateively toward Rauh. And when a prominent conservative would vote the same way, Rauh would nod in Garment's direction.[58] The rider was rejected by a vote of 208 to 156 in the House, and by a vote of 39 to 29 in the Senate.[59] It was a smashing victory for the Nixon Administration, Joseph Rauh, the A.D.A., and the New Racism.

The Nixon Administration was reported to be moving to extend some of the features of the Philadelphia Plan to virtually all work done under federal contract. The plan was spurring negotiations for "home-town solutions" in cities across the country, with arm-twisting "hints" that the plan would be instituted in those cities if no "home-town solution" was reached.[60]

In the summer of 1969, more than $60 million in construction at more than a dozen sites was halted in Chicago by a coalition of black organizations, which vowed to close all construction in the city until job discrimination in the building trades was ended.[61] *Jet* wrote, "Small numbers of police are usually on hand for the invasions of up to 200 persons, but they offer no resistance to the protesters." Among the invaders were the members of such Chicago street gangs as the Blackstone Nation, Black Disciple Family of Nation, Conservative Vice Lords, and Cobras, all of whom, the Negro magazine insisted, "act as protection for the demonstrators."[62] *The New York Times* was much more blunt about it:

> The shock forces of the demonstrations have been members of the Blackstone Rangers and other street gangs, and frequently they have stormed onto a site and ordered the workers off the job. The workers have left.[63]

And the *National Observer* described the typical scene, "repeated more than 20 times in the past four weeks . . . ," stating:

At a public-housing project under construction on this city's south side, the carpenters, masons, plumbers, and other craftsmen suddenly are interrupted at their work. A group of shouting demonstrators appears, many of them wearing berets identifying them as members of street gangs. "Okay, buddy, pack up and go home," one demonstrator tells a carpenter. "That's it fellow; you're not working any more today," a plumber is told. Within minutes, the construction site is still. No work is being done.[64]

About 1,200 workers stayed home, and many of them said they were afraid to return to work despite promises of police protection. Contractors said that many of these workers were black.[65] A spokesman for the Black Coalition for United Community Action warned that "we are going to be included in the building unions, or they are not going to build in our community."[66]

The coalition was demanding that 10,000 on-the-job training positions be made available to Negroes within 90 days, that Negroes with four years of construction experience be made foremen on construction in black communities, that construction in Negro areas be approved by the community, and that the union referral system of assigning jobs be abolished.[67] Up till then, most of the blacks who worked in construction were in the so-called mud trades—common labor, trench digging, foundation excavation—trades *Jet* called "the mostly going nowhere, cul-de-sac jobs that pay the lowest wages and are least desirable to whites."[68]

Ralph Abernathy threatened, "We will shake the very foundations of this city until the racism in the trades unions is ended and Black people assume their rightful place in building Chicago."[69]

In mid-August, a circuit court judge prohibited picketing by more than six persons.[70] The injunction was obeyed for about three weeks, at which time Jesse Jackson and four other members of the Black Coalition were arrested after they refused to lead about 500 demonstrators away from a new building being constructed.[71] Jackson had asserted that if there was any publicly financed construction in Negro areas, "we are going to do it."[72]

On September 22, Chicago had its first "black Monday." A

crowd estimated at from three to four thousand Negroes rallied in Civic Center Plaza to emphasize their demands for more skilled jobs in Chicago's construction trades. Members of the street gangs ringed the plaza and mingled with the crowds.[73] The *Chicago Tribune* wrote, "The real rally support was from youths wearing the berets symbolic of the youth gangs."[74]

A few days later, Assistant Secretary of Labor Fletcher attempted to hold hearings in Chicago on building-trades discrimination. He first tried to hold the hearings at the LaSalle Hotel. But white construction workers packed the conference room, and after trying for 45 minutes to quiet them, Fletcher gave up and adjourned the meeting. The following day, Fletcher shifted the site of the hearings to the U.S. Custom House, but there, more than 2,000 white construction workers jammed the sidewalks, scuffled with the police, and prevented Negro leaders from appearing to testify.[75] The white workers' counter-protest went into a third day, as they filled the sidewalks outside the Federal hearing room, jeering and shouting at witnesses. At lunch time, a column of shouting workers, stretching for nearly six blocks, wound through crowds in the Loop, stopping traffic on several of the busiest streets. The police were out in force and prevented the white workers from blocking the door, so that witnesses were able to enter the building.[76]

Several workers told reporters they were protesting any attempt to bring Negroes into the unions without regular journeyman training. One white worker declared, "I had to wait my turn and spend my turn getting my apprenticeship. Why should these guys be given special consideration, just because they happen to be black?"[77]

Later, a contingent of construction workers arrived at the *Chicago Sun-Times–Daily News* building. Sweeping into the building chanting "We want the truth," they knocked over a display of photographs from the walls and tore up copies of the papers on sale in the lobby.[78]

With all the subtlety of a karate chop, Assistant Secretary of Labor Fletcher vowed that if job discrimination did exist in Chicago, and if the trade unions did not show good faith and cooperate with federal efforts to eliminate it, he would see to it that all federally financed construction in Chicago—

worth some $2.5 billion—was closed down.[79]

In January, after months of negotiations and conflict, a program to train Negroes in skilled construction jobs was agreed upon by leaders of the black community, and by union and construction industry officials in Chicago. The Chicago Plan was expected to bring 4,000 Negroes into jobs in the building trades. A thousand who could qualify as apprentices or journeymen were to be put to work immediately. A second thousand were to start on-the-job training as quickly as possible, and another thousand were to begin journeyman training to full rating as skilled workers. The final thousand were to be given a special pre-apprentice training program to qualify them for basic construction skills. The three principals agreed that they would work toward the Negro goal of proportionate minority representation in the skilled building trades by 1975.[80]

It was an unconditional surrender to the New Racism— crammed down the throats of the companies and the unions by all the coercive powers of the federal government. But George Meany was practically ecstatic about the entire agreement. In a letter to the *New York Times,* Meany wrote:

> Tom Wicker's comparison . . . of the Chicago and Philadelphia plans for expanding minority employment in the building trades demonstrates that a columnist should know what he is talking about before he sits down to his typewriter. Far from disproving my National Press Club remarks, the Chicago plan can do what the Philadelphia plan cannot do—provide employment for minority group workers in the area work force with equality of skills, wages, standards, and opportunity. The A.F.L.-C.I.O. Civil Rights Department helped conceive, negotiate and execute the Chicago agreement. I expect and pray that it will be a success and I have already, on the record, pledged the continued cooperation and assistance of the A.F.L.-C.I.O. No one in the A.F.L.-C.I.O. denies discrimination existed in the building trades unions in the past. I deplore it, even though I recognize discrimination exists in other unions and throughout society as a whole. But the building trades unions have been doing a conscientious job of eliiminating discrimination. I am as proud, however, of what they have accomplished as I am convinced that much more remains to be done. . . . There is not now nor has there ever been an ample number of black skilled tradesmen ready, willing

and able to go to work in Chicago or anywhere. The Chicago plan, therefore, goes beyond the shortage for a solution. It will recruit those who have had some experience as well as young people who have no experience. The Philadelphia plan relies on a thinly disguised quota system for employment on jobs Federally funded. It trains no one, puts no one into the area work force and could be called a success if not a single additional black got a job. And of course it lasts only as long as it takes to complete construction of each Federal facility. Instead of pointing an erring finger of scorn at others who are trying to right an ancient wrong, Mr. Wicker might be well advised to look at his own profession and its record and responsibilities. How many blacks, for example, are editors or editorial writers or hold other management, supervisory, or policy making positions on the Times? How many of Mr. Wicker's fellow columnists on the Times are black?[81]

George Meany may have been turning handsprings over the Chicago agreement, but it is highly doubtful that most rank-and-file union members shared his enthusiasm. From their viewpoint, the Philadelphia Plan and Chicago agreements both provided for racial quotas. The only difference—if it could be called that—was that one quota was enforced by government, while the other quota was enforced by the unions. But either way—for a specified number of jobs in the building trades— black was not only beautiful but positively mandatory for gainful employment.

Of course the federal government was hardly bereft of business allies in its enforcement of the New Racism. Some of the most respected and powerful business leaders in the country were eagerly scanning the job market like talent scouts, dredging up employment opportunities for the hardcore. To these business executives—and to the Urban Coalition and National Alliance of Businessmen that could not have existed for a week without them—it was never really wrong to discriminate; it was only wrong to discriminate against blacks.

Whatever the Urban Coalition may be today, there can be no doubt that it was conceived in a climate of fear and nurtured in a time of hate and violence still haunting our cities. It was in the summer of 1967—that summer when race riots threatened to annihilate Newark and Detroit, and promised more and more Molotov cocktails in city after city, more burning, more looting, more wanton destruction. Towards the end of the summer of 1967, Whitney Young wrote:

> This summer's racial violence has caused a crisis of leadership. The riots have made it easy for "backlashers" to justify resistance to necessary social changes. But this leads to a dangerous polarization of attitudes which could lead to more violence.... There are signs that some leaders realize the urgency of the situation and are willing to join with others to form the coalition so desparately needed if our country is to have peace and progress. I took part in a recent meeting to form just such a group. It is called the Urban Coalition, and our first meeting included leaders of business, labor, religion, city mayors, and civil rights groups. Out of this meeting came proposals for an emergency work program to provide jobs and training for the unemployed, the establishment of job centers in cities, and the commitment of private industry to take all steps necessary to insure full employment.[82]

The members of the Urban Coalition Steering Committee included mayors John Lindsay of New York and Jerome Cavanagh of Detroit, George Meany and Walter Reuther, Young and Roy Wilkins, and such business leaders as Irwin Miller, David Rockefeller, and Henry Ford.[83] The Ford Foundation became the chief financial supporter of the Urban Coalition, making a first grant of $100,000, a second grant of $1 million, and a third grant of $2.25 million.[84]

Like Whitney Young, Henry Ford made it perfectly obvious that "violence works"—that fear of renewed violence was a crucial motivating factor in the founding of the Urban Coalition. "It is already clear," Ford wrote, "that the summer of 1967 will prove to have been a turning point in the history of our nation's long and halting quest for equal opportunity. After the holocaust, which swept Detroit and Newark, and other cities last summer, things can never again be the same. Whether they change for the better, or for the worse, remains to be determined."[85]

Ford envisioned the corporate personnel office as a kind of traveling road show using all its powers of persuasion to sell ghetto residents on the idea of working in its plants:

I believe that employers must take aggressive steps to overcome such barriers [lack of confidence, lack of knowledge of job openings]. It is not enough to provide technically equal employment opportunities. Management should be willing to go directly into the city, to seek out the unemployed, to make sure that hiring standards are not unnecessarily or unrealistically restrictive, and to lend a helping hand in adjusting to the work and the work place.[86]

Virgil E. Boyd, president of Chrysler Corporation, disclosed that "each of the automobile companies quickly opened employment centers in the inner city" following the riots in Detroit, in the belief that "unemployment and underemployment demanded immediate attention if we are going to resolve the urban crisis."[87]

The auto companies became the industrial backbone of the Urban Coalition and its twin, the National Alliance of Businessmen. By February 1, 1969, *Business Week* was reporting that "in terms of the goals set by the National Alliance of Businessmen, early results are impressive. General Motors, Ford, and Chrysler have all passed their first-year hiring quotas with months to spare, and the margin grows weekly."[88] *Business Week* also noted:

Between last April and December, the three major auto makers hired 38,600 persons classified as "hard core unemployed" by NAB standards. Briefly this means they were out of work and came from disadvantaged backgrounds. About 65% were non-white. The Detroit figures constitute 31% of the latest NAB total of 125,000 newly hired hardcore unemployed. The Big Three's original quota was 22,-338.[89]

Inevitably, this discrimination in favor of black workers at times boomeranged against white job applicants. The *Wall Street Journal* noted:

Company efforts to hold down sharply rising costs, plus pressures on businessmen to permanently hire the hardcore unemployed, may limit summer openings, figures a New York State employment official. . . . The summer job tightness threatens to pinch the better-off white kids who aren't rated needy. Mayor Daley's summer-jobs hunter says 65% of the 35,000 openings sought in Chicago companies will go to"disadvantaged" youths. Wisconsin Telephone Co. workers are told first call on summer jobs will go not to their own kids but to poor youngsters. A West Coast company says its summer hiring of college students had been cut by two-thirds while the firm gives priority to employing minority youth.[90]

In a kind of last hurrah for the outgoing administration, on January 10, 1969, the National Alliance of Businessmen told President Johnson that cooperating employers had already hired 125,000 hardcore unemployed, exceeding LBJ's goal of 100,000 job placements by June 30.[91] By September, the National Alliance of Businessmen reported that it had so far placed a total of 229,679 men and women—white, black, red, and yellow—from the nation's urban slums and rural poverty pockets.[92] But some corporate officials dismissed it as a "phony numbers game." The numbers were held to include hiring that would have been done in any case and to credit companies with high employee turnovers as having more recruits.[93] The *New York Times* stressed, "The major problem with alliance programs is that very little can be double-checked. Thus if the alliance says 268,920 persons have been placed in jobs or if a businessman says he has hired 50 disadvantaged persons, there is no precise means of confirmation."[94]

The program of the National Alliance of Businessmen was divided into two areas. The first was a drive to enlist businessmen to pledge jobs to the hardcore jobless. The other was a contract program in which businesses were reimbursed by the Department of Labor for the cost of training and other expenses for handling problems associated with the unemployed. As of October 1969, the government had paid out $300 million in reimbursements.[95]

Negroes and some NAB members complained that the Labor Department provided reimbursement for training for such jobs as busboy, porter, maid, parking-lot attendant, housekeeper, laborer, and airlines baggagemen. The critics said they could not understand what training would be needed for these jobs, and thought companies should not get money for them.[96] But Donald Kendall, chairman of the NAB, told Presidential ad-

viser Arthur Burns that unless companies were given government money to finance on-job training, many firms would simply make do with fewer workers.[97]

Most NAB officials saw nothing wrong with the practice, including its executive vice chairman, Paul W. Kayser. "There is
nothing wrong with a $1.60-an-hour job, so long as it leads
someplace. I would certainly not discourage such jobs where
efforts are made to make certain there is upward mobility. A
low-level job is better than no job at all."[98]

Some black militants expended a great deal of time and effort
in biting the paternalistic hand that fed them. On July 12, 1968,
an estimated 2,000 Negro workers left their jobs at the Chrysler
Corporation plant in Hamtramck, Michigan, in protest against
alleged "racism." Chrysler said a production line that turned
out Barracudas and Chargers had been halted because of
"excessive absenteeism." Among the Negro dissidents' demands were the appointments of a Negro plant manager, 50
Negro foremen, and 10 Negro general foremen.[99]

Undoubtedly, demands such as these were arousing more
white unionist support for George Wallace than the United
Auto Workers cared to admit. In October of that Presidential
election year, UAW Local 599—representing 16,000 workers at
the Buick works in Flint, Michigan—held a Presidential preference poll in which more than 8,000 rank-and-file members participated. Of those union men voting, 49 percent chose Wallace,
39 percent selected Humphrey, and 12 percent voted for
Nixon.[100] This was in staggering contrast to a vote by elected
union delegates that had given Humphrey 87.8 percent of its
ballots, 10.2 percent to Wallace, and 1 percent to Nixon.[101]

The *New York Times* wrote: "The size of the Buick vote was
the real test of Mr. Wallace's strength among the union membership, and the results indicate the union is underestimating
his appeal or at least not publicly admitting to it."[102] Flint was
the home of tens of thousands of Southern-born factory workers, but ironically, it was also the first city in the nation to
approve an open housing law in a popular referendum. And,
too, it had an appointed Negro mayor.[103]

The UAW was obviously most reluctant to tangle openly with
George Wallace. At Wallace rallies, in Flint, Kalamazoo, Lans-
ing, and Grand Rapids there were no union men handing out

anti-Wallace literature, no UAW-for-Humphrey signs, and no "truth squad" trailers.[104]

A few days after the union rank-and-file vote for Wallace, Richard Nixon came to Flint, and asked:

"Do you just want to make a point or do you want to make a change?

"Do you want to get something off your chest, or do you want to get something done?

"Do you want to get a moment's satisfaction by your vote of protest or do you want to get four years of action?"[105]

Quite obviously, the last thing these workers wanted was a change to a racial quota for union labor; the last thing they wanted done was a retooling of all the forms of reverse discrimination that had come off the paternalists' assembly line under Lyndon Johnson. Quite obviously, their idea of "four years of action" was *not* four years of the New Racism.

White union workers had undoubtedly been incensed by wildcat strikes triggered by militant black unionists in defiance of their white leadership, strikes which had temporarily shut down auto production at Chrysler Corporation's biggest Detroit plant.

One of the most fanatical of these black militant groups was the Dodge Revolutionary Union Movement (DRUM). The *Wall Street Journal* wrote that DRUM's "literature, written in shrill, often obscene language, warns of conflicts, bloodshed, possibly even destruction of plants." With a bow to Malcolm X, a DRUM manifesto declared, "Before peace and tranquility can prevail our demands must be met and our goals achieved, *by any means necessary*"[106] (emphasis added) Among DRUM's demands were more black foremen, black plant managers, black union representatives, and even a black board chairman at Chrysler Corporation.[107] Marcellius Ivory, the first Negro elected a regional director of the UAW, felt there was "a real polarization between white and black auto workers as a result of DRUM and other Negro activities." Said Ivory, "To be frank with you, I'm scared. I don't know where the hell this is leading." Ivory probably owed his election to UAW President Walter Reuther's concern with advancing Negroes into union leadership posts. Reuther had persuaded two white candidates to drop out of the election contest, thus assuring that either Ivory or another black man would win.[108]

The preamble to DRUM's constitution said, "We do here proclaim our solemn duty to take this the first step on the road to final victory over the great common enemy of humanity: i.e. the monstrous U.S.A. and the . . . system of exploitation and degradation."[109] DRUM said its purpose and objective was "to break the bonds of white racist control over the lives and destiny of black workers" as a step toward eventual "relief" for "people all over the world oppressed by our common enemy." In this connection, DRUM said it would be necessary to "get rid of the racist, tyrannical, and unrepresentative UAW as representation for black workers, so that . . . we can deal directly with our main adversary, the white racists, owners of the means of production" and "bring down this exploitative system."[110]

Black militants had disrupted production for short periods in plant demonstrations in several industries.[111] Chrysler would not comment on reports reaching *Business Week* that DRUM members and sympathizers engaging in guerrilla warfare had scratched paint on new cars and left nuts and bolts untightened. But the company did admit that production machinery had been sabotaged.[112] And UAW found it necessary to warn auto unionists, "Sabotage can be deadly."[113]

Some militants were demanding multi-million-dollar "reparations from industry" for "exploited blacks." Among the suggestions was one that corporations turn over up to 10 percent of their common stock to be used to improve the blacks' lot.[114]

To these militants, control and domination "by any means necessary" were not merely rhetoric. A black industrial relations man was stabbed in a Chrysler plant for "Tomism" when he notified a black militant that he was suspended.[115] And DRUM boasted of a contingent of 200 "storming a union hall and taking over the executive board meeting," and of "a sit-down protest by 50 black workers at Solidarity House, headquarters of the UAW."[116]

In an unprecedented action, the International Executive Board of the UAW adopted a statement, which read in part:

A group now exists in a few plants where UAW represents the workers which calls itself a black revolutionary movement and whose goals are the complete separation of the races in the shop and the destruction of our Union through the tactics of violence, fear and intimidation. In recent weeks, a tiny handful of people, not all of them auto workers or members of the UAW, attempted to shut down the Eldon Ave. Axle plant of Chrysler Corp. by picketing the gates, carrying picket signs with racist slogans. They were unsuccessful in shutting the plant down, but hundreds of workers lost wages as a result of this illegal and unwarranted picket line. Incidents of violence, including knifings and physical assaults, have occurred in both the Hamtramck Assembly and Eldon Axle plants of Chrysler, perpetrated by members of this so-called revolutionary group. Fires have been started inside the plants which, had they not been brought under control, could have meant the loss of workers' lives and the loss of jobs. . . . The UAW will continue to fight all forms of discrimination and will provide the fullest protection to workers who have legitimate grievances. *The UAW, however, will not protect workers who resort to violence and intimidation with the conscious purpose of dividing our Union along racial lines; for these workers would undermine our Union, the principles upon which our Union was founded and put into jeopardy the jobs which our members hold.* [117]

*Business Week* considered the UAW statement "a direct attack on DRUM—and a warning against support for the self-styled revolutionary group."[118]

A month and a half after the warning, about 500 Negro workers, protesting alleged racism, stayed off the job and forced the closing of the Ford assembly plant in Mahwah, New Jersey. Workers were sent home after the 4:00 p.m. shift began, and assembly lines that would have produced 425 cars by midnight came to a halt. The walkout was called by the United Black Brotherhood of Ford Mahwah, after a Negro worker charged that a supervisor had insulted him with a racial epithet. The protest produced a split between the Negro production-line employees and Local 906 of the UAW, which urged its members to return to work.[119]

A spokesman for Ford denied that there were bigotry and racial discrimination in the plant. He said that the Ford Motor Company had a long history of employing Negroes in its plants and that throughout the United States, 25 percent of its employees were Negroes. He disclosed that at the Mahwah plant nearly 50 percent of the employees were Negroes.[120]

UAW officials reported that the supervisor who had allegedly used racial epithets had been suspended. But this did not quite square with Ford's version—that the supervisor was on vacation, a vacation proposed following the incident.[121]

Ken Bannon, director of UAW's Ford Department, charged that at Mahwah, the militants "threatened to beat up wives and children of Negro workers, including union leaders, if they refused to cooperate."[122] But most white workers, and an estimated half or more of all blacks, heeded Ford and UAW urgings to stay on the job.[123]

*Newsweek* emphasized that "the health of the job program depends upon the continued health of the economy," and quoted one Labor Department administrator who had observed, "If the economy takes a nose dive, this program is going to go to hell."[124]

In March 1969 the economy was transmitting early warning signals. Production curtailments resulted in indefinite layoffs for several hundred hardcore workers among the estimated 7,800 hired and retained by Ford. Two of their special hiring centers in Detroit's inner city were closed.[125] At the time, it was thought that the move would be temporary, as the outlook for auto sales was "bullish." General Motors and Chrysler were reducing overtime, shortening the work week, and closing plants temporarily.[126]

With union seniority provisions in full force and effect, the hardcore would inevitably be among the first to be laid off, or fired—unless the seniority rules were turned upside down for the new Negro employes; unless inverted seniority was made part of company policy and the UAW contract. UAW proposals for inverted seniority were made—and lost—in the 1964 and 1967 auto negotiations.[127] Now the issue was raised again by a UAW request that Ford apply reverse seniority to hardcore workers only.[128]

UAW official Ken Bannon said that when a layoff occurred, a high-seniority worker in a particular job classification should be able to volunteer to take time off, while a new hardcore worker, who normally would have to go, would be permitted to stay on the job.[129] Under the company-union supplemental unemployment benefit program (SUB), the senior man who elected to be laid off would receive 95 percent of his regular weekly take-home pay, minus $7.50—to offset savings for work-related expenses—for up to 52 weeks.[130]

A management official objected that applying inverse seniority meant "we would almost have to pay double on a man-to-man basis."[131] Another problem was state laws that required people out of work and receiving unemployment compensation to be available for and to seek work. And an industry executive wondered where it would stop, considering that others might be hard-off, whether or not they were hardcore. For example, he said, what if you hired 1,000 workers, one-third hardcore, and two-thirds not, although many might come close to the classification. "You can't deal differently with the two-thirds than the one-third," he argued. Another auto man added, "Would you also have to set up special layoff programs for women supporting families or older workers tired of working?"[132]

The auto companies were also concerned about possible loss of efficiency. Executives argued that the new employees from the tight labor market of recent years were not as capable or flexible as earlier workers. They feared that in temporary layoffs, a plant department might end up short, and in a highly integrated industry that could be disastrous.[133]

It was probably for reasons such as these that Ford, on April 11, 1969, rejected the UAW proposal to create a reverse seniority program.[134] In January 1970 the job program was running out of gas. *Business Week* reported, "Layoffs are threatening nationwide efforts to rehabilitate people once thought unemployable. . . . The focus of concern now is the auto industry, where the nation's most highly touted program for hiring the unhireables is grinding to a halt in the wake of depressed car sales. This week, 10,000 workers at GM and Chrysler plants were on indefinite or permanent layoffs. These are aside from short furloughs for some 110,000 GM, Ford and Chrysler workers this month . . . and plans to close Ford's Dallas assembly plant permanently at the end of February. . . ."[135] *Business Week* noted that of the 38,600 hardcore unemployed originally hired by the auto companies, only 16,356 remained—a rather lackluster retention rate of 42 percent.[136]

Once a worker was on the job for four months, he was no

longer classified as a "hardcore unemployable," which closed that channel for new employment. There was no NAB program for finding new employment for laid-off black workers.[137] It was hoped that "four or five months' experience may be enough to give them the confidence and motivation to get another job." But *Business Week* underscored the fact that "Many—probably most—have never found a job on their own."[138]

The future could scarcely be grimmer. If the jobs program is not successful enough, it will arouse the fierce resentment of ghetto residents who will roundly denounce Whitey for "jiving" him again. If the jobs program is too successful, it will arouse the fierce resentment of white workers who will see a black skin as a passport to privilege in the plants and factories. Either way, the program must inevitably engender wall-to-wall hostility—a hostility of which private industry has only recently become aware. A study made for the American Foundation on Automation and Employment expressed concern with "high turnover and worker restlessness," and with the discontent of "the white, lower-middle-class industrial worker who flirted so longingly with the George Wallace for President drive in the last election."[139] The study warned:

> The introduction of hardcore workers and minority-group members into the lower levels of the mainstream of American economic life is creating pressures from the blacks who want to move up in the system and resentment among whites over special favoritism accorded to blacks.[140]

The study concluded that "evidence of job dissatisfaction by those at the lower level seems destined to increase."[141] The resentments, the dissatisfactions, the hostility—all are very much like a political time bomb set to explode with considerable force in 1972. And some time very soon, the White House advisers had better tear themselves away from the polls and TV cameras—and all other political manifestations of "mirror, mirror on the wall"—and consider this very real possibility: that a double-standard in enforcing civil rights laws may become the political Achilles' heel of Richard M. Nixon; that white workers who were lured away from George Wallace in 1968 may very well cast their lot with the Alabamian (or a reasonable facsimile) in 1972, *even knowing he will lose.* In the bluntest possible terms, they may very well vote for their jobs and unstitch the fragile coalition that sent Nixon to the White House.

For no matter what his entourage may say or think, his hold on the White House is not unshakable. It will be indeed ironic if—after having waited eight long years for vindication at the polls—it is the New Racism that inflicts upon Richard Nixon the most crushing defeat of his career, the second-rate historical status of a one-term President.

# CHAPTER 15

# The New Racism

THIS IS THE END OF MY BOOK—BUT IT IS HARDLY the end of the New Racism.* A year has elapsed between my writing of the Introduction and the words I am writing now, and more than ever, I am convinced that the New Racism will become the tidal wave of the 1970's—a wave that could very well engulf our cities in such unbearable torment and tension that in this decade, armed conflict may be almost inevitable. And I am equally convinced that the more favoritism that is shown the Negro, the more inevitable this tragic conflict will become.

Call them the White Lower-Middle Class. Call them the White Working Class. Give them any name you like, but know that some of them are ready to fight—with a toughness, a fury, a recklessness, and a courage that are a match for the most militant black men in the ghetto—even in my own native New York City, which is still virtually the national capital of American liberalism.

The working-class white is not an insatiable reader. He is likely to bypass the best-seller lists and book reviews for the sports page—but he has read about Malcolm X, the Black Pan-

*This last chapter is a mixture of documented fact and personal opinion. To underscore this, it is written in the first person.

thers, and the Black insurrections at San Francisco State, Cornell, and CCNY. He believes that when the Black Panthers talk about revolution, they *mean* revolution. He sees black studies as a Seminar in Rebellion. He sees civil rights laws being strictly enforced to prevent job discrimination against blacks, and sees those same laws stretched like an accordion to accept the Philadelphia Plan, with its job discrimination against whites. He sees community control beaten down by court edict in Mississippi, and flourishing in Harlem and Bedford-Stuyvesant, and knows it depends upon whose racial ox is being gored. He remembers the Granddaddy of the racial study groups—the National Advisory Commission on Civic Disorders—warning that "our Nation is moving toward two societies, one black, one white—separate and unequal," and he feels that the Kerner Commission got its conclusion right, but its colors wrong—that in the 1970's, it will be the *black* society that will acquire superior rights and benefits at his expense. And he knows that if one of America's most famous conservatives is correct, we will even choose a President because of the color of his skin.

The September 1969 issue of *Ebony* carried a most illuminating article titled, "Urban League Conducts A Guided Tour." It was about Urban League sponsorship of "a tour of carefully chosen journalists to black communities in selected cities across the country...." Among those who went on the tour were reporters or columnists from the *New York Times, Wall Street Journal,* and *Look,* and William F. Buckley Jr. of *National Review.* A photo in *Ebony* showed Buckley chatting with Ed Goff, director of Watts' Urban Workshop.

The magazine noted:

> The black communities greeted the touring mass communicators with varying degrees of hostility and ill-concealed skepticism. The most hostile reception the journalists received was in San Francisco from members of the Black Student Union, the Third World Liberation Front, and the Joe Hill caucus of Students for a Democratic Society (SDS).

Apparently, Buckley was subjected to one of the most hostile receptions of all, and "was called some rather choice names." *Ebony* quoted Buckley as saying of an especially vitriolic group, "I had the feeling that there wasn't anything of a human quality there. There was a gang bang mentality. I can see those people in a Castro tribunal sentencing people to death. There was also a great bullying instinct present." *Ebony* could hardly resist the temptation to comment, "Many black people, of course, have this same kind of reaction about Buckley and many of his supporters."[1]

The announced purpose of the tour was for the journalists to "acquaint themselves with the needs of Black America."[2] And apparently, somewhere between the first leg of the tour and the first issue of *Look* in 1970, William F. Buckley Jr. decided that what black America needed was a four-year lease on 1600 Pennsylvania Avenue.

Buckley's article appeared in *Look* and was titled, "Why We Need a Black President in 1980." It was written with all the usual Buckley wit and brilliance and charm—but with all its rhetorical artistry, it could just as appropriately have been titled, "Why We Need the New Racism in the White House." Buckley wrote:

> The outstanding charge against America is hypocrisy. It is greatly exaggerated, beyond even the exaggeration that always marks the distance between national practice and national ideal. But where the Negroes are concerned, the practice of inequality directly belies the vision of equality of opportunity so that the election of Negro public officials (yes, because they are Negro) is a considerable tonic for the white soul. . . .

Buckley believed that it was from the ranks of

> young Negro leaders who work in the ghettos . . . who are arguing that progress is possible within the system. . . . It is from the ranks of these young men now 30, 35, 40 years old that I can imagine someone rising, in the next decade, to national prominence as a presidential candidate. When it happens, I think that it is quite possible that he will be greeted gladly by those who, having satisfied themselves that the point they are about to make will not be at the expense of the survival of the Republic, will join in a quite general enthusiasm over his election as President of the United States; who will celebrate his achievement of the highest office in the world as a personal celebration, as a

celebration of the ideals of a country that by this act alone,
would reassert its idealism. . . .

Buckley believed that in electing such a Negro president, those
"seeking to alleviate the sorrow of the few [would] lighten the
burden of the many.[3]

For years, William F. Buckley Jr. has discoursed upon almost
every subject as a spokesman for American conservatism. But
I do not think he was speaking for most rank-and-file conservatives when he wrote this article. Buckley would make the Presidency the Gold Watch for 350 years of faithful service—the
Super-Reparation that surpasses anything James Forman has
ever demanded. He would make the Presidency the Supreme
Premium in the paternalist gift catalog, to redeem the green
stamps of rage of practically every black militant in the country.

What Buckley called "idealism" was just a glowing mirage,
in an article that was woefully barren of the cool-headed logic
that had distinguished his writings for many years. It was not
just that William F. Buckley's emperor had no clothes, but that
there never was any emperor at all. You simply cannot en-
throne the New Racism without enthroning virtually every
other form of discrimination since time began. You simply cannot *condone* anti-white discrimination in seeking the highest
office in the land, and then *condemn* anti-black discrimination,
and expect to retain the trust or confidence of either the ghettos
or the suburbs.

To be sure, Buckley tidily inserted the proviso that those welcoming a black President *because* he was black should satisfy
themselves that "the point they are about to make will not be
at the expense of the survival of the Republic. . . ." But it was
difficult to see how supporters of the Buckley proposal could be
all that sure. Harvard Negro educator Martin Kilson wrote that
the Black Panther Party (BPP)

is entering a second phase of political development, including organization among Negro workers, community
development activity, campus organization, and some
electoral activity. But it is doubtful that the limited educational and technical skills possessed by the paraintellectual leaders of the BPP will allow it to evolve very far in

this new direction without outside aid from more skilled groups.... At this point enter the established Negro intelligentsia as the source of the second type of black politician able to facilitate the political institutionalization of black nationalism. A new crop of professionally educated black politicians is now emerging to urban ghettos—and the growth of this group seems certain as more Negroes enter and complete college. Lawyers currently predominate in the new group of Negro professional politicians; Hatcher in Gary, Stokes in Cleveland, Thomas Atkins in Boston, Conyers in Detroit, and Tom Bradley in Los Angeles are among the best. These men are fashioning a black militant style of their own, within the established framework of urban politics; and as they perfect the assimilation of a black ethnicity to the basic patterns of American politics, *they may prove legitimate recipients of alliance with such paraintellectual elements as the Black Panther party.*[4] [Emphasis added]

So the ambitious black politician may be carrying water on both shoulders—with one bucket marked "moderate" and the other marked "Black Panther Party." And the white voter who views this with alarm will probably be denounced as a racist for his pains.* He may even view with alarm some officials in moderate civil rights organizations. Cleveland is, after all, a city with a black mayor now serving his second term in office. Yet Joseph Battle, director of the Urban League's Project Equality fair housing office in Cleveland had this to say about his contribution to the revolution: "Maybe I won't throw the firebomb but I damn sure will give the gasoline and the money. . . . The chips are down. We know whose side we're gonna be on."[5] Would a black candidate for the Presidency, such as Buckley envisions, be able to repudiate such a statement without being castigated as an "Uncle Tom" by ghetto militants? And

---

*This was exactly the strategy followed by Kenneth Gibson, Newark's first black Mayor, during his successful election campaign in 1970. Along with a great many Negro notables in the political, sports, and entertainment fields, the June 20, 1970, edition of the *Amsterdam News* noted that "There are more black nationalists, who are dribbling in from everywhere to give the black candidate . . . their assistance." Among these black nationalists was one of Gibson's earliest supporters—LeRoi Jones. And in Cleveland, retired Negro Air Force General Benjamin O. Davis, Jr. resigned after 6 months as safety director in charge of the police and fire departments. Davis charged that the administration of Negro mayor Carl Stokes was providing "support and comfort" to the enemies of the police.

if he refused to repudiate it, would he deserve the support of white voters?

Buckley has never had any personal experience with poverty —he has never known what it is to be *white* and poor, or even white and middle-class, and to scan the budget to see whether he can put Peter off another week to pay Paul. Perhaps this is why he finds it so impossible to understand that many whites in this country have no feelings of guilt about the Negro. Having been poor themselves, these whites see no reason to be held personally liable for the poverty of Negroes. Never having functioned as landlord or employer, these whites reject the idea that Negro deprivations should be laid at their door. It is true enough that some of them may have blocked Negro efforts to enter certain unions or to move into certain neighborhoods, but it is also true that these have been the very blocs that tended to vote liberal—enabling Congress to pass all manner of civil rights laws and fund all manner of anti-poverty programs. Yes, there is some white guilt in this country, and the Buckley article is like a human pincushion of guilt feelings; but as Nathan Perlmutter, associate director of the American Jewish Committee, once observed, "We don't help blacks by hurting whites."[6]

We sometimes forget how demeaning paternalism is—that the white paternalist is, in effect, saying to the Negro that he is not intelligent enough or able enough or mature enough to be judged by the same standards as we judge other men. From the viewpoint of pride and self-respect, the Negro is better off in a shack built with his own two hands than a mansion built for him by the Urban Coalition, by the government, or even by William F. Buckley. And if someday a Negro runs for President (and this is not impossible), it would be the supreme moment of pride if he were elected because of his ability and popularity, but it would be the supreme condescending insult if he were elected primarily because of the color of his skin.

With conservative leaders vying with liberals to see who can be more paternalistic, it is small wonder that some members of the white middle class no longer refer to themselves as the silent majority, but the forgotten majority. One Brooklyn welfare worker commented:

It's become annoying. The white man doesn't mind competing with the black man for a job—they're annoyed because they feel it's not a fair competition when they compete with someone of lower intelligence and lower educational background and then lose out to the black. Friends of mine who work for utility companies see Negroes with less capability, less seniority, getting higher positions, and they don't like it.[7]

Congressman Hugh Carey, the Brooklyn Democrat whose district includes a large number of working-class whites, made this perceptive comment:

The average working stiff is not asking for very much. He wants a decent apartment, he wants a few beers on the weekend, he wants his kids to have decent clothes, he wants to go to a ball game once in a while, and he would like to put a little money away so that his kids can have the education that he never could afford. That's not asking a hell of a lot. But he's not getting that. He thinks society has failed him and, in a way, if he is white, he is often more alienated than the black man. At least the black man has his own organizations, and can submerge himself in the struggle for justice and equality, or elevate himself, whatever the case might be. The black man has hope, because no matter what some of the militants say, his life is slowly getting better in a number of ways. The white man who makes $7,000 a year, who is 40, knows that he is never going to earn much more than that for the rest of his life, and he sees things getting worse, more hopeless. John Lindsay has made a number of bad moves as mayor of this town, but the alienation of the white lower-middle class might have been the worst.[8]

When the existence of working-class whites is even acknowledged by the media, it is often with the most thinly veiled hostility and contempt. Reporters, columnists, commentators almost automatically deplore them, denounce them, ridicule them as latter-day Neanderthals—doing everything except trying to understand them. From their intellectual vivisections—delivered to hushed and breathless audiences in the most weighty publications and television programs—one gathers that the proper function of the white workers is to fight the country's wars, pays the country's taxes, vote for the most lib-

eral candidates on Election Day, and keep their mouths shut
the rest of the time.

But this Silent—or Forgotten—Majority is beginning to find
its voice. The voices are not glossily articulate. The accents are
not those of Harvard or Yale, but of the docks, the corner bar,
the American Legion Hall. The prose may be studded with ex-
pletives, and totally devoid of scholarly reference, but it makes
a compelling point that can no longer be swept under the Urban
Coalition rug.

Pete Hamill of the *New York Post* wrote:

> All over New York City tonight, in places like Inwood,
> South Brooklyn, Corona, East Flatbush and Bay Ridge,
> men are standing around saloons talking darkly about
> their grievances, and even more darkly about possible
> remedies. Their grievances are real and deep; their reme-
> dies could blow this city apart.

To Hamill, these were *not* the "murderous rabble" of "American Demonology." He wrote:

> Basically, the people I'm speaking about *are* the working
> class. That is, they stand somewhere in the economy be-
> tween the poor . . . and the semi-professionals and profes-
> sionals who earn their way with talents or skills acquired
> through education. The working class earns its living with
> its hands or its backs; its members do not exist on welfare
> payments; they do not live in abject, swinish poverty, nor
> in safe, remote suburban comfort. They earn between $5,-
> 000 and $10,000 a year. And they can no longer make it in
> New York.[9]

Pete Hamill wrote about an ironworker friend named Eddie
Cush, who was averaging "about $8,500 a year—pretty good
money. I work my ass off, but I can't make it." Cush told Hamill:

> I come home at the end of the week, I start paying the bills.
> I give my wife some money for food. And there's nothing
> left. Maybe, if I work overtime, I get $15 or $20 to spend on
> myself. But most of the time there's nothin'. They take $65
> a week out of my pay. I have to come up with $90 a month
> rent. But every time I turn around, one of the kids needs
> shoes or a dress or something for school. And then I pick

up a paper and read about a million people on welfare in
New York or spades rioting in some college or some fat
welfare bitch demanding—you know, not askin', *demanding*—a credit card at Korvette's. . . . I *work* for a living
and I can't get a credit card at Korvette's. . . . You know,
you see that, and you want to go out and strangle someone."[10]

Hamill himself is "a son of the white working class" and
displays a basic, and sometimes sympathetic, understanding of
what his old boyhood friends are saying. But he has moved up
in the world, and apparently finds it more difficult to make the
transition from a cocktail party on the Upper East Side to a
saloon in Bay Ridge. He swigs beer with them, but concludes
that New York politicians must "begin to deal with the growing
alienation and paranoia of these people."[11] He faithfully quotes
them but just as faithfully falls back on the old liberal bro-
mides in rebuttal:

> It is very difficult to explain to these people that more than
> 600,000 of those on welfare are women and children; that
> one reason the black family is in trouble is because outfits
> like the Iron Workers Union have practically excluded
> blacks through most of their history; that a hell of a lot
> more of their tax dollars go to Vietnam or the planning for
> future wars than to Harlem or Bed-Stuy [Bedford-Stuyve-
> sant, the largest Negro neighborhood in Brooklyn] . . . that
> they are paying taxes to relieve some forms of poverty
> because of more than 100 years of neglect on top of 300
> years of slavery.[12]

I too am "a son of the white working class," and now live in
a white working-class neighborhood (after residing for some
five years in a heavily integrated neighborhood). And I think I
know why Hamill's arguments fell on such stonily deaf ears. If
it is true that "more than 600,000 of those on welfare are women
and children," it is also true that a number of these women gave
birth to more children than they could support, and then demanded that the government support them. But the act was
theirs—the poverty which arose from it was theirs—and the
fault, if fault there was, was theirs. Of course, the government
cannot abandon children in need, but at the very least we can
stop flogging white society for actions in the maternity ward

that are totally beyond its control. And at least let us give the welfare mothers credit for enough intelligence to realize from the very start that they would *have* to go on welfare to support themselves and their families.

Hamill's point about racial discrimination by the Iron Workers Union is a valid one, but must be carefully counterbalanced by the practices of other unions that for years have admitted Negroes, and of still other unions that for years have discriminated against certain white religious or ethnic groups. It cannot be too often repeated that various white groups in this country have known discrimination, but would be laughed into oblivion if they ever presented a bill for reparations.

And now we come to the quintessence of white guilt—the catch phrase repeated with the glib persistence of a Madison Avenue advertising slogan—"that they are paying taxes to relieve some forms of poverty because of more than 100 years of neglect on top of 300 years of slavery." It is reasonable to ask whether it was Eddie Cush who held any Negro in slavery. It is reasonable to ask whether all the Eddie Cushes in this country should feel personal guilt for acts in which they took no part —for slavery which began and ended before they were born (and, in many cases, before their families even came to this country). As for "100 years of neglect," the phrase requires further definition. *Neglect* implies failure to fulfill an obligation, and the burden of proof is on Hamill to show that his friends were *obligated* to help the Negro (even though no one ever seemed obligated to help working-class whites).

Working-class whites are acutely aware that today's black militants are enjoying educational advantages they never had. Hamill describes it very well:

> Usually, the working-class white man is a veteran; he remembers coming back from the Korean War to discover that the GI Bill only gave him $110 a month out of which he had to pay his own tuition; so he did not go to college because he could not afford it. Then he read about protesting blacks in the SEEK program at Queens College, learns that they are being paid up to $200 a month to go to school, with tuition free, and he starts going a little wild.[13]

The working-class white sees a torrent of radicalism flooding the campus, and attributes much of it to black students. That picture of armed blacks filing out of the building at Cornell said more to him that a fileful of learned articles about student rebellion. He reads about Black Panther leaders being welcomed, if not lionized, at far too many colleges, and whether he articulates it or not, sees America in the first stages of moral and political decay. He reads about the calls to violence that have become part of the standard repertoire of invective of many young black political leaders. He reads about black Georgia State Representative Julian Bond, who told more than 1,000 Princeton students that America is in for a "violent era" in politics—Julian Bond who told the students, "When government becomes unrepresentative and unresponsive, we have not only the right but the duty to rise up against it and strike it down."[14] And he reads that, far from becoming a political pariah, white girls join black girls "in jostling for his necktie and cuff links at rallies as if he were a young Frank Sinatra or Bobby Kennedy." Bond was mobbed by admirers four or five times on campuses where he was in demand as a speaker.[15]

The working-class white is perhaps vaguely aware that the overwhelming majority of Negroes are not revolutionaries or separatists—that most Negroes work just as hard, take just as much pride in their homes and families, and worry just as much about crime and predatory drug addicts as he does. But it is not the hard-working, responsible Negro family man, but some Panther leader seething with hatred of "the system" who gets the headlines, and carves out a niche for himself in one of those ponderous TV specials. The working-class white sees these Black Hucksters of Hate threatening the destruction of his country, while a potpourri of the Beautiful People and V.I.P.'s offer their rapt admiration. He hears about higher crime rates in some integrated neighborhoods, and fears for the safety of his wife and children. He adds up the facts, the rumors, the whispers, the personal experiences, and ultimately may feel he has only one of two choices: take arms or take flight.

A Brooklyn welfare worker, thirtyish, earning about $8,500 a year, told William J. McKean, *Look* senior editor:

What are the whites doing about all this violence? We make sure that we're protected with bats and guns. I have an unregistered gun, and I'd use it—I'd do anything to protect my life, legal or otherwise. I wouldn't stop at anything. I carry a gun all the time. I have it in the trunk of my car, brand new .38—never used—in from Mexico. I would rather take the chance of going to jail than being dead. All my friends have guns. I think the average white is carrying a gun for the same reason I'm carrying one—to protect myself from the extremist black man, 'cause that's who's causing all the trouble.

The white welfare worker told the *Look* editor:

I can show you a neighborhood in south Brooklyn where I know, for a fact, there are organizations that will not allow a Negro family to move in that neighborhood. I know they're doing it 'cause I'm part of the movement. By now, a hundred guns could be brought here in five minutes—in case of a confrontation between blacks and white wives or daughters. These people will not move out—they're going to stay and fight. They're not moving—a line has been drawn.[16]

*Look* Senior Editor McKean practically implored,

The politicians, in whom the people are losing faith, must deal with the situation before the shooting starts. They have to find new ways to divert the endless drain on the descendants of people who came here to escape terror, to find a better way of life. *They must also shatter the double standards of equality that plague those whose ancestors' voyage to this country was a nightmare in chains.*[17] [Emphasis added]

The working-class white has a deep-seated suspicion that some stories reporting black militant terror tactics are either buried in the back pages, or killed by the editor. Certainly, under the New Racism, it sometimes becomes necessary to look the other way—to pretend not to see, not to hear or know about, incidents which are practically crying out to be reported. A chilling article about what was *not* reported during the New York City school strike appeared in the November 1969 issue of the *Quill,* the monthly magazine of Sigma Delta Chi, the

professional journalistic society. It was written by Martin
Gershen, New York bureau chief for the Newark (N. J.) *Star-
Ledger,* and chairman of the Freedom of the Press Committee
of the Newspaper Reporters Association of New York City, Inc.
Gershen wrote:

> The true story has never been told of what happened in
> 1968 inside New York's public schools and on its campuses
> during the teachers strike and student rebellion that swept
> this city like the plague. It was never told because in too
> many instances, newsmen on the scene were not permit-
> ted to bear eyewitness testimony to the events. . . . The eye
> of the storm hovered over two experimental school dis-
> tricts in predominately black neighborhoods. The teachers
> were predominately white. . . . A black-white confronta-
> tion was imminent. Police were powerless. They weren't
> permitted on the campuses and apparently were under
> orders not to get too involved at the public schools.[18]

One veteran of the school "wars" told Gershen, "We never got
across one-tenth of the troubles that went on." The press was
considered an enemy by college students and black militants.
The police department's green card of accreditation made the
reporters not only *personae non gratae,* but part of the "Establishment press" or "pig press."[19]

One newsman, Dell Wade, a reporter for ABC-TV's Eyewitness News, was knocked out by a black militant in front of the
headquarters of Rhody McCoy in Ocean Hill-Brownsville. The
assailant, apparently a bodyguard, beat Wade up after he had
tried to enter one of the public schools to interview a leader of
the governing board. The following day, Wade was knocked to
the floor again. ABC assigned a bodyguard to stay with him for
the duration of the school strike.[20]

Gershen said that another New York newsman, who didn't
want his name mentioned, was threatened with death because
demonstrators did not like his reporting of a scene at the same
Brooklyn site. This reporter said:

> My bosses supported me. But I always had to fight like hell
> to get my stories out because they were ready to accept the
> word of the militants like it was the gospel truth. The
> trouble is the brass was never on the streets. They were

never the targets of bottles and bricks and fists. They
didn't know what was going on. All they said was they
didn't want to blow things out of proportion. So they would
water down my stories—*which were already watered
down*—because we too didn't want to blow things out of
proportion.[21]

At least one member of the press corps began carrying a gun
and a couple had blackjacks because of fear.[22]

Tommy Zumbo, UPI's city editor, said he was aware that his
reporters could not enter the public schools where the most
serious incidents were occurring. He said he contacted all the
parties involved and pleaded with them to allow at least one
pool reporter to enter. He was turned down.[23]

In his article, Gershen did not charge that members of the
local community governing board had actively aided and abet-
ted in these terrorist assaults on newsmen. Gershen called the
chairman of one of the governing boards, who explained that
he took orders from the people and the people didn't want reporters. "I can't help it," the chairman said. "I have to take
orders from the community and they don't want you." Community "representatives" apparently came in all ages and sizes. In
one of the very rare press conferences, each reporter was given
a mimeographed statement from the unit administrator, and
"those of us who worked fast even were able to talk to him for
a moment or two and get some quotes." Then a member of the
community ordered, "OK, all police, press, FBI and CIA, get
out." And a little boy who couldn't have been over 13 walked up
to Gershen and snarled: "OK, press man. You got your story.
Now get out."[24]

A week later, Tom Poster of the New York *Daily News,* and
president of the Newspaper Reporters Assocation, sent tele-
grams to Mayor Lindsay, the city school superintendent, the
new state Board of Education representative in the city, and
Rhody McCoy and Charles Wilson, the two unit administrators
of the school districts in conflict. The telegram outlined the
problem and urged "that arrangements be made immediately
to authorize the press full access to the public schools involved
in the current crisis. . . ." The mayor, McCoy, and Wilson never
replied to the telegram. The *New York Times* ran one paragraph about the complaint at the bottom of their school story

on the "jump page" (the page on which the story was continued). WINS radio carried something on it. As far as Gershen knew, there was no other mention of the story. Gershen considered the press protest "in vain, for New York's news managers spiked the story."[25] He concluded:

> New York is supposed to be one of the most enlightened and sophisticated cities in the world. Why then have its leaders permitted news to be withheld or managed in the interest of public safety? And why must a school news reporter have to gain experience as a war correspondent before he can feel qualified for the job?[26]

The greatest tragedy is that so many of the Negroes in the ghetto are being shoved, pulled, and pushed into one supermilitant bag, by far too many of the press and TV pundits. But no one speaks for the 22 million Negroes in this country. If there are some Negroes who practically worship the Black Panthers, there are many others who deplore their activities. If there are some Negroes who are counting the hours until they can "seize the time" and "make the revolution," there are a great many other Negroes who realize their primary salvation is in law and order—that much-reviled phrase—because only in an orderly society can laws favorable to a minority be enforced.

I believe there are countless Negro moderates who are neither Uncle Toms nor revolutionaries. And I believe they never felt more abandoned by white society—white liberals included —than they do today. In our fascination with the Newtons, the Cleavers, the Seales, we have almost forgotten that the black moderate exists. Probably more often than we could ever know, he has fought unpublicized battles in the ghetto against radical fanatics who seek to bend him to their will, or at least "neutralize" him as an opponent. The black moderate hears that phrase "power to the people," and has a pretty good idea which people are going to get that power, and what they'll do with it—and what they'll do to him. And he might recognize something of himself in this letter a Cornell student wrote about C. David Burak, leader of the local SDS chapter:

> I would begin by thanking Mr. Burak for having the audacity to preclude the choices I have and the decisions

I must make in my lifetime. Today he seeks to prevent me from being induced by the Department of Defense into becoming a "lower echelon murderer." What choices will he take from me and what decisions will be made for me tomorrow? I can only shudder at the possibilities. Let me clearly state that under no circumstances would I work for the Defense Department nor do I intend to serve in the armed forces. But this is a decision I must make by myself. Mr. Burak must not make it for me. How dare he try?

While I may not have Mr. Burak's apparently extensive knowledge of political philosophy, I can only respond to both Mr. Burak and Plato with this excerpt from Tocqueville: "Each individual possesses the degree of intelligence necessary to manage those affairs which concern him exclusively—this is the great principle on which civil and political society rests."

"Power to the people" is a fine goal. But I would think one of the very first powers that each person desires would be the power to decide what kind of life he shall lead.[27]

The black moderate knows that with just a change or two, he could have written that letter himself. And he knows that if the black revolutionaries ever manage to "seize the time" and seize the ghetto, hardly a Soul Brother will be able to call his soul his own. The black moderate believes it *can* happen here, and so does the middle-class white. On that much at least, from different vantage points and for very different reasons, they can agree.

The working-class white sees black separatism as a human battering ram against majority rule, a step-by-step takeover of first the inner, then the outer city. He fears that he and his family could be next, that his job might be next, if the black revolutionaries ever seized power. And his fears are not allayed by the soothing verbal tranquilizers of various long-distance liberals—and conservatives—who take care to live in areas far removed from racial conflicts. And he is in no mood to be coaxed by the vague generalities of politicians who seem to be playing both racial ends against the middle. And if some quickly label his fears paranoid, the working-class white has an all too obvious rejoinder: how many of today's headlines, and how many of today's front-page stories, would have been dismissed as paranoiac fantasies just ten short years ago?

It is predictable that if today's political leaders and political parties fail those whose families, jobs, and property are threatened by the New Racism, other leaders will be found, and other political movements will be created in the 1970's. They may turn to someone who says "Dese," "Dem," and "Dose," someone whose alma mater is the School of Hard Knocks, someone who will fight hatred with hatred, threat with threat, violence with violence. He may not be the man on horseback, but he could very well unseat some of the most powerful leaders in the country. He may not be one of the Beautiful People, but he will look beautiful to more and more frightened and angry white Americans. He may not yet have arrived on the political scene, or he may be someone who is already the subject of deeply apprehensive newspaper and magazine articles—someone like George Wallace, who, says one top Republican strategist, "is going to run for President again in 1972 as sure as I'm sitting here"—or, in the urban arena, someone like ex-marine and ex-karate instructor Anthony (Tony) Imperiale of Newark.

Imperiale first achieved renown shortly after the Newark riots, when he organized the North Ward Citizens Committee, a group with an estimated membership of some 1,000 white males from the predominantly Italian North Ward of the city. Its major purpose was to patrol the streets of the ward nightly in private cars. Later, he was elected to the Newark City Council, where he became known as one of the staunchest supporters of the police.[28]

Robert Curvin, a former president of Newark's CORE, said of Imperiale, "Of course he's a racist, but he's very clever. His ability to portray himself as honest and sincere since his election as councilman . . . amounts to genius. . . . Imperiale is a demagogue and nothing more." Certainly Imperiale has made racist remarks. At a meeting, he referred to Dr. Martin Luther King as "Dr. Martin Luther Coon." He has said, "These are violent times. Maybe we need a violent man, a tough man." But he insists that "Negroes and whites can live together in peace. We've got to talk to each other and be honest with each other." Imperiale supported George Wallace in the 1968 Presidential election—but when he took his turn at evening patrols, he responded as vigorously to calls for help from Negro residents and businessmen in the integrated North Ward as to pleas from whites. At a public meeting in strife-torn Vailsburg High

School, Imperiale had to talk twice when an overflow crowd filled the parking lot as well as the auditorium. But his concern was with "the radicals, *black and white,* that are disrupting this town." Imperiale kept 40 guns at home, cached in every room of his house. He warned, "Should a breakdown of law and order occur, we have an arsenal." He would not disclose its size or location. Two attempts had already been made on his life.[29]

Imperiale contended that "a lot of whites and conservative Negroes feel like I do. We're willing to fight and go to jail to preserve the peace. If it comes to all-out war, and we have to kill some of the black and white animals, we'll kill 'em."[30]

Imperiale said, "We can use a mayor who uses a few deses and dems and 'I'll kick you in the butt.' Gentlemen don't get nowhere. We could overplay being a gentleman. If a mayor didn't wear lace on his panties, he could do better."[31]

"This is me," said Tony Imperiale, "take it or leave it."[32]

Frankly, I'd rather leave it. I would also rather leave the mayor with "lace on his panties." I hope there's still a middle ground between them. I hope the New Racism has not yet kicked the middle ground out from under me—me and perhaps hundreds of thousands of other voters.

Curiously, the same white paternalists who rationalized black militant violence roundly condemned the Tony Imperiale kind of counterviolence—just as those who winked covertly at the black separatist movement were the first to wring their hands in anguish over the *white* movement toward separation in Gary, Indiana.

Since his election in November 1967, Negro Mayor Richard G. Hatcher of Gary, Indiana, has set an indoor and outdoor track record for edging out the competition and winning more federal aid to his city than all past administrations combined. He has cracked down hard on organized crime, and been instrumental in persuading U. S. Steel, the city's largest employer, to play a bigger role in helping Gary solve its problems.[33]

But for a growing number of people in Glen Park, an overwhelmingly white residential section, it was not enough. Glen Park was not the most affluent part of town, but it did contain neatly kept homes and lawns of mill and office workers. The Glen Park people were mostly of East European ancestry:

Czechs, Poles, Croatians, Slovaks, and Greeks, with a sprinkling of newcomers from Appalachia.[34]

Supported by city councilman Eugene Kirtland and GOP district captain Robert K. Stephenson, a movement began to "disannex" Glen Park from Gary. In effect, this would be a form of secession, since Gary annexed the Glen Park area in 1910.[35]

If the movement was successful, Hatcher stood to lose 20 percent of his population and probably a large percentage of his tax base. Kirtland attributed the disannexation move to neglect by City Hall. Glen Park residents complained that municipal services, such as garbage collection and road repairs, were poor, and he said the complaints went unheeded. Kirtland asserted, "Glen Park residents simply are not enjoying the upswing of the surrounding community in building new development and shopping centers."[36]

But those opposing disannexation claimed the real issue was racism. As proof, they cited the fact that support for disannexation didn't begin gathering momentum until Hatcher moved to rezone large vacant sections of Glen Park for public housing.[37] Some 20 or 30 black families were scattered throughout the area, and Kirtland believed that Glen Park could assimilate Negroes who moved there under "natural" conditions, "but we couldn't handle the forced integration of public housing."[38]

With a population of 40,000 in its five-square-mile area, Glen Park gave Hatcher only 9 percent of its vote in the Gary mayoral election 17 months before. Many of the area's residents had fled racially changing inner-city areas. Now they felt threatened again by Hatcher's low-income housing proposals.[39]

To disannex from Gary, supporters would have to gather signatures from at least 51 percent of the lot owners in Glen Park. The petition would then be presented to Gary's Board of Public Works for a vote. If the board failed to approve the petition, the next step would probably be the courts.[40]

Kirtland himself was not circulating petitions. He firmly believed politicians should respond to their constituents, not lead them, and was waiting to see if 51 percent in fact signed up to get out of Gary.[41] (Polls showed that 75 to 90 percent of Glen Park residents favored disannexation.)[42]

The councilman supported decentralization of big cities. He believed most governments had grown too big, and that the voice of the individual was lost. Kirtland described the movement as "an interesting exercise in basic democracy to see whether 40,000 people who have become disenchanted with the city administration can separate themselves and govern themselves."[43]

Indiana law required a minimum three-mile buffer zone between incorporated areas. A bill abolishing the regulation was passed in both houses of the state legislature in 1969—at the height of the controversy in Gary—but the bill literally vanished as it was being taken to the governor's office for signature.[44] Since the Indiana legislature held only one 61-day session every two years, Glen Park could not incorporate before 1971, even if disannexation took effect earlier.[45]

Mayor Hatcher was trying to scuttle the movement, and was able to count on the help of a small group of Glen Park residents, among them Mrs. Pauline Schwegel. "What most people don't understand yet," she said "is how much this version of the Berlin Wall would cost. We'd have to set up our own fire department, scavenger service, planning and zoning commission and local government." And while Glen Park waited to incorporate, it would be governed by Lake County, which currently was able to assign only a single patrol car to the area.[46]

Mrs. Schwegel, and others opposing disannexation, formed the Glen Park Information Committee. In a pamphlet, the commitee stated that Glen Park could secede from the "civil city" but not from the school district, the library, the sanitary districts, and the redevelopment commission. So the total tax rate in a separate Glen Park could be reduced initially by only one-fifth, and then the new city would have to provide its own municipal services, making a sharp tax rise "absolutely certain."[47]

Hatcher saw disannexation as a move "toward disunity at a time when we should be doing all we can to unify our city." Said Ray Wilde, an aide to the mayor, "Those favoring disannexation have never presented a list of grievances to us, they have never talked to us. But they seem very upset that Mayor Hatcher spends OEO and poverty funds where the poverty is. It all points to a thinly veiled case of racism."[48] Or it may have pointed to disenchantment with Hatcher's use of former convicts in anti-poverty programs.[49]

Charges of racism were rejected by Joseph Zimmerman, a Democratic Party precinct worker and supporter of disannexation. He said, "We know we can't keep the colored out of here, and we're not trying to. But we want our streets fixed and our gargage picked up without it being necessary to get a petition for it every time. We think we can do the job better by setting up an independent community."[50]

Beyond any question, the Award of the Year for consummate gall should have been presented to *Muhammad Speaks,* which championed black separatism but moaned that the action of Glen Park residents "might spur latent plans by whites living in other areas peripheral to Black inner cities to parcel themselves off."[51] Blacks made up 50 to 55 percent of Gary's 178,000 residents, and sociologists forecast that the next census would show nearly that percentage of Negroes in Baltimore, Detroit, Newark, St. Louis, Trenton, Oakland, and Cleveland.[52] Would Glen Park be only the first of other *white* separatist movements?

Hatcher called the Glen Park movement "another attempt at American apartheid. It is clearly a manifestation of some very strong racist sentiment. There is no place to run anymore, and there is no place to hide."[53]

GOP district captain Stephenson said that at one point, 70 to 80 percent of the Glen Park homeowners signed the petitions when asked to do so. Then, there was an uproarious Gary City Council meeting in which members of black youth gangs shouted their support of Mayor Hatcher, and seemed to threaten whites who opposed him. The result, said Stephenson, was that the percentage of contacted Glen Park residents who signed the petition soared above 90 percent.[54] The *National Observer* concluded that Hatcher "knew Glen Park was hostile to him, but he misjudged the depth of hostility and the resourcefulness of Mr. Kirtland. And the mayor perhaps failed to understand how the threats of black militants could intensify the fear in Glen Park."[55]

In the 1970's, will our cities have to choose between a pistol-packing strong man—a mayor with "lace on his panties"—and black or white separatist movements? I hope not, but I think there is only one alternative left. We have tried paternalism. We have tried flattery. We have tried programs with failure built right in. We have tried various forms of political guile. I suggest that now, as a last resort, we try honesty.

I suggest we say honestly and even bluntly that we are not going to abandon majority rule in the cities to placate some ghetto militants; that we insist workers be hired because of ability or experience, not because of their color, and not because of any guideline or tacit racial quota; that admissions to college will be based upon grades and objective tests of intelligence, and that in fairness to other students, poverty (however deplorable) cannot be accepted as an equivalency diploma; that those college students, black or white, who, after appropriate warnings, remain so alienated that they seriously disrupt the lives and studies of other students will be given the choice of voluntary withdrawal or expulsion; that the Black Panthers and other such groups will be regarded as thugs and demagogues rather than martyrs.

Of course, the paternalist will argue that this would mean a return to lily-white schools and lily-white jobs, and end political dissent. But I have considerably more faith in the ability of the Negro to meet competition on the basis of merit—and to make the necessary social adjustments—in the universities, in industry, anywhere, and everywhere. I have considerably more faith in the ability of Negroes to appreciate the truth of the saying, "Freedom to move your arm about ends where someone else's nose begins."

In any case, the struggle must be waged and won; the struggle against all forms of discrimination that favor one racial group at the expense of another; the struggle against all forms of guilt that pile the racial burdens of three centuries on the shoulders of those who are living today—the struggle against the demeaning academic and employment handouts that treat the Negro as if he were an intellectual basket case, unable to think or act for himself.

And if the struggle is lost? I think of words that once meant something to this country—words of the Declaration of Independence: "We hold these truths to be self-evident, that all men are created equal"; of the Gettysburg Address: "government of the people, by the people, for the people." I think of phrases like "equal rights" and "equal protection of the laws," and I realize that in our lifetime, they could all be buried in some dead and forgotten page of history. For the New Racism can win only if the meaning of America is lost. The New Racism can triumph only if our democratic ideals go down to defeat. Ultimately, its differences cannot be compromised or papered over, submerged or ignored. Ultimately, in Lincoln's phrase, it will become "all one thing or all the other." And I am profoundly convinced of this—if we lack the will and the courage to end it, the day will come when the New Racism will end every dream of liberty and equality our country has ever had.

# Appendix

Black Panther Plans for Control
of Black High School Students

The Chairman. Will you identify yourself for the record, please?

Mr. White. My name is Stanley White. I am a sergeant in the Oakland, Calif., Police Department, in charge of the intelligence section.

The Chairman. How long have you been in the police department?

Mr. White. I have been in charge of the intelligence section for a year and a half. I have been with the department for approximately 18 years.

****

Activists in Black Student Unions (BSU's), which are now proliferating across the country in high schools and in colleges, are coming more and more under Black Panther Party domination, the prime example of this being the San Francisco State

College riots, in which George Murray (minister of education of the Black Panther Party) took a key role. Local disturbances and demands of black students can be directly attributed to the Black Panther Party mainly due to an organizational outline for Black Student Unions that was prepared and distributed by the Black Panther Party in December 1968.

Mr. Chairman, there follows an outline of that on this and the succeeding pages.

The Chairman. That will be printed in the record.

Mr. White. I would like to emphasize that copies of the outline were found at San Francisco State and in high schools in the city of Oakland, and in the mailboxes of black instructors.

\*\*\*\*

## Exhibit No. 383
## Organization of the Black High School Student—Some Basic Guidelines

The high school is one of the most important components in these early stages of the Black Liberation Struggle. It is one of the few places where you have a true cross-section of at least one segment of the Black community: the youth. The purposes of organizing the Black high school student is to: (1) Create an atmosphere at the school where students can learn to think, (2) Establish a base area from which to operate in other sections of the Black Community, and (3) Recruit cadres for other areas of activity in the Black Liberation Struggle. This paper is designed to give some basic guidelines for high school organization, and should be treated only as a guide and not a rule book. The most important factor is the initiative of those organizing to assess the situation of the particular high school he is organizing at and come up with particular methods in that situation.

### I. Hard Core Steering Committee

This committee must be made up of trained, disciplined bloods who attend the high school. They should meet as many times a week as possible with a member of the B.P.P.N.C., who will provide the link between them and the party. Also, these hard-core bloods should attend party meetings and should be active members of the party, if possible. For security reasons the groups should be small, possibly five or six. They should be as uptight or more uptight than the average party member, because it will be their role to recruit the masses of students at the high school. This is the most important component of the high school organization, and several months of intensive study and training should be taken with them before they will be able to carry on the functions of the party at their school. Their first loyalty must be to the B.P.P.N.C., from which they will receive direct orders.

## II. Off-Campus Group

These hard-core Brothers will comprise the Central Committee of a Black Nationalist organization (OCG) of members of the particular high school, who will hold their meeting off-campus initially, will be made up of those who will be doing the day-to-day work of the organization; passing out leaflets, selling newspapers, talking to fellow Black students, etc. Efforts should be made to put to use any skills which come out of the group, such as photography, artistic ability, writing ability, etc. The members of this group, of necessity, cannot be worked with as much as the hard-core group, but they must be given at least one session a week in lecture and discussion of such things as Black History, political Philosophy, Organizing Techniques, Karate, and any other subjects which the party leaders see as being necessary. The most important thing to realize is that this will be an organization chiefly of workers. The policy of the group will be set and determined by the B.P.P.N.C. through the hard-core steering committee, all the time inviting discussions, criticisms, and suggestions, from members of the OCG. The only way there will be any discipline in the organization is if the members realize that the steering committee is the leader but the only way the group will be of any success is if the steering committee realizes that it must listen to the demands of its group and of the masses of Black students on the campus. Only with this interaction can here [there?] be any progress made in organizing the Black students in the high school.

### III. Umbrella Organization

The first job of the OCG should be to create some sort of organization on campus and instantly make all Black students at the high school a part of this organization. This would be a meeting ground where all Black students could come, despite class or other differences, and talk out their problems without having to thump on them. It must be understood that this is a Black organization, no whites allowed, and that the reasons for this are not racist, but simply that Black People must learn to come together themselves to discuss their collective problems. ... An interaction from all sides of the picture should be encouraged, and no Black student should be forced out as long as he is sincere in trying to get the problems solved. This is the place where the OCG would find out just what the interested Black students at the school are thinking about, and from these meetings plans of action can be drawn up. Also, this Umbrella Organization can be a powerful force during negotiations with the school, which will usually come at one point. The purpose of the Umbrella Organization will be to bring about a united front of the bourgeois and ghetto Black factions at the school, and so for purposes of reaching the most students its meetings should be held on-campus. Bloods for the OCG could be recruited from those who attend its meetings. Through this organization, strikes, boycotts, and rallies could be started.

### IV. School Bulletin

A Black school bulletin should immediately be started by the OCG. This should be distributed free to the Black students at the high school as often as possible and with as many pages as possible, without, of course, sacrificing quality. This bulletin would announce Black activities on and off campus, give the positions of the OCG, and aid in politicizing Black students at the school and raising their consciousness.

### V. Reaching the Masses of Black Students

Along with the school bulletin, other efforts should be made to mobilize and politicize the masses of Black students at the school. The most important thing which can be done by the OCG is the day-to-day blowing to the bloods on campus. There can be no substitute for this! At lunch time, before and after school and when possible during classroom time, discussions on topics ranging from world to school to personal problems should be encouraged by the OCG organizers. Those who appear the most interested should be encouraged to come either to the Umbrella Organization meetings or the OCG meetings or both.

BLACK POWER! Newspapers should be sold, and other literature passed out. Discussions should be started in classrooms as much as possible, and OCG members, should press their teachers to let them lead discussion on Black Nationalism, Black History, World Problems, or other topics as they come up. When specific problems arise, such as if the OCG and the Umbrella Organization decide to key on the bad food at the cafeteria, this should be the topic that the organizers direct their attention to. Everything should be done to make the average Black student feel a part of a Black Student Confederation at the school and everything should be done to politicize him.

## VI. Political Candidates

The OCG should definitely run an all-Black slate of candidates for school elections, either for all offices or for the offices that the OCG considers the most important at that particular time. Coalitions and deals should be definitely be [sic] made with all bloods who have political power at the school already, but the OCG should shy away from making deals with white students unless it is absolutely necessary. Black students. These candidates would be directly representing the OCG if possible, but in any case directly responsible to the organization. The candidates would run on a well-thought-out ticket answering to the needs of the masses of Black students, and once in office they would continue to work for the interests of the Black students through direction from the OCG.

## VII. Black Athletes Union

Because the Black athletes are either in actuality or in potentiality the most powerful student forces at the school, attempts should be made either to neutralize them or to bring them over to the side of OCG. (It should be realized that during a riot or other disturbances among Black students these are the mercenary forces which Whitey uses to patrol the halls or otherwise quell the violence.) If there is already an athlete's union (such as Block C, etc.) the Black members should be approached and urged to take it over. The most radical members of the union should be recruited for the OCG, so that their understanding of the struggle will increase. Coalitions should be definitely be [*sic*] made with the most popular athletes and they should be urged to exert their influence to get bloods to join the OCG. Whether there is an athlete's union already or not, Black athletes at the school should be urged to start their own separate union. Special efforts should be made to politicize all Black athletes, so that if any trouble starts they will realize whose side they are really on. The threat of all the Black athletes walking off the field during a school boycott can be a very powerful weapon when negotiating with school officials, but a lot of groundwork must be laid because this is usually the most reactionary element of the high school.

## VIII. Social Events

The OCG should sponsor dances and other social events and should try to bring blood entertainers to the school under their name. This is an invaluable tool for getting bloods to support your cause. Also, the OCG should not overlook sponsoring special days where bloods are urged to do special things, such as bring watermelons to eat for lunch or something of that sort. By themselves these things will do nothing to further the Black Liberation Struggle, but in conjunction with the other activities suggested in this paper they can serve to keep the school administration off balance as well as increase support among the Black students at the school for the OCG. The OCG should also support any all-blood events at the school (except completely reactionary ones), and should form coalitions with Black social clubs at the schools. Remember, the more sides you hit the Black student from, the harder it will be for him to escape reality.

## IX. Lectures and Discussions

The OCG should hold regular, on-campus lectures and discussions, if possible. Outside speakers should be invited, and the topics should be such things as Black History, Political Philosophy, and topics along those lines. World Problems would be another area to be discussed. This would be just another way of politicizing the Black students.

## X. Turning the School Black

Every symbol at the school should be turned into a Black symbol if possible, so as to further get the Black students looking to the OCG to solve his [sic] problems and to further increase his [sic] identification with the other Black students at the school. The OCG should organize, or get the bloods themselves to organize Black functions in the areas in which they are interested. Black talent productions, bongo drummer corps, theatrical groups, etc.; all should be organized and pushed up tempo. They can then be later used by the OCG to further hit bloods from all sides. The OCG should realize that it should put its hands in everything, as long as it will not overextend the organization and as long as by so doing it will increase the consciousness of Black students at the school. Coalitions should be made with every Black function already at the school (probably through the Umbrella Organization) and either these forces should be neutralized or brought over to the side of the OCG.

## XI. Action

Initially, action should be taken in places where it has been determined by the OCG that Black students at the school are interested and have shown that they are willing to be committed. This commitment, of course, will have to be pushed up tempo by the OCG organizers, as stated before. The OCG must constantly come up with new areas to protest and mobilize with, so that they aren't continually calling for the same old thing such as a school boycott. Boycotts can be effective, but only if the groundwork for them is laid and only if they are used sparingly. Mass rallies are another area that can be used to good effect. One tactic could be to have 200 or 300 bloods break up to the School Board meeting to protest a certain action. It should be remembered that no plan of action should be taken if it can be used to alienate the OCG from the masses of students. For this reason, in the initial stages of organizing anything of a mass nature should be kept to a minimum, until a sufficient amount of sympathetic forces are built around the OCG. Such action as burning the school down or jumping on white students should only be taken at later stages of the struggle, and only if the OCG is not directly involved in the rebellions (publicly). The thing the OCG must always remember is that its function is to mobilize the Black students to take over their school, only to destroy that school if the administration forces give it no alternative.

BLACK POWER!!!
A CHANGE GONNA COME!!!

Mr. White. It is highly significant to note that the National Black Student Union business address is the same as the National Black Panther Party Headquarters, 3106 Shattuck Avenue, Berkeley, Calif.

[Source: Permanent Subcommittee on Investigations of the Senate Committee on Government Operations, *Riots, Civil and Criminal Disorders,* Part 19, June 18, 1969, pp. 3826, 3849–3853.]

# "If I Were Black Today, I'd Be ..." — Nixon

The following article appeared on page 5 of the August 27, 1970, issue of *Jet*. It is reprinted here, without addition or deletion, exactly as it ran in that magazine.

The private President Richard M. Nixon is definitely different from the hard-nosed public Nixon, noted syndicated columnist Carl T. Rowan. In a recent column, Rowan says that a Cabinet member said that President Nixon listened with compassionate interest to the plights of Blacks during a meeting with two campus advisers, Chancellor Alexander Heard of Vanderbilt University and Howard University President Dr. James E. Cheek. The President was reported to have slammed the table with his fist and bristled, "Damn it, if I were a Black man today I'd be a revolutionary, too!" Afterwards, press secretary Ronald Ziegler reportedly said, "If that comment gets into the press, we're dead." When JET asked whether Rowan's account was true or false, Ziegler, who claimed he was in and out of the conference room, said he did not personally hear the statement and ended the discussion by saying, "No further comment." Rowan wrote of other private chats with President Nixon which contradict his public position. Whether President Nixon will show his private side publicly is debatable, which may be why the Administration requests that people "judge us by what we do, and not by what we say."

# *Notes*

CHAPTER 2
*The Black Muslims*

1. *Muhammad Speaks,* November 7, 1969, pp. S-1, S-2, S-3.
2. *Time,* March 7, 1969, p. 21.
3. Ibid.
4. *Muhammad Speaks,* November 28, 1969, pp. 3, 5, 7, 9, 11, 14.
5. Ibid., October 3, 1969, p. 3.
6. Ibid., July 4, 1969, p. 20.
7. Ibid., July 11, 1969, pp. 20, 21.
8. Ibid., August 22, 1969, p. 20.
9. Ibid., September 12, 1969, pp. 20, 21.
10. Ibid., July 11, 1969, p. 21.
11. Ibid., September 12, 1969, p. 21.
12. Ibid., October 10, 1969, pp. 20 and 21.
13. Ibid., p. 19
14. Ibid.
15. Ibid., June 13, 1969, p. 21.
16. Ibid., August 22, 1969, p. 21; September 12, 1969, p. 21; September 19, 1969, p. 21.
17. Ibid., October 31, 1969, p. 18.
18. Ibid., November 21, 1969, p. 16.
19. *Amsterdam News,* September 27, 1969, p. 40. See also ibid., August 23, 1969, p. 4.
20. Ibid., August 23, 1969, p. 4.
21. Ibid.
22. *Muhammad Speaks,* September 26, 1969, p. 3.
23. *Amsterdam News,* September 27, 1969, p. 1.
24. *Muhammad Speaks,* October 10, 1969, p. 14.
25. Ibid., September 26, 1969, pp. 3, 38.
26. Ibid., October 10, 1969, p. 13
27. Ibid., November 28, 1969, p. 32.
28. *National Observer,* December 1, 1969, p. 5. See also *New York Times,* November 23, 1969, p. 39.
29. *New York Times,* November 23, 1969, p. 39.

30. *National Observer,* December 1, 1969, p. 5.
31. *Wall Street Journal,* November 25, 1969, p. 1. See also *New York Times,* November 23, 1969, p. 39.
32. *National Observer,* December 1, 1969, p. 5. *Wall Street Journal,* November 25, 1969, p. 1.
33. *New York Times,* November 23, 1969, p. 39.
34. *Wall Street Journal,* November 25, 1969, p. 1. Also see *New York Times,* November 23, 1969, p. 39.
35. *New York Times,* November 23, 1969, p. 39.
36. *National Observer,* December 1, 1969, p. 5.
37. Ibid.
38. *Wall Street Journal,* November 25, 1969, p. 1.
39. Ibid.
40. Ibid.
41. Ibid., pp. 1, 33.

CHAPTER 3
*Malcolm X*

1. John Hope Franklin, *From Slavery to Freedom,* 3rd ed. (New York: Alfred A. Knopf, 1967), p. 159.
2. Ibid., pp. 240, 241.
3. Ibid., p. 490.
4. *Newsweek,* March 3, 1969, p. 27.
5. Ibid.
6. Ibid.
7. Ibid.
8. Malcolm X, *Malcolm X Speaks* (New York: Grove Press, 1966), p. 18.
9. *New York Times,* July 30, 1964, p. 1.
10. Malcolm X, op. cit., p. 25.
11. Ibid., pp. 26, 27.
12. Ibid., p. 56.
13. Ibid., pp. 28, 155.
14. Ibid., p. 57.
15. Ibid., pp. 155, 156.
16. Ibid., pp. 168, 169.
17. Ibid., p. 107.
18. Ibid., pp. 107, 108.
19. Ibid., pp. 163, 214.
20. Ibid. pp. 195, 196.

21. Ibid., p. 31.
22. Ibid., p. 53.
23. Ibid., pp. 54, 55
24. Ibid., p. 173.
25. Ibid., pp. 70, 71.
26. Ibid., p. 208.
27. Ibid., pp. 25, 26.
28. Ibid., p. 26.
29. Ibid., p. 32.
30. Ibid., p. 149.
31. Ibid., p. 66.
32. Ibid., pp. 166, 167.
33. Ibid., p. 167.
34. Ibid., p. 50.
35. Ibid., p. 116.
36. Ibid., pp. 145, 134.
37. Ibid., pp. 76, 77.
38. Ibid., p. 111.
39. Ibid., p. 49.
40. Ibid., p. 134.
41. Ibid.
42. Ibid., p. 106.
43. Ibid., pp. 165, 168.
44. Ibid., p. 32.
45. Ibid., p. 68.
46. Ibid., pp. 52, 218.
47. Ibid., p. 103.
48. Ibid., p. 129.
49. Ibid., pp. 129, 130.
50. Ibid., p. 72.
51. Ibid., pp. 72–77.
52. Ibid., p. 84.
53. Ibid., pp. 85, 86.
54. Ibid., p. 87.
55. Ibid., p. 177.
56. Ibid., pp. 162, 163.
57. Ibid., p. 194.
58. *New York Times,* News of the Week in Review, February 21, 1965, p. 10E.
59. Ibid., February 15, 1965, pp. 1, 21.

60.   Ibid., February 16, 1965, p. 18.
61.   Ibid., February 22, 1965, p. 10.
62.   Ibid., January 15, 1965, p. 19.
63.   Ibid.
64.   Ibid., February 22, 1965, p. 10.
65.   Ibid.
66.   Ibid.
67.   Ibid., March 14, 1965, p. 57.
68.   Ibid.
69.   Ibid.
70.   Ibid., February 22, 1965, p. 10.
71.   Ibid., February 16, 1965, p. 18.
72.   Ibid., February 22, 1965, p. 10.
73.   Ibid., February 22, 1965, pp. 1, 11.
74.   Ibid., February 22, 1965, p. 10.
75.   Ibid., February 24, 1965, p. 31.
76.   Ibid., February 22, 1965, pp. 1, 10.
77.   Ibid.
78.   Ibid.
79.   Ibid.
80.   Ibid. See also ibid., February 23, 1965, p. 20.
81.   Ibid., February 22, 1965, pp. 1, 10.
82.   Ibid, p. 10.
83.   Ibid., February 22, 1965, p. 10.
84.   Ibid., February 23, 1965, p. 20.
85.   Ibid., p. 1.
86.   Ibid., February 24, 1965, p. 1.
87.   Ibid., February 27, 1965, pp. 1, 10.
88.   Ibid., p. 10.
89.   Ibid., February 25, 1965, p. 1.
90.   Ibid., February 27, 1965, p. 10.
91.   Ibid., February 28, 1965, p. 72.
92.   Ibid., December 6, 1965, p. 46.
93.   Ibid.
94.   Ibid., March 1, 1966, pp. 1, 33.
95.   Ibid., p. 33.
96.   Ibid.
97.   Ibid., March 11, 1966, p. 16.
98.   Ibid., March 3, 1966, p. 24.
99.   Ibid., March 11, 1966, p. 1.

100.  Ibid., April 15, 1966, p. 36.
101.  Ibid., February 27, 1965, p. 10.
102.  *Muhammad Speaks,* October 3, 1969, pp. 20, 21.
103.  *Harvard Today* (Spring 1968), p. 31.

CHAPTER 4
*Republic of New Africa*
   1.  Malcolm X, *Malcolm X Speaks,* p. 177.
   2.  *Ebony,* September 1968, p. 93.
   3.  Ibid.
   4.  Ibid.
   5.  Subcommittee on Investigations of the Senate Committee on Government Operations, *Riots, Civil and Criminal Disorders,* Part 20, June 26, 30, 1969, p. 4192. See also *New York Times,* March 31, 1968, p. 32.
   6.  *Congressional Record* (unbound), January 6, 1969, p. H79.
   7.  *Riots, Civil and Criminal Disorders,* p. 4189.
   8.  Ibid., p. 4187.
   9.  *Combat,* April 15, 1969.
  10.  *New York Times,* August 29, 1961, p. 21.
  11.  *Combat,* October 15, 1969.
  12.  A copy of the May 1968 *Crusader* is in the author's possession.
  13.  *Jet,* September 12, 1968, p. 5. See also *Riots, Civil and Criminal Disorders,* p. 4364.
  14.  *Jet,* May 30, 1968, p. 16.
  15.  Ibid.
  16.  Ibid., pp. 14, 15.
  17.  *Human Events,* June 14, 1969, p. 14.
  18.  *Riots, Civil and Criminal Disorders,* p. 4262.
  19.  Ibid., pp. 4265, 4266.
  20.  Ibid., p. 4266.
  21.  *Jet,* January 23, 1969, p. 30.
  22.  *Congressional Record* (unbound), January 6, 1969, p. H84.
  23.  *Riots, Civil and Criminal Disorders,* pp. 4367, 4368.
  24.  *New York Times,* September 30, 1968, pp. 1, 50.
  25.  *Riots, Civil and Criminal Disorders,* pp. 4253, 4255.
  26.  Ibid., pp. 4252, 4253.
  27.  *Amsterdam News,* March 22, 1969, p. 25.
  28.  *Riots, Civil and Criminal Disorders,* pp. 4252, 4263. See

       also *Amsterdam News,* October 7, 1967, p. 43.
29.    *Riots, Civil and Criminal Disorders,* p. 4252.
30.    Ibid., p. 4368.
31.    Ibid.
32.    Ibid., pp. 4205, 4206.
33.    *Detroit News,* April 20, 1969, p. 1A.
34.    Ibid., p. 14A. See also *Muhammad Speaks,* April 18, 1969,
       p. 5.
35.    *Amsterdam News,* April 19, 1969, p. 23.
36.    *Detroit News,* April 20, 1969, p. 1A.
37.    Ibid., p. 14A.
38.    *New York Times,* April 3, 1969, p. 36.
39.    *Muhammad Speaks,* April 25, 1969, pp. 23, 25.
40.    *New York Times,* April 2, 1969, p. 24.
41.    Ibid., March 31, 1969, p. 24.
42.    Ibid.
43.    Ibid., p. 1.
44.    *Detroit News,* March 31, 1969, p. 4A.
45.    *Muhammad Speaks,* April 18, 1969, p. 5.
46.    *Jet,* April 24, 1969, p. 9.
47.    *Muhammad Speaks,* May 2, 1969, p. 13.
48.    Ibid.
49.    *Amsterdam News,* April 19, 1969, p. 23.
50.    *Detroit News,* March 31, 1969, p. 4A.
51.    *Human Events,* June 21, 1969, p. 8.
52.    *National Observer,* April 7, 1969, p. 4.
53.    *Muhammad Speaks,* April 18, 1969, p. 6.
54.    *U.S. News & World Report,* April 14, 1969, p. 10.
55.    *Human Events,* June 21, 1969, p. 8. See also *National
       Observer,* April 7, 1969, p. 4.
56.    *National Observer,* April 7, 1969, p. 4.
57.    *Human Events,* June 21, 1969, p. 8.
58.    *New York Times,* April 1, 1969, p. 19.
59.    Ibid., p. 18.
60.    Ibid.
61.    Ibid.
62.    *Jet,* April 24, 1969, p. 9.
63.    *Jet,* June 19, 1969, p. 15.
64.    *Human Events,* April 19, 1969, p. 3.
65.    *Combat,* April 15, 1969.

66. *Muhammad Speaks,* May 9, 1969, p. 17. See also *Jet,* May 15, 1969, p. 4.
67. *New York Times,* September 21, 1968, p. 14.
68. Ibid.
69. *Muhammad Speaks,* June 13, 1969, p. 2. See also *Jet,* June 19, 1969, p. 25.
70. *Jet,* September 25, 1969, p. 8. See also *New York Times,* September 13, 1969, p. 22.
71. *New York Times,* September 13, 1969, p. 22.
72. Ibid.
73. Ibid.
74. *Washington Post,* September 15, 1969, p. A4.
75. *Human Events,* October 11, 1969, p. 19.
76. *Muhammad Speaks,* September 26, 1969, p. 5.
77. *Washington Post,* September 15, 1969, p. A1.
78. *Muhammad Speaks,* October 3, 1969, p. 9.
79. Ibid.
80. Ibid., p. 30.
81. *Zambia Mail,* July 5, 1968, p. 5.
82. *Amsterdam News,* August 30, 1969, p. 46.
83. *New York Times,* January 30, 1965, p. 10.
84. *Jet,* December 18, 1969, pp. 6, 7.
85. *Detroit Free Press,* December 4, 1969, p. 15B.
86. Ibid.
87. *New York Times,* May 30, 1967, p. 1. See also *Muhammad Speaks,* November 7, 1969, p. 11.

CHAPTER 5
*The Black Panthers*

1. *New York Times,* December 5, 1969, pp. 1, 34.
2. Ibid.
3. Ibid.
4. Ibid.
5. Ibid., December 7, 1969, p. 68.
6. Ibid.
7. *Jet,* December 25, 1969, p. 31.
8. *New York Times,* December 11, 1969, p. 50.
9. Ibid., December 16, 1969, p. 20.
10. Ibid.
11. *Wall Street Journal,* December 12, 1969, p. 1.

12. *New York Times,* August 1, 1968, p. 18.
13. *Newsweek,* August 4, 1969, p. 32.
14. *National Observer,* December 15, 1969, p. 7.
15. *New York Times,* January 1, 1970, p. 13.
16. *Black Panther,* December 13, 1969, p. 4.
17. *U.S. News & World Report,* December 22, 1969, p. 25.
18. *New York Times,* August 8, 1969, p. 13.
19. Ibid., September 9, 1968, p. 55.
20. Ibid., August 23, 1968, p. 43.
21. Ibid., August 15, 1968, p. 20.
22. Ibid.
23. Ibid., September 6, 1968, p. 58.
24. Ibid., September 9, 1968, p. 1.
25. Ibid., September 28, 1968, p. 34.
26. Ibid., November 21, 1968, p. 35.
27. Ibid.
28. Ibid.
29. Ibid.
30. Ibid.
31. Ibid.
32. Ibid.
33. Ibid., November 29, 1968, p. 37.
34. Ibid.
35. Ibid., November 28, 1968, p. 1.
36. Ibid., December 11, 1968, p. 30,
37. *Jet,* January 9, 1969, p. 4.
38. *New York Times,* October 23, 1969, p. 24.
39. Ibid., October 28, 1969, p. 24.
40. Ibid. See also ibid., News of the Week in Review, November 2, 1969, p. 7E.
41. Ibid.
42. Reprinted in *Human Events,* August 30, 1969, p. 5.
43. *Black Panther,* October 4, 1969, p. 5.
44. *Combat,* November 15, 1969.
45. Ibid.
46. *New York Times,* October 29, 1969, p. 27.
47. Ibid., October 30, 1969, p. 1.
48. Ibid., p. 39.
49. Ibid.
50. Ibid., October 31, 1969, p. 38.

51. Ibid., News of the Week in Review, November 2, 1969, p. 7E.
52. Ibid., November 1, 1969, p. 34.
53. Ibid., November 4, 1969, p. 22.
54. Ibid., November 5, 1969, p. 30.
55. Ibid., November 6, 1969, pp. 1, 54.
56. Ibid.
57. Ibid. See also *U.S. News & World Report,* November 17, 1969, p. 69.
58. *Washington Post,* November 9, 1969, pp. A1, A4.
59. *Black Panther,* November 22, 1969, pp. 10, 11.
60. Ibid.
61. *New York Times,* December 4, 1969, p. 37.
62. Ibid.
63. *The Progressive,* July, 1969, p. 20.
64. *Combat,* July 1, 1969.
65. *Black Panther,* July 5, 1969, p. 20.
66. *Oakland Tribune,* July 19, 1969, p. 3E.
67. *Human Events,* August 23, 1969, pp. 8, 9.
68. *New York Times,* News of the Week in Review, July 27, 1969, p. 6E.
69. *Black Panther,* June 14, 1969, p. 21.
70. Ibid., August 2, 1969, p. 21.
71. Ibid.
72. Reprinted in *Congressional Record* (unbound), March 3, 1969, p. H1372.
73. *U.S. News & World Report,* May 19, 1969, p. 36.
74. *Black Panther,* June 28, 1969, p. 8.
75. Ibid., May 31, 1969, p. 8.
76. *Washington Post,* May 5, 1969, pp. B1, B9.
77. *Black Panther,* November 22, 1969, p. 15.
78. Ibid., June 28, 1969, p. 7.
79. Ibid., June 14, 1969, p. 16.
80. Ibid., September 6, 1969, p. 2.
81. *New York Times,* September 11, 1969, p. 56.
82. Ibid.
83. Ibid.
84. Ibid., September 5, 1968, pp. 1, 94.
85. Ibid.
86. Ibid., September 7, 1968, p. 1.

87.  Ibid., September 6, 1968, pp. 1, 49.
88.  Ibid., September 7, 1968, p. 38.
89.  Ibid.
90.  *Amsterdam News,* September 14, 1968, p. 23.
91.  *New York Times,* September 11, 1968, p. 56.
92.  Ibid., October 20, 1968, p. 40.
93.  Ibid., November 14, 1969, p. 28.
94.  Ibid. See also *Jet,* November 27, 1969, p. 50.
95.  *New York Times,* November 15, 1969, p. 18.
96.  *Black Panther,* October 4, 1969, p. 20.
97.  *Human Events,* June 21, 1969, p. 7.
98.  *New York Times,* News of the Week in Review, December 7, 1969, p. 4E.
99.  *Black Panther,* June 7, 1969, p. 6.
100. *Jet,* October 23, 1969, p. 5.
101. *Black Panther,* August 16, 1969, p. 16.
102. *New York Times,* News of the Week in Review, December 7, 1969, p. 4E.
103. *New York Times,* December 21, 1969, p. 47.
104. Ibid.
105. *Black Panther,* August 23, 1969, p. 4.
106. Ibid. See also *The Nation,* May 5, 1969, p. 558.
107. *The Nation,* May 5, 1969, pp. 558 and 559.
108. *New York Times,* January 22, 1969, p. 24.
109. *Jet,* November 13, 1969, p. 58.
110. *Black Panther,* September 6, 1969, p. 10.
111. *New York Times,* May 23, 1969, p. 24. See also *Newsweek,* September 1, 1969, p. 22A.
112. *New York Times,* May 23, 1969, p. 24.
113. Ibid.
114. *New York Times,* August 20, 1969, p. 15. See also *New York Times,* August 28, 1969, p. 25.
115. *New York Times,* December 2, 1969, p. 59. See also *Amsterdam News,* August 30, 1969, p. 1.
116. *Amsterdam News,* August 30, 1969, p. 1.
117. Ibid., pp. 1, 46.
118. *Black Panther,* August 30, 1969, p. 12.
119. Ibid., p. 13.
120. *New York Times,* August 28, 1969, p. 25.
121. Ibid., December 2, 1969, p. 59.

122. Ibid.
123. Ibid., November 30, 1969, p. 59.
124. Ibid., May 23, 1969, p. 24.
125. Ibid., April 3, 1969, pp. 1, 36.
126. Ibid., p. 36.
127. Ibid.
128. Ibid. See also (New York) *Daily News,* April 3, 1969, p. 3.
129. *New York Times,* April 3, 1969, p. 36.
130. (New York) *Daily News,* April 3, 1969, p. 3.
131. *Combat,* April 15, 1969.
132. *Amsterdam News,* April 5, 1969, p. 1.
133. Ibid.
134. *New York Times,* April 4, 1969, p. 46.
135. Ibid., April 12, 1969, p. 42.
136. Ibid. See also *Muhammad Speaks,* April 18, 1969, p. 24.
137. *New York Times,* June 12, 1969, p. 35.
138. *Muhammad Speaks,* April 18, 1969, p. 24.
139. Ibid.
140. Ibid., May 2, 1969, p. 5.
141. *Amsterdam News,* September 27, 1969, p. 40.
142. *New York Times,* July 7, 1969, p. 22.
143. *Black Panther,* June 7, 1969, p. 9.
144. *New York Times,* October 17, 1969, p. 27.
145. Ibid., November 18, 1969, p. 33.
146. *Black Panther,* September 20, 1969, p. 3.
147. Ibid.
148. Ibid., August 16, 1969, p. 5.
149. *New York Times,* April 9, 1969, p. 44.
150. Permanent Subcommittee on Investigations of the Senate Committee on Government Operations, *Riots, Civil and Criminal Disorders,* Part 19, June 18, 1969, p. 3791.
151. Ibid., p. 3788.
152. Ibid., p. 3822.
153. Ibid., p. 3819.
154. Ibid., pp. 3823–24.
155. Ibid., p. 3798.
156. Ibid., p. 3793.
157. Ibid., p. 3796.
158. Ibid., p. 3797
159. Ibid., pp. 3791, 3798.

160. Ibid., pp. 3798, 3799.
161. Carl Rowan's column, *Pittsburgh Press,* August 27, 1969, p. 30.
162. Ibid.
163. A committee copy of Mr. Cannon's testimony is in the author's possession. See also *Jet,* July 10, 1969, p. 30.
164. *Jet,* July 10, 1969, p. 30.
165. *Sepia,* July 1969, p. 64.
166. Ibid., p. 65.
167. *Newsweek,* August 25, 1969, p. 20A. See also *New York Times,* July 24, 1969, p. 41.
168. *New York Post,* September 24, 1969, p. 54.
169. *Newsweek,* August 25, 1969, p. 20B.
170. Ibid. See also *Congressional Record* (unbound), July 31, 1969, p. H 6662.
171. Ibid. See also *Congressional Record* (unbound), August 4, 1969, p. H 6879.
172. *Congressional Record* (unbound), July 31, 1969, p. H 6662.
173. Ibid.
174. *New York Post,* September 24, 1969, p. 54.
175. Ibid.
176. *New York Times,* August 15, 1969, p. 23.
177. Ibid.
178. *Congressional Record* (unbound), July 31, 1969, p. H 6662.
179. Ibid.
180. *New York Times,* August 10, 1969, pp. 1, 67.
181. Ibid.
182. *Amsterdam News,* August 16, 1969, p. 1. See also *Newsweek,* August 25, 1969, p. 20B.
183. *New York Post,* September 24, 1969, p. 54.
184. *New York Times,* August 10, 1969, p. 67.
185. Ibid., July 29, 1969, p. 19.
186. *Black Panther,* September 20, 1969, p. 2.
187. *Amsterdam News,* August 16, 1969, pp. 1, 43.
188. *New York Times,* January 4, 1970, p. 57.
189. Ibid., News of the Week in Review, August 17, 1969, p. 6E.
190. Ibid., August 16, 1969, pp. 1, 14.
191. Ibid.
192. Ibid.
193. Ibid., September 4, 1969, p. 39.

194. Ibid., August 16, 1969, p. 14.
195. Ibid.
196. Ibid.
197. Ibid., September 4, 1969, pp. 1, 39.
198. *Jet,* September 25, 1969, pp. 22–25.
199. *Amsterdam News,* October 25, 1969, p. 1.
200. *Black Panther,* August 16, 1969, p. 9.
201. Ibid., November 22, 1969, p. 16.
202. Testimony of Cannon, op. cit.
203. *Black Panther,* September 6, 1969, p. 19.
204. Ibid., August 16, 1969, p. 11.
205. *Combat,* July 15, 1969.
206. *Washington Post,* June 25, 1969, p. A8.
207. Ibid.
208. Permanent Subcommittee on Investigations of the Senate Committee on Government Operations, *Riots, Civil and Criminal Disorders,* Part 19, June 25, 1969, pp. 4161–4173.
209. *Washington Post,* June 25, 1969, p. A8.
210. *New York Times,* July 16, 1969, p. 17.
211. Ibid., December 14, 1969, p. 64.

CHAPTER 6
*The Black Rebellion on Campus*

1. *Negro Digest,* September 1965, p. 13.
2. Ibid., p. 14.
3. Ibid., p. 17.
4. *Jet,* February 29, 1968, p. 20.
5. *New York Times,* April 9, 1967, pp. 1, 55.
6. Ibid.
7. Ibid.
8. Ibid.
9. Ibid., April 10, 1967, p. 19.
10. Ibid.
11. Ibid., p. 1.
12. Ibid., November 9, 1967, p. 41.
13. Ibid., November 15, 1967, p. 37.
14. Ibid.
15. Ibid.
16. Ibid.

17.   Ibid.
18.   Ibid.
19.   Ibid.
20.   Ibid.
21.   *Amsterdam News,* November 25, 1967, p. 2.
22.   *New York Times,* November 15, 1967, p. 37. See also *Amsterdam News,* November 25, 1967, p. 2.
23.   *Amsterdam News,* December 2, 1967, p. 2.
24.   Ibid.
25.   *U.S. News & World Report,* July 31, 1967, p. 38.
26.   Ibid.
27.   Ibid., p. 39.
28.   *Congressional Record,* May 4, 1965, p. 9406.
29.   Ibid.
30.   Ibid.
31.   *Negro Digest,* December 1967, p. 21.
32.   Ibid., pp. 21, 22.
33.   Ibid., p. 22.
34.   Ibid.
35.   Ibid., November 1966, p. 91.
36.   Ibid., December 1967, p. 22.
37.   *U.S. News & World Report,* July 31, 1967, p. 39.
38.   *Negro Digest,* December 1967, p. 22.
39.   Ibid., p. 23.
40.   *U.S. News & World Report,* July 31, 1967, p. 38.
41.   *Negro Digest,* December 1967, p. 23.
42.   Ibid., p. 24.
43.   Ibid., p. 25.
44.   *U.S. News & World Report,* May 22, 1967, p. 65.
45.   *Negro Digest,* December 1967, p. 25.
46.   Ibid., pp. 25, 26.
47.   Ibid., p. 27.
48.   Ibid.
49.   Ibid.
50.   Ibid.
51.   Ibid.
52.   Ibid., p. 28.
53.   Ibid.
54.   Ibid.
55.   *Amsterdam News,* August 5, 1967, p. 6.

56.  *Amsterdam News,* September 23, 1967, p. 1.
57.  *Jet,* July 13, 1967, p. 53.
58.  *Negro Digest,* December 1967, p. 27.
59.  Ibid., March 1968, p. 45.
60.  Ibid., December 1967, p. 29.
61.  *Jet,* July 13, 1967, p. 53.
62.  *U.S. News & World Report,* July 31, 1967, p. 38.

CHAPTER 7
*The Black University*

1.  *Negro Digest,* March 1968, p. 97.
2.  Ibid., p. 29.
3.  Ibid., p. 97.
4.  Ibid., pp. 5–8.
5.  Ibid., pp. 8, 9.
6.  Ibid., p. 9.
7.  Ibid., p. 12.
8.  Ibid., pp. 33–36.
9.  Ibid., p. 37.
10.  Ibid., pp. 21, 23, 24, 25.
11.  Ibid., pp. 15, 16, 18, 19.
12.  Ibid., pp. 64, 65.
13.  Ibid., p. 65.
14.  Ibid., p. 65.
15.  Ibid., pp. 67, 69.
16.  Ibid., p. 69.
17.  Ibid., p. 13.

CHAPTER 8
*San Francisco State College*

1.  *Negro Digest,* May 1965, pp. 4 ff.; August 1964, pp. 5 ff.
2.  Ibid., July 1964, pp. 10 ff.
3.  Ibid., January 1965, p. 17 ff.
4.  Ibid., p. 22.
5.  *U.S. News & World Report,* May 22, 1967, p. 68.
6.  Statement of Dr. S. I. Hayakawa before the House Special
     Subcommittee on Education, February 3, 1969.
7.  Ibid.
8.  Ibid.
9.  *Dissent* (March–April 1969), p. 167.

10.   Ibid., p. 168.
11.   Ibid.
12.   *National Review,* February 25, 1969, p. 167.
13.   *Dissent* (March–April 1969), p. 167.
14.   Ibid.
15.   Ibid., p. 169.
16.   Ibid.
17.   House Committee on Un-American Activities, *Subversive Influences in Riots, Looting and Burning,* Part 6, June 27, 28, 1968, p. 2168.
18.   Ibid., p. 2168.
19.   Ibid., p. 2166.
20.   Ibid., pp. 2163, 2165.
21.   Ibid., p. 2165.
22.   Ibid.
23.   Ibid., p. 2166.
24.   Ibid.
25.   Ibid.
26.   Ibid., p. 2172.
27.   Ibid., p. 2168.
28.   Ibid., pp. 2168, 2169.
29.   Ibid., p. 2167.
30.   Ibid., p. 2170.
31.   Ibid.
32.   Ibid.
33.   Ibid., p. 2172.
34.   Ibid.
35.   Ibid.
36.   *The Nation,* January 8, 1968, p. 39.
37.   Ibid., p. 2173.
38.   Ibid.
39.   Ibid., p. 2174.
40.   Ibid., p. 41.
41.   *Subversive Influences in Riots, Looting and Burning,* p. 2172.
42.   Ibid.
43.   Ibid.
44.   Ibid., p. 2174.
45.   Ibid., p. 2175.
46.   Ibid.

47. Ibid., p. 2178.
48. Ibid., pp. 2176, 2177.
49. Ibid., p. 2177.
50. *The Nation,* January 8, 1968, p. 40.
51. *Subversive Influences in Riots, Looting and Burning,* pp. 2177, 2183.
52. Ibid., p. 2177.
53. Ibid., pp. 2177, 2178.
54. Ibid., p. 2177.
55. Ibid.
56. *The Nation,* January 8, 1968, p. 40.
57. *Subversive Influences in Riots, Looting and Burning,* p. 2178.
58. Ibid., p. 2167.
59. Ibid., p. 2147.
60. Ibid., p. 2154.
61. Ibid.
62. Ibid., p. 2148.
63. Ibid., p. 2150.
64. Ibid., p. 2149.
65. Ibid., pp. 2154, 2155.
66. *Dissent* (March–April 1969), p. 170.
67. *Public Interest* (Fall 1968), p. 23.
68. Ibid., p. 28.
69. Ibid., pp. 28, 29.
70. Ibid., p. 29.
71. Ibid., p. 31.
72. Ibid., p. 27.
73. Ibid.
74. Ibid., pp. 27, 28.
75. Ibid., p. 31.
76. Ibid., p. 32.
77. Ibid., p. 36.
78. Ibid.
79. Ibid., p. 37.
80. Ibid.
81. Ibid.
82. *New York Times,* March 8, 1969, p. 13.
83. Ibid., p. 1.
84. Ibid.

85.   Ibid., p. 13.
86.   Ibid.
87.   *Public Interest* (Fall 1968), p. 33.
88.   *Dissent* (March–April 1969), p. 171.
89.   Ibid.
90.   *Wall Street Journal,* November 27, 1968, p. 18.
91.   Ibid.
92.   *Human Events,* November 23, 1968, p. 12.
93.   *Wall Street Journal,* November 27, 1968, p. 18.
94.   Ibid.
95.   Ibid.
96.   Ibid.
97.   *Dissent* (March–April 1969), pp. 171, 172.
98.   Ibid.
99.   *San Francisco Chronicle,* November 7, 1968, p. 1.
100.  Ibid.
101.  Ibid.
102.  Ibid., pp. 1, 12.
103.  Ibid., p. 12.
104.  Ibid.
105.  Ibid., p. 30.
106.  Ibid.
107.  Ibid., pp. 1, 30.
108.  Statement of Dr. Hayakawa, op. cit.
109.  *Educational Record* (Spring 1969), p. 127.
110.  Ibid., p. 128.
111.  *Dissent* (March–April 1969), p. 172.
112.  *New York Times,* November 13, 1968, p. 37.
113.  *National Catholic Reporter,* December 11, 1968, p. 10.
114.  *New York Times,* November 15, 1968, p. 29.
115.  Ibid., November 19, 1968, p. 30.
116.  Ibid.
117.  Ibid.
118.  Ibid., November 20, 1968, p. 27.
119.  Ibid., November 21, 1968, p. 35.
120.  *National Catholic Reporter,* December 11, 1968, p. 10.
121.  *Dissent* (March–April 1969), p. 172.
122.  *New York Times,* November 27, 1968, p. 25.
123.  Ibid.
124.  *Wall Street Journal,* November 27, 1968, p. 18.

125. *National Observer,* December 9, 1968, p. 7.
126. *New York Times,* November 28, 1968, p. 37.
127. Ibid., December 1, 1968, p. 76.
128. Ibid., December 3, 1968, p. 29.
129. Ibid.
130. Ibid.
131. Ibid.
132. Ibid., December 4, 1968, p. 26.
133. Ibid.
134. *Trans-Action,* March 1969, p. 22.
135. *Educational Record* (Spring 1969), p. 129.
136. *New York Times,* December 4, 1968, p. 26.
137. Ibid. See also ibid., December 5, 1968, p. 36.
138. Ibid., December 6, 1968, pp. 1, 39. See also *Human Events,* January 25, 1969, p. 14.
139. *New York Times,* December 7, 1968, p. 31.
140. Ibid. See also ibid., December 8, 1968, p. 66.
141. *New York Times,* December 9, 1968, p. 23.
142. *National Observer,* December 9, 1968, p. 3.
143. *New York Times,* December 10, 1968, p. 43.
144. Ibid., December 11, 1968, p. 31.
145. Ibid., December 14, 1968, p. 40.
146. Ibid.
147. Ibid., December 28, 1968, p. 16.
148. *Human Events,* December 28, 1968, p. 4.
149. *U.S. News & World Report,* December 30, 1968, p. 49.
150. *New York Times,* January 9, 1969, p. 53.
151. Ibid., January 4, 1969, p. 24.
152. Ibid.
153. *Human Events,* January 25, 1969, p. 14.
154. Ibid.
155. *New York Times,* January 4, 1969, p. 24.
156. Statement by Dr. John H. Bunzel, before the Special Sub-committee on Education, House Committee on Education and Labor, March 25, 1969.
157. *Dissent* (March–April 1969), p. 174.
158. Ibid.
159. Ibid.
160. Statement of Dr. Bunzel, op. cit.
161. *New York Times,* January 5, 1969, p. 57.

162. *Educational Record* (Spring 1969), p. 128.
163. *New York Times,* January 5, 1969, p. 57.
164. Ibid.
165. *National Observer,* January 13, 1969, p. 4.
166. *New York Times,* January 7, 1969, p. 24.
167. *National Observer,* op. cit.
168. *Harvard Crimson,* February 19, 1969, p. 4.
169. *New York Times,* January 7, 1969, p. 24.
170. Ibid., January 11, 1969, p. 17.
171. Ibid., January 8, 1969, p. 36.
172. *Human Events,* January 25, 1969, p. 8.
173. *Educational Record* (Spring 1969), p. 129.
174. *New York Times,* January 9, 1969, p. 49.
175. Ibid., January 9, 1969, p. 17.
176. Ibid., January 10, 1969, p. 33. See also ibid., January 11, 1969, p. 17.
177. *Trans-Action,* March 1969, p. 61.
178. *New York Times,* January 15, 1969, p. 26.
179. Statement of Dr. Bunzel, op. cit.
180. *New York Times,* January 16, 1969, p. 41.
181. Ibid., January 17, 1969, p. 45.
182. Ibid., January 19, 1969, p. 25.
183. *Educational Record* (Spring 1969), pp. 128, 129.
184. *Human Events,* January 25, 1969, p. 14.
185. *New York Times,* February 3, 1969, p. 52. See also ibid., February 5, 1969, p. 26.
186. Ibid., February 5, 1969, p. 26.
187. February 7, 1969, p. 20.
188. Ibid.
189. *Newsweek,* February 10, 1969, pp. 56, 57
190. *Wall Street Journal,* May 15, 1969, p. 1.
191. Ibid.
192. *New York Times,* February 17, 1969, p. 26.
193. *Trans-Action,* March 1969, p. 62.
194. *San Francisco Chronicle,* February 15, 1969, p. 12.
195. Ibid., pp. 1, 12.
196. *New York Times,* March 1, 1969, p. 21. See also *National Observer,* February 24, 1969, p. 5.
197. *San Francisco Chronicle,* February 15, 1969, pp. 8, 12.
198. Ibid., p. 8.

199. *New York Times,* February 18, 1969, p. 25.
200. Ibid.
201. *National Observer,* February 24, 1969, p. 5.
202. *San Francisco Chronicle,* March 1, 1969, p. 8. See also *San Francisco Examiner,* March 1, 1969, pp. 1, 4.
203. *San Francisco Chronicle,* March 1, 1969, p. 8.
204. Ibid.
205. *San Francisco Examiner,* March 7, 1969, p. 4.
206. Ibid.
207. Ibid., March 1, 1969, p. 1. *New York Times,* March 3, 1969, p. 18. See also *New York Times,* March 4, 1969, p. 88.
208. *New York Times,* March 2, 1969, p. 51.
209. *San Francisco Examiner,* March 7, 1969, p. 1.
210. *New York Times,* March 7, 1969, p. 1.
211. Ibid. See also *San Francisco Chronicle,* March 7, 1969, p. 9.
212. *San Francisco Chronicle,* March 7, 1969, p. 9.
213. Ibid., March 21, 1969, pp. 1, 28.
214. Ibid., p. 28.
215. Ibid., March 22, 1969, pp. 1, 14.
216. Ibid., p. 14.
217. *Jet,* March 13, 1969, p. 53.
218. *San Francisco Chronicle,* March 22, 1969, p. 14. See also *New York Times,* March 22, 1969, p. 23, and *National Observer,* March 24, 1969, p. 11.
219. *New York Times,* March 22, 1969, p. 23.
220. *Washington Post,* May 17, 1969, p. A19.
221. *New York Times,* May 14, 1969, p. 30.
222. *Jet,* June 26, 1969, p. 24.
223. *New York Times,* April 15, 1969, p. 31.
224. *San Francisco Examiner,* June 28, 1969, p. 5. See also *Jet,* July 17, 1969, p. 46.
225. *San Francisco Examiner,* June 28, 1969, p. 5.
226. *San Francisco Chronicle,* July 10, 1969, p. 1.
227. Ibid.
228. *New York Times,* March 8, 1969, p. 13.

CHAPTER 9
*Federal City College*

1.  "Higher Education for One World or for Two?" Speech by David Dickson at the General Meeting of the National Association of State Universities and Land Grant Colleges, November 12, 1968.
2.  Ibid.
3.  *Wilson Library Bulletin* (February 1969), p. 528.
4.  Ibid.
5.  *Science,* September 6, 1968, p. 994.
6.  *Southern Education Report* (May 1969), p. 20.
7.  "Higher Education for One World or for Two?" pp. 1, 2.
8.  Ibid., p. 3. See also *Wilson Library Bulletin* (February 1969), p. 530.
9.  *Wilson Library Bulletin* (February 1969), pp. 530, 531.
10. "Higher Education for One World or for Two?" pp. 3, 4.
11. *New York Times,* November 17, 1968, p. 76.
12. *Washington Post,* March 6, 1969, p. A10.
13. House Committee on Un-American Activities, *Subversive Influences in Riots,* Looting and Burning, Part 6, June 27, 28, 1968, p. 2172.
14. *Washington Post,* March 6, 1969, p. A10.
15. *New York Times,* November 17, 1968, p. 76.
16. *U.S. News & World Report,* May 12, 1969, p. 40.
17. Ibid.
18. Focus on the Federal City College, February 1969.
19. Ibid.
20. Ibid.
21. Ibid.
22. *Washington Post,* March 6, 1969, p. A1.
23. Ibid., pp. A1, A10.
24. Ibid., p. A10.
25. Ibid.
26. Ibid. See also *Harvard Crimson,* March 10, 1969, p. 8.
27. *Washington Post,* March 6, 1969, p. A10.
28. Ibid.
29. *Muhammad Speaks,* September 12, 1969, p. 35.
30. A.C.E. Special Report, "Black Studies Programs and Civil Rights," April 8, 1969, pp. 7, 8.
31. *Washington Post,* March 7, 1969, p. C1.

32. Ibid.
33. Ibid., March 6, 1969, p. A10.
34. *The Nation,* May 12, 1969, p. 595.
35. *Wilson Library Bulletin* (February 1969), p. 533.
36. *Southern Education Report* (May 1969), p. 18.
37. Ibid., p. 23.
38. *Washington Post,* March 8, 1969, p. B1.
39. *Harvard Crimson,* March 10, 1969, pp. 1, 8.
40. *Southern Education Report* (May 1969), p. 20.
41. *U.S. News & World Report,* May 12, 1969, p. 40.
42. *Congressional Record* (unbound), March 27, 1969, p. E2470.
43. *Washington Post,* May 24, 1969, p. B8.
44. Ibid.
45. Ibid., p. B1.
46. Ibid.
47. Ibid., May 28, 1969, p. C2.
48. Ibid., May 27, 1969, p. A1.
49. Ibid., May 28, 1969, p. C2.
50. Ibid.
51. *Muhammad Speaks,* June 27, 1969, pp. 29, 30.

CHAPTER 10
*Cornell University*

1. *National Catholic Reporter,* July 23, 1969, p. 6.
2. *Cornell Alumni News,* June 1969, p. 11.
3. *Newsweek,* October 9, 1967, p. 59.
4. Ibid.
5. House Committee on Un-American Activities, *Subversive Influences in Riots, Looting and Burning,* Part 6, June 27, 28, 1968, p. 2162.
6. Ibid.
7. Ibid.
8. Ibid., p. 2146.
9. Ibid., p. 2164.
10. Ibid.
11. *New York Times,* September 8, 1969, p. 57. See also ibid., October 17, 1968, p. 59; October 19, 1968, p. 1.
12. Ibid., September 8, 1969, p. 57.
13. Ibid., Magazine Section, April 6, 1969, p. 26.

14. Ibid.
15. Ibid.
16. Ibid., pp. 26, 60.
17. The Report of the Special Trustee Committee on Campus Unrest at Cornell, submitted to the Board of Trustees, Cornell University, September 5, 1969, p. 32.
18. Ibid., pp. 34, 35.
19. Ibid., p. 38.
20. Ibid.
21. Ibid.
22. *New York Times,* April 24, 1969, p. 34.
23. Ibid., June 3, 1968, p. 51.
24. *Cornell Alumni News,* June 1969, p. 12.
25. *New York Times,* May 23, 1968, p. 36.
26. Ibid., May 12, 1968, p. 37.
27. Ibid.
28. Ibid.
29. Ibid.
30. Ibid., June 3, 1968, p. 51.
31. Ibid., Magazine Section, April 6, 1969, p. 65.
32. Ibid.
33. Ibid. See also ibid., December 9, 1968, p. 27.
34. Ibid., December 9, 1968, p. 27.
35. Ibid., Magazine Section, April 6, 1969, p. 65.
36. Ibid. See also *Trans-Action,* June 1969, p. 30.
37. *New York Times,* Magazine Section, April 6, 1969, p. 65.
38. Ibid., December 14, 1968, p. 40.
39. Ibid., Magazine Section, April 6, 1969, p. 65.
40. Ibid.
41. Ibid., March 1, 1969, p. 28. See also ibid., Magazine Section, April 6, 1969, p. 26.
42. Ibid., Magazine Section, April 6, 1969, p. 75.
43. Ibid.
44. Ibid., March 18, 1969, p. 30.
45. *Cornell Alumni News,* June 1969, p. 12.
46. *Muhammad Speaks,* May 30, 1969, p. 26.
47. Ibid., May 16, 1969, p. 13.
48. Ibid., September 12, 1969, p. 27. See also *New York Times,* May 28, 1969, p. 30.
49. *Newsweek,* May 5, 1969, p. 27.

50.  *New York Times,* April 14, 1969, p. 49.
51.  *Cornell Daily Sun,* April 11, 1969, p. 14.
52.  *New York Times,* Magazine Section, April 6, 1969, p. 76.
53.  Ibid., May 28, 1969, p. 30.
54.  Ibid., Magazine Section, April 6, 1969, p. 76. See also *Trans-Action,* June 1969, p. 31.
55.  *New York Times,* April 22, 1969, p. 35.
56.  *Trans-Action,* June 1969, p. 31.
57.  *Cornell Daily Sun,* April 18, 1969, p. 1.
58.  Ibid. See also *Cornell Alumni News,* June 1969, p. 15.
59.  *New York Times,* April 19, 1969, p. 16.
60.  *National Catholic Reporter,* July 23, 1969, p. 6.
61.  *New York Times,* April 19, 1969, p. 16.
62.  Ibid.
63.  *Washington Post,* May 1, 1969, p. A19.
64.  *Muhammad Speaks,* May 23, 1969, p. 18.
65.  Report of the Special Trustee Committee, p. 5.
66.  Ibid.
67.  Ibid., p. 6.
68.  *Muhammad Speaks,* May 23, 1969, p. 14.
69.  *New York Times,* April 20, 1969, p. 1.
70.  Ibid.
71.  *Cornell Alumni News,* June 1969, p. 14.
72.  *New Leader,* May 12, 1969, p. 12.
73.  *New York Times,* April 20, 1969, p. 77.
74.  *Muhammad Speaks,* May 23, 1969, pp. 14, 18.
75.  *New York Times,* May 28, 1969, p. 30.
76.  *New Leader,* May 12, 1969, p. 12.
77.  Report of the Special Trustee Committee, p. 7.
78.  Ibid., p. 11.
79.  *Muhammad Speaks,* May 23, 1969, p. 14.
80.  *Cornell Daily Sun,* April 22, 1969, p. 4.
81.  *New York Times,* April 20, 1969, p. 77.
82.  Report of the Special Trustee Committee, pp. 7, 18.
83.  Ibid., p. 18
84.  *New York Times,* April 20, 1969, p. 77.
85.  Ibid.
86.  *National Catholic Reporter,* July 23, 1969, p. 6.
87.  *Cornell Alumni News,* June 1969, p. 14.
88.  *Muhammad Speaks,* May 23, 1969, p. 14.

89. Report of the Special Trustee Committee, p. 11.
90. *National Catholic Reporter,* July 23, 1969, p. 6.
91. *Cornell Daily Sun,* April 21, 1969, p. 9.
92. Report of the Special Trustee Committee, p. 22.
93. *National Catholic Reporter,* July 23, 1969, p. 6.
94. *Muhammad Speaks,* May 16, 1969, p. 24.
95. *New York Times,* April 21, 1969, p. 35.
96. *National Observer,* May 5, 1969, p. 22.
97. *Congressional Record* (unbound), April 21, 1969, p. E3187.
98. Report of the Special Trustee Committee, p. 12.
99. Ibid., pp. 12, 13.
100. Ibid., pp. 13, 14.
101. *Cornell Daily Sun,* April 21, 1969, pp. 1, 9.
102. Ibid., p. 9
103. Ibid.
104. Report of the Special Trustee Committee, pp. 14, 15.
105. *Cornell Daily Sun,* April 30, 1969, p. 1.
106. Ibid., April 21, 1969, p. 9.
107. Ibid., April 21, 1969, p. 4.
108. Ibid., April 21, 1969, p. 4.
109. Ibid., April 22, 1969, p. 1.
110. Ibid., p. 7.
111. *New York Times,* April 23, 1969, p. 30.
112. Ibid., April 22, 1969, pp. 1, 34.
113. Ibid. See also *Newsweek,* May 5, 1969, p. 29.
114. *Cornell Alumni News,* June 1969, p. 18.
115. *New Leader,* May 12, 1969, p. 14.
116. Ibid.
117. Ibid.
118. *Ithaca Journal,* April 22, 1969, p. 8.
119. *Cornell Daily Sun,* April 22, 1969, p. 9.
120. *Ithaca Journal,* April 22, 1969, p. 11.
121. *New York Times,* April 23, 1969, pp. 1, 30.
122. *Cornell Daily Sun,* April 23, 1969, pp. 1, 7.
123. *New York Times,* April 23, 1969, p. 30.
124. Ibid. See also *Cornell Alumni News,* June 1969, p. 20.
125. *Washington Post,* May 1, 1969, p. A19.
126. *Congressional Record* (unbound), May 6, 1969, p. E3646.
127. *New York Times,* April 23, 1969, p. 30.
128. *Cornell Daily Sun,* April 23, 1969, pp. 1, 11.
129. *Trans-Action,* June 1969, p. 35.

130. *New Leader,* May 12, 1969, p. 14.
131. *Cornell Daily Sun,* April 23, 1969, p. 11.
132. *New York Times,* April 23, 1969, p. 30.
133. *Ithaca Journal,* April 26, 1969, p. 8.
134. *Cornell Daily Sun,* April 23, 1969, p. 11.
135. Ibid.
136. *New Leader,* May 12, 1969, p. 14.
137. Ibid.
138. *Ithaca Journal,* April 23, 1969, p. 15.
139. *Cornell Daily Sun,* April 24, 1969, p. 7.
140. *New York Times,* News of the Week in Review, June 8, 1969, p. 11E.
141. *Washington Post,* May 1, 1969, p. A19.
142. *New York Times,* April 24, 1969, pp. 1, 34.
143. *Ithaca Journal,* April 24, 1969, p. 19.
144. *New York Times,* April 24, 1969, p. 1.
145. *Cornell Alumni News,* June 1969, p. 21.
146. *New York Times,* April 24, 1969, p. 34.
147. *Cornell Daily Sun,* April 24, 1969, p. 16.
148. Ibid.
149. *New York Times,* April 24, 1969, p. 34.
150. *Cornell Daily Sun,* April 24, 1969, p. 1.
151. *Newsweek,* May 5, 1969, p. 30.
152. *Cornell Daily Sun,* April 24, 1969, p. 16.
153. *New York Times,* April 24, 1969, p. 34.
154. Ibid.
155. Ibid. See also ibid., May 28, 1969, p. 30.
156. *Cornell Daily Sun,* April 25, 1969, p. 4.
157. *New York Times,* April 24, 1969, p. 34.
158. *Ithaca Journal,* April 24, 1969, p. 19.
159. *New York Times,* April 24, 1969, p. 34. See also *Cornell Daily Sun,* April 24, 1969, p. 8.
160. *Ithaca Journal,* April 24, 1969, p. 19.
161. Ibid.
162. *New York Times,* April 24, 1969, p. 34.
163. Ibid., May 28, 1969, p. 30.
164. *Ithaca Journal,* April 24, 1969, p. 20.
165. Ibid.
166. *New York Times,* May 11, 1969, p. 56. See also ibid., May 13, 1969, p. 32; May 14, 1969, p. 31.
167. Ibid., Magazine Section, May 18, 1969, pp. 60, 61.

168. *Cornell Daily Sun,* April 25, 1969, p. 1.
169. Ibid., p. 16.
170. Ibid.
171. *New York Times,* April 25, 1969, p. 30.
172. *Congressional Record* (unbound), May 6, 1969, p. E3646.
173. Ibid.
174. *Cornell Daily Sun,* April 29, 1969, p. 1.
175. *Muhammad Speaks,* September 12, 1969, p. 27.
176. *Cornell Daily Sun,* April 25, 1969, p. 5.
177. *New York Times,* April 25, 1969, p. 1.
178. Ibid., p. 30.
179. *Ithaca Journal,* April 25, 1969, p. 11.
180. Ibid., April 26, 1969, p. 8.
181. *New York Times,* April 27, 1969, p. 64.
182. Ibid.
183. Ibid.
184. Ibid.
185. *Cornell Daily Sun,* May 1, 1969, p. 1.
186. *New York Times,* April 26, 1969, p. 14.
187. *The Nation,* June 16, 1969, p. 757.
188. *Cornell Daily Sun,* April 29, 1969, p. 10.
189. *New York Times,* April 30, 1969, p. 28.
190. *Cornell Daily Sun,* May 2, 1969, p. 4.
191. *New York Times,* June 2, 1969, p. 35. See also *Amsterdam News,* June 14, 1969, p. 30.
192. *New York Times,* June 1, 1969, p. 1.
193. Ibid.
194. Ibid., June 9, 1969, p. 67.
195. Ibid., May 3, 1969, p. 22; May 4, 1969, p. 1; May 6, 1969, p. 32.
196. Ibid., June 1, 1969, p. 68.
197. A Letter from Northwestern Department of Public Relations, Northwestern University, May 29, 1968, p. 1.
198. Ibid.
199. Ibid., pp. 1, 2.
200. Ibid., p. 3.
201. Ibid.
202. Ibid.
203. Ibid.
204. *New York Times,* May 31, 1968, p. 10.

205. *Muhammad Speaks,* February 14, 1969, p. 11.
206. *New York Times,* June 1, 1969, p. 68.
207. Ibid.
208. Ibid.
209. *New York Post,* July 21, 1969, p. 37.
210. Ibid.
211. Ibid.
212. Ibid., July 30, 1969, p. 44.
213. *Jewish Press,* August 8, 1969, p. 10.
214. *New York Times,* July 26, 1969, p. 1.
215. *National Catholic Reporter,* July 23, 1969, p. 7.

CHAPTER 11
*The City College of New York (CCNY)*

1. *Saturday Review,* June 21, 1969, p. 70.
2. *New York Times,* April 30, 1969, p. 28.
3. Ibid., January 2, 1968, p. 34.
4. *Amsterdam News,* November 18, 1967, p. 1.
5. Ibid., p. 37.
6. *New York Times,* October 29, 1967, p. 65.
7. Ibid.
8. Ibid., November 2, 1967, p. 50.
9. City University of New York, Admission Procedure for Special Programs (application for admission).
10. Ibid. See also *New York Times,* April 5, 1968, p. 93, and *Educational Record* (Fall 1968), pp. 382 ff.
11. *New York Times,* August 3, 1968, p. 16.
12. Ibid., p. 1.
13. Ibid., p. 16.
14. Ibid.
15. *Change* (March-April 1969), p. 11.
16. *New York Times,* February 14, 1969, p. 24.
17. Ibid.
18. Ibid.
19. Ibid., pp. 1, 24.
20. Ibid., p. 24.
21. Ibid., February 15, 1969, p. 16.
22. *Amsterdam News,* February 22, 1969, p. 2.
23. *New York Times,* February 18, 1969, p. 28.
24. Ibid.

25.   *Amsterdam News,* February 22, 1969, p. 2.
26.   Ibid.
27.   Ibid.
28.   *New York Times,* April 18, 1969, p. 30.
29.   *The Campus* (CCNY undergraduate newspaper), April 22, 1969, pp. 1, 2.
30.   Ibid., p. 2.
31.   Ibid.
32.   Ibid.
33.   Ibid.
34.   *New York Times,* April 23, 1969, p. 1.
35.   Ibid.
36.   Ibid.
37.   Ibid., pp. 1, 31.
38.   Ibid., p. 31.
39.   *New York Post,* May 29, 1969, p. 3.
40.   Ibid.
41.   Ibid.
42.   *New York Times,* November 18, 1968, p. 46.
43.   Ibid., May 5, 1969, p. 29.
44.   Ibid., April 24, 1969, p. 34.
45.   Ibid.
46.   Ibid., p. 1.
47.   Ibid., April 25, 1969, p. 29.
48.   Ibid.
49.   Ibid., April 26, 1969, p. 15.
50.   Ibid.
51.   Ibid.
52.   Ibid., April 29, 1969, p. 30.
53.   *New York Post,* April 29, 1969, p. 3.
54.   *New York Times,* April 29, 1969, p. 30.
55.   Ibid., May 2, 1969, p. 27.
56.   Ibid., May 3, 1969, p. 23. See also ibid., May 4, 1969, p. 74.
57.   *The Campus,* May 6, 1969, p. 5.
58.   *New York Times,* May 5, 1969, pp. 1, 29.
59.   Ibid., p. 29.
60.   Ibid.
61.   Ibid.
62.   Ibid.

63. Ibid.
64. Ibid.
65. *Amsterdam News,* May 10, 1969, p. 54. See also *New York Times,* May 6, 1969, pp. 1, 32.
66. *Amsterdam News,* May 10, 1969, p. 54.
67. *New York Times,* May 7, 1969, p. 1.
68. Ibid., p. 32.
69. *New York Post,* May 8, 1969, pp. 3, 14, 15.
70. Ibid.
71. *New York Times,* May 8, 1969, p. 42.
72. *New York Post,* May 8, 1969, p. 15.
73. *New York Times,* May 8, 1969, p. 42.
74. *New York Post,* May 8, 1969, p. 15.
75. *New York Times,* May 10, 1969, p. 15.
76. *Amsterdam News,* May 17, 1969, p. 1.
77. *The Campus,* May 16, 1969, p. 7.
78. *Liberator,* January 1969, p. 6.
79. *Muhammad Speaks,* May 16, 1969, p. 11.
80. *The Campus,* May 16, 1969, p. 7.
81. *New York Times,* News of the Week in Review, May 11, 1969, p. 1E.
82. Ibid., May 8, 1969, p. 42.
83. Ibid.
84. Ibid.
85. Ibid., May 9, 1969, pp. 1, 28.
86. Ibid.
87. Ibid.
88. *New York Post,* May 9, 1969, p. 37.
89. Ibid.
90. *New York Times,* May 9, 1969, p. 29.
91. Ibid., June 6, 1969, p. 22.
92. Ibid., May 10, 1969, pp. 1, 15.
93. *The Campus,* May 16, 1969, p. 6.
94. Ibid., May 22, 1969, p. 1.
95. Ibid., May 16, 1969, p. 6.
96. *New York Times,* May 11, 1969, p. 1.
97. Ibid., p. 54.
98. Ibid.
99. Ibid. See also ibid., May 12, 1969, p. 50.

100. *New York Post,* May 12, 1969, pp. 1, 3.
101. *New York Times,* May 12, 1969, p. 1; May 13, 1969, p. 1.
102. Ibid., May 14, 1969, p. 1.
103. Ibid., pp. 1, 30.
104. Ibid.
105. Ibid., May 16, 1969, p. 50.
106. Ibid., May 18, 1969, p. 1.
107. Ibid.
108. Ibid., May 19, 1969, p. 33.
109. Ibid., May 18, 1969, p. 76.
110. Ibid., May 19, 1969, p. 33.
111. Ibid., May 20, 1969, p. 33.
112. Ibid., May 18, 1969, p. 76.
113. Ibid.
114. Ibid.
115. Ibid., May 20, 1969, p. 33.
116. Ibid.
117. Ibid., May 22, 1969, pp. 1, 19.
118. Ibid., p. 19.
119. Ibid., May 23, 1969, p. 31.
120. Ibid., May 24, 1969, p. 1.
121. Ibid.
122. Ibid., p. 22.
123. Ibid.
124. *New York Post,* May 24, 1969, p. 1.
125. *New York Times,* May 25, 1969, p. 68.
126. *New York Post,* May 24, 1969, p. 1.
127. Ibid., p. 3.
128. *New York Times,* May 25, 1969, p. 1.
129. Ibid., p. 68.
130. Ibid.
131. Ibid., May 27, 1969, p. 30.
132. Ibid.
133. Ibid.
134. Ibid.
135. Ibid.
136. Ibid.
137. Ibid., May 27, 1969, p. 46.
138. Ibid., June 2, 1969, p. 44.
139. Ibid., May 27, 1969, p. 31.

140. Ibid.
141. *Amsterdam News,* May 31, 1969, pp. 1, 16.
142. *New York Times,* May 28, 1969, p. 1.
143. Ibid., p. 31.
144. *New York Post,* May 28, 1969, pp. 1, 3.
145. *New York Times,* News of the Week in Review, June 1, 1969, p. 9E.
146. *New York Post,* May 29, 1969, p. 3.
147. Ibid.
148. Ibid.
149. *New York Times,* February 13, 1970, p. 19.
150. Ibid.
151. Ibid., June 13, 1969, p. 31.
152. Statement of Admissions Policy Adopted by the Board of Higher Education, November 12, 1969.
153. *The Campus,* November 19, 1969, p. 1.
154. *New York Times,* October 21, 1969, p. 96. See also ibid., October 23, 1969, p. 53.
155. Statement of Admissions Policy.
156. *New York Times,* December 28, 1969, p. 58.
157. *Jewish Press*, November 28, 1969, p. 10.
158. Ibid.
159. *New York Times,* December 14, 1969, p. 78.
160. *Jewish Press,* November 28, 1969, p. 4.
161. Ibid.

CHAPTER 12
*The "Impossible" Revolution*

1. *Ebony,* September 1969, p. 97.
2. Ibid., August 1969, p. 142.
3. Ibid., pp. 143, 144, 145.
4. Ibid., p. 143.
5. Ibid.
6. Ibid.
7. Ibid.
8. Ibid.
9. Ibid., September 1969, p. 98.
10. Ibid., pp. 98, 100.
11. Ibid., p. 100.
12. Ibid., August 1969, p. 141.

13.   Ibid., p. 142.
14.   Ibid., September 1969, p. 98.
15.   Ibid., p. 102.
16.   Ibid., p. 97.
17.   Ibid., p. 104.

CHAPTER 13
*Black Anti-Semitism and the New York Mayoralty*

1.    *Jewish Press,* February 28, 1969, p. 3.
2.    *New York Post,* April 28, 1969, p. 6.
3.    *Jewish Press,* July 11, 1969, p. 3.
4.    Ibid., May 16, 1969, pp. 1, 2.
5.    Ibid.
6.    Ibid.
7.    Ibid.
8.    Ibid.
9.    *New York Times,* December 9, 1968, p. 57.
10.   Ibid., June 25, 1969, p. 25.
11.   Ibid., May 18, 1969, p. 81.
12.   *Jewish Press,* June 20, 1969, p. 20.
13.   *The Flame* (newspaper of the Jewish Student Union at CCNY), November 5, 1969, p. 2.
14.   A copy of this "Internal Release" is in the author's possession.
15.   *National Observer,* July 28, 1969, p. 3.
16.   *Jewish Press,* May 30, 1969, p. 27.
17.   Ibid., June 27, 1969, p. 4.
18.   Ibid., July 18, 1969, p. 4.
19.   *Anti-Semitism in the New York City School Controversy,* a preliminary report of the Anti-Defamation League of B'nai B'rith, January 1969.
20.   *Columbia Journalism Review* (Fall 1969), p. 26.
21.   Ibid., pp. 26, 27.
22.   *Harlem on My Mind* (New York: Random House, 1968), Introduction.
23.   *Anti-Semitism in the New York City School Controversy.*
24.   Ibid.
25.   Ibid.
26.   *New York Times,* February 15, 1967, p. 1.
27.   Ibid., December 18, 1968, p. 38.

28.   Ibid., January 30, 1969, p. 41.
29.   Ibid.
30.   Ibid., February 5, 1969, p. 1.
31.   *African-American Teachers Forum* (November-December 1967), p. 1.
32.   *New York Times,* July 25, 1968, pp. 1, 29.
33.   Ibid., March 13, 1968, p. 37.
34.   Ibid., July 25, 1968, p. 1.
35.   Ibid., p. 29.
36.   Ibid., July 27, 1968, p. 28.
37.   Ibid., August 10, 1968, p. 1.
38.   Ibid., p. 15.
39.   Ibid.
40.   Ibid., pp. 1, 15.
41.   Ibid., October 9, 1968, p. 1.
42.   Ibid., October 11, 1968, p. 1.
43.   *African-American Teachers Forum* (November 1968), p. 2.
44.   *Anti-Semitism in the New York City School Controversy.*
45.   Ibid.
46.   Ibid.
47.   *New York Times,* January 22, 1969, p. 1.
48.   A copy of this memo is in the author's possession.
49.   *Time,* January 31, 1969, p. 58.
50.   Ibid.
51.   *New York Times,* February 2, 1969, p. 38.
52.   Ibid., February 3, 1969, p. 34.
53.   Ibid., November 24, 1969, p. 36.
54.   *New York Post,* June 18, 1969, p. 3.
55.   Ibid.
56.   *New York Times,* News of the Week in Review, July 13, 1969, p. 5E.
57.   Ibid.
58.   Ibid.
59.   Ibid., October 6, 1969, p. 38.
60.   Ibid.
61.   Ibid., September 15, 1969, p. 50.
62.   Ibid.
63.   Ibid.
64.   Ibid.

65. Ibid., Magazine Section, November 2, 1969, p. 26.
66. *New York Times,* August 28, 1969, p. 32; October 15, 1969, p. 1; September 1, 1969, p. 11; October 6, 1969, p. 43; *New York Post,* September 25, 1969, p. 4; September 26, 1969, p. 5; *New York Times,* October 1, 1969, p. 28; October 8, 1969, p. 36; *New York Daily News,* October 22, 1969, p. 5; *Village Voice,* October 23, 1969, p. 1; *New York Times,* October 8, 1969, p. 37.
67. A copy of this campaign literature is in the author's possession.
68. *New York Times,* October 6, 1969, p. 35.
69. A reprint of "20 Questions" is in the author's possession.
70. *Jewish Press,* October 24, 1969, pp. 1, 23.
71. *New York Times,* October 28, 1969, p. 1.
72. Ibid., October 31, 1969, p. 30.
73. *New York Daily News,* November 6, 1969, p. 5.
74. Ibid., October 31, 1969, p. 2.
75. Ibid., October 30, 1969, pp. 2, 24.
76. *New York Times,* October 30, 1969, p. 40.
77. Ibid.
78. Ibid., October 31, 1969, p. 30.
79. Ibid., September 30, 1969, p. 28.
80. Ibid., October 28, 1969, p. 30.
81. Ibid., November 1, 1969, p. 1.
82. *New York Daily News,* October 24, 1969, p. 22.
83. *Washington Post,* October 29, 1969, p. A25.
84. *New York Times,* November 6, 1969, p. 40.
85. Ibid., August 5, 1969, p. 34.
86. Ibid., November 23, 1969, p. 48.
87. Ibid.
88. *New York Daily News,* November 6, 1969, p. 5.
89. *New York Times,* November 6, 1969, p. 37.
90. Ibid.
91. Ibid.

CHAPTER 14
*Black Help Wanted*

1. *Nation's Business,* January 1967, p. 35.
2. Ibid.
3. Ibid.

4. Ibid.
5. Ibid., March 1968, p. 78.
6. Ibid.
7. Ibid.
8. Ibid.
9. *U.S. News & World Report,* May 16, 1966, p. 9.
10. *Barron's,* December 23, 1968, p. 9.
11. Ibid., p. 16.
12. Ibid.
13. *Human Events,* March 15, 1969, p. 8.
14. Ibid.
15. Ibid.
16. Ibid.
17. Ibid.
18. Ibid.
19. Ibid.
20. Ibid.
21. Ibid.
22. Ibid.
23. Ibid.
24. Ibid.
25. Ibid.
26. Ibid., pp. 8, 10.
27. Ibid., p. 10.
28. Ibid.
29. Ibid., p. 8.
30. *New York Times,* March 28, 1969, p. 31.
31. Ibid., March 29, 1969, p. 23. See also ibid., April 10, 1969, p. 1.
32. Ibid., March 28, 1969, p. 31.
33. Ibid., July 18, 1969, p. 10.
34. Ibid.
35. *Amsterdam News,* August 16, 1969, p. 2.
36. *New York Times,* July 18, 1969, p. 10.
37. Ibid.
38. Ibid., August 7, 1969, p. 23.
39. Ibid.
40. Ibid., September 23, 1969, p. 56.
41. Ibid., August 9, 1969, p. 17.
42. Ibid.

43. *Amsterdam News,* August 30, 1969, p. 15.
44. *U.S. News & World Report,* August 18, 1969, p. 64; October 6, 1969, p. 72. See also *National Observer,* September 29, 1969, p. 6.
45. *New York Times,* September 24, 1969, pp. 1, 18.
46. Ibid., p. 18.
47. Ibid., p. 1.
48. Ibid., September 30, 1969, p. 1.
49. Ibid., October 29, 1969, p. 27.
50. Ibid.
51. Ibid., November 9, 1969, p. 29.
52. Ibid.
53. Ibid.
54. Ibid., December 21, 1969, p. 39.
55. Ibid.
56. Ibid., December 26, 1969, p. 20.
57. Ibid.
58. Ibid.
59. Ibid.
60. Ibid., January 25, 1970, pp. 1, 71.
61. *Jet,* August 14, 1969, p. 17.
62. Ibid.
63. *New York Times,* August 22, 1969, p. 21.
64. *National Observer,* August 18, 1969, p. 5.
65. Ibid.
66. Ibid.
67. *New York Times,* August 22, 1969, p. 21.
68. *Jet,* September 25, 1969, p. 16.
69. *Muhammad Speaks,* August·29, 1969, p. 33.
70. *New York Times,* September 9, 1969, p. 44.
71. Ibid.
72. Ibid., September 23, 1969, p. 56.
73. Ibid. See also *Chicago Tribune,* September 23, 1969, p. 9.
74. Ibid.
75. *New York Times,* September 26, 1969, p. 25.
76. Ibid., September 27, 1969, p. 18.
77. Ibid.
78. Ibid.
79. *Jet,* October 9, 1969, p. 14.
80. *New York Times,* January 13, 1970, p. 28.

81. Ibid., February 7, 1970, p. 28.
82. *Amsterdam News,* August 19, 1967, p. 16.
83. *Outlook,* January 1969, p. 1.
84. *New York Times,* July 11, 1969, p. 13.
85. *Outlook,* June 1968, p. 9.
86. Ibid., p. 20.
87. *Outlook,* October 1968, p. 1.
88. *Business Week,* February 1, 1969, p. 32.
89. Ibid.
90. *Wall Street Journal,* March 25, 1969, p. 1.
91. *New York Times,* November 11, 1969, p. 18.
92. *Newsweek,* September 8, 1969, p. 65.
93. *New York Times,* March 25, 1969, p. 44.
94. Ibid., October 27, 1969, p. 38.
95. Ibid.
96. Ibid.
97. *U.S. News & World Report,* August 25, 1969, p. 19.
98. *New York Times,* October 27, 1969, p. 38.
99. Ibid., July 13, 1968, p. 28.
100. Ibid., October 6, 1968, p. 75.
101. Ibid.
102. Ibid.
103. Ibid.
104. Ibid.
105. Ibid., October 9, 1968, p. 1.
106. *Wall Street Journal,* November 29, 1968, p. 1.
107. Ibid.
108. Ibid., pp. 1, 16.
109. *Business Week,* May 24, 1969, p. 56.
110. Ibid.
111. Ibid., p. 54.
112. Ibid.
113. Ibid.
114. Ibid.
115. Ibid., p. 56.
116. Ibid.
117. Statement adopted by the UAW International Executive Board, March 10, 1969.
118. *Business Week,* May 24, 1969, p. 56.
119. *New York Times,* April 29, 1969, p. 23.

120. Ibid., April 30, 1969, p. 26.
121. Ibid.
122. *Business Week,* May 24, 1969, p. 56.
123. Ibid.
124. *Newsweek,* September 8, 1969, p. 66.
125. *Business Week,* March 22, 1969, p. 41.
126. Ibid.
127. Ibid., March 29, 1969, p. 82.
128. Ibid.
129. Ibid.
130. Ibid.
131. Ibid.
132. Ibid., pp. 82, 84.
133. Ibid., p. 84.
134. *New York Times,* April 12, 1969, p. 72.
135. *Business Week,* January 17, 1970, p. 29.
136. Ibid.
137. Ibid.
138. Ibid., pp. 29, 30.
139. *New York Times,* February 8, 1970, p. 61.
140. Ibid.
141. Ibid.

CHAPTER 15
*The New Racism*

1. *Ebony,* September 1969, pp. 48, 52, 54.
2. Ibid., p. 48.
3. *Look,* January 13, 1970, p. 59.
4. *Dissent* (July-August 1969), pp. 309, 310.
5. *Jet,* December 4, 1969, p. 34.
6. *New York Times,* October 6, 1968, p. 30.
7. *Look,* September 9, 1969, p. 69.
8. *New York,* April 14, 1969, p. 28.
9. Ibid., p. 24.
10. Ibid.
11. Ibid.
12. Ibid., p. 26.
13. Ibid.
14. *Jet,* November 6, 1969, p. 11.
15. Ibid., January 22, 1970, p. 44.
16. *Look,* September 9, 1969, p. 69.

17. Ibid., p. 70.
18. *Human Events,* January 17, 1970, p. 12.
19. Ibid.
20. Ibid.
21. Ibid.
22. Ibid.
23. Ibid.
24. Ibid., p. 22.
25. Ibid.
26. Ibid.
27. *Cornell Daily Sun,* November 11, 1969, p. 4.
28. *Look,* September 9, 1969, p. 64.
29. Ibid., pp. 65, 66, 67.
30. Ibid., p. 66.
31. Ibid., p. 65.
32. Ibid.
33. *Business Week,* April 19, 1969, p. 40.
34. *National Observer,* May 19, 1969, p. 4.
35. *Business Week,* April 19, 1969, p. 40.
36. Ibid., pp. 40, 41.
37. Ibid., p. 41.
38. *National Observer,* May 19, 1969, p. 4.
39. *Business Week,* April 19, 1969, p. 41.
40. Ibid.
41. *New York Times,* April 13, 1969, p. 50.
42. *National Observer,* May 19, 1969, p. 4.
43. *New York Times,* April 13, 1969, p. 50. See also *National Observer,* May 19, 1969, p. 4.
44. *Business Week,* April 19, 1969, p. 41.
45. Ibid.
46. Ibid.
47. *National Observer,* May 19, 1969, p. 4.
48. *Business Week,* April 19, 1969, p. 41.
49. *New York Times,* April 13, 1969, p. 50.
50. *Business Week,* April 19, 1969, p. 41.
51. *Muhammad Speaks,* April 25, 1969, p. 4.
52. *National Observer,* May 19, 1969, p. 4.
53. *Muhammad Speaks,* March 7, 1969, p. 5.
54. *National Observer,* May 19, 1969, p. 4.
55. Ibid.

# Index